13.35.

THE PSYCHOLOGY OF VISUAL PERCEPTION

Holt, Rinehart and Winston, Inc.
New York   Chicago   San Francisco   Atlanta   Dallas
Montreal   Toronto   London   Sydney

THE PSYCHOLOGY OF VISUAL PERCEPTION

RALPH NORMAN HABER / MAURICE HERSHENSON

The University of Rochester   *Brandeis University*

This book is dedicated to Ruth and Amy.

Copyright © 1973 by Holt, Rinehart and Winston, Inc.
All Rights Reserved
Library of Congress Catalog Card Number: 72–11627
ISBN: 0–03–081413–8
Printed in the United States of America
4 5 6   071   9 8 7 6 5 4 3 2

acknowledgments

We are grateful to the following publishers and authors for permission to reprint copyrighted material:

Academic Press Inc. for our Figures 2.11, 2.20, 3.8, 4.4, 6.13, 11.1, 15.2, and 15.3. From Cornsweet, T. N., *Visual perception*, 1970, figures 8.11, 12.3, 12.20, pp. 174, 315, 341; Lindsay, P., and Norman, D., *Human information processing*, figure 4.11, p. 168; Davson, H., *The eye*, vol. 3, 1962, figure 2, p. 4; Posner, M. I., Abstraction and the process of recognition, in G. H. Bower and J. T. Spence (Eds.), *The psychology of learning and motivation*, 1969, figure 2, p. 51; Salapatek, P., and Kessen, W., Visual scanning of triangles by the human newborn, *Journal of experimental child psychology*, 1966, 3, figures 2 and 3, pp. 160–163. Reprinted by permission of the publisher and the authors.

Academic Press Inc. (London) Limited for our Figures 6.8 and 9.11. From Haber, R. N., and Standing, L. G., Direct measures of short-term visual storage, *Quarterly journal of experimental psychology*, 1969, *21*, figure 1, p. 44; Morton, J., The effects of context upon speed of reading, eye movements, and eye-voice span, *Quarterly journal of experimental psychology*, 1964, *16*, figure 2, p. 343. Reprinted by permission of the publisher and the authors.

Allyn and Bacon, Inc., for our Figures 5.6 and 5.7. From Hurvich, L. M., and Jameson, D. *The perception of brightness and darkness*, 1966, figure 1, p. 8. Reprinted by permission of the publisher.

American Association for the Advancement of Science for our Figures 6.10, 9.3, 10.6, and 14.1. From Schmidt, M. W., and Kristofferson, A. B., Discrimination of successiveness: A test of a model of attention, *Science*, 1963, *139*, figure 1, p. 113, Copyright 1963 by the American Association for the Advancement of Science; Mackworth, N., and Kaplan, I. T., Visual acuity when eyes are pursuing moving targets, *Science*, 1962, *136*, figure 1, p. 387, Copyright 1962 by the American Association for the Advancement of Science; Posner, M., and Keele, S. W., Decay of visual information from a single letter, *Science*, 1967, *158*, pp. 137–139, figure 1, Copyright 1967 by the American Association for the Advancement of Science; Sekular, R. W., and Ganz, L., Aftereffect of seen motion with a stabilized retinal image, *Science*, 1963, *139*, figure 1, p. 419, Copyright 1963 by the American Association for the Advancement of Science.

The American Physiological Society for our Figure 2.13. From ten Doesschate, J., and Alpern, M., The effect of photoexcitation of the two retinas on pupil size, *Journal of neurophysiology*, 1967, *30*, pp. 562–576, figure 3.

American Psychological Association for our Figures 4.11, 5.18, 5.21, 5.22, 8.11, 8.12, 8.14, 8.15, 11.4, 11.5, 11.6, 11.7, 11.8, 14.9. From Hurvich, L. M., and Jameson, D., An opponent-process theory of color vision, *Psychological review*, 1957, *64*, pp. 384–402, figure 2; Graham, C. H., and Bartlett, N. R., The relation of size and intensity in the human eye: II. Intensity thresholds for red and violet light, *Journal of experimental psychology*, 1939, *24*, figure 1, p. 577; Heinemann, E. G., Simultaneous brightness induction as a function of inducing- and test-field luminance, *Journal of experimental psychology*, 1955, *50*, figures 1, 3, pp. 90, 92; Attneave, F., Some informational aspects of visual perception, *Psychological review*, 1954, *61*, figures 1, 2, pp. 183, 184; Hochberg, J., and McAlister, F., A quantitative approach to figural "goodness," *Journal of experimental psychology*, 1953, *46*, figure 2, table 1, p. 363; Hershenson, M., Stimulus structure, cognitive structure, and the perception of letter arrays, *Journal of experimental psychology*, 1969, *79*, figures 1, 5, pp. 329, 331; Hershenson, M., Perception of letter arrays as a function of absolute retinal locus, *Journal of experimental psychology*, 1969, *80*, figure 1, p. 202; Mewhort, D. J. K., Merikle, P. M., and Bryden, M. P., On the transfer from iconic to short-term memory, *Journal of experimental psychology*, 1969, *81*, figures 1, 2, pp. 91, 92; Hay, J., and Pick, H., Jr., Visual and proprioceptive adaptation to optical displacement of the visual stimulus, *Journal of experimental psychology*, 1966, *71*, figure 3, p. 157.

Bell Telephone Laboratories for our Figure 8.13.

Butterworth & Company, Limited, for our Figure 7.3. From Averbach, E., and Sperling, G., Short-term storage of information in vision, in C. Cherry (Ed.), *Symposium on information theory*, London, 1961, figure 5. Reprinted by permission of the author.

Canadian Journal of Psychology for our Figures 6.9 and 11.11. From Haber, R. N., and Standing, L. G., Direct estimates of apparent duration of a flash followed by visual noise, *Canadian journal of psychology*, 1970, *24*, figure 1, p. 219; Mooney, C. M., Age in the development of closure ability in children, *Canadian journal of psychology*, 1957, *11*, pp. 219–226, figure 1. Reprinted by the permission of the editor and the authors.

Chapman & Hall, Ltd., for our Figures 2.16 and 4.4. From Pirenne, M. H., *Vision and the eye*, London: 1948, figure 29, plate IV, pp. 30, 6–7.

Clark University for our Figures 2.18 and 5.25. From Hecht, S., Vision: II. The nature of the photoreceptor process, figures 11, 29, pp. 727, 774 in Carl A. Murchison (Ed.) *A Handbook of General Experimental Psychology* (Worcester, Mass.: Clark University Press, 1934; reprinted New York; Russell & Russell, 1969).

Cold Spring Harbor Laboratory for our Figure 4.10. From Wald, G., and Brown, P. K., Human color vision and color blindness, *Cold Spring Harbor symposium on quantitative biology*, 1965, *30*, figure 10, p. 353. Reprinted by permission of the publisher and the author.

W. H. Freeman and Company for our Figure 8.3. From Stabilized images on the retina, by Pritchard, R. M., *Scientific American*, 1961, *204*, figure on p. 75. Copyright © 1961 Scientific American, Inc. Reprinted with permission.

Houghton Mifflin Company for our Figures 12.7 and 13.26. From James J. Gibson: *The Senses Considered as Perceptual Systems*. Houghton Mifflin Company, 1966, figure 10.10, p. 207; James J. Gibson: *The Perception of the Visual World*. Houghton Mifflin Company, 1950, figure 55, p. 123. Reprinted by permission.

Human Factors Society for our Figure 6.7. From Sperling, G., A model for visual memory tasks, *Human factors*, 1963, *5*, pp. 19–34, figure 4.

The Institute for Perception for our Figures 9.6 and 9.7. From Sanders, A., *The selective process in the functional visual field*, 1963, figures 3, 6, pp. 46, 51. Reprinted by permission of the Institute for Perception, TNO, Soesterberg, Netherlands, and the author.

International Universities Press, Inc., for our Figures 14.4, 14.5, 14.6, and 14.7. From Kohler, I., The formation and transformation of the perceptual world (tr. by H. Fiss), *Psychological issues*, 1964, *3*, no. 4, pp. 48, 49, 50, 97. (Originally Über Aufbau and Wandlungen der Wahrnehmungswelt, Vienna: R. M. Rohrer, 1951.)

Journal of the Optical Society of America for our Figures 4.13, 4.14, 6.3, and 6.12. From DeValois, R. L., Abromov, I., and Jacobs, G. H., Analysis of response patterns of LGN cells, *Journal of the Optical Society of America*, 1966, *56*, pp. 966–977, figures 9, 10, 15, 16; Boynton, R. M., Sturr, J. F., and Ikeda, M., Study of flicker by increment threshold technique, *Journal of the Optical Society of America*, 1961, *51*, figure 3, p. 199; Kelly, D. H., Visual responses to time-dependent stimuli, *Journal of the Optical Society of America*, 1961, *51*, pp. 422–429, figures 4, 5.

The Journal of Physiology for our Figure 9.1. From Robinson, D. A., The mechanics of human smooth pursuit eye movements, *Journal of physiology*, 1965, *180*, figure 5, p. 577. Reprinted by permission of the publisher and the author.

The Journal Press for our Figures 11.2 and 11.3. From Miller, G. A., Bruner, J. S., and Postman, L., Familiarity of letter sequences and tachistoscopic identification, *Journal of general psychology*, 1954, *50*, table 1, figure 1, pp. 133, 135. Reprinted by permission of the publisher and the author.

The M.I.T. Press for our Figures 2.19 and 15.10. From Boynton, R. M., Some temporal factors in vision, in W. Rosenblith (Ed.), *Sensory communication*, 1961, Figure 4, p. 746; Hershenson, M., Kessen, W., and Munsinger, H., Ocular orientation in the human newborn, in W. Wather-Dunn (Ed.), *Models for the perception of speech and visual form*, 1957, figure 3, p. 286.

North-Holland Publishing Company, Amsterdam, for our Figure 7.4. From Sperling, G., Successive approximation to a model for short-term memory, *Acta psychologica*, 1967, *27*, pp. 285–292, figure 3, part c.

Perceptual and Motor Skills for our Figure 14.11. From Held, R., and Hein, A. V., Adaptation of disarranged hand-eye coordination contingent upon re-afferent stimulation, *Perceptual and motor skills*, 1958, *8*, figure 1, p. 88.

Pergamon Press, Ltd., for our Figure 9.2. From Latour, P. L., Visual threshold during eye movements. *Vision research*, 1962, *2*, figure 1, p. 261.

Plenum Publishing Corporation for our Figures 9.9 and 9.13. From Yarbus, A. L., *Eye movements and vision*, 1967, figures 125, 109, pp. 197, 174.

Psychonomic Society, Inc., for our Figures 9.12 and 15.5. From Mackworth, N. H., and Morandi, A. J., The gaze selects informative details within pictures, *Perception and psychophysics*, 1967, *2*, figure 1, p. 548; Tronick, E., Stimulus control and the growth of the infant's effective visual field, *Perception and psychophysics*, 1972, *11*, figure 2, p. 374.

The Rockefeller University Press for our Figures 5.15, 5.16, 5.17, and 5.24. From Mueller, C. G., Frequency of seeing functions for intensity discriminations at various levels of adopting intensity, *Journal of general physiology*, 1951, *34*, pp. 463–474, figure 2; Hecht, S., Peskin, J. C., and Patt, M. Intensity discriminations in the human eye. II. Relationship between $\Delta I/I$ and intensity for different parts of the spectrum, *Journal of general physiology*, 1938, 22, pp. 7–19, figure 2; Crozier, W. J., and Holway, A. H., Theory and measurement of visual mechanisms. I. A visual discriminometer. II. Threshold stimulus intensity and retinal position, *Journal of general physiology*, 1939, 22, figure 4, p. 356; Hecht, S., and Mintz, E. U., The visibility of single lines at various illuminations and the retinal basis of visual resolution, *Journal of general physiology*, 1939, 22, figure 3, p. 601. Reprinted by permission of the publisher and the authors.

The Royal Society for our Figure 2.15. From Dowling, J. E., and Boycott, B. B., Organization of the primate retina: Electron microscopy, *Proceedings of the Royal Society* (London), Series B, 1966, *166*, figure 23, p. 104. Reprinted by permission of the publisher and the author.

Taylor & Francis, Ltd., for our Figure 2.14. From Ditchburn, R. W., Eye movements in relation to retinal action, *Optica acta*, 1955, *1*, figure 5, p. 174.

The University of Chicago Press for our Figures 2.17 and 9.10. From Polyak, S., *The verterbrate visual system*, 1958, figure 161, p. 276; Buswell, G. T., Fundamental reading habits: A study of their development, *Supplementary educational monographs*, vol. 21, 1922, table 1.

The University of Illinois Press for our Figures 8.5, 8.9, 8.16, 10.2, 10.4, and 11.10. From Boring, E. G., Appratus notes—A new ambiguous figure, *American journal of psychology*, 1930, 42, p. 444; Beck, J., Similarity grouping and peripheral discriminability under uncertainty, *American journal of psychology*, 1972, *85*, figure 1, p. 3; Hochberg, J., and Brooks, V., The psychophysics of form: Reversible-perspective drawings of spatial objects, *American journal of psychology*, 1960, *73*, plate I, p. 340; Neisser, U., Decision-time without reaction-time: Experiments in visual scanning, *American journal of psychology*, 1963, *76*, figures 1, 3, pp. 377, 385; Gibson, E. J., Pick, A. D., Osser, H., and Hammond, M., The role of grapheme-phoneme correspondence in the perception of words, *American journal of psychology*, 1962, *75*, figure 1, p. 562.

John Wiley & Sons, Inc., for our Figure 4.7. Judd, D. B., and Wyszecki, G. W., *Color in business, science and industry* (1952, 1st edition), 1963, figure 12.

preface

This book grew out of our need for a textbook that could be used primarily at an undergraduate level—one that would cover the new area of the study of perception called information processing, and that at the same time would provide the basic information in the more traditional fields of perception. We have attempted to meet this need with a book directed at this level, but detailed enough to provide a solid foundation for the beginning graduate student. To fulfill this aim, we have had to ignore a few of the older traditional topics of perception and also to be selective with respect to specific experiments and theories within each topic. We have not tried to write a handbook, but rather a book that touches on as many aspects of visual perception as possible.

But breadth of coverage has not been our only goal. We also have tried to present an integrated view of the visual functioning of the human being. Thus, wherever possible, we have interpreted material from the information-processing point of view using such concepts as storage, encoding, strategies, and so forth. We hoped that in this way we could bring together the seemingly different disciplines of visual physiology, sensory psychophysics, visual cognition, perceptual organization, and the perception of the world around us. The book is organized in three sections to reflect the major areas within the discipline. While many readers may be tempted to skip one chapter or another, or even whole sections, we hope to dissuade them from this practice. It is our belief that an understanding of visual perception at any level requires an understanding of the fundamental operation of the visual system at all levels. Therefore we would hope that the student and the scholar alike would read the book straight through.

This book is not without its pet notions, nor its seeds of controversy. Because the audience we have had in mind looks more like students and teachers, and not exclusively active researchers, we have occasionally yielded to the temptation to delete some of the qualifiers for the sake of the unity and the flow of the discussion. But we claim no special insight, nor greater access to truth. Wherever we could, we have tried to find a unity that would encompass more of this broad field than has been apparent before, without having to sacrifice parts of the discipline, or some of its disciples. In most instances, decisions were made on pragmatic grounds: Does this material make sense here?

In selecting the topics to be covered, we have specifically omitted a number, either because they could not fit into the flow of the material (for example, the perception of causality or of time) or because the flow would have to be broken for elaborate explanations (for example, the nature of imagery, of the visual illusions, or of figural aftereffects). We have not attempted to place arguments in their historical context unless the context itself seems to add to our understanding of the problem under discussion. Neither have we included controversies for the sake of controversy—those which affect the field broadly have been included; those which affect only a small portion of the field are included where relevant.

Perhaps the most glaring omission is formal definition of terms. Arguments over the definition of perception and related concepts have caused much difficulty in the history of the study of perception. We decided at the outset that we would present the material without becoming embroiled in formal definitions and the inevitable controversies that follow. Instead, we hope terms and concepts will become clear when the context of their use is understood. To help the student in this regard, we have italicized in the subject index at the end of the book those pages where the defining characterizations of concepts may be found.

As a further aid to the reader, each chapter ends with a brief summary of the material covered, and an annotated list of sources for additional study or research. Some of these will be general, covering part or all of the range of material in that chapter. We have tried to indicate the level of difficulty, but in most cases all such references are to more advanced sources. We also have included some more specialized references when they are particularly important contributions or if they provide a thorough discussion of the problem at hand or contain a good set of references for further research. It is our hope that this section at the end of each chapter will provide a good starting point for additional study of the topics in that chapter.

It is our special privilege to acknowledge our great appreciation for the benefits we have received from a number of persons who helped us throughout the course of our writing. The original draft of the manuscript was read in its entirety by Julian Hochberg, Douglas Matheson, William Epstein, and Eckart Scheerer. In addition, Robert Boynton read several of the chapters. Each helped us to shape our exposition more clearly and to avoid at least some of our errors. Needless to say, the ones that remain are those we were too obstinate to change or recognize. Many students at both Rochester and Brandeis read parts of the manuscript, and of course were guinea pigs to its content in various courses and seminars; their suggestions are reflected throughout the book. Leslie Chopek and Linda Handler assisted us at numerous and essential stages, for which we owe a special debt of gratitude. We also would like to thank the editorial and production staff at Holt, Rinehart and Winston for their unfailing support and efforts, and especially their good humor when we exercised our dubious rights as authors to change at the last minute what we had already agreed was immutable. Finally, to our wives Ruth and Amy we dedicate this book. They have paid the greatest price for its birth, without ever a complaint or reproach . . . well, hardly ever.

Rochester, New York   R.N.H.
Waltham, Massachusetts   M.H.
January 1973

contents

chapter
1
introduction to the study of visual perception

We shall start this book with only a very brief introduction because we wish to dispense with some of the more traditional topics of typical introductions. We are bypassing the history, the formal definitions, the development of major theoretical viewpoints, the methodological perspectives, and most of the other concerns that usually precede the substantive content. We do this because we believe context must provide the perspective from which to consider topics of history, theory, methodology, and so forth. To this end, we plan to jump directly into the study of visual perception. Along the way these other concerns will come up in their appropriate contexts, not as ends in themselves, but as means toward a more complete understanding of the study of visual perception.

Having said this, we do wish to add a few words to help the reader, both the beginning as well as the advanced student of visual perception, to anticipate what he will find in this book, and to understand our point of view. We have set our task in writing this book as follows: To show the student of visual perception how light transmits information about the environment to the eye of the perceiver, how that information is received and processed by the perceiver, and finally, how that information results in both conscious experience of the external world and in behavior based on that experience. The problem of perception is stated in this way because it emphasizes the fact that the perceiver must take part in perceiving—the information received from the environment must be processed. The contribution of the perceiver as a processor of information is the central focus in our study of the psychology of visual perception.

We will discuss many different kinds of research problems, some of which will seem far removed from the ordinary everyday perceiving we are used to. Nevertheless, it is our intention to direct our study as much as possible to perceptions that are reported by real people in a real world and that may have real consequences for them. This will be reflected by our selection of topics to be discussed and by our emphasis within that discussion. Thus, we will point out many examples in which the explanations offered or the demonstrations presented are contrived, restricted, or so specific to the circumstances that they will not survive generalization from the laboratory to the real world of real perceivers.

We approach the study of visual perception from an information-processing point of view. This is rightly called an approach and not a theory, for it

1

stresses analysis in terms of a sequence of processes without specifying what the processes have to or should be. When specific processes are suggested to explain a certain phenomenon, the sequence is called a theory or a model. We will meet many of them in the course of our study.

The general approach treats stimulation as information and attempts to specify what happens to that information. In the study of perception, the information will eventually affect the experience and behavior of the perceiver. The researcher in perception can observe only the behavior of the perceiver. The task of such a researcher is to try to determine what happened to the information, how the perceiver worked on it, stored it, experienced it, and perhaps ultimately made use of it in an overt act. Thus, the information-processing approach simply provides the student of perception with a starting point and a loose conceptual framework from which to begin his study.

The framework will be applied to the many different areas of the study of visual perception. We hope it will lend unity to the book, and will permit the student to gain some insight into the phenomena with fewer concepts than would otherwise be possible. It is our hope that, in this way, the solutions to seemingly unrelated problems will grow out of the same general principles.

For example, there are certain fundamental constraints on the visual system which apply to all of its functions—sensory reception, spatial perception, or visual cognitive tasks. The consequences of these constraints will provide a pervasive theme in our discussion. For example, because our eyes continually sample the visual world, making many rapid movements and corresponding fixations, visual information is not obtained continuously, but rather in successive inputs. Thus, a temporal factor is always present in the information available in stimulation. Therefore, the effects of time and of the integration of sequential information must always be considered at all subsequent stages of information processing. It is this temporal aspect of information reception which will be the basis for the suggestion, in many parts of the book, that the visual system integrates information or constructs percepts. But the first chapter is not the place to present the entire picture. It is sufficient at this point to have given you a glimpse of the direction the book will travel.

THE STRUCTURE OF THE BOOK

The topics to be discussed in our study of visual perception fall into three categories. Therefore, the book contains three sections: The first focuses upon the reception of information by the visual system; the second concerns the integration of that information in the perception of forms and the understanding of symbols; and the third considers the perception of a three-dimensional world. In selecting these three major problems of visual perception, we have ignored others (such as the perception of time and of causality) and have limited our discussion of some others. The discussion of perceptual development, for example, is almost entirely restricted to the development of space perception.

The three sections of the book may be read separately, but this is not recommended. It is important to read the section on sensory organization first, for not only does it provide the basic understanding of the anatomy, physiology, and general receptive functions of the visual system, but it does so within the framework of the general approach used throughout the book. Thus, we show immediately how sensory information is encoded, enhanced, and inhibited at the very first stage in the receptive process. When these processes underlying sensory organization are clearly understood, they are less likely to confound the reader when he deals with the more complex application of processing sequences in understanding perceptual recognition or the perception of space.

Additional sources of information about the topic discussed will be suggested at the end of each chapter. We will mention general sources rather than specific research articles in order to permit the student to locate information detailed enough to meet his needs. Under the heading "Readings" will be found references to review chapters on the specific topics or to other books. References to the specific experimental articles or books cited in the text will be given at the end of the book.

Finally, we have tried to construct the subject matter index at the end of the book as an additional learning aid. Rather than set up a glossary or list of formal definitions, we have used bold-faced type for the page references for every important term or concept to indicate the place in the book where it is first introduced, or where it is defined or used in the most illustrative manner.

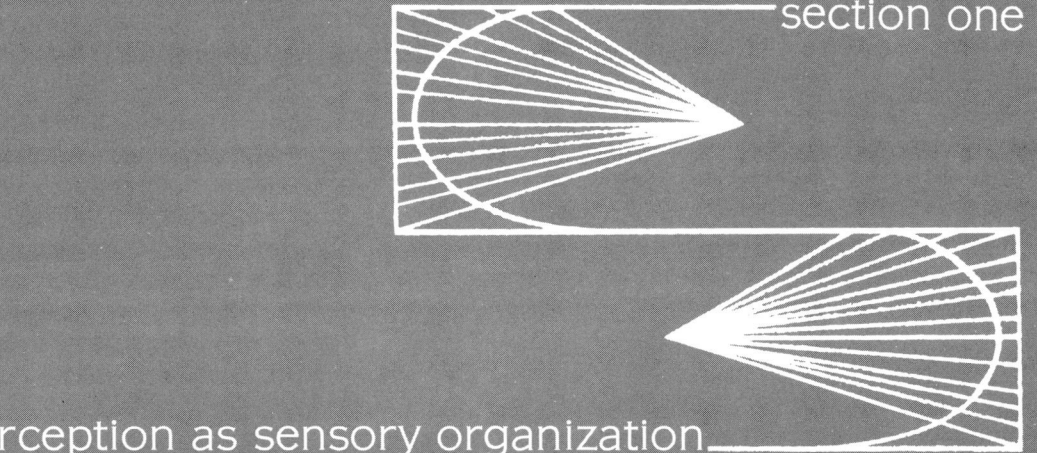

section one

perception as sensory organization

Chapters 2 through 6 begin our study of visual perception. In each we are concerned with different aspects of the properties of energy and objects as the stimuli for our perception of the visual world, with the mechanisms by which this stimulation is sensed and encoded by the visual system, and with some of the more basic functional relationships between stimulation and their effects. Chapter 2 examines the properties of light that convey information about the visual world, the receptor systems that transduce the electromagnetic energy of light into neural signals, and the transformations and pathways by which these signals reach the visual cortex of the brain. Chapter 3 focuses more directly on the mechanisms by which the different characteristics of the light energy reaching the eye are encoded as neural signals. Specifically, it is concerned with the processes by which important information is saved and even emphasized, while redundant or trivial information is thrown away. Chapter 4 concentrates on the perception of color as one of the most important dimensions of perceptual experience. In this chapter we examine the prerequisites for color perception, the properties of stimulation that are capable of producing different experiences of color, the receptor processes and the neural encoding needed to differentiate these properties of stimulation, and finally, some of the characteristics of the experience of color. Chapter 5 will concentrate on the functional relationships between stimulation and perception. First, we will consider some of the problems in the measurement of the effects of stimulation—the psychophysics of visual perception. Then we will use these principles of psychophysics to examine the sensitivity of the visual system to changes in the intensity of light, and its visual acuity— the ability to perceive small details. Finally, Chapter 6 explores the basic temporal dimension of visual stimulation, with respect both to how long perceptual processing takes, and to how well we can perceive the temporal extent of stimulation that has a time dimension.

These five chapters will serve as an introduction to the more complicated problems of perception, problems that involve properties of stimulation more complex than simple energy, wavelength, and spatial extent and problems of perception that are more complex than simply whether something was perceived or not.

2
sensory processes in visual perception

INTRODUCTION

In this chapter, we will first consider the characteristics of light as stimulation: its source, how it is measured and specified, and how it reaches the visual receptors. Then we will look at the receptor systems themselves, and the pathways by which the initial information is transmitted to the cortex of the brain. Finally we will examine how light energy is transduced by a receptor into neural excitation.

SPECIFICATION OF VISUAL STIMULATION

Sources of Light

There are relatively few objects in the universe that produce or radiate light. Usually light sources are hot, such as a candle, a filament in a light bulb, or a fiery sun or star. Some gases, however, are fluorescent and glow, especially when electrically stimulated. Although these sources are all important to human beings, they represent a very small proportion of the objects in the visual environment. Nearly everything that we can see is not in itself an emitter of light, but is reflecting light from the sun or from man-made sources such as light bulbs, or the gases in fluorescent tubes. Thus, the light that reaches our eyes is a function both of the characteristics of the sources of light and of the surfaces of objects that reflect it.

It is possible to conceptualize light in two different ways. One is to think of light as traveling in waves of varying wavelengths. In this sense, light is electromagnetic energy that arises from the excitation of electrons. The electromagnetic spectrum contains energy with wavelengths varying from many kilometers (certain types of radio waves) to cosmic waves that are so short that millions of them together would be less than one meter long. The visible portion of this spectrum, the only part properly called light, contains wavelengths from about 700 nanometers (billionths of a meter) down to about 400 nanometers. Figure 4.1 illustrates the electromagnetic spectrum, emphasizing the visible portion. The wavelength of light is a critical property of stimulation necessary for the perception of color, and we shall postpone further discussion of this property of light until Chapter 4.

The second physical description of light is in terms of the amount of energy radiated. In general, electromagnetic energy is described by the number of quanta radiated. A quantum of energy is called a photon when describing visible light. When we are concerned with the intensity of a light source, we will have to consider the number of photons being radiated from that source.

Photons as light energy are radiated from a source and travel in different directions. The number of photons traveling in any particular direction provides a measure of the intensity of the light in that direction. Photons travel in straight lines for all intents and purposes, and will continue to do so until they interact with matter along the way. Objects placed in their path will either absorb the photons, in which case they die (usually being transformed into heat), reflect them off in some other direction, or refract them through the matter and out the other side in a new direction. Light rays of photons can be considered to travel at such great speed that, at least on Earth, man is potentially in instantaneous visual contact with all objects, no matter how far away they are.

Although most sources of light have some size to them, it is usually convenient to think of them as point sources, and to think of them as emitting photons in all directions. Most objects in the path of photons have the property of being diffusely reflecting, meaning that light reflected in various directions is largely independent of the angle of incidence of the light onto the surface. In this way it is relatively easy to see the light as belonging to the surface, rather than as belonging to the light source, even when in fact there is no light being emitted by the surface itself.

When a surface is very smooth, the dispersion of the reflected photons is much narrower. In the extreme, a perfect mirror surface reflects photons in only one direction, opposite to the direction from their source and at the same angle of reflectance as the angle of incidence. Figure 2.1 illustrates several of the rays of photons radiating from a light source and being reflected from a number of surfaces and objects.

The reflectance of a surface is the ratio of the amount of light reflected to the amount of light incident. Objects with high reflectances appear very bright, since the eye receives nearly all of the light that falls on the object. On the other hand, objects with low reflectances appear dark, since the amount reflected from them is relatively small. Thus black surfaces appear dark no matter how much light falls on them since nearly all of it is absorbed (which is also why they feel warm in sunlight).

In a typical visual environment, photons are flying in all directions from light sources, and bounding off objects in all directions, some of them being lost through absorption in the process. From any given point on any surface, photons are being reflected in virtually all directions. If an eye is placed in this environment, every point in space in a straight line to the eye is capable of being a pathway of a stream of photons from that point to the eye. Thus, while light is diverging from every point in space, from the vantage point of an eye light is converging on it from every point in space.

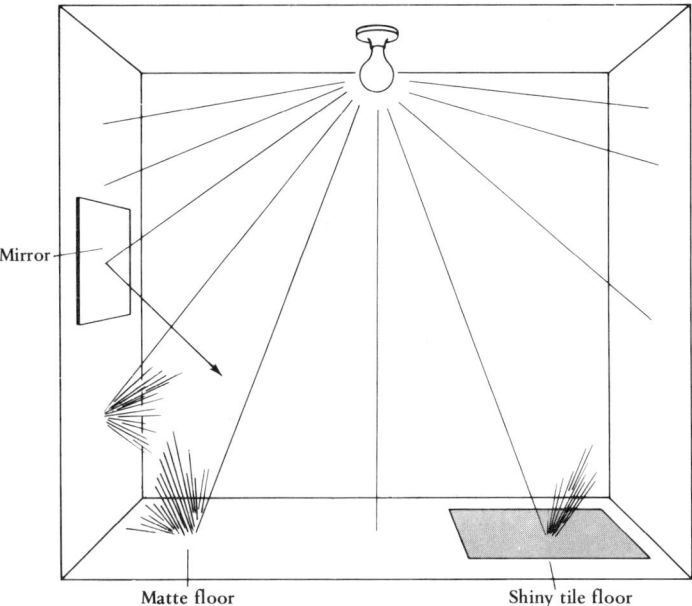

FIGURE 2.1   Rays of photons radiating from a light source and being reflected from various surfaces.

Projections of Objects

With all of these flying photons, how can the eye as an optical instrument capture any of them? A brief digression into the workings of a simple box camera may be helpful. Imagine the eye as a pinhole camera (see Figure 2.2). The pupil opening at the front is very small, and there is no focusing lens. We point our

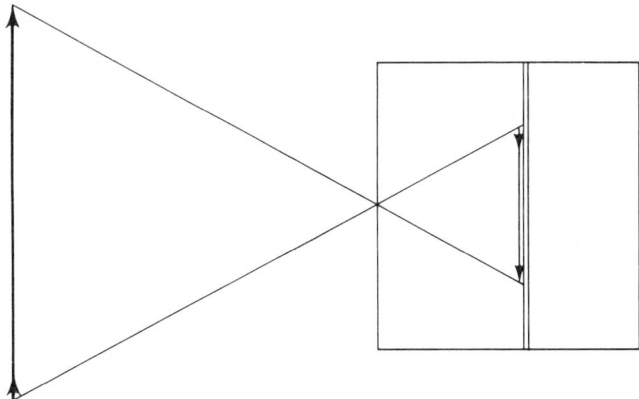

FIGURE 2.2   Schematic representation of a box camera with a pinhole to admit light and a projection surface on which film would normally be placed.

camera-eye at a stick in front of us. Light from the sun is being reflected in all directions from every point along the stick. What will our eye see? From any given point on the stick, of all the possible streams of photons only one of them could fit through the pinhole. Figure 2.2 shows only the streams from the two tips of the stick, but obviously there are an infinite number of streams of photons in between. These are all projected on the surface at the back of the inside of the camera, forming an optical image of the stick upside down. There is no reason why our eye could not function in principle in this manner. In fact, the pinhole camera has much to recommend it in simplicity, but because the hole is so small, very little light can get into it. In this sense, such a device is not particularly useful except under very high levels of illumination.

One could try to solve that problem by increasing the size of the hole, as in Figure 2.3. The problem here is that the object projected on the rear surface of the camera is now a hopeless blur, since from any given point on the stick a large number of different streams of photons going in slightly different directions manages to get through the hole. Thus, any given point on the projection surface may receive photons from a number of different points on the stick and there would never be any way to sort them out. As the hole is enlarged the blur will get progressively worse, even though brighter. Thus, the bigger-hole procedure creates more problems than it solves.

Figure 2.4 illustrates how a focusing lens placed in a relatively large opening in the front of the camera now is able to capture more light, but without blurring the projection. The lens refracts light by bending it, the amount bent being a function of the angle at which the light hits and leaves the surfaces of the lens. A perfect lens would be one that would take all of the different streams of photons from any given point on the object, and bend them in such a way that they all come back to a single point on the projection surface on the other side of the lens. In this way there would be no resulting blur, but a very sharp outline of a stick (still upside down). It would also be much brighter because it

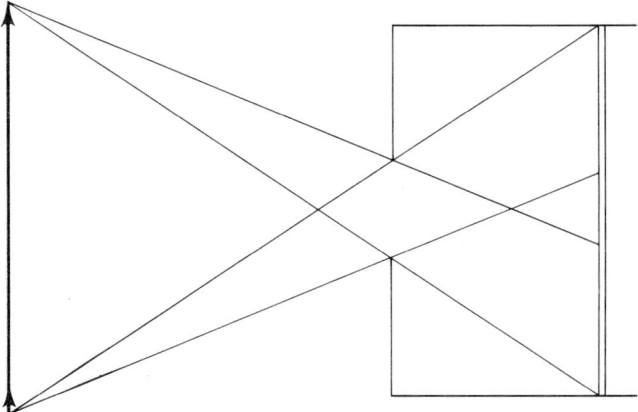

FIGURE 2.3   A box camera with a large opening in order to admit more light.

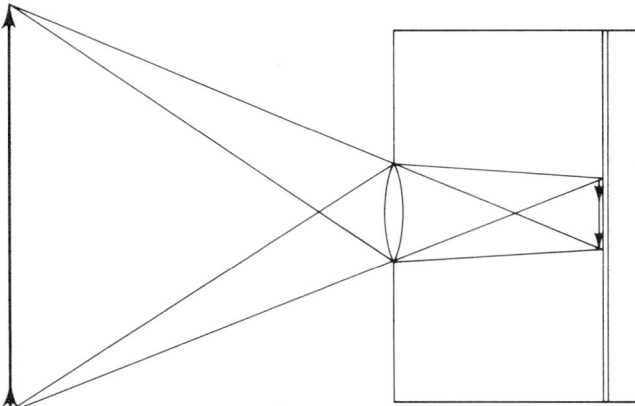

FIGURE 2.4   A box camera with a lens in the opening to focus the light rays on the projection surface.

is composed of many different streams of photons. The focal length of a lens describes the distance from the lens to the projection surface needed to give an object in space a sharply focused quality. The focal length is obviously a function of the curvature of the lens.

The human visual system has an outer covering of the eye, called the cornea, which provides the bulk of refraction of light. The shape of the cornea is relatively fixed and unchanging. Behind the cornea is a lens that is changeable in shape and provides a finer accommodation correction. The focal length for a typical human eye is about 17 millimeters. If the lens is fixed in shape and the distance between the lens and the retinal surface at the back of the eye is also fixed, then objects only at a certain distance would produce a sharp projection on the retinal surface. Since the diameter of the eyeball is relatively fixed, we can maintain clearly focused projections on the retina only by changing the shape of the lens as objects move closer or farther away, or as we shift our attention from near to far ones. We will consider the accommodation control later in this chapter.

THE REPRESENTATION OF VISUAL
STIMULATION IN THE RETINAL PROJECTION

We have considered, although briefly, how photons flying about in a visual environment might end up in the eye, or more precisely, on the retinal surface in the inside of the eye. We shall see shortly how photoreceptors embedded in this retinal surface transduce the photic energy, first into photochemical events and then into neural signals. But before we can tackle that process, we need to examine some of the properties of the retinal projection, especially in terms of the way it represents and preserves information about the objects radiating or reflecting photons. First we will see how changes in the intensity of light — the number of photons from a particular direction—are specified in the retinal projection. A second characteristic of objects is their size or extent, and a third is the sharpness of their edges and contours as well as the uniformity of their surfaces. We will take each of these up in turn. A fourth characteristic, the wavelength of the photons, will be postponed until Chapter 4.

Intensity of Light

We will need to use several measures to describe intensity of light (see Figure 2.5). We talk about light in terms of the number of photons being emitted from a light source. These are usually referred to in standard units of candlepower. The candlepower of a light-emitting object is a function of the number of photons being emitted per unit time. This is rarely a useful measure in the study of perception, however, since we are not concerned with light sources as such. Rather, we are interested in how many candlepower reach and illuminate a surface or the eye. This measure is called illuminance, specified as meter-candles, and is equal to the number of candlepower radiated from a source divided by the square of the distance in meters from the source to the surface or the eye. This says that the farther the light source is from a surface of a given size, the less light reaches it. The correction for distance is needed because when the surface or eye is farther from a source, fewer streams of photons are captured because the solid angle formed by the streams is smaller. Specifically, the number of streams of photons (defined as the size of the solid angle made by the surface to the source) varies inversely with the square of the distance from the source to the surface. From this geometric relationship, the illuminance is defined as candlepower divided by the square of the distance.

In terms of units one should have about 100 meter-candles on a desk surface in order to read comfortably. Ten meter-candles are adequate for normal street lighting at night. One could obviously increase the number of meter-candles from a street light by shortening the pole on which the light is mounted.

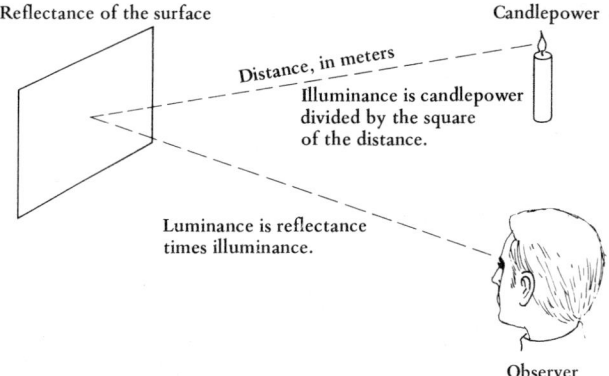

FIGURE 2.5 Measures to describe the intensity of light at the source, at a surface being illuminated, and as reflected from a surface to the eye.

This would increase the illumination or illuminance on the ground around the base of the light, although to the degree that the light is focused downward, a shorter pole would reduce the area on the ground illuminated.

Illuminance tells us how much light falls on a surface, or on the eye when looking directly at the source. But most light that we see enters the eye after being reflected from surfaces rather than coming directly from a light source. How much light reaches the eye depends upon how much of the incident light from the source is reflected from the surface to the eye. Reflectance is the ratio of light reflected from a surface to the light that reaches the surface. It is usually expressed as a percentage—100 percent reflectance signifying a perfectly reflecting surface.

The light reaching the eye from a surface is called its luminance, which will be determined by the product of its illuminance and the reflectance of the surface. The unit of luminance is a millilambert. Notice that luminance is not affected by the distance of an observer from the reflecting surface. Thus, the screen in a movie theater looks equally bright from the front or back row. However, the appearance of a screen changes dramatically if the projector is moved forward or back. If a light source radiated many photons in one direction it would be much more intense in that direction. Thus the solid angle over which the photons are emitted also determines its intensity. So if you take the same number of photons and concentrate them into a smaller area by focusing them with a reflector or a lens, the light will become more intense, as also happens when a light source moves closer to the surface. However, this is not the same as changing the size of the portion of the surface that is reflecting light, as would happen when you move closer or farther away from that surface. Since this does not change the number of photons being reflected from each point on the surface, the luminance of the surface is not affected. Thus, neither illuminance nor luminance is concerned with the area over which light is incident to or reflected from a surface.

Occasionally it is important to know not only how much light reaches an object or how much light is reflected from it, but how much reflected light actually enters the eye. This will be a function of the area of the pupil, and is called the retinal illuminance, specified in trolands. Retinal illuminance is equal to the luminance times the area of the pupil, measured in square millimeters. Hence, holding luminance constant, as the pupil opens, more light gets onto the retina, producing an increase in the number of trolands.

It should be obvious that if the eye looks directly at a point source of radiant energy, the intensity of light reaching the eye will be the same as if the light were first reflected from a mirror with 100-percent reflectance. Thus when the eye is looking directly at sources of light, the luminance of the light reaching the eye is the same as its illuminance.

Figure 2.6 presents some light levels found in normal environmental stimulation. These are reported as luminance in millilamberts. As can be seen, there is a range of 10^{13} millilamberts over which the visual system can normally respond. This is divided into a photopic range, increasing from about 1 milli-

FIGURE 2.6.   Typical light levels found in a normal visual environment.

	Scale of luminance in millilamberts	
Sun's surface at noon	10^{10}	
	10^{9}	Damaging
	10^{8}	
Tungsten filament	10^{7}	
	10^{6}	
	10^{5}	
White paper in sunlight	10^{4}	Photopic
	10^{3}	
	10^{2}	
Comfortable reading	10	
	1	Mixed
	10^{-1}	
White paper in moonlight	10^{-2}	
	10^{-3}	
White paper in starlight	10^{-4}	Scotopic
	10^{-5}	
Absolute threshold	10^{-6}	

lambert (10^{0}) to 10 million millilamberts (10^{7}), and a scotopic range, descending from about 1/10 of a millilambert (10^{-1}) down to absolute threshold of around 1/1,000,000 of a millilambert (10^{-6}). Given this large range of sensitivity, it is usually not possible to plot graphs in luminance values directly. Instead, a logarithmic transformation is made, which in effect plots the exponents to the base 10 of luminance. Hence a luminance of $1 = \text{Log}_{10}\ 1 = \text{Log}_{10}\ 10° = 0$ in the log scale; a luminance of $100 = \text{Log}_{10}\ 100 = \text{Log}_{10}\ 10^{2} = 2$ in the log scale; and a luminance of $1/10,000 = \text{Log}_{10}\ 1/10,000 = \text{Log}_{10}\ 1/10^{4} = \text{Log}_{10}\ 10^{-4} = -4$ in the log scale. In this sense, the range of sensitivity is 13 log units. To say that sensitivity was decreased by one log unit means that whatever light intensity was initially needed, now ten times as much intensity is needed to achieve the same perceptual effect.

There are other units with which the intensity of light can be specified, but we will not require their formal definitions in this book.

The term brightness refers to the psychological appearance of luminance, and will vary with luminance under many conditions. But it can also be a function of variables other than simply the reflectance of a surface and the illuminance of the light incident to it. We will consider some of these determinants of brightness in Chapter 5.

The Size of Objects

One can specify an object's size out in space with a measuring instrument, such as a ruler. Such measurements are useful if we are concerned with describing the environment. However, if we want to describe our perception of the environment, then we need to know something about the size of objects as a function of how far they are from the eye, and the magnitude of their projection on the retina.

For simplicity, we can consider the eye again as a pinhole camera, and can draw lines representing streams of photons from the extremities of an object through the pinhole and spread out again on the retinal surface at the back of the eye, as in Figure 2.7. An object of size S will produce a retinal projection of size s. If the real size S of the object is held constant, but the object is moved farther away from the eye, s will decrease in size. Consequently, the size of an object S in meters is not typically a useful measure. Rather, what we need is the angle subtended by rays of light converging on the eye from the extremities of an object. As seen in Figure 2.7, the tangent of this angle A is equal to S/D.

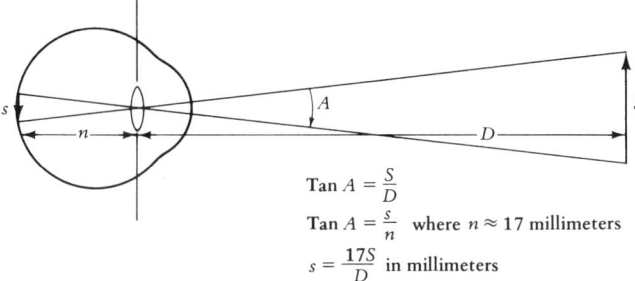

$$\text{Tan } A = \frac{S}{D}$$

$$\text{Tan } A = \frac{s}{n} \quad \text{where } n \approx 17 \text{ millimeters}$$

$$s = \frac{17S}{D} \quad \text{in millimeters}$$

FIGURE 2.7 Schematic representation of the relationships between the physical size of an object (S) at a distance (D) from the eye, the visual angle (A) formed by rays of photons reflected from its extremities, and the size of the retinal projections (s).

To determine the size of the retinal projection s, note that its angle is the same as A. For the average adult eye, the distance from the nodal point in the eye to the retinal surface is about 17 millimeters. Thus, the tangent of A equals $s/17$. Since the tangent of A is also equal to S/D, s equals $17S/D$. Thus, for any known object of size S, it is possible to determine the visual angle it subtends and the size of its retinal projection in millimeters.

Figure 2.8 presents some typical visual angles in relation to object sizes in the environment. Visual angles are reported in degrees, minutes, and seconds of arc. A complete circle is 360 degrees, and a right angle has 90 degrees. In each degree is sixty minutes, and in each minute is sixty seconds. Looking straight ahead with both eyes, we can see objects spread over about 200 degrees across the visual field.

Sharpness of Contour

We have already considered intensity of light being reflected from an object, expressed as luminance, and the size of an object, expressed as visual angle. If we stopped here we would be assuming that the intensity distribution over an object was uniform, and that the nature of the edges of the object was unimportant. However, these are of critical importance for perception, so we

FIGURE 2.8.   Some visual angles of common objects at specified distances from a perceiver.

Fovea is about 2° in diameter.

Your thumbnail at arm's length is between 1.5° and 2°.
   ($D = 60$ centimeters, $S = 1.5$ centimeters, Tan $A = 1.5/60 = .025$, $A \approx 1.5°$)

A four-letter word in this book held at 50 centimeters (20 inches) viewing distance is about 0.7°.

If you move the book to 25 centimeters, $A \approx 1.4°$.

Each letter is 0.16 centimeters wide, or about 12 minutes of arc at 50 centimeters.

One letter at 50 centimeters is 0.05 millimeters on the retina.

Sun and moon are each 30 minutes of arc. While the sun is nearly 400 times farther away, it is much larger, too.

A quarter coin at arm's length is 2°, at 85 meters is 1 minute, and 5 kilometers is 1 second. Under optimal conditions, an object the width of a quarter could be seen at 10 kilometers distance from the eye.

---

need to consider how such changes can be described and how they are represented in the optical information reaching the retina.

As a useful analogy consider what happens when the light output from a surface is measured with a photometer, such as a photographer's light meter. When the opening that admits light is relatively small, Figure 2.9 would represent the output of a photometer that is moved slowly in a horizontal direction along a picket fence seen against the sky. Using the sky as a reference point of 100 percent, only 10 percent as much luminance is being reflected from the bars in the fence as from the sky behind it. Notice that the edges of the bars do not show up sharply, but are rounded off. Further, the bars themselves are not uniform in intensity, since the photometer picks up much more light

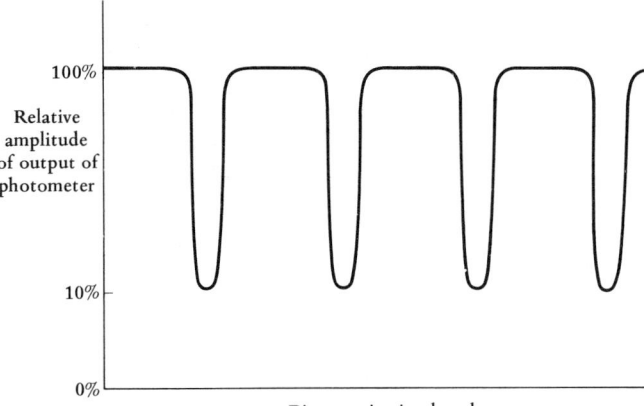

FIGURE 2.9   Hypothetical output of a photometer, describing the amount of light reaching the photometer as it is moved slowly over a picket fence seen against the sky.

near their edges than in their centers. While both of these characteristics could be due to a large opening in the photometer, it could also be due to gradual changes in luminance at the edges. The same measurements on a row of capital letter I's, such as might be printed on this page, would yield a distribution of light intensity similar to that of Figure 2.9, no matter how small an opening in the photometer was used. This is because the ink near the edges of the lines will not appear as dark as in the center of the lines.

Theoretically, any edge or contour can be specified by its luminance distribution. Figure 2.10 shows several different examples. It is obvious that other things being equal, edge *b* should be easier to notice than edge *c*, with edge *a* somewhere in between. This is reasonable even though the absolute difference in luminance from the left-hand side to the right-hand side of the edges is the same in each example. We would typically call edge *c* fuzzy, and edge *b* sharp. It would also be reasonable to expect that for edges of equal sharpness, those with a larger luminance difference would be more prominent or noticeable than those with a smaller difference.

Although the luminance distribution over a surface such as those plotted in Figure 2.10 provides a description of the sharpness of the contour of objects, there has been a mathematical description available for some time that appears to offer several benefits for the understanding of contour effects in perception. Although the details go far beyond the scope of this book, a Fourier analysis shows that any wave form, such as any of the edges in Figure 2.10 or the bars in Figure 2.9, can be described by the summation of several sine waves of varying amplitude and frequency. As a simple example, Figure 2.11 shows how a sharp edge (or one cycle of a square wave) can be constructed by adding more and

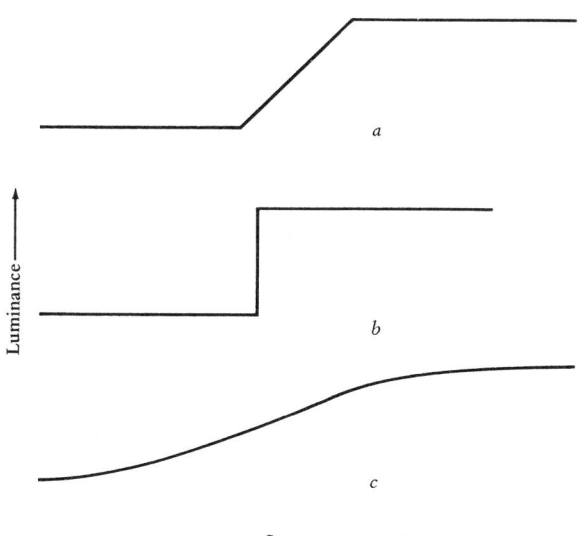

FIGURE 2.10 Several hypothetical luminance distributions at the intersection of two surfaces of unequal intensity.

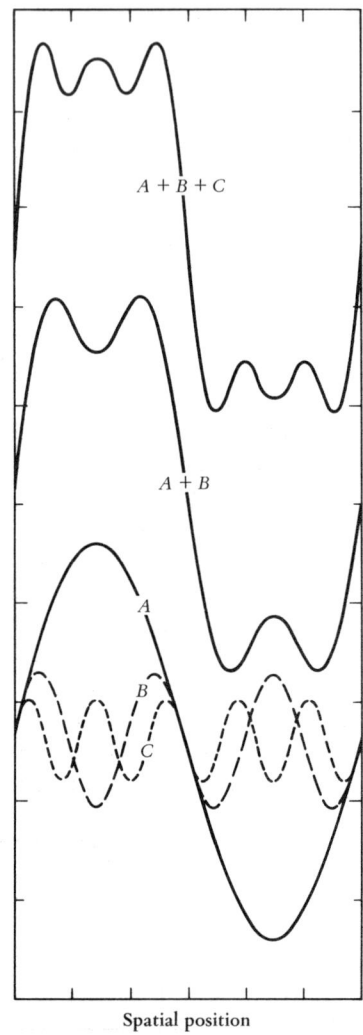

Spatial position

FIGURE 2.11   The construction of a square wave luminance distribution by a series of sine waves of varying frequency and amplitude (from Cornsweet, 1970).

more sine waves together. If you take a sine wave with a frequency F (where frequency is the reciprocal of the wavelength) and with amplitude A (where amplitude is the intensity of the peak as measured against the average or zero intensity), and add to it sine waves of $3F$, $5F$, $7F$, . . . , each with corresponding amplitudes of $1/3A$, $1/5A$, $1/7A$, . . . , the sum of these waves will approach the shape of the square wave edge.

Although this may appear to be only a mathematical nicety, we will consider in subsequent chapters some evidence to suggest that the visual system may be sensitive to these different frequencies. Hence, we may not respond to the sharpness of an edge directly, but rather to the frequencies of which the edge is composed. In that case our ability to see a sharp edge would depend on our sensitivity both to high as well as to low frequencies. But the sharpest part of the edge depends only on the high frequencies. If we could not resolve high-frequency wave forms, then we would not be able to see a very sharp edge. We will return in Chapter 3 to some of the uses of this type of spatial frequency analysis of edges.

THE VISUAL NERVOUS SYSTEM

We will consider three components of the visual nervous system—the structure and anatomy of the eye, the neural structure of the retina, and the visual pathways from the eye to the cortex.

Visual Anatomy

Figure 2.12 illustrates the principal components of the human eye. We will discuss them as we trace the path that light takes as it enters the eye. The eyeball is about 25 millimeters in diameter and is covered with an opaque layer called the sclera, the white of the eye that we see from the outside. The outside opening at the front of the eye is covered by a clear membrane called the cornea. Behind the cornea is the iris, a sphincter muscle which can open and close, changing the amount of light that can enter the eye. The iris is the pigmented part of the front of the eye whose color is determined genetically. The opening in the iris, called the pupil, appears to be controlled by a light reflex, which is

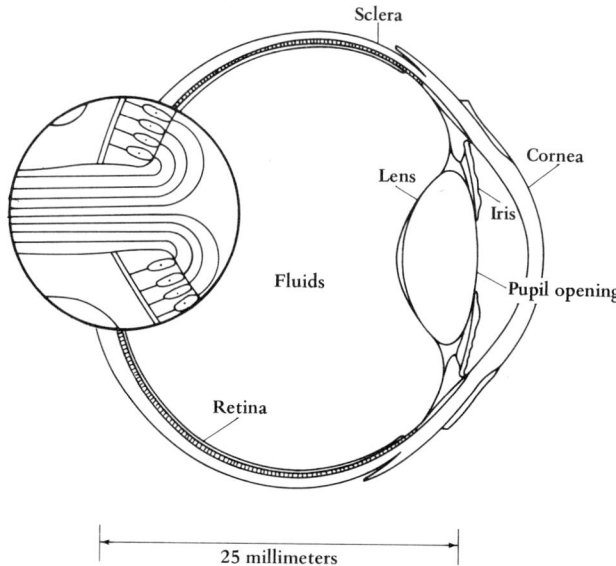

FIGURE 2.12 The principal anatomical components of a human eye.

virtually identical to the intensity sensitivity function of the eye. Thus, if light can be seen then the pupil contracts, and if the light changes in energy, then the pupil changes. Figure 2.13 shows the change in normal pupil size as a function of retinal illuminance, specified in trolands. The normal range of pupil change is from about 2 to 8 millimeters in diameter, or about a sixteenfold change in area (about a 1.2 log-unit change). Thus, while the change in pupil size might be useful over small changes in energy, a 1.2 log-unit adjustment obviously cannot be very useful over a full sensitivity range of thirteen log units of the visual system.

Notice that there appear to be two components to the pupil-size function of Figure 2.13. The one at the lower illuminance level represents adjustments caused by light falling on those photoreceptors primarily concerned with perception under dim illumination. The right-hand function of the curve represents further adjustments in illuminance from the light falling on the photoreceptors that respond only to high illumination. These two sections correspond to the scotopic and photopic aspects of sensitivity in the visual system, a characteristic that we will notice in many functions.

If the iris mechanism is understood only as a device to adjust the visual system for variation in light intensity, then it would not seem to have much importance. The visual system is sensitive to intensity changes many billion-fold (from 10^{-6} to 10^7 millilamberts), yet the iris can produce only a sixteen-fold change. Further, adjustment in pupil size is quite slow, with latencies up to ten seconds or longer for full excursion. It seems more likely that the iris serves a smaller yet still important function that is only partially related to the adjustment to light intensity. We saw with a pinhole camera that the sharpest retinal projection occurs with the smallest pupil opening. This will be true even with a lens in the opening. Further, the depth of field is greatest with a smaller

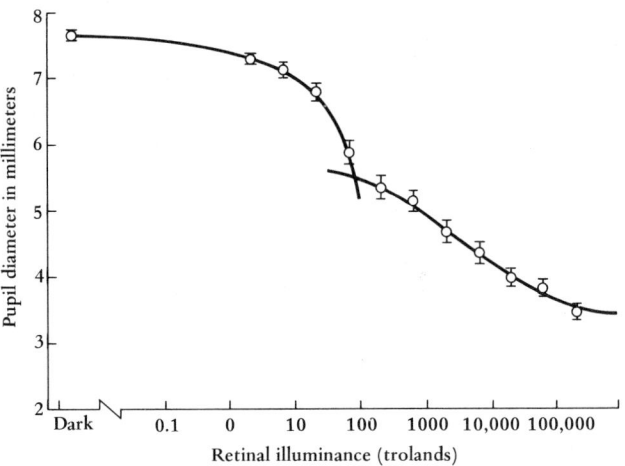

FIGURE 2.13   The change in pupil size as a function of retinal illuminance (from ten Doesschate and Alpern, 1967).

opening. Finally, given the various imperfections of the lens of the human eye, accurate focusing deteriorates sharply for those paths of light that enter the eye off-center. For all of these reasons, then, keeping the entrance part of the eye as small as possible will increase the sharpness of focus of the retinal projection. However, when the intensity of light drops too low, this sharpness must be sacrificed in order to capture enough photons. It is then that a variable opening is needed. It is for this reason that much of the responsiveness of the iris is to low light levels, as seen in the left-hand portion of Figure 2.13.

There has also been some evidence recently that the iris changes as a function of emotional and attentional variables, including those involved in thinking and problem solving. Although empirical relationships have been studied, their importance and possible cause-effect significance is not at all clearly understood yet (see Goldwater, 1972).

After light passes through the pupil, it next encounters the lens. Although most of the refraction of light occurs as it passes from the air into the cornea, some remaining focusing is accomplished by varying the thickness and hence the refractive power of the lens. This process is called accommodation. The lens consists of a number of transparent crystalline layers arranged much like the layers of an onion. They are held in a sac which can be tightened or relaxed by the tension of the muscles holding the sac in place. If you close one eye and while looking at your finger at arm's length slowly move your finger toward your nose, you can feel the tension as the thickness of the lens is increased to keep the projection on the retina in focus. Focus breaks down close to your eye, and a blurred image results.

The stimulus for accommodation changes appears to be retinal blur, but we do not yet know how this stimulus is picked up and signaled to the muscles. It is a relatively slow process, requiring nearly four-tenths of a second for a complete change from near to far accommodation, or vice versa. Further, the precision of the adjustment is relatively crude. However, given all of the other optical imperfections in the visual system, finer refractive power of the lens does not appear to be needed.

After the light exits from the lens it passes through the fluids in the center of the eyeball and is focused on the inside surface of the ball. The purpose of the fluids is to maintain the shape of the eye, and also to provide a medium with a similar refractive index to that of the lens, so that no further refraction of light occurs as the light exits from the lens.

The retina surrounds nearly 200 degrees inside the eye. Embedded in the retina are the photoreceptors and their neural support, as is shown in the enlarged insert of Figure 2.12. The most sensitive portion of the retina to pattern is the fovea, shown as a small indentation at the back of the eye. The blind spot, or optic disk, is an area of several degrees on the retina. It has no receptors because the nerve connections from the receptors exit from the eye at this point to form the optic nerve tract connecting to higher centers in the brain.

Neither the cornea nor the lens is a very good optical instrument. This means that they are incapable of producing very sharp projections on the retinal surface. Further, the fluids inside the eye lead to some refraction of light as well, scattering it around the inside of the eyeball. Not only is a substantial amount of energy lost in this way, but it blurs the retinal projection. Further, the blood vessels supplying the nervous structure of the retina and all of the nerve cells themselves lie in front of the receptors, so that light must pass through them to get to the part of each receptor where a photochemical reaction can occur. Some light energy is absorbed by this mass, and more is refracted and bent again. Consequently, only a small percentage of the energy in light impinging on the cornea actually reaches the receptors, and that which does is no longer in sharp optical focus. We will look at this optical spreading effect again in Chapter 5 when we consider our ability to notice very fine detail.

Each eye is held and controlled in a bony socket by six muscles acting somewhat as three antagonistic pairs. One pair roughly controls up-and-down movement, another side-to-side movement, and a third rotational movement about the foveal-pupil axis of the eye itself. The muscles are controlled and coordinated by brain-stem centers, but we do not yet know very much about the details of the neural systems that provide signals to these centers.

There are three types of eye movements of great importance in our perception of the visual world around us: convergence movements that keep both eyes pointing at whatever is our center of attention; saccadic movements that shift both eyes to a new center of interest; and pursuit movements that follow an object moving in space or maintain fixation on an object as we move in space. We will consider these three types of movements in substantial detail in later chapters on visual search and on perception of space and motion.

One final set of eye motions is relevant to our present discussion, however. If the position of the eye is precisely monitored by attaching a mirror directly to the eye and photographing deflections of a light from the mirror as the eye moves, it is known that the eye undergoes almost continuous movements, even when the perceiver is attempting to maintain precise fixation on an object in space. Riggs, Armington, and Ratliff (1954) showed that the eye can shift by an amount equivalent to three minutes of arc during a one-second recording interval. During a one-tenth of a second interval, the excursion is nearly one-half minute of arc, about the distance between two cones in the center of the fovea. These movements are physiological tremors, and probably represent the irreducible minimum precision in trying to hold the eye in position with the balance of six very strong muscles all pulling on it. As will be expected, the direction and distance of the tremors are independent over time.

In addition to these tremors found during fixations, the eye will also drift off the fixation point quite slowly. After it has moved some distance, perhaps ten or twenty cones, a microsaccadic movement will rapidly jerk it back toward the fixation point again. Figure 2.14 illustrates a brief sequence of tremors, drifts, and microsaccades.

It should be clear that given these small and somewhat independent movements, the retinal projection imaged on the retinal surface by the cornea and

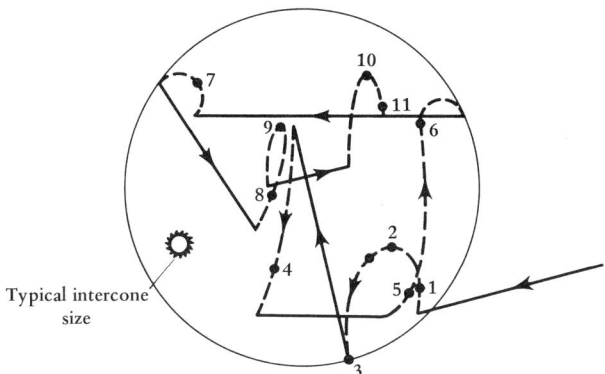

FIGURE 2.14   Displacements of the retinal projection of a point source of light caused by a brief sequence of tremors, drifts, and microsaccades (from Ditchburn, 1955).

lens is never stationary with respect to specific receptors. We shall examine the impact of this for sensory coding and visual acuity in Chapters 3 and 5, respectively.

Retinal Structure

Figure 2.15 illustrates the arrangement of receptors and neurons in the retina. The receptors themselves are imbedded in the back of the retina, with all of the nervous connections and blood supply in front of them. Consequently, the light passes through all of the supporting structure before reaching the receptors.

The two kinds of photoreceptors in the visual system are called rods and cones. There are about 120 million rods and nearly seven million cones. Figure 2.16 shows the distribution of each type of photoreceptor across the retina. The center of the fovea, covering an area of perhaps 1 degree, contains only cones. The number and proportion of cones falls off rapidly with many fewer cones present beyond 10 degrees. On the other hand, no rods are found in the center of the fovea. They reach their highest frequency at about 16 degrees on either side, with decreasing numbers out to about 100 degrees at the edge of the retina on either side of the fovea.

The density of cells also varies across the retina. In the center of the fovea cones are packed very tightly together, so that the center-to-center distance is about 22 seconds of arc, or .002 millimeters, or 2 microns. In general, receptors are less tightly packed as one moves farther from the fovea. Figure 2.17 shows the high density over a portion of the center of the fovea.

Each receptor is connected to a bipolar cell via a synapse. In the fovea, usually only one cone is connected to one bipolar. Outside of the fovea there will be many receptors connected to one bipolar. This approaches a convergence of hundreds of rods onto one bipolar beyond 20 degrees into the periphery. This great pooling of receptors onto a single bipolar cell in the periphery

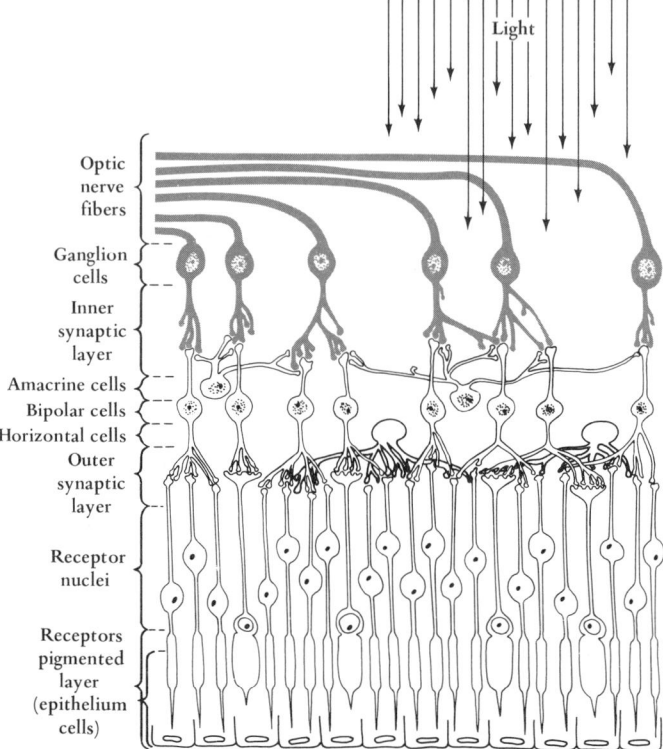

FIGURE 2.15   Schematic diagram of the neural interconnections among receptors and bipolar, ganglion, horizontal, and amacrine cells (from Dowling and Boycott, 1966).

means that any particular bipolar cannot determine which of its many receptors had been stimulated by light. In the center of the fovea there is very little pooling, resulting in virtually perfect specificity of excitation.

Each bipolar cell is connected to a ganglion cell via a second synapse. The ganglion cell has an elongated body that forms one of the fibers of the optic nerve. There are less than one million ganglion cells leaving the retina in this manner. Again, in the fovea each bipolar generally connects to one ganglion, whereas in the periphery a number of bipolars will converge on a single ganglion cell.

Figure 2.15 also shows the interconnection among the bipolar and ganglion cells via horizontal and amacrine cells. While these interconnections are not on the direct pathway between receptor and cortex, they are involved in critical functions regulating the pattern of excitation in the retina, especially concerning inhibitory processes. We will consider some of these in detail in Chapter 3.

A few of the photons traveling through the media of the eye are absorbed by those media, by the blood vessels, or by the neural tissues that lie in front of the receptors. A much larger number pass through these materials and

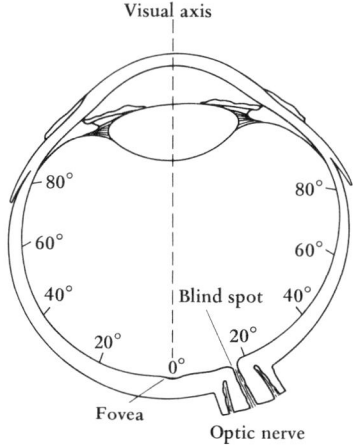

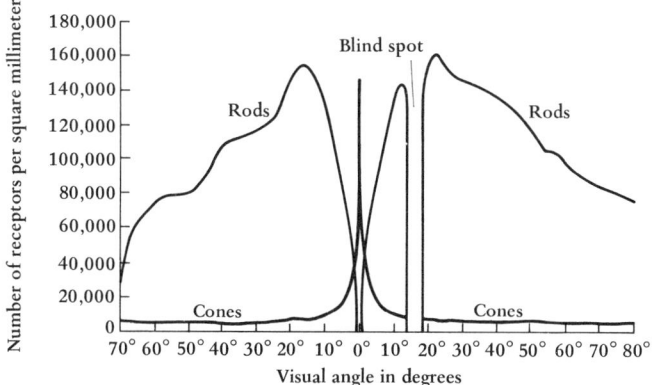

FIGURE 2.16   Density distributions of rod and cone receptors across the retinal surface (from Pirenne, 1967).

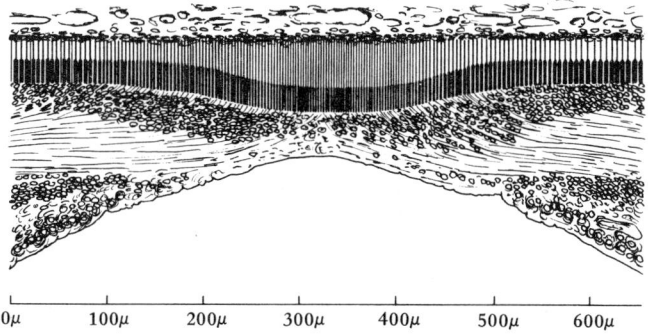

FIGURE 2.17   Schematic representation of a microscopic section of the central portion of a human retina. The diagram covers about 2 degrees, or about ⅔ millimeter (from Polyak, 1957).

also pass through the receptors themselves, and are absorbed by the dark inner lining around the inside of the eye. None of these photons have any consequences at all for visual perception. Some other photons are reflected off of the back of the eye, pass back through the receptors again unnoticed, and bounce around inside the eye until they are finally absorbed by some of the media, by the lining of the eye at some other point, by pigment molecules in some other receptor, or exit back through the pupil and out into the world again. Of course, the degree to which any of this scattered light excites receptors represents substantial error.

Even under the most optimal conditions, only a small percentage of the photons incident on the cornea actually have any visual impact on a photoreceptor. But it is these few that do that account for all of the phenomena of visual perception, for there can be no vision without photons exciting receptors.

We still do not understand the details concerning how the energy in photons is transduced into electrical activity in neurons. This is an area of intense research interest and we will add only a few comments. The first stage requires absorption of a photon by a molecule of photopigment in a photoreceptor. The photopigment in rod receptors is called rhodopsin, or visual purple. (We will postpone consideration of cones and the absorption of photons of different wavelengths until Chapter 4.) Each of the four million or so molecules of rhodopsin in each rod will undergo a molecular change when it absorbs a photon. This change occurs effectively instantaneously with absorption. Somehow, and we do not yet know the mechanism, the products of this change are capable of producing a neural charge across the synapse between the photoreceptor and the bipolar cell it connects to. The neural charge probably is a logarithmic function of the number of photons absorbed, thereby producing an output as a graded potential of the input.

When a molecule of rhodopsin absorbs a photon, that molecule is bleached in color, rendering it temporarily unable to absorb another photon. Thus, when rods are exposed to intense light much of the rhodopsin will be bleached, thereby reducing the sensitivity of those rods to subsequent stimulation. Current evidence (see Cornsweet, 1970, for a discussion) suggests that once a molecule has been bleached, it has a 50-percent chance of regenerating within five minutes. This means that following very intense prolonged stimulation, in which virtually all of the molecules of every rod are bleached, it will take nearly forty minutes in total darkness before they all regenerate. In the normal visual environment, light is not so intense and relatively few molecules are bleached at any one time. Consequently, most visual functioning occurs during times when most of the molecules are in an unbleached, and therefore responsive, state. Nevertheless, the responsiveness of the visual system can be dramatically altered as a function of exposure to light levels that cause very little bleaching. We will consider these effects on adaptation below.

As we will show in Chapter 5, the minimum sensitivity of the visual system is such that if only about ten rods absorb one photon each, that will be sufficient for the awareness that visual stimulation has occurred. But each rod has upwards of four million pigment molecules, each capable of absorbing a photon. The more of these that absorb photons, the larger the output of the receptor, although as indicated above, we do not yet know how that output is produced. But its effect on the remaining neural units in the retina is somewhat more clearly understood, in part because the different kinds of neurons in the retina share great similarities to the properties of other neural units in the rest of the nervous system.

Specifically, we know that some synapses are excitatory and some are inhibitory in their effects. Thus the firing of a neuron may either increase or decrease the probability that the next neuron will fire, depending on the nature of the neural transmitter substance released at the synapse. Further, we know that the more cells converging on a neuron that are active, the greater is the likelihood that the neuron will fire. Thus, we should expect spatial summation effects throughout the retina. In this sense, a many-to-one interconnection will pool excitation. Inhibition can also summate in the same manner, as we will see in Chapter 3.

For many reasons, all neurons will show some activity, even in the absence of normally effective stimulation. Thus, retinal ganglion cells have a resting or spontaneous rate of firing on the order of several responses per second. Consequently, all measures of activity or effects of stimulation must be taken against a baseline of the spontaneous activity level. This is especially important because an increase in inhibition may be signaled by a decrease in the firing rate below that of the baseline rate.

Adaptation to Retinal Stimulation

We know that if the photoreceptors are suddenly deprived of photons, the sensitivity of the visual system to subsequent stimulation will increase. This process is called dark adaptation, the gain in sensitivity as the eye remains in the dark. As we will see, this is a relatively slow gain, taking over forty minutes to complete. Light adaptation is the loss in sensitivity when a dark-adapted eye is suddenly placed in the light. Complete light adaptation is much faster, with much of its effect occurring in less than a second, and the whole process needing only several minutes.

The great importance of adaptation changes stems from the rather narrow operating, or dynamic, range of sensitivity of the visual system at any one moment in time. As we will see in Chapter 3, while visual perception can occur over a range of intensity covering thirteen log units, we are sensitive at any one time to a dynamic range of only about two log units. If the light level varies more widely than this narrow range, the visual system becomes momentarily blind and unable to respond to photons. Adaptation refers primarily to the stability of this narrow dynamic range, and how the visual system changes to a new dynamic range.

Dark Adaptation

Dark adaptation refers to the time course of the increase in sensitivity of an eye when illumination is terminated. This is what happens when you walk from outside into a darkened movie theater. The classic dark-adaptation function was obtained by Hecht in 1934. In a typical experiment, the perceiver would first look at a fixation point at the center of a large screen, uniformly illuminated at some value. Periodically a small increment spot would be flashed on this background, and the perceiver indicated whether he saw it. The luminance of the spot was adjusted until it was just barely detectable. Then the background light was turned off, and the increment spot again flashed in the center of the now blank screen. The luminance of the spot was again adjusted so as to be just at threshold. Figure 2.18 shows that the amount of energy needed in the small spot decreases rapidly over the first minute or so, and then more slowly after that, finally flattening out over a range in which there are no further increases in sensitivity. This first ten minutes or so represents changes in the sensitivity of the cones and shows an increase of about one and one half log units. We know this is a cone function since no change in adaptation over this time would have been found if the spot had been presented only in the periphery in the relatively more cone-free areas.

During this ten minutes, the rod receptors have also been increasing in sensitivity, although they do not start as fast as do the cones. But this early portion of the rod adaptation function is difficult to show, since it is difficult to measure activity of the rods alone without involving the cones. Aguilar and Stiles (1954) have by very careful procedures managed to follow the early stages of rod adaptation without cone involvement, and they have shown the dotted portion of the rod function of Figure 2.18.

In any event, after about ten minutes no further sensitivity increase is possible for the cones. From then on, all further increases in sensitivity are due to changes in the rod receptors. They produce an increase of another three log units. After about thirty minutes, sensitivity has increased to its maximal

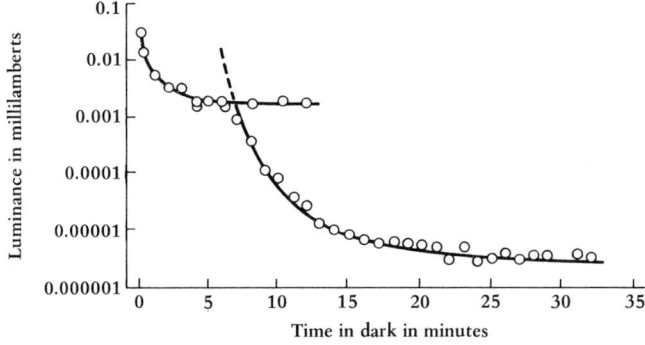

FIGURE 2.18   The time course of dark adaptation as shown by the decrease in luminance threshold as a function of time after the exposure of a human eye to an intense light (from Hecht, 1934).

value, given the size, wavelength, duration, and location of the increment spot. The overall change in the course of the thirty to forty minutes is about a 10,000-fold increase in sensitivity. The rod component of dark adaptation will not be observed if the increment spot is only presented in the rod-free center of the fovea, nor if the light is red, to which rods are relatively insensitive (see below and Chapter 4).

Since the course of dark adaptation is very long relative to light adaptation, a dark-adapted perceiver will lose his high sensitivity quickly if the lights are turned on even briefly, and will have to remain in the dark again for a long period of time to regain that sensitivity. As a practical point, people who have to work in the dark but occasionally must turn on the lights have a serious problem in maintaining sensitivity. A typical example might be a soldier on patrol at night who must periodically glance at a map. Every time he turns on a flashlight even briefly to read the map, he will become effectively blind for as long as ten to twenty minutes before he can again see in the dark. Since he is primarily concerned with seeing in the dark, it is the rods that he must protect from light adaptation. If the map is examined under long wavelength light, such as when wearing red goggles, the soldier will be able to see the map with foveal vision, which is sensitive to long wavelength light, while at the same time leaving the rods unstimulated, as they are relatively insensitive to such light. When the long wavelength light is then turned off, the rods will still be at their maximum sensitivity, and the perceiver will not have to wait for them to readapt. Of course, the soldier will lose his foveal vision in the dark because the long wavelength light has adapted the cones. But since his cones are not useful for seeing in the dark anyway, he has had no actual loss.

Mechanisms of Dark Adaptation

Is dark adaptation a change in the photochemistry of the receptors, or is it a neural effect? We now know it is both, although up to the 1930s a photochemical effect seemed to be the whole answer. Thus, if each photon bleached a molecule of photopigment, which then took up to forty minutes to return to the unbleached state, this would nicely account for the shape of Hecht's data. This model of bleaching was very consistent and appealing, but it fails to account properly for the time course of adaptation. The sensitivity of the rods can change even when there is no change in the concentration of rhodopsin. In fact, bleaching effects occur rather slowly and reverse themselves rather slowly. Hence, this type of photochemical model can account for the long-term changes in dark-adaptation curves, but not the very rapid changes. This is especially true for light adaptation, where the loss of sensitivity following the onset of light begins to occur within 100 microseconds of the light onset. These times are much faster than are ever observed for the photochemical processes. Hence, at least part of the adaptation functions must be due to some kind of neural effect. Dowling (1967) has argued that there is a pooling of excitation of receptors, probably at the bipolar levels, and that this pooling is responsible for the more rapid adaptation changes. The details of this are just becoming clear in research. It appears now that when the neural processes are combined with the photochemical effects, the two together can provide a more satisfactory explanation of dark adaptation.

Light Adaptation

To some extent light adaptation is the mirror image of dark adaptation, except that it occurs very rapidly. It also has several other interesting properties. Figure 2.19, taken from Kandel (1958), shows the changes in luminance threshold for the onset of light to an eye that has been in the dark long enough to be fully dark adapted. The functions shown are for several intensities of the adapting light. There are three important characteristics to these functions. First, the threshold begins to rise up to 100 milliseconds before the adapting light is turned on. This is very puzzling on the surface, since it suggests that the effect of the onset of light acts backward in time to affect events that occurred up to one-tenth of a second earlier. Second, there is the large overshoot. Hence, to the onset of the adapting light, not only is there a loss in sensitivity which occurs rapidly, but the loss is greatest just at the point when the light comes on, and then settles down to a lower asymptotic level. Third, the shape of the time course of light adaptation is virtually the same, regardless of the intensity of the adapting light. The more intense the adapting light, the greater and more rapid the loss in sensitivity and the lower the ultimate level of sensitivity after the transient effects have ended.

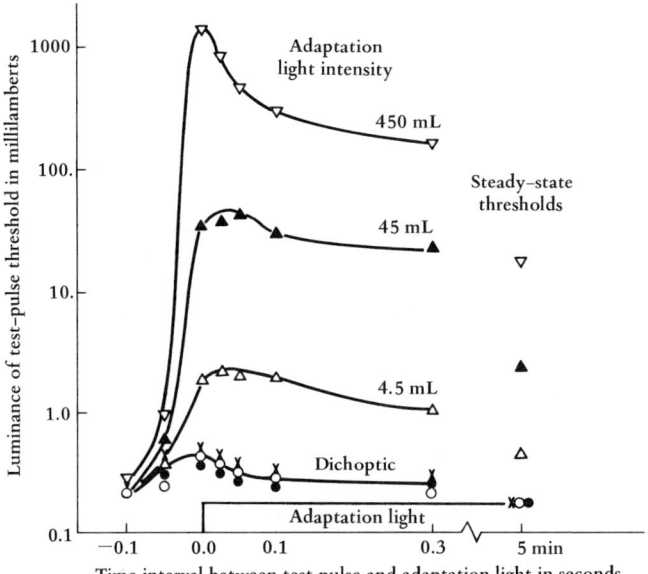

FIGURE 2.19   The time course of light adaptation as shown by the changes in luminance threshold produced by the onset of light presented to a dark adapted eye (from Kandel, 1958, reprinted in Boynton, 1961).

We will postpone most of our discussion of these transient effects until Chapter 6 on temporal factors, because they have greater implications for temporal processing, especially visual masking phenomena. The main point to note here is the rapidity of light adaptation. It is especially due to this finding that the photochemical models of adaptation are by themselves inadequate.

Visual Pathways to the Brain

Figure 2.20 shows the neural interconnections between each eye and the brain. Within each eye there are two synapses, one between the receptor and bipolar cells, and one between the bipolar and the ganglion cells. There are also cross-

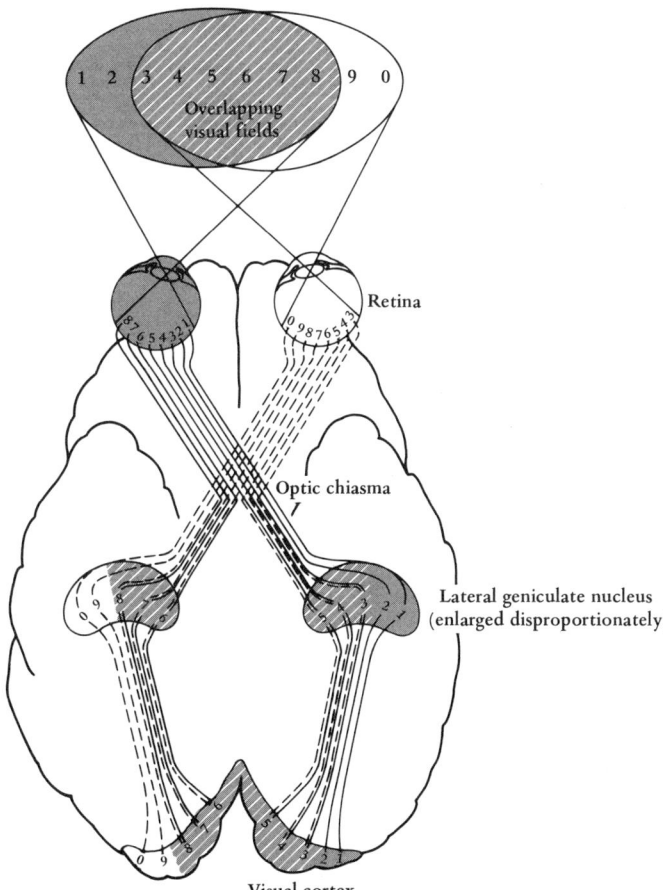

FIGURE 2.20 Schematic representation of the visual pathways from each eye to the visual cortex, via the optic chiasma and the lateral geniculate nucleus. The parts of the visual field represented at each level are indicated by tracing the numbers through the system (from Lindsay and Norman, 1972).

synapses with horizontal and amacrine cells. The ganglion nerves are several inches long, and do not form their next synapse until they reach the lateral geniculate body in each hemisphere of the brain.

The nearly one million fibers in the optic nerve are anatomically separated according to the side of each half of the retina from which they originated. One can think of each retina as divided vertically through the fovea into two halves. All of the ganglion cells connected to receptors from the temporal side of each retina (closest to the ears) go to the lateral geniculate nucleus in the same side of the brain as that eye. All of the ganglion cells from receptors on the nasal side of each retina (closest to the nose) cross at the optic chiasma so that they go to the lateral geniculate body of the hemisphere opposite to the side the eye is on. If the eyes are looking straight ahead, an object that is to the left will project onto the nasal side of the left eye and the temporal side of the right eye. Both of these sets of receptors will have ganglion cells which end up in the right visual hemisphere. Likewise, with the eyes straight ahead, an object to the right will project onto ganglions on the nasal side of the right eye and the temporal side of the left eye, and both will end up in the left side of the brain. With the eyes straight ahead, objects which are themselves straight ahead will fall on both sides of each retina, and consequently will be projected into both brain hemispheres.

From the lateral geniculate nucleus, visual radiations project out to the striate cortex, known as area 17, the primary visual cortex.

In spite of all of the mixings and crossings, there is an approximate point-for-point representation between the retinal ganglion cells, the lateral geniculate nucleus, and the striate cortex. In the fovea this point-for-point representation continues all the way down to the receptor cells themselves, since they have a one-to-one interconnection with ganglion cells. With only one million ganglion cells in each optic nerve, the majority of which are connected individually to single receptors in the fovea, the largest proportion of the striate cortex is taken up with foveal representations.

The lateral geniculate nucleus and the striate cortex have their cells arranged in layers and in columns. Some of the importance of this will be seen in Chapter 3 on coding mechanisms, since the handling of pattern coding appears to differ from layer to layer.

The striate cortex projects to the association cortex, areas 18 and 19, which integrate other senses with memory and pattern. Other areas of the brain are concerned with language and symbols and these are connected to areas 18 and 19. The hemispheres are also interconnected.

Some of the optic nerve fibers do not go to the lateral geniculate body, but are pulled out at the pregeniculate nucleus adjacent to the lateral geniculate nucleus (not shown in Figure 2.20). These appear to control pupillary eye movement, accommodation, and other eye functions, although their entire operations and structures are not very well understood yet.

SUMMARY

This chapter has provided the introduction to our study of visual perception by focusing at the most basic level of analysis. First we examined the nature of light as energy that is radiated from sources and reflected from surfaces of objects. Some of these reflected rays enter the eye and are focused on the photosensitive retina around the inside of the eyeball. We indicated how basic information about the sources and reflecting surfaces of light are represented in light on the retina. Intensity must be defined at the source, as light incident to a surface, as the amount of light reaching the eye, and as the amount of light that actually enters through the entrance pupil of the eye. The distribution of light over the retina can provide information about the size of the surface reflecting light to the eye. The distribution is specified in visual angle, which permits us to consider together both the physical size of an object or surface and its distance from the eye. In addition to the intensity and distribution of light on the retina, information is available about the boundedness or contour of the reflecting surface. This is specified by the abruptness and the texture changes in the luminance discontinuities in the light as it is spread out over the retina.

Following this consideration of light as it can provide information at the retina about the visual world, we turned to a discussion of some of the basic properties of the visual nervous system. First we looked at the anatomy of the eye, especially the functions of each component as light enters and passes through to the retina. The neural structure of the retina and the visual pathways to the cortex were examined, both in terms of its different types of cells and in the mechanisms by which photic energy is transduced into neural signals which are then transmitted to the cortex. We digressed briefly to consider the specific response of the photoreceptors to light, and the adaptation processes inherent in prolonged exposure to light and to darkness.

With these basic principles and mechanisms, we can now consider in somewhat more detail the means by which information conveyed by light is coded and represented in the visual nervous system. This is the topic for Chapter 3.

Readings

We can suggest a number of general or advanced textbooks, handbooks, and articles that form the basis of this chapter. For the physics of light, Monk (1963) provides a general introduction. Cornsweet (1970) has a good discussion of the representation of objects in space on the retinal projection. For the greatest detail on the neuroanatomy of the retina, Polyak (1957) is still the classic, with Brindley's 1960 and 1972 books, though difficult, providing a detailed discussion of most of the relevant topics covered in this chapter. The various movements of the eye are discussed by Alpern (1971 and 1972), and in an article by Robinson (1968). Barlow (1972) has an excellent advanced treatment of adaptation.

There are several handbooks that contain useful sections or chapters on topics covered here. We will list several here, and they will come up in subsequent chapters. Davson's four-volume work (1962), Graham (1965), Woodworth (1938), Woodworth and Schlossberg (1954), Kling and Riggs (1971), Jameson and Hurvich (1972), and Carterette and Friedman (1973, 1974) have many relevant chapters, though usually at advanced levels. Stevens (1951), while older, is still quite useful.

For general texts on neurophysiology, including the visual system, see Stevens (1966) or Milner (1970).

chapter
3
sensory coding mechanisms

INTRODUCTION

This book is primarily concerned with visual perception. Nevertheless, we believe it is important to begin with an understanding of receptive processes and visual neurophysiology because, on the one hand, the processes set the limits of visual functioning, and on the other, they provide models for higher-level visual processing. We will discover here how information is represented in the visual system—how it is coded, refined, abstracted, and how some of it is lost.

The coding task in vision is enormous. There are nearly 130 million photoreceptors in the retina, each theoretically capable of being active at the same time, and refiring at rates approaching 1000 times per second under optimal circumstances. The 130 million cells converge, diverge, and interconnect among the neural cells into which they feed. Ultimately, less than one million fibers in the optic nerve are available to represent the activities of all of the photoreceptors and all of their supporting neural structures. No matter how complex a computer system is available, and the brain is undoubtedly the most complex one, it could not handle all of this information if each signal had to be monitored and treated independently. If this were not enough, we have also already seen that the optics of the eye are none too good. A point of light in space results in a spread of excitation on the retina, with a large amount of random scatter and loss of energy.

Following this logic, as well as other lines, we cannot reasonably expect the visual system to maintain information about the state of individual receptors in some type of code. Rather, we should expect to find ways in which the characteristics of the visual world around us can be represented in a sensory code, without at the same time demanding that the state of each receptor be known at each level in the visual nervous system. This chapter will explore some of these sensory coding processes.

We shall use the concepts of code and representation interchangeably to stand for storage and transformation of information. We are obviously interested in the transformations that reduce the amount of different events that have to be represented without sacrificing anything that is important. We shall not be preoccupied with definitions of "importance," hoping that it will be as obvious to the reader as it is to us what the advantages and disadvantages are of particular coding processes. Almost all reasonable usages of

35

concepts of coding imply some kind of trade-off where some information is retained or enhanced at the expense of other information. Some codes are reversible in that one can retrieve the original state from knowledge of later stages. This is rarely possible in the coding processes that we will be examining, so the trade-offs are real.

Perhaps at this point one brief word is necessary about surplus meanings which may accrue to the concept of coding strategy. Everything we will discuss in this chapter concerns interactions among sensory neurons, based on neurophysiological evidence. Thus, the use of the word strategy in no sense implies a higher order homunculus, or little man in the head, who decides how to process or code information.

We can begin by seeing what kinds of information must be coded. What are the qualities of visual stimulation that we need to know about in order to perceive the visual world? We must know something about the location of objects in space, where they are, and whether they have moved. We need to know something about their spatial extents, their sizes, shapes, and texture. We need to know something about the scale of space, the distances between objects and their relative sizes, and the organization of space. We need to know something about serial order, about what happened before and what is happening next. And we need some way to integrate across the successive retinal projections that occur when our eyes move.

It is obvious that the individual receptors themselves cannot tell us anything about this kind of information. To show that this is so, let us look at the limitations of an individual receptor in providing even the simplest information about the light that falls on it. Where is the light source? From which direction in space did the light come? Where on the retina did the light fall? What is the light's intensity, what is its wavelength, how large is it? What is its duration? For all of these simple characteristics of light, only two can be partially specified by a particular receptor alone—the intensity of the light and its duration. All of the other properties require more complex coding than that available in a single receptor.

As we noted in the previous chapter, the absorption of light energy or photons is the only stimulus event relevant to visual perception. If there is no absorption, then there is no way in which the visual system can have any information at all about the presence of light and thereby about the visual world around us. But when a receptor absorbs some photons, it can represent information about only two things—how many photons it absorbed, and for how long. The number of photons absorbed is coded by the output of the receptor, and the duration of the light by the time course of that output. These are circumstances in which the number of photons absorbed by a receptor will be monotonically related to the number of photons being radiated or reflected to the eye. When that is the case, then the output of this receptor will be informative about the intensity of the light. But in the majority of circumstances, this relationship does not exist. There may be many photons in the light, but a particular receptor may absorb only a few of them. Or there may be only a few photons and the receptor may catch most of them. But much more important, the vigor of the response of an individual receptor may be uncorrelated with the magnitude of the overall coding for the intensity of light reaching the retina.

Even so, intensity coding by a receptor at least can start in the receptor itself. What about the other aspects? The problem is that once a photon is absorbed, the receptor has no way of providing any information at all about that photon. While rhodopsin will be more likely to absorb photons of 500 nanometers of wavelength than those of 600 nanometers, once absorbed the result is exactly the same, and there is no way for the receptor to code the wavelength of the photon. Likewise, the direction from which the photon came, the path it followed upon entering the eye, is not coded. That path will affect the probability of its being absorbed, at least by cone receptors, but once absorbed the same photochemical events are set in motion.

What about location on the retina—can a receptor provide information about its position on the retina? It cannot do this alone, because a single receptor cannot encode spatial information. The location of a receptor is specified only in terms of coordinates provided by a higher-level combination of outputs of receptors. In order to specify that light hit the right-hand side of the retina, the output of at least one other receptor must be taken into account.

Without further detail it is obvious that a single receptor can produce a wide variety of responses, but that by itself, it is not very informative about even the simplest properties of the light that gave rise to those outputs. We have developed this point to show first that complex sensory coding is necessary before we can know anything about the light in the retinal projection. Even more important, there is little reason to try to preserve the separate states of the separate receptors, since those states by themselves tell us very little. Thus, we should be looking for coding processes that quickly go beyond the states of individual receptors.

STRATEGIES FOR CODING

As our previous discussion suggests, we need to look for coding strategies in the visual system by which the overwhelming magnitude of potential information can be reduced to manageable proportions, while at the same time abstracting in an economical fashion the critical information needed in order to perceive the visual world. We will distinguish three principal strategies that the visual system could follow. Each focuses on a slightly different aspect of coding, and each offers different advantages and disadvantages. After we have described each briefly, we will discuss them in detail in light of known facts about how the visual system actually follows the strategies concerned.

Ignore All Steady-State Stimulation

If a group of adjacent receptors are all in the same state, then knowing the state of one would allow us to predict the state of all of the others. If this is the case, there is no reason to encode all of them, and they can be ignored. Thus, it is really only necessary to transmit information about a gradient or a discontinuity in stimulation. Only when there is a receptor that is excited adjacent to one that is not excited should the visual system take notice. The same concern for discontinuity should occur for the time domain. If a particular receptor does not alter its output over time, then it can be safely ignored. One needs information about the state of a receptor only when it changes state. In general, steady-state excitation is redundant; it has no information value. Since our environment is relatively unchanging in relation to the density of spacing and to the temporal resolution of the receptors, such a strategy alone would reduce the amount of neural coding and transmission to a fraction of its potential without any loss of information about the environment.

Specialize the Visual System for Different Functions

There is no reason why all parts of the retina should perform all functions equivalently, or why they should be performed at each moment in time. It seems quite reasonable to expect that evolution would have selected some aspects of the environment-perceiver interaction to be more important than others. For example, in the environment man typically finds himself, except for the detection of moving objects, fine temporal resolution in vision is usually not necessary. Hence, we could dispense with the ability to detect rapidly flickering light when its spatial position is unchanged. Further, being primarily a daytime animal, man rarely needs to make fine acuity judgments in darkness. Hence, acuity could be specialized for high levels of illumination, but not for perception at night. Many other trade-offs of this variety may be possible and for each one of them a great reduction in information transmission would occur.

Precode Critical Visual Features

Evolution has probably played a major role in selecting mechanisms to encode the aspects of the visual environment which are most important. These salient aspects of the visual environment have been called critical visual features. If the coding can be carried out in the retina, then a much simpler representation of the information can be transmitted to the cortex. Recent research has already identified several critical visual features, including the presence of color, edges, lines, motion, and orientation. We will see that each of these is probably precoded in the retina, so that the cortex can acquire information about their presence in the visual field with minimal information transmission.

These are not the only possible coding strategies, but they are the most important ones. We will now see how each of these solutions or coding strategies is worked out to reduce the transmission of excitation without valuable information loss.

MECHANISMS TO IGNORE STEADY-STATE EXCITATION

What is required to ignore steady-state information is a neural device to permit adjacent receptors to interact. The visual system shares with all parts of the nervous system two mechanisms that go a long way by themselves to accomplish this—lateral summation and lateral inhibition. Lateral here refers to the property of affecting other neural elements nearby in space. Their properties represent a most important coding mechanism in vision.

Lateral Summation and Inhibition

We have already described in Chapter 2 how synaptic connections between two neurons can be either excitatory or inhibitory. If a group of receptors is connected to a bipolar cell only with excitatory synapses, then the likelihood that the bipolar would become active would increase in direct proportion to the number of its receptors that absorb photons. Likewise, if the interconnections among bipolars and ganglions only involved excitatory synapses, a further pooling of excitation would occur. Such interaction is called lateral summation. This process would be very useful in maximizing responses to light of very low energy levels. We will show in Chapter 5 that, especially for small areas in the periphery of the retina, there is a complete reciprocity between area and intensity of stimulation. That is, the probability of detecting the presence of a light could be held constant even with a decrease in luminance if the area is increased by a comparable amount. This is a very useful device for noticing the presence of light even if it is in the extremes of the periphery.

Some of the connections between receptors and neurons include inhibitory synapses as well. Now instead of summation between adjacent receptors, we would find inhibition. In Figure 3.1, receptor A forms an excitatory synapse with bipolar cell X, so that when the receptor is active it excites the bipolar. But receptor B has an inhibitory synapse with bipolar X. Thus when a light falls on A and B together, the probability that the bipolar will be excited is reduced. Notice that if B is stimulated alone it will inhibit X, dropping it below its resting or spontaneous level of firing. The point is that when A and B are both stimulated, they inhibit each other as far as their impact on X is concerned. (Notice that receptor A is not inhibited by B. A's response is still entirely a function of the number of photons it absorbs. What is inhibited is the effect of A on X).

If any rod receptor in the periphery has inhibitory synapses, then the amount of lateral summation would be greatly reduced or entirely absent. Thus, for pooling of receptors to occur, either inhibition must be absent

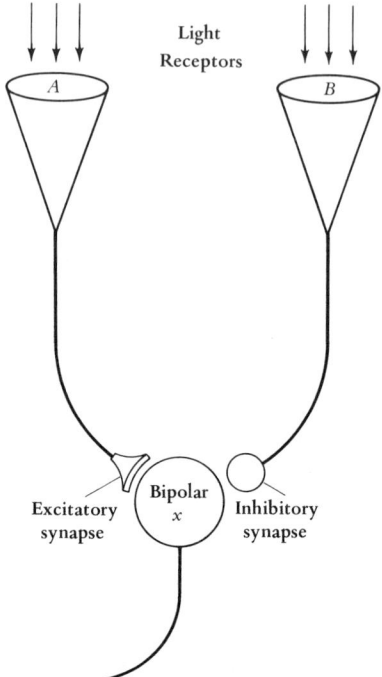

FIGURE 3.1 Schematic representation of an excitatory synapse between a receptor on a bipolar cell and an inhibitory synapse between a receptor and a bipolar cell.

in the periphery or not involved during low-intensity stimulation. We now know that the latter is correct, and that inhibitory processes come into play only when light levels are quite high. Hence, we see an example of specialization—summation to capture small amounts of light, and inhibition to provide more complex coding when light levels are high.

The classic research on lateral inhibition by Hartline (for example, Hartline and Ratliff, 1957) was performed on the horseshoe crab, Limulus. Nearly all of the properties Hartline reported seem to apply to the nervous systems of virtually every species studied. When he recorded from a single optic nerve fiber he found excitation to be roughly a logarithmic function of the intensity of the light falling on the receptor for that fiber. If a second spot of light stimulated other receptors, the output of the first receptor decreased as the second light moved closer, or as the second light was made more intense. Each of these findings suggests lateral inhibition—the output of one receptor's ganglion cell is inhibited by the activity of another nearby receptor. Hartline found no evidence of any lateral excitatory interactions in Limulus such as those we have described for the peripheral human retina.

Cornsweet (1970) has presented the schematic description of the inhibition in Limulus shown in Figure 3.2. Light falling on receptors A and B excites ganglion cells A' and B', respectively, through their excitatory synapses. The outputs of the two ganglion cells travel to the brain. But those outputs each have two forks, one of which forms an inhibitory synapse with an adjacent ganglion. Consequently, as light falls on *A* it not only excites *A'*, but also inhibits *B'*. If light also falls on *B*, *B'* is excited and *A'* inhibited. Thus mutual inhibition of *A'* and *B'* will tend to reduce the level of activity of both, well below what they would have been if *A* or *B* alone were absorbing photons.

Lateral inhibitory effects have been found in every species studied. Except for man, most of the research has involved electrophysiological procedures in which a microelectrode records the activity level in a neural unit while light is applied to one or more receptors. In man psychophysical procedures have been used to supply similar evidence. Suffice it to say that there is overwhelming evidence for the presence of lateral excitatory and lateral inhibitory effects in man, as well as in other animals.

How does lateral inhibition help reduce steady-state excitation? With no more of a mechanism than we have seen in Limulus, several very powerful effects can be described. If all receptors have light falling on them, although

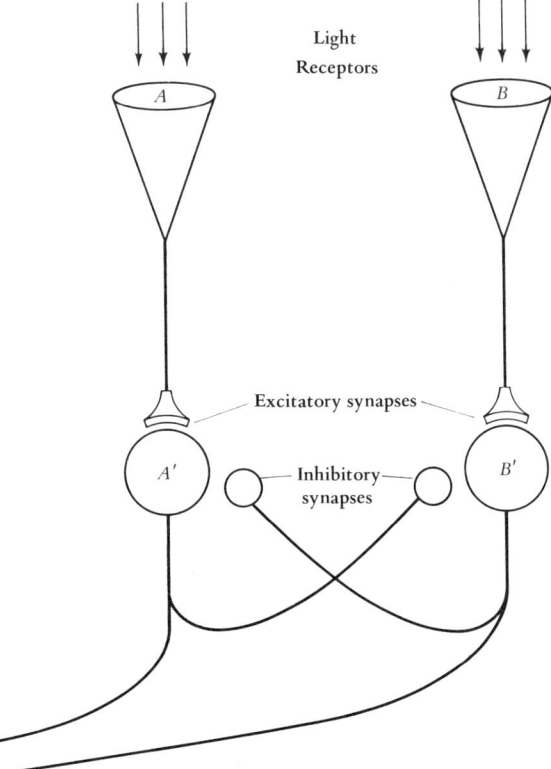

FIGURE 3.2 Schematic representation of excitatory synapses between two pairs of receptors and ganglion cells and mutual inhibitory synapses between the two ganglion cells, as a description of the type of lateral inhibition found in Limulus.

each will be active, their ganglions will tend to inhibit one another. Under optimal circumstances their inhibitions and excitations will be so balanced that no change in output will occur over that of the spontaneous level. Here, then, a uniform excitation across the receptors produces little or no effect at the ganglion cell level.

To see even more powerful coding that can be built up from inhibitory interactions among neural units, we need a brief digression to consider the concept of a receptive field.

Receptive Field Organization

The visual systems of many species are organized in such a way that collections of neurons act as functional units. When one attempts to determine the functional inputs to a particular neural unit, one is looking for the receptive field for that unit. If the visual nervous system were a completely noninteracting system, then there would be a different cell in the cortex for each receptor in the retina. Thus, the receptive field of each of the cortical cells would be a single retinal receptor in each case. To locate the receptive field of one such cortical cell, a microelectrode could be embedded in the cortical cell, and then a small spot of light moved over the retina until the receptor was found that would produce a response in the cortical cell being recorded. While this example is implausible, the principle is applied to the search for inputs to any neural unit.

Figure 3.3 presents the general procedure for mapping out a receptive field in a visual system by electrophysiological recordings. The methods are the same whether one looks for receptive fields of a ganglion cell, a cell in the lateral geniculate nucleus, a cell in area 17 of the cortex, or in other parts of the brain. For example, to locate a receptive field of an area-17 cortical cell, a recording microelectrode is placed in the cortical cell and then light of a particular intensity and size is presented to some area of the retina. If the responsiveness of the cortical cell changes, this light can be considered to be stimulating part of the receptive field of that cortical cell, and so this light is a

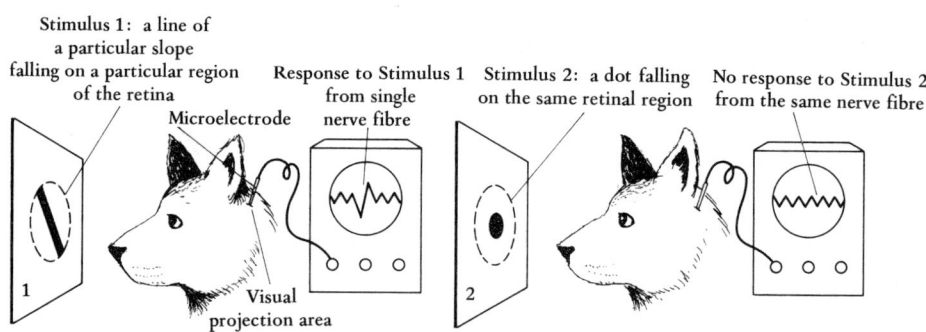

Stimulus 1: a line of a particular slope falling on a particular region of the retina

Response to Stimulus 1 from single nerve fibre

Microelectrode

Stimulus 2: a dot falling on the same retinal region

No response to Stimulus 2 from the same nerve fibre

Visual projection area

1

2

FIGURE 3.3 A schematic representation of the procedure for mapping a receptive field in the visual system electrophysiologically.

stimulus for that cell. The light is then moved to a new location, repeating the process, to find all areas of the retina to which the cortical cell responds. This then provides a map of the receptive field of that cell for that particular pattern of light. The light can then be changed in intensity or size or shape or pattern of movement, and the process repeated until receptive fields for that cell are mapped out for all different stimulus characteristics. Usually, however, a particular cell will respond to only one type of light pattern. When this mapping is done, the electrode is moved to another cell and the process is repeated. Note that this is a map of the retina, not of the cortex. It is the locus of all points on the retina that are capable of exciting the cortical cell from which a recording is being taken. Electrophysiological recording cannot be used with human beings, but it has been used with animals from primates to frogs.

We shall consider a number of specialized receptive fields when we talk about the third coding strategy later in this chapter. Here we have looked at the simplest and most general case.

On-Off Receptive Field Structures

Consider the receptive field of a mammalian ganglion cell for a small spot of light seen on an otherwise dark background. This field is mapped by recording the activity of a ganglion cell with a microelectrode while moving the spot of light around on the retina. When the ganglion's activity level changes, then the receptors being stimulated will be considered part of the receptive field of the ganglion cell. Figure 3.4 shows schematically an on-center, off-surround receptive field. When one is recording from such a cell, a certain amount of spontaneous activity will be found, even in the absence of stimulation. This is

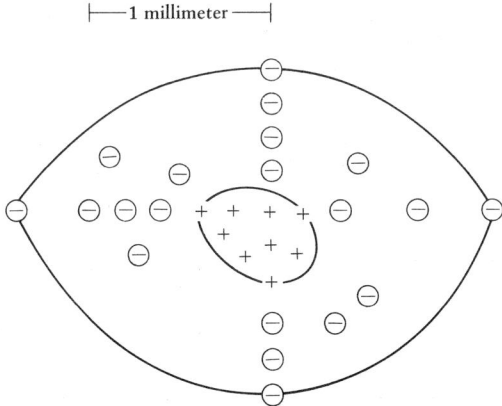

FIGURE 3.4   A schematic drawing of an on-center, off-surround concentric receptive field at the ganglion cell level. Plus signs indicate that an elevation in activity of the cell is found when light falls on that portion of the receptive field, and minus signs indicate a decrease in activity.

pictured in Figure 3.5, at the top *(a)*. If a small spot is presented only to the on-center, the rate of firing is initially increased (panel *b*) but then returns to the spontaneous level. Note that no change in firing occurred as the light is left on, or when it is turned off. If a small spot falls only on the off-surround, then the rate of firing is affected only at the offset of the light, at which time there is a brief decrease in activity level (panel *c*). In each of these cases, the ganglion cell does not change its response to the steady state, either when the light is left on or left off. Further, if the spot of light is sufficiently large so that it falls on both the on-center and the off-surround, then the two parts of the field tend to cancel each other and the total change in response of a ganglion cell may be zero (panel *d*).

The particular receptive field illustrated in Figure 3.4 is called an on-center, off-surround concentric field because of the pattern of responses observed when it is stimulated. The opposite variety is also common, in which the surrounding part of the receptive field signals the onset of light. Notice that large stimuli would tend to produce no response from either variety of this type of receptive field, since the light would fall on both parts and they would mutually inhibit each other. The most effective stimulus for this cell is a bright spot of about the size of the on-center portion.

As a general rule, there are relatively few receptive fields that continue to signal the presence of unchanged light. Further, as with Limulus, the mechanism of inhibition occurs above the level of the receptor itself. Each receptor continues to fire, but its effect at the ganglion level is changed, either being enhanced or inhibited, depending on the pattern of light and the shape of the receptive field.

There are three important characteristics of the on-off inhibitory mechanisms as found at this level of the visual system. The first is that when light falls only on an on-center, it tends to increase the level of activity in the ganglion cell above its spontaneous firing rate. When the light falls only on the off-surround area it tends to depress the level of activity in the ganglion cell below its spontaneous firing rate. Thus, the center is an excitatory area and the surround is an inhibitory area.

Second, when light falls primarily on the on-center, there is an increase in the activity level of the ganglion cell at the time of the onset of the light. The ganglion then returns rather rapidly to its spontaneous level, even if the light is left on. When the light is turned off, there is no further change in activity. If the light falls primarily in the off-surround area, there will be no change in the resting level of the ganglion cell when the light is turned on. When the light is turned off, however, there will be a rapid depression in activity which again will rather quickly return to baseline level, even if the light is left off. In this sense, then, the two parts of the receptive field are sensitive to the leading and trailing edges of stimulation over time, rather than to steady-state levels.

Third, there is a mutual inhibitory characteristic to the two parts of the receptive field. Thus, light falling on the on-center area will tend to inhibit responses to light falling in the off-surround area and conversely. This effect does not show strikingly until light falls on both areas simultaneously, in

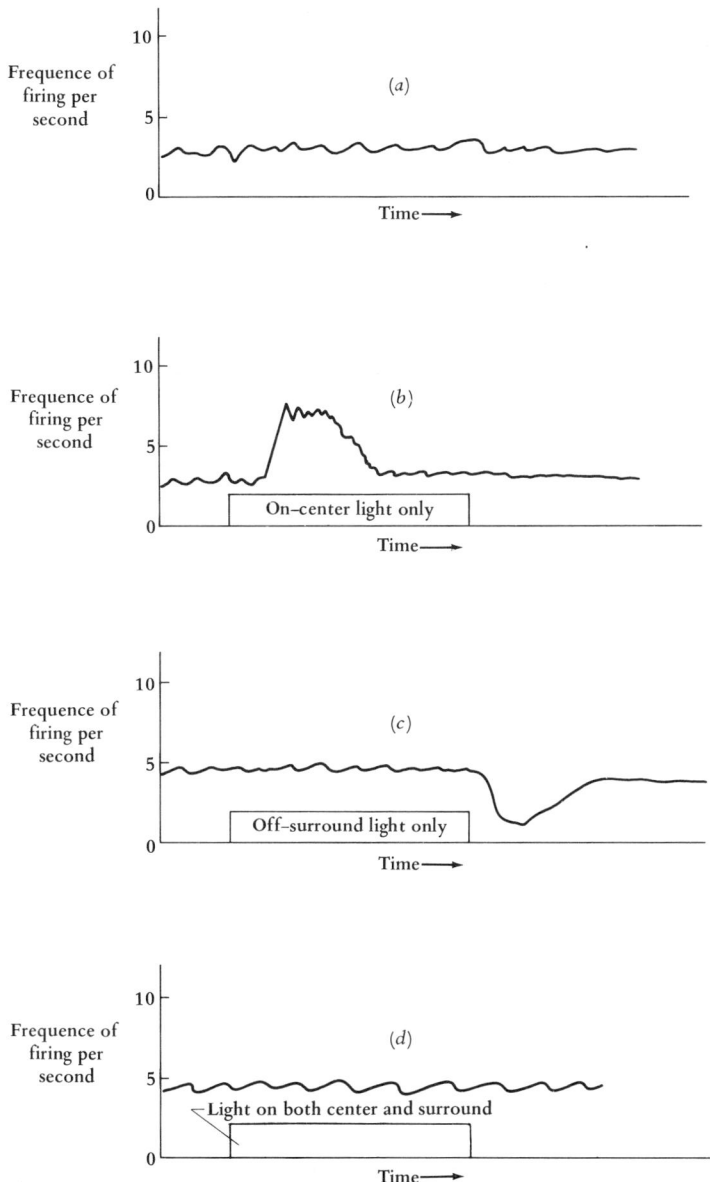

FIGURE 3.5 Four hypothetical functions illustrating the changes in activity level of a ganglion cell when: (a) no light is present in its receptive field; (b) when light covers only its on-center; (c) when light covers only the off-surround; and (d) when light covers the entire receptive field uniformly.

which case we find a canceling effect being roughly proportional to the relative amounts of stimulation falling in both areas. In this sense, then, the on-center, off-surround receptive field is designed to be mutually inhibitory for large uniform illumination. It serves as an ideal mechanism by which the visual system can ignore spatial redundancy. Symmetric receptive fields of this kind will only be active when there is some spatial discontinuity in the stimulation falling on that part of the retina.

Temporal Steady-State Inhibition

So far, we have been considering spatial steady-state coding, although it should be clear that the on-off receptive field system as outlined above also will serve to reduce temporal steady-state information transmission. As we saw in Figure 3.5, a ganglion cell with such a receptive field will show a change in activity only when there is some temporal change in the stimulus impinging on its receptors. This would occur whenever the light is turned on or off, or whenever the position of the eye is changed relative to the stimulus spot of light. In general, most of the receptive fields recorded at the ganglion level or beyond do not signal temporal steady states. Unless the light changes over time, such a system acts very much as if there is no stimulus out there at all.

There is another device for minimizing transmission about unchanging events over time. We have already seen that the receptors are capable of responding to very high rates of temporal change. We will see in Chapter 6 that the brain receives information about temporal discontinuities at far lower precision—under the best of circumstances, rarely more than 100 changes per second, and usually more on the order of ten changes per second. Temporal discontinuity more rapid than this will not be signaled to the central visual system. Thus, it is apparent that somewhere between the eye and the brain information is sampled rather coarsely in time.

One suggestion advanced by Stroud (1956) is that time is integrated into perceptual moments of about 100 milliseconds in length. All the energy stimulating the visual system within the moment would be integrated, that is, received and processed as a single unit. Rather than taking separate time samples of excitation every millisecond or so, an average would be taken over all excitation during intervals of time up to as much as 100 milliseconds. Thus two brief pulses of light occurring close in time would be added together and seen as one brighter flash, rather than two separate ones. We will return to the idea of a perceptual moment in Chapter 6 which is devoted entirely to a detailed discussion of temporal processes in vision. In the present context, we should note that the perceptual moment represents a loss in temporal information, and that this loss is another way of reducing the bombardment of excitation to the brain.

This section has looked briefly at various techniques for ignoring steady-state information, and even of ignoring discontinuities in time when they are very rapid. Before turning to the next coding strategy, it is important to note that the inhibitory mechanisms just discussed which help to ignore steady-state excitation are most useful for enhancing spatial discontinuities in the stimulus pattern on the retina. We will consider two examples of these processes.

Edge-Enhancement Techniques

It is possible to think of the receptors in the central portions of the retina as interconnected in a mutually inhibitory fashion, such as suggested in Figure 3.2. Thus the activity level generated in a ganglion cell by a particular receptor will be lowered if receptors adjacent to it are also active. Such a system has a very interesting property. Suppose we present a pattern consisting of two areas of adjacent luminance, one more intense than the other, with a fairly sharp edge formed by the junction of the luminance differences. This describes the physical stimulus intensities, but what will the brightnesses look like? Specifically, what will we see at the edge? Figure 3.6 shows the stimulus schematically. Notice that there appears to be a brighter band on the bright side of the edge, and a darker band on the dark side. Hence, the brightness contrast at the edge is greater in our perception than it is in the physical intensity distribution itself. The edge has been enhanced. This is an example of a Mach band, named after Ernst Mach, who first discovered and studied them in 1865.

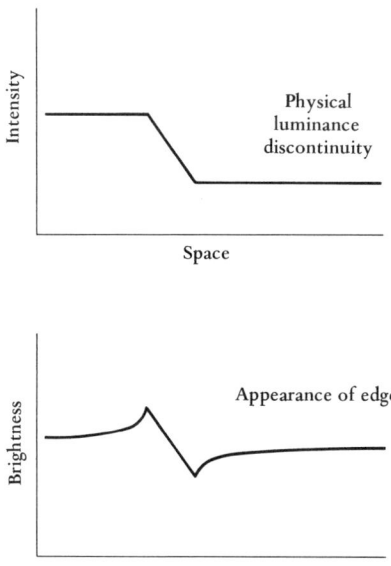

FIGURE 3.6 Schematic representation of a spatial distribution of luminance from an edge (top) and its resulting discontinuity in brightness (bottom) illustrating the Mach band phenomenon.

Mach bands depend for their functioning on the inhibitory network of the retina. If we imagine that our fovea is fixated on the left side of this intensity discontinuity, well into the more intense part, all the receptors will have substantial levels of excitation on them, with no differences among adjacent receptors. Given the lateral inhibition present, the ganglions in this area will be less active than if only a few receptors were stimulated. Now imagine that we shift our eye toward the edge, but still focused just on the bright side. There will be little inhibition from the adjacent receptors that happen to be over the edge on the dark side, since much less light falls on them. Thus, the total amount of inhibition on the receptors near the edge on the bright side will be less than the inhibition away from the edge. This will leave a band of greater brightness along the edge on the bright side.

Just the converse happens on the dark side. Away from the edge, there is little excitation, nor much inhibition, and the area looks uniform and dim. As the eye moves toward the edge but on the darker side, it will begin to pick up substantial inhibition from the adjacent receptors that happen to be over the edge on the bright side. Thus, the total amount of inhibition on the ganglions near the edge on the dark side will be greater than inhibition away from the edge on the dark side. This will produce a perception of a dark band along the edge on the dark side, just as we see in Figure 3.6.

Mach bands are one example of how the visual system selects spatial discontinuities and sharpens them so they stand out in perception even more than they might otherwise. Ratliff (1965) reports a substantial amount of work on Mach bands, and Cornsweet (1970) provides a more general discussion.

The visual system has another very important edge-enhancement process that also depends on inhibitory properties, especially of the type found in on-off receptive field organizations. Imagine a small spot of light that covered part of the center of a concentric on-center receptive field. This field would provide a vigorous signal when the spot appeared, and then would return to an activity level near its spontaneous rate. But we already know that the eye is not perfectly still. The physiological tremors, drifts, and microsaccades will shift the receptors of the eye relative to the retinal projection by one or two receptors every 10 to 100 milliseconds. This change will be irrelevant in the center of the spot of light, but at its edge it will move one side of the spot onto a receptor that had just previously been unstimulated, and will move the other edge off of a receptor that had been stimulated. If both of these receptors are in the on-center, the first one will cause the ganglion cell to become more active. Of course, a few milliseconds later the eye may shift back again, and the other receptor will signal. If one of the receptors is in the off-surround area, then it will create a signal when the edge leaves it but not when it returns.

What these small eye movements do is to produce a continual signaling of the presence of the edge of a continuous spot of light even from a receptive field organization that cannot respond to a steady state. These movements are very small, only on the order of a receptor or two, but they do provide a very powerful mechanism of edge enhancement.

The discussion of coding strategies to remove steady-state redundancy has not been very detailed. This has been in part because of the scope of the present book, but also in part because some of these details are not yet well known, especially in man. But the general principles seem reliable enough, and certainly go a long way to bring the task of coding sensory information within reasonable bounds.

MECHANISMS TO SPECIALIZE THE VISUAL SYSTEM FOR DIFFERENT FUNCTIONS— TRADE-OFFS

It is clear that if we can trade off some functions for others then the amount of transmission about excitation can potentially be reduced. We will consider four such trade-offs that appear to occur in the human visual system.

Sensitivity to Low Illumination as Opposed to Color and Acuity

In order to achieve high sensitivity to low illumination the visual system appears to pool many rod receptors onto each bipolar and ganglion cell. When this occurs, however, it is difficult for the ganglion cell to convey information about precisely which receptors in its pool were active. Consequently, if the coding of color and fine detail depends upon knowing which particular receptors were excited, then it will not be possible both to pool receptors and at the same time resolve color and acuity.

Most of the periphery of the retina is organized so that the majority of rod receptors are pooled onto bipolars. Consequently, the rods would not be able to mediate color discrimination or the perception of fine detail very accurately. The rods seem to be specialized in every possible way to capture photons efficiently when there are not many around to capture. To maximize sensitivity to low illumination levels, this part of the visual system appears to have traded away almost everything else it could potentially learn about the light incident to the retina—it cannot resolve detail or time very precisely, nor can it tell very much about color. While this may seem to be a large price to pay, it does permit the visual system to be the most sensitive instrument known to man to detect small numbers of photons.

The converse of this trade-off is also very clear. Central vision is practically blind, except at relatively high light levels. But once these levels are achieved, it has an incredible ability to discriminate fine detail. It can notice a line whose width is only one-fiftieth the width of a foveal cone, and can discriminate among an infinite number of different wavelengths specifying different hues. As we will see in a moment, it achieves these high levels of shape and color acuity at the expense of temporal resolution.

This distinction between central versus peripheral functions reflects one made earlier between the photopic and scotopic systems. There are a number of components of this distinction, and Figure 3.7 lists several of them. They refer to different receptors, cones versus rods, to color versus achromatic perception, to discriminative versus summative organization, to high versus low visual pattern acuity, and so forth. Each of these differences represents another variety of trade-off.

FIGURE 3.7. Some anatomical and functional differences between scotopic and photopic processes.

Scotopic		Photopic
Rods	versus	Cones
Night	versus	Day
Achromatic	versus	Color
Summative	versus	Discriminative
Low Acuity	versus	High Acuity

Wide versus Dynamic Range of Sensitivity

The human eye has an overall range of sensitivity of thirteen log units of luminance, that is, from 10^{-6} to 10^7 millilamberts. At the lower bound, one photon of light per rod over only a dozen or so rods will produce a sensation of light under conditions of maximum sensitivity.

However, at any one time the range of sensitivity rarely needs to exceed more than about two log units. Thus, in normal room illumination, with reflectances of objects rarely varying from no less than 10 percent to no more than 90 percent, the luminances reaching the eye might vary from say, 1 to 100 millilamberts, or if one is outdoors, from 10 to 1000, or at night from 1/100 to 1, and so forth. This represents the dynamic range of visual sensitivity and is a result of variation in reflectances of surfaces that one can expect when only a single source of light is available.

When we are confronted with a sudden shift in luminance that is larger than two log units, the eyes become functionally blind for brief periods of time. This is the familiar experience of going from bright sunlight into a movie, or coming from a movie into bright sunlight. Perhaps one way the visual system can provide such a very large range in overall sensitivity is to work at any one time with only a relatively small range of dynamic sensitivity. The penalties incurred with this processing trade-off between an incredibly large total range and a small dynamic range are normally not very severe, since in typical environments we rarely undergo sudden luminance changes of more than two log units.

Central Acuity versus Peripheral Attention

There is usually no necessity to have acute vision over the entire retina. High acuity can be concentrated in one section of the retina but it will result in certain structural and functional trade-offs. Up to some limit, as we will see in Chapter 5, acuity should improve if the receptors are packed tightly together, as is the case in the fovea. Also, discrimination should be better if there are fewer interconnections between receptors and their relay neurons at higher levels. But this lowers the number and complexity of receptive field structures that can be established since fewer interconnections would be available.

A very severe penalty is paid for the concentration of receptors in the fovea and their one-to-one connections. Since nearly all are located in a small area of the retina, how can the perceiver notice anything in any other part of the retinal projection? Further, how does our perception of the visual world avoid having a fish-eyed look, in which the center of the field is greatly magnified out of proportion, with the rest a hopeless blur of indistinct, color-less, and unresolvable confusion? This concern is apparent when considering Figure 3.8 which shows the dramatic fall-off of visual acuity, even at less than 1 degree from the center of the fovea.

The figure illustrates two separate problems. First, it is important that the periphery provide cues about where details might be found rather than about their actual detail. That is, it provides information about where to look next. The periphery must be sensitive to movement since this is a critical detail that stimulates an immediate eye movement. So we see a very powerful trade-off between the central portion of the retina analyzing visual stimulation in detail while the peripheral portion of the retina provides information to the visual system about where to look next to get more information.

How to provide a perceiver with a panoramic visual world when in each instant only part of it is seen clearly is a more complex problem. It will be a recurrent theme in a number of chapters in this book—what is the relationship between the information available in a single instant or glance and in the inte-gration over several fixations, each producing a retinal projection of a dif-ferent part of the visual world? That we must worry about this distinction is due in part to this trade-off.

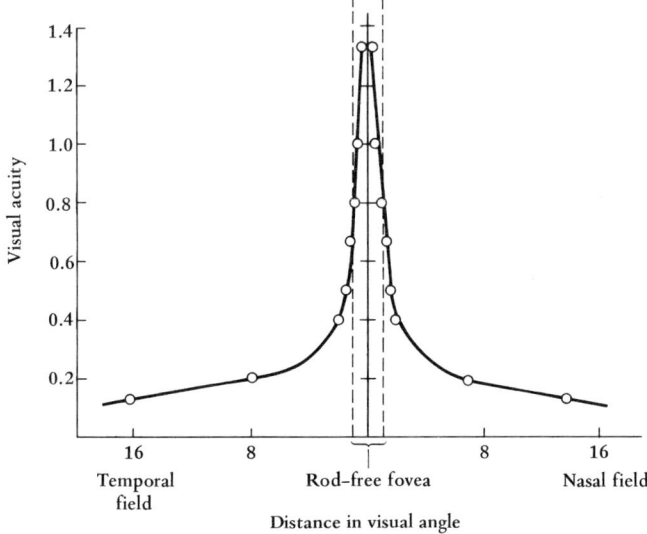

FIGURE 3.8 Changes in visual acuity for stimulation on different locations across a horizontal meridian of a human retina (from Alpern, 1962).

Temporal versus Spatial Resolution

The human visual system usually does not need fine temporal resolution, except to detect movement. Consequently, one would expect it to be relatively insensitive to nonspatial changes. We do not need to see rapid flicker, and in fact we do not. But we do need to be very good at noticing spatial variation down to widths of less than one cone. There are a number of other instances in which the visual system appears to make spatial-temporal trades. We will examine some of these in detail in Chapter 6.

A number of other trade-offs occur in the visual system. Each of them sacrifices some information in order to preserve other information. Evolution appears to have been the selective device for deciding which information is critical. The importance here is that the trade-offs all provide mechanisms for reducing the amount of excitation to the brain, hopefully without serious loss of information.

PRECODED CRITICAL VISUAL FEATURES

Precoding is probably the most important of the strategies for information reduction. There is no reason to believe that the interconnections between and within the various neural layers in the visual system are at all random. We have already seen good evidence for specialization. We should expect that with the inhibitory as well as excitatory components among neurons that there can be very specific feature-detection systems. A receptive field organization with an on-center and off-surround is one such specialization. This receptive field is maximally sensitive only to a small regular spot of light, and will not respond much to a large area of light. But there are other much more sophisticated feature detectors.

There have been two basic research techniques employed to discover and study the receptive field structure of the visual system in order to look at coding properties of luminance discontinuities. One has been electrophysiological work, primarily on cats, monkeys, and apes, in which microelectrodes are used to record the activity of neurons as they respond to stimulation on the retina. The other, primarily with humans, has used selective adaptation to particular patterns of stimulation as a way of attenuating a feature-detecting system, thereby lowering the sensitivity for features in that type of pattern. We will briefly review basic research using each approach.

Electrophysiological Studies of Receptive Fields

What kinds of receptive fields have been discovered? Much of this research has been done by Hubel and Wiesel (1962, 1965, 1968). When a receptive field of a ganglion cell is mapped, as has been described above, such fields are nearly all concentric in shape, with the center excitatory and the surround inhibitory, or vice versa (see Figure 3.4). Such a receptive field is maximally sensitive to a small spot that falls entirely within the center or the surround without spilling over into the other part. Further, this type of field is summative, in that the energy in two spots that fall within the center will be added together. But if one is in the center and one in the surround, they may even cancel out, so the net response of the receptive field is zero.

As we have seen in Chapter 2, the next level in the visual system up from the ganglion cell is the terminus of the optic nerve in the lateral geniculate nucleus. When cells there have their receptive fields mapped, they have shapes and properties substantially similar to those at the ganglion level.

An optimal response from a ganglion or a geniculate cell usually depends only on the size, intensity, and location of a spot of light on the retina. If the spot is too large, the threshold for a response increases, but even diffuse light will produce some response if the light is intense enough. This latter property is found less at the geniculate level, where the penalty for exceeding the critical size is more severe. But at both of these levels, no shapes other than circular ones seem relevant, and no direction of movement seems better than any other. Thus, the specificity of the coding at these levels is not too great.

Most of the work of Hubel and Wiesel has been with recordings of the receptive fields of cortical cells, and with these the patterns of coding are quite different. Such cells have been described as simple, complex, and hypercomplex, depending on their properties. We shall briefly consider each type in terms of its shape and the types of visual features to which it is sensitive.

The simple cortical cells have antagonistic regions as do the geniculate and ganglion cells, but their shapes are elongated rather than circular. Figure 3.9 shows several examples of simple cells. These will, of course, respond to a spot of light anywhere within a single region, but the cell is obviously most responsive to an elongated stimulus, either an edge or a bar oriented in parallel with the axis of the receptive field of the cell. Thus, in cell A a maximal response will occur to a narrow lighted bar at 45 degrees to the right, whose width matches the width of the on-center area. Cell B requires a dark bar on a lighted background. For most of the simple cells, misalignment by only 5–10 degrees of orientation will no longer excite the cell. Notice that cell C will be most sensitive to an edge separating two stimuli of unequal intensity. It will not matter what side is more intense, except that the polarity of the output will be reversed. But the vigor of the response will be the same.

All simple cortical cells will respond to a moving stimulus, but the orientation of the direction of movement is critical and specific to the orientation of the receptive field. In most cases the direction of movement did not matter, except for a few fields which had some asymmetry in the flanking regions (cell D of Figure 3.9). Some simple cells also had some specificity with respect to the rate of movement. This occurred when there was marked variability in the width of the center region. For example, cell E would respond more vigorously

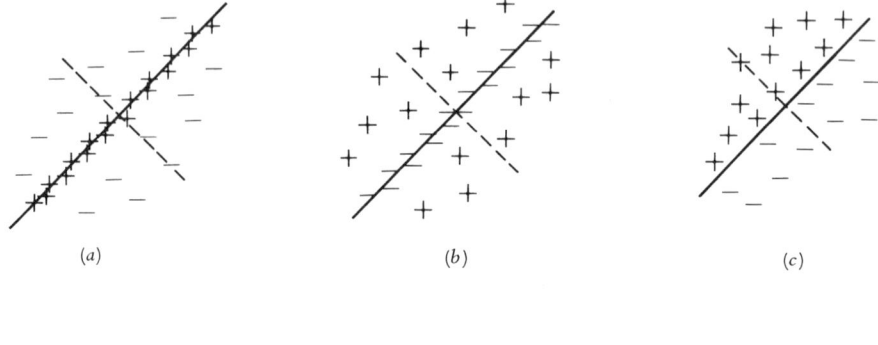

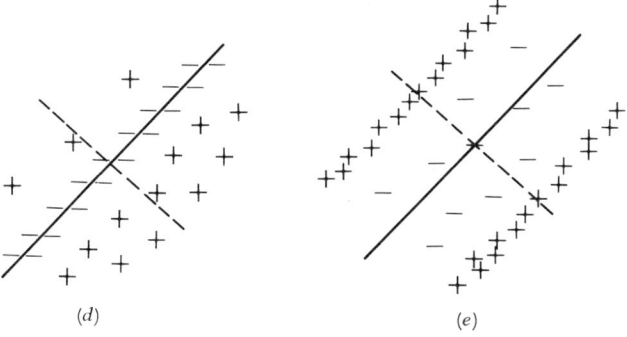

FIGURE 3.9 Schematic representation of the receptive field shapes of several types of simple cortical cells. Plus signs indicate locations in the receptive field where stimulation will increase the activity of the cortical cell, and minus signs indicate locations where activity will decrease. All examples are for diagonal orientation, but all other orientations have also been discovered.

to a rapid as compared to a slow movement because with the former, the three transitions from + to − and back to + would be close together in time only with rapid movement.

It takes little imagination to describe these simple cortical fields as edge detectors and line detectors. They are sensitive to lines of specified widths and orientations and edges of specified orientations. For most, the orientation and rate of movement is also specified. The sizes of these simple fields are relatively small, averaging about 2 degrees, with many as small as 15 minutes. They are found over most areas of the retina. Each field is specific to stimulation in its area — hence these can provide information about where on the retina a pattern is located.

The complex cortical receptive fields show two major differences from the simple cells. Their fields are larger, averaging 5–10 degrees, and often approaching 20–30 degrees. Second, while they are generally sensitive to the same kinds of features as those for the simple cells, it does not matter where in the receptive field the feature is placed. Thus, a field might be selective for a line 12 minutes wide at 45 degree orientation, but that line will produce a large response when presented anywhere within the field. Thus such a field remains a feature detector, but is indifferent within a large latitude to where on the retina the line appeared. As Cornsweet (1970) suggests, the output of such complex receptive fields directly codes slant, regardless of the location of the line on the retina.

The hypercomplex cortical cells look as if they are the output of combinations of complex cells, in that they code combinations of stimulus features. For example, cells have been found that respond to the angles between two lines, rather than to the lines alone. Such cells are most likely to be found above area 17. Also, cells have been found which respond only if the patterns falling on the receptors of the two eyes are not in perfect alignment. This is most likely to occur when both eyes are focused on a nearby object. Because the eyes are separated by about two inches in our heads, slightly different retinal projections will fall onto the two retinas. A cell responding to the retinal disparity could provide coding for binocular stereoscopic depth.

The implications of these findings are that the activity of a single cell in the cortex can tell us about a retinal projection that represents the changing activity of millions of retinal receptors sampled over a long time. This type of specialization obviously represents an incredible level of complexity in coding, with an equally incredible saving in transmission to the cortex.

We mentioned in Chapter 2 that cells in area 17 and in the lateral geniculate nucleus are arranged in layers and columns. When an electrode is put into a cortical cell, one can locate its receptive field. If the electrode is now moved one layer farther down, that is, down a column, we will pick up a new receptive field. Generally, the new field would respond to a line of the same orientation, but in a new location on the retina. Thus, columns form a functional unit even across the eyes, since they tend to map onto both eyes.

We have talked about the receptive field organization as being tuned to certain visual features and there is substantial evidence about a few. These include edge detectors that locate discontinuities in luminance and may also respond specifically to orientation. There are line detectors, which can be specified in terms of their orientation and width. There are movement detectors for both edges and lines that describe a path of movement of a particular velocity and even acceleration. Binocular disparity is also coded as a feature. In Chapter 4 we will see how color coding is handled by receptive fields of the lateral geniculate bodies.

The location of a particular visual feature is indicated by the receptive field which signals it. Since receptive fields overlap a great deal, the same receptors may be part of hundreds of different receptive fields, each capable of representing a different aspect or critical feature.

Selective Adaptation Studies

Arguing by analogy from the effects of light and color adaptation, we should expect that prolonged viewing of a stimulus consisting of a particular visual feature (for example, a line of a given width, orientation, color, and so on), should selectively adapt the detecting mechanism for that feature. This would render the visual system less sensitive to that feature in subsequent patterned stimulation. Weisstein (1969) has reviewed some of the evidence for such selective adaptation. For example, Gilinsky and Cohen (1972) have shown that reaction times to a line of the same orientation as an adapting pattern are elevated by as much as several hundred milliseconds, compared to lines with different orientations. Comparable selective adaptation studies have been carried out for color-feature detectors (McCollough, 1965; and Harris and Gibson, 1968), and for motion detectors (Sekuler and Pantle, 1967).

Weisstein (1969) has argued that a visual masking paradigm would produce evidence for the existence of feature detectors. That is, rather than selectively adapting a specific feature detector, a brief presentation of a patterned stimulus could be followed by a masking stimulus consisting of the particular feature to be detected or recognized. Thus, a bar stimulus might be followed by a mask made up of a grating of a particular spatial frequency, orientation, size, and color. This procedure will not adapt the feature detector, but rather interfere with its processing of a target containing that feature. Weisstein reports several studies with supporting evidence.

This review of both the electrophysiological and the adaptation research is quite selective, designed primarily to illustrate the different techniques and effects, rather than to cover all of the relevant work. Research using both approaches is rapidly growing, so that today's new feature may be tomorrow's footnote.

What is important in these types of coding systems is that complex information on the retina is signaled directly to single cells in the cortex and represented there by the activity of those cells. What about even more complex visual features? There is no evidence yet that there are receptive fields for curved lines or for simple shapes like squares or circles. It may be that such receptive fields exist, but they have not yet been found. It is also possible that such figures would be signaled by combinations of cortical cells, or more complex organizations.

This is rather likely, since most of the research with electrophysiological recordings in animals have not used very complex patterns of light in mapping out receptive fields, nor has much recording been done from sites in area 18 and beyond. Thus, there is a certain artificiality in the extent of the list available to date. On the one hand, the features identified are certainly basic and important ones and represent fundamental sets of building blocks. Further, almost all complex properties of form could be derived from cortical operations and combinations performed on these features. But it seems even more likely to us that the next few years will provide evidence of even higher-order features that are coded by a receptive field structure as the activity level of single cortical cells.

We can probably look to the selective pressures during evolution to predict which features are yet to be discovered. While it may be unlikely that we have a detector for squares as compared to triangles, evolutionary arguments suggest that curved features are fairly basic units of form, and should be organized in the retina. Even more important, the last section of this book on the perception of space will argue strongly for a perceived scale of space, built up primarily from information about texture changes in the retinal projection. Hence, we should expect that texture itself would be a visual feature for which we would have feature detectors. Further, with such texture detectors, we should have higher-order texture gradient detectors that would signal when a texture is changing over one part of the receptive field to another part.

Such reasoning is still speculative, but this is no more so than the entire state of this work was less than a decade ago. Given the fact that relatively few broad explorations of features have been undertaken, it is not surprising that few have yet been found.

Feature versus Frequencies

In Chapter 2 we mentioned the possibility that the visual system may respond to spatial frequencies, and that intensity discontinuities that make up edges and contours can be shown mathematically to be composed of a series of spatial frequencies. Are spatial frequencies another variety of visual features, or are they something different? The answer to this is not yet clear—again we are still too much in the middle of a rapid accumulation and change in research data to know the final story. There is rather clear evidence that the visual system detects bars of specific widths and orientations, and also that it detects grating patterns of specific spatial frequencies. It is possible that these are quite independent properties of patterns that the visual system is tuned to detect, but parsimony would suggest some relationship should be found between them.

We have much less electrophysiological evidence on the shapes of receptive fields for different spatial frequencies. Recordings taken from Robson (1972) have shown when recording from ganglion cells or at the lateral geniculate nucleus in cats indicates that some cells have receptive fields that are maximally responsive to a given spatial frequency, and are less responsive to both higher and lower frequencies. At these levels in the visual nervous system there appears to be no orientation specificity (Robson, 1972). It did not matter whether the bars making up the grating pattern were horizontal, vertical, or oblique. Presumably, this type of ganglion cell is responding to a group of concentric center-surround receptive fields in which the distance in any direction between the centers would give the frequency of the maximum response. Thus if a group of center-surround receptive fields were aligned so that their centers were 1 degree apart, then any ganglion cell fed by all of these receptive fields would respond maximally to a grating pattern in which the bars were one cycle per degree apart. Since the alignment might be in any direction, the orientation of the grating would be irrelevant.

However, Robson finds when recording from cortical cells that the orientation of the gratings is critical, just as we have seen from single bars or edges in the work of Hubel and Wiesel. Thus, he finds different cortical cells to have maximum responsiveness to gratings of different frequencies, but only when he has the orientation properly aligned. This suggests that the receptive fields for these cortical cells are alternating stripes of excitatory and inhibitory regions.

Robson mentions that the responsiveness of the cortical cell increases with the number of bars present in the grating, holding their spatial frequency constant. This suggests that for these cortical cells, the receptive fields are quite large, so that with more bars more exitatory and inhibitory stripes are covered, thereby yielding a larger response.

The above work by Robson suggests the mechanism by which the visual system could code the spatial frequencies of luminance distributions in the retinal projection. The electrophysiological evidence from cats and monkeys strongly suggests that such coding takes place. Further, spatial frequency adaptation studies in man lend even stronger support.

The question that is unclear at the moment is what the visual system does with the frequency information it seems to be extracting in these ways? If the visual world were primarily made up of striped patterns, then having detectors tuned to the different spatial frequency of stripes would be very efficient in much the same way that having edge and angle detectors seems to be efficient. While no one has done the kinds of ecological analyses of frequencies of repeating gratings in the normal visual environment, we suspect that the modal number of bars would be one, or perhaps two when considering parallel sides of many shapes. To the extent that this is true, then having a finely tuned frequency detector does not seem to be critical. However, at another level of analysis, the texture found on surfaces is primarily of high spatial frequency, being repeating patterns of relatively high numbers of cycles per visual angle. Since texture is difficult to code in terms of its features, and the features of a particular texture are probably irrelevant, a frequency code would be very useful. But this speculation requires substantial experimental verification.

The next decade should see major advances in our understanding of how critical aspects of stimulation are coded by the visual system. Presumably we will find more evidence both for features and for frequencies. Hopefully we will also gain some insight into how some of these sources of information are used by the visual system. During this time of rapid growth of knowledge, much of the speculation, including some in this book, will turn out in retrospect to be silly, inaccurate, or even wrong. But other aspects will have been very useful in guiding new and fruitful work and theorizing. We will have to see.

SUMMARY

The previous chapter described some of the basic processes by which light could reach the retina and excite photoreceptor cells so that they produced neural signals to be transmitted through the visual nervous system. The present chapter has been concerned more specifically with how neural signals are encoded or represented in the nervous system so that they efficiently convey the information in the light about the visual world around us without so overloading the nervous system that communication would be all but impossible.

We need the visual nervous system to code something about the location of objects in space, their rate and direction of movement, their sizes, shapes, and textures, the relative and absolute distances in visual space, and the temporal order and succession of events.

We discussed in some detail several strategies that can be observed, by which the visual nervous system reduced the coding of 130 million photoreceptors to manageable proportions while providing the kinds of information just enumerated.

The first strategy is to ignore all spatial and temporal steady-state stimulation. If adjacent receptors are in the same state, ignore them, and if the state of a receptor does not change, ignore it. Only when a change is detected does it have to be coded. This encoding strategy is accomplished primarily by the lateral inhibitory mechanisms at the ganglion cell level. This is seen best in the receptive field organization of the retina, which provides a means of encoding simple features of stimulation. Lateral inhibition also is used to enhance luminance discontinuities so that contours are sharpened (Mach bands).

The second strategy concerns various specializations and trade-offs of functions, so that many different aspects of stimulation can be emphasized, though not simultaneously. The scotopic-photopic division at the structural and functional levels reflects this specialization to the greatest degree— peripheral vision detects low levels of illumination and movement, while the fovea, functioning only under high illumination, is specialized more for color, and fine visual acuity.

The third strategy focuses on ways in which certain visual features of stimulation are precoded by the retina so that they are represented in the cortex as the activity of single cells. Again, the receptive field organization is the principal mechanism that accomplishes this encoding. We considered some of the research on different levels or complexity of this coding.

Readings

Most of the general references included at the end of Chapter 2 are relevant here, although the point of view is somewhat different. Cornsweet (1970) is perhaps the most useful. For more specific references on lateral inhibition, the two best sources are Ratliff's book on Mach bands (1965), and von Bekesy's book on sensory inhibition (1967). A more technical one is Fiorentini (1972). Dodwell (1971) has collected many papers on sensory coding of pattern, and many of the advanced chapters in Rosenblith (1961) are excellent, especially those by Boynton; Barlow; Rushton; and Lettvin, Maturana, Pitts, and McCollough. A recent collection by Uttal (1972) contains papers on many of the topics of this chapter.

4

the perception of color

INTRODUCTION

Color is an impossibly large and complex topic. It is an important and pervasive part of our normal perceptual experience of the visual world. Not only does color effect our ability to differentiate among objects, but it changes our moods and feelings, distorts our preferences, and influences our esthetic experiences as can no other single aspect of vision. We have more vivid descriptors of color, and more words available to us for experiences of color than for any other dimension of vision or any dimension of any of our other senses. These characteristics of color are known, but not well understood.

In this chapter we will first consider the prerequisites needed for the perception of color to occur. Using these prerequisites as a guide, we will first examine the physical dimensions of light and objects that lead to the perception of color, and then the dimensions of that color experience. We will devote substantial space to the receptor processes underlying color perception and color coding beyond the receptors. In the last section we will look at a number of phenomena of color perception, including adaptation, contrast, constancy, and color-defective vision.

Although a perceiver with normal color vision might think he would have little difficulty defining color perception, in theory it is more complex. Some of the more technical definitions heighten these complexities, so we will follow a straightforward definition. Any noticeable difference between two fields of luminance other than spatial, temporal, or intensity variation is due to differences in color. For a normal perceiver, it is what differentiates black and white from color movies or television. One way to demonstrate this is to present two different wavelengths of light in two halves of the visual field. There are no adjustments that a normal perceiver can make to either half of the field that will make the two sides appear alike. This difference can be considered as the definition of the presence of color. It is possible for a color-defective perceiver to believe he sees differences in color when in fact it is intensity differences he notices. In this test such a color-defective perceiver might be able to match the two sides with an appropriate adjustment in intensity to one of the sides.

PREREQUISITES FOR THE PERCEPTION OF COLOR

Boynton (1971) has distinguished five prerequisites normally needed for the occurrence of the perception of color. First, there must be variation in the wavelength of the light sources illuminating the eye and the visual world. Second, there must be variation in the spectral reflectances from surfaces and objects. Third, there must be two or more receptor processes which differ in their absorption of various wavelengths that comprise visible light. Fourth, there must be coding in the receptor processes that is then transmitted to the cortex in such a way as to preserve the information about the spectral composition of light reaching the receptors. And fifth, there must be separate and unique perceptual experiences attached to this information reaching the cortex. We will discuss each of these prerequisites in turn, several of them in detail.

It seems obvious to the naïve observer that colors are on the surface of objects. To say that color is an experience only in the visual system seems meaningless. But we have already observed other visual properties of objects that are not part of the objects themselves. For example, the brightness of an object will be, at least in part, a function of its reflectance—the proportion of incident light that is reflected to the eye. The light is not on the surface or in the surface. We can know nothing visually about objects except insofar as light is reflected from them and collected in our eye so that photoreceptors are excited by it. So it is with color. Red is not on the surface of an apple nor in the photons of the light rays themselves. Rather, it is a perceptual experience that arises as a function of particular properties of light reaching the receptors and selectively exciting different types of receptors which in turn are encoded selectively.

WAVELENGTH COMPOSITION OF LIGHT— THE STIMULUS FOR COLOR

We noted in Chapter 2 that physicists describe electromagnetic radiation in terms of its energy and in terms of its wavelength. Up to this point we have focused primarily on its energy component, as specified in photons. But all electromagnetic radiation can also be thought of as traveling in rays or waves, the waves having a frequency specified by the distance from wavecrest to wavecrest, usually measured in meters. Figure 4.1 shows the entire spectrum of electromagnetic radiation, with gamma and X rays at the shortest end and radio waves near the long end. Different parts of the human body are responsive to several sectors of this spectrum. Only the photoreceptors embedded in our retinas, however, have evolved a receptor system for a particular segment of the spectrum. These photochemical sensors produce a neurochemical response to a narrow range of electromagnetic radiation. This range is called the visible

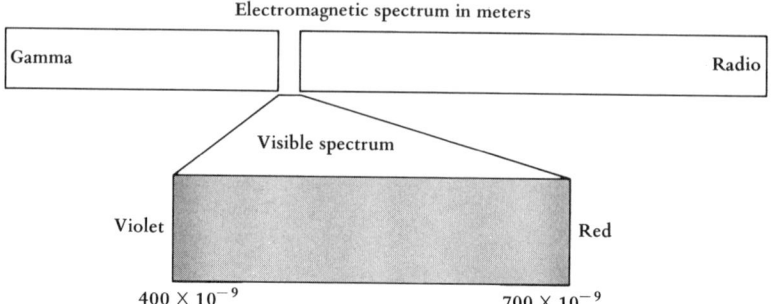

FIGURE 4.1   The electromagnetic energy spectrum indicating the visible portion.

spectrum, or light, and is enlarged in Figure 4.1 to show it more clearly. The color labels are added to show the perceptual correlates of these wavelengths.

The shortest wavelength that can be perceived is about 400 nanometers, or 400 billionths of a meter. Wavelengths shorter than about 400 nanometers are absorbed primarily by the lens, so as to avoid the effect of their harmful radiation properties on the retina. Such wavelengths never reach the receptors so that the visual system cannot have any knowledge about such stimulation. By convention, electromagnetic radiation of wavelengths shorter than 400 nanometers (or longer than 700) is not called light. Our response to the upper end of the spectrum is limited for a different reason. As we will see below, the amount of energy in each photon of radiation varies inversely as a function of its wavelength. Thus, while wavelengths longer than 700 nanometers can reach the retina, they are unable to excite the photoreceptors. We may feel this radiation as heat, and the thermal receptors throughout the body can respond to infrared radiation, but the photoreceptors in the retina are not sufficiently sensitive to such photons to produce a photochemical reaction.

The great physicist Newton, in about 1700, first reported evidence on the wave properties of light. Part of his work included the discovery that a very narrow beam of intense sunlight produces a spectrum of colors after passing through a wedge-shaped prism. Figure 4.2 illustrates in principle what he did, an experiment that can easily be repeated with a prism and a white-light source. It is necessary to use intense light—sunlight is easy to come by—and pass it through a narrow slit first. Without the slit, a number of partially overlapping spectra will be produced and only the edges will have colored fringes. The rainbow that we observe during a rainstorm is sunlight being refracted through raindrops, and the effect shows some of the same properties as Newton observed.

The colors seen are called spectral colors. They are separated because light waves passing from a medium of one density (air) into a medium of another density (the prism) are bent or refracted. The amount they are bent will be a function of their wavelength. In Figure 4.2 one can see that the shorter wavelengths are bent more than the longer ones. Thus if all the wavelengths are mixed together, as in white light, and then refracted, the different wavelengths

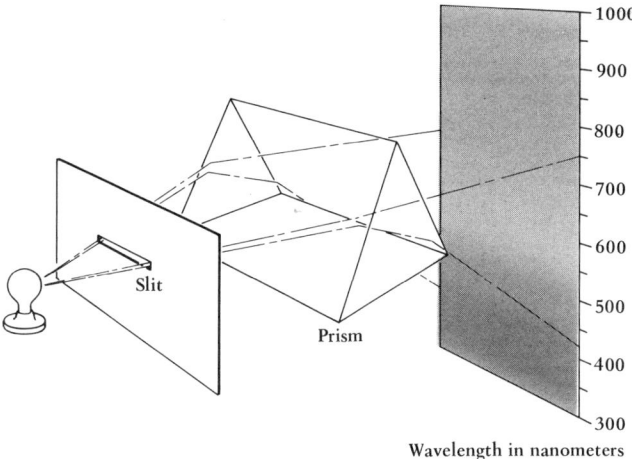

FIGURE 4.2   Refraction of light into its component wavelengths by a prism.

will be separated and can be seen one by one. Figure 4.3 shows that a lens can be used to refocus the separated wavelengths, combining them into light that again appears white. The recombination is accomplished by the same principle —differential refraction as a function of the wavelengths—as was the dispersion.

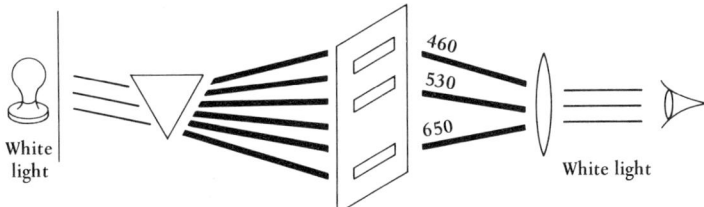

FIGURE 4.3   Illustration of a prism refracting light into separate wavelengths and of a lens refocusing into white light again.

Newton was aware of several of the important properties of the wavelengths of light. But there were some properties that were not known until later, especially through the work of Young (1807), Helmholtz (1867), and Maxwell (1860). These properties are critical for an understanding of the perception of color, so we will cover several of them, although without regard to their historical discoverers.

We have already mentioned that white light contains a mixture of wavelengths. Light sources differ in their spectral composition, that is, the different wavelengths they radiate, depending on the methods whereby they generate their radiation. Light from the sun contains radiations of all of the wavelengths in the visual spectrum, as well as substantial components of longer and shorter ones.

Being able to mix wavelengths together results in some interesting properties that are quite different from other mixtures with which we are familiar. For example, we can mix sound waves of different frequencies, but can still easily perceive the different frequencies in the mixture. It does not yield a new sound, but what we call a chord, made up of perceptually separable frequencies. However, no amount of practice or attention will permit us to see the different wavelengths in white light without some physical device to isolate them. Paint pigments can also be mixed together so that the mixture will produce a new color. But unlike mixing wavelengths of light, the pigments cannot be separated again into the original ones. With light we can arrange an infinite series of prisms and lenses so that an input of white light can be separated into its component wavelengths and then remixed over and over. This process is limited only by the precision of the refracting surfaces, the prisms, lenses, and the medium through which the light travels.

Another means to separate wavelengths is by an optical filter that will selectively pass some wavelengths through it while absorbing others. Thus if white light illuminates a filter, the only light that will be seen through the filter will be the wavelengths that it transmits. Although in principle a filter could be so selective as to be monochromatic, transmitting only a single wavelength, in practice even the best filters pass a narrow band of wavelengths rather than a single one. Thus, while we may refer to monochromatic light in this chapter, this reference should be taken as shorthand for a narrow range of wavelengths. In this sense, then, a 500-nanometer filter will pass wavelengths from perhaps 495 to 505 nanometers, but no other ones. Since light of these wavelengths appears green, we can call this a green filter, but we must recognize that it is not the wavelength of the light transmitted or the filter itself that is green. Rather, calling the filter green refers to the fact that, under normal circumstances, light of these wavelengths produces a perception of greenness.

Boynton's second prerequisite for color perception concerns another characteristic of different wavelengths, over and beyond selective refraction and selective filtering. We noted in Chapter 2 that virtually all of the light that reaches our eyes is reflected light from nonradiating surfaces. We observed that the brightness of a surface is a function of its reflectance. When we consider that the light reaching a surface may be composed of many different wavelengths, we can now be more precise about reflectance. The chemical and atomic structure of a surface is such that it will reflect or absorb different wavelengths in varying amounts. There are some surfaces which will absorb most of the wavelengths that reach them. Such surfaces will appear very dark or black. The flattest blackest surface will still reflect 3 or 4 percent of the light falling on it. Usually any surface that reflects less than 10 percent of the light that falls on it will look black.

Most surfaces reflect wavelengths differentially. Figure 4.4 shows examples of several different spectral reflectance distributions. From these functions we can begin to predict how the surfaces will appear. A surface that

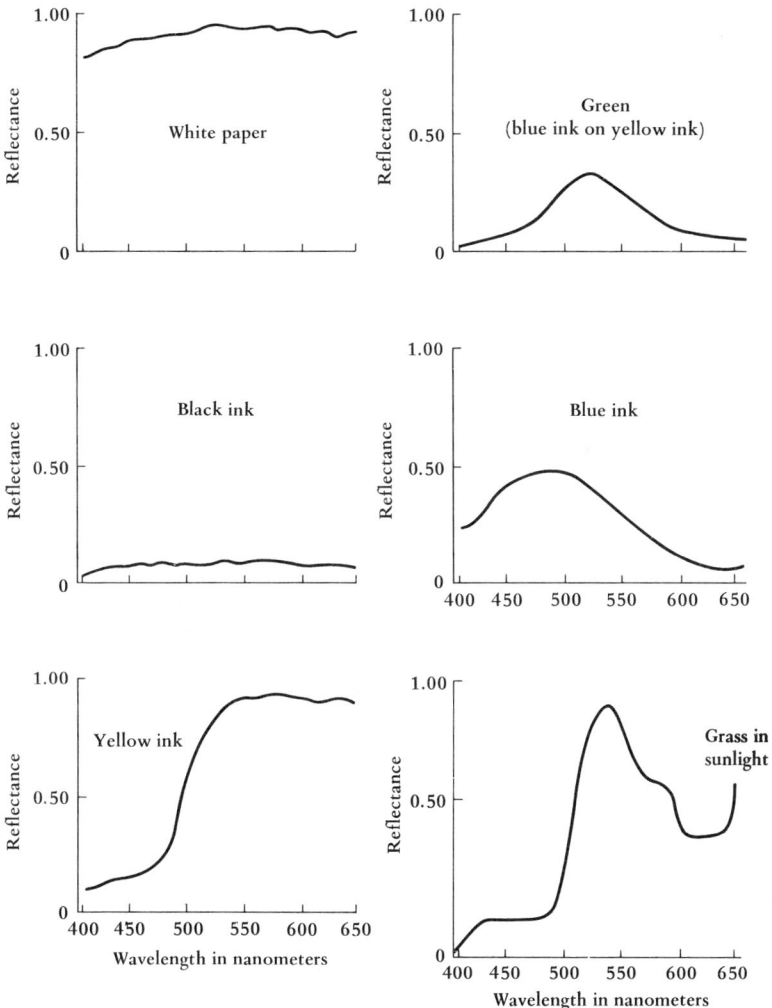

FIGURE 4.4   Several spectral reflectance distributions that result from white light being reflected from grass (taken from Cornsweet, 1970); and from several different colored inks on white paper (from Pirenne, 1948).

reflects primarily long-wavelength light (when illuminated by white light) will tend to appear to be red in color because the light that reaches our eyes is limited to those wavelengths which produce the perception of red. If the light reaching the surface does not contain any of the wavelengths that the surface reflects, then the surface will appear black, since no light will be reflected from it at all. Thus surfaces are selective with respect to wavelengths, reflecting some and absorbing the rest. It is this selectivity that determines the colors of surfaces.

We have now considered Boynton's first two prerequisites for the perception of color. Before turning to the remaining prerequisites we will briefly examine the ways in which our experience of color is described. This information will be used to explain the effects of mixing different wavelengths.

THE DESCRIPTIONS OF COLOR

Throughout the book we have tried to distinguish carefully between the physical properties of the light entering the eye and the psychological characteristics of the perceiver's experience of or response to that light. This distinction is extremely important in the description of color perception. In this chapter we will be even more explicit about the distinction, because we will be seeking ways in which to describe the perceiver's experiences that we call color perception, and to trace these back to the characteristics of the light that gave rise to them.

The intensity of light incident to the eye is called luminance. Its magnitude is proportional to the number of photons contained in the light. The psychological concomitant of luminance is the brightness of the light, and whenever we use the term brightness we will be concerned with the appearance of light, not its physical intensity. We have discussed several aspects of the psychophysical relation between luminance and brightness already, and will consider more of these in Chapter 5.

In addition to intensity of light, we will discuss two other dimensions of the light entering the eye that lead to two different characteristics of the experience of color. We have already noted that light may be composed of a number of different wavelengths. If a narrow band of light is isolated (as with a filter or a prism), then we can specify a dominant wavelength. The psychological correlate of this physical measure is hue, since each narrow band of wavelengths gives rise to a different sensation of hue. For example, light of 500 nanometer wavelength has a blue-green hue, while light of 650 nanometer wavelength has a reddish hue.

The third dimension is the purity of the light and the saturation of its color. A pure light is one with little or no white light mixed with the narrow band of wavelengths. This will give rise to the perception of a highly saturated color.

We shall discuss each of these dimensions of light and its perceptual correlates in turn.

Luminance and Brightness

As we noted in Chapter 2, the relation between luminance and brightness is not perfect. This is especially true when wavelength of light is varied, and for two independent reasons. The energy in each photon is a linear decreasing function of the wavelength of the radiation. Thus, each photon of light from the short wavelengths has nearly twice the energy as a photon from a long wavelength. Further, the photoreceptors are not equally sensitive to all wavelengths. Hence, both energy in the photons and sensitivity of the receptors differ as a function of wavelength.

The sensitivity of the receptors to photons of different wavelengths is described by a spectral sensitivity function. The procedure for deriving the function involves presenting a small bipartite field, usually about a 2-degree spot which is divided in half so that each side is illuminated separately. One side contains the standard energy value of a given wavelength. The perceiver adjusts the energy of the other side for each wavelength presented until the two sides look equally bright. The observer is told to ignore differences in hue or saturation in making his match. Figure 4.5 shows the foveal (cone) spectral sensitivity function for a typical normal observer. The ordinate is the relative sensitivity of the eye to each of the wavelengths shown on the abscissa. The wavelength of the greatest sensitivity is given a value of 1.0, and all others are proportionate values. Thus, for any wavelength the observer is asked to add the least amount of energy needed to match it with the standard light.

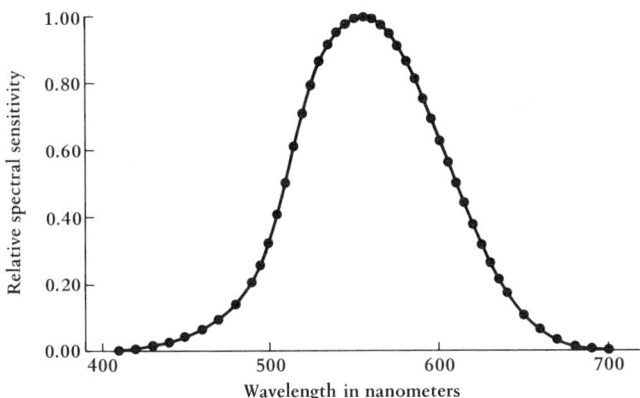

FIGURE 4.5   A foveal spectral sensitivity function for a normal observer.

As can be seen, the fovea is most sensitive to wavelengths in the middle of the spectrum, around 555 nanometers. The relative luminance of all other wavelengths is related to their appropriate ordinate values. Hence a light of 480-nanometer wavelength has only 20 percent of the luminance of a 555-nanometer light. This means that to make these two wavelengths appear equally bright, five times as much 480-nanometer light will have to be presented as 555-nanometer light.

Dominant Wavelength and Hue

In addition to the luminance-brightness dimension, light can be described in terms of its spectral composition and its corresponding appearance. We have already introduced terms for hue, for whenever we name a color by its appearance, we are referring to its hue. When a number of wavelengths are mixed together, the resulting light has no dominant wavelength and its hue is white or gray. As soon as one wavelength is more heavily represented than any other then light takes on the appearance of color, which we call hue. Thus, light of 650 nanometers has a red hue, while light of 450 nanometers has a blue hue.

What happens to the appearance of light when different wavelengths are mixed together? Most demonstrations and experiments in which lights of different wavelengths are mixed (called colorimetry) use selective filters that pass only a narrow band of wavelengths of light. Empirically, results of such experiments have been known for centuries, but it has only been in the last 100 years that any rational scheme for their understanding has begun to develop. That development is not yet complete, since no system of describing colors has been able to account for all of the phenomena of the perception of colors. We shall cover only the most salient features; see Boynton (1971) for a description of the principal systems.

If the spectral wavelengths are portrayed in a circular display, as in Figure 4.6, we can illustrate some of the important aspects of color mixing. When wavelengths corresponding to colors opposite to each other on the circle are mixed in equal amounts, then the resulting hue will appear gray or white. Such opposites are called complementary hues. If the amounts are unequal, the result will be the hue of the predominant wavelength, but less saturated (as if white or gray light had been added to it—see below). If any two lights from the

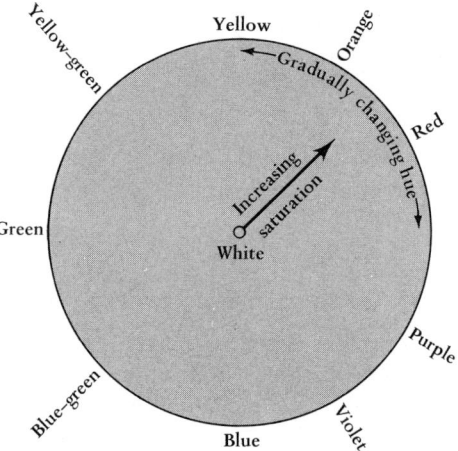

FIGURE 4.6 A psychological color circle.

same side of the circle are mixed, the result will be a hue intermediate between the two.

Notice that the hues in the lower right quadrant of the circumference of the circle are nonspectral colors. These are not seen when light is passed through a spectrum, and hence are not wavelengths contained in white light. But they can be made by mixing different combinations of long and short wavelengths together. They are needed in the circle so that mixing complementaries will always produce gray. To get gray or white from a mixture of a wavelength of green hue and some other wavelength, the other light must be a mixture of long and short wavelengths, a mixture that has a purple hue. It is obvious from the continuity of the hues around the circle that the nonspectral colors do fit. Red, blue, green, and usually yellow are often called primary colors because they are unique and do not look like any other colors, although such names are often arbitrarily applied. We already described how mixing two exact complementaries in equal amounts will produce white. For example, a 609-nanometer (orange) light and a 496-nanometer (blue-green) light will yield white when mixed. So will a 575-nanometer (yellow) light and a 474-nanometer (blue) light.

If one mixes any three primaries in varying amounts, this mixture of wavelengths can be made to match any wavelength. Using equal amounts it produces white. The light from most radiant sources has a number of wavelengths in it, so that most sources look white. This will be true even if they are deficient in some wavelengths. As long as there is a balance from several different parts of the spectrum the light appears white.

These colorimetry demonstrations are important, for they have formed the basis for most of the research on the perception of colors. They help determine whether color perception is normal or defective, they are the basis of tests of the receptor processes, and they allow measurement of the effects of chromatic adaptation, to give just a few examples.

Purity and Saturation

The final pair of descriptors is the purity of the spectral composition and the resulting subjective experience of saturation. A pure light is one with a narrow band of dominant wavelengths, but with little white light mixed with it. This gives the appearance of great saturation. The spectral colors are the most saturated ones obtainable, but they differ from one another in their appearance of saturation even at their state of complete purity. Thus spectral red looks very saturated. If some white light is added it becomes desaturated and looks pink. The more white light is added, the more desaturated it becomes, until with a sufficiently large amount of white all traces of hue disappear. To show that the spectral colors differ in saturation, much more white light has to be added to spectral blue or spectral red than to spectral yellow before they completely desaturate. Hence, spectral yellow is considered less saturated.

In fact it is very difficult to get a yellow to be as saturated as red under any circumstances.

All three sets of psychological descriptors are illustrated graphically in Figure 4.7 in a color solid. The vertical dimension corresponds to brightness, the circumference to hue, and the radius to saturation.

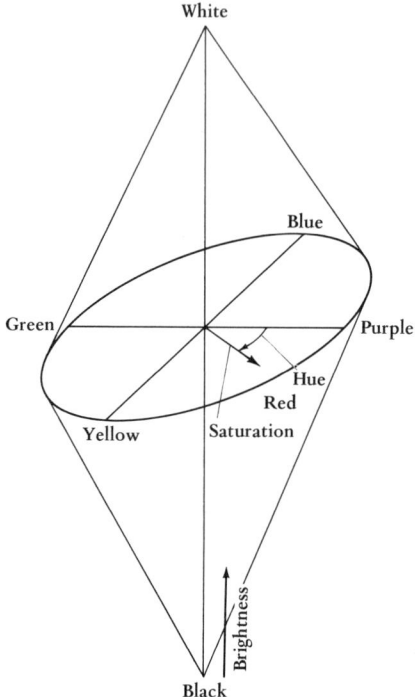

FIGURE 4.7   A psychological color solid (from Judd and Wyszecki, 1952).

THE RECEPTORS FOR COLOR PERCEPTION

Boynton's third prerequisite specifies that there must be two or more receptor processes that differ in their absorption of the various wavelengths. A photo-receptor collects photons—any kind of photons. It is a nonselective radiation detector in the sense that its response contains no information about any of the properties of the photons that excited it. Its response is the same whatever the wavelength of the photon. But photons of different wavelengths have different probabilities of being absorbed. We saw this in the spectral luminosity or sensitivity function in Figure 4.5.

Although the data in Figure 4.5 were collected in a psychophysical experiment, they could also be considered the absorption function of a receptor. As such, they would show the percentage of photons absorbed at each wavelength relative to the amount absorbed at the wavelength of greatest sensitivity, or the probability of absorption of a single photon by the receptor. Thus if all receptors have the same absorption function as in Figure 4.5, then if five times as many photons of 480-nanometer light illuminate one side of a bipartite field as 555-nanometer light on the other side, then the two sides would look equally bright. With only one absorption function, different wavelengths would produce only brightness differences, not hue differences.

Consequently, in order to get different hues, we have to have at least two different receptor types. Hence Figure 4.5 must be a composite of several separate ones. For example, Figure 4.8 shows two separate luminosity functions, one for a receptor system most sensitive to long (red) wavelengths and another to medium (green) wavelengths. According to the figure, a photon of 650-nanometer light has four times as great a chance of exciting a long-wave receptor as it does a medium-wave receptor. Conversely, a 500-nanometer photon would be much more likely to be absorbed by a medium- than by a long-wave receptor. In the hypothetical example here, color perception would be related to the ratio of absorption of photons by the two receptor systems. All receptors can absorb some of the wavelengths, since both of the curves extend over the entire visible range. But they absorb wavelengths in different amounts. As the wavelength of the photons changes, there would be a change in the relative output of the two receptor systems.

Figure 4.8 is a hypothetical example of a two-receptor system. We now know from several independent lines of evidence that the normal human fovea contains three different receptor systems with respect to the absorption of wavelengths. The methods used to determine this are themselves of some interest, and although we will not examine them in detail, some appreciation of how these measurements are made is useful to understanding the receptor mechanisms themselves.

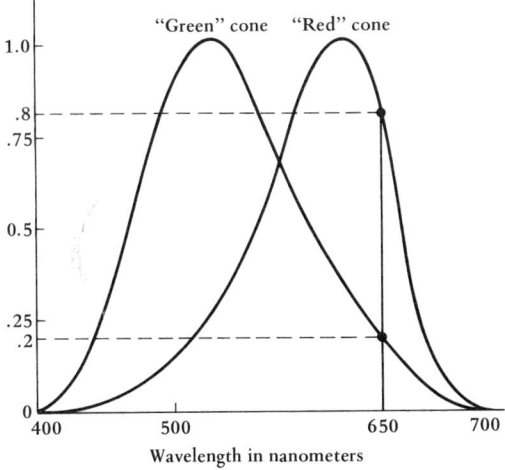

FIGURE 4.8 Two hypothetical spectral luminosity functions: one for receptors maximally sensitive to long wavelength light, and the other to medium wavelength light.

It should be obvious that the hypothetical data of Figure 4.8 could not be collected as were the actual data of Figure 4.5. To do so, one would need a spot of light that could be focused so precisely and on such a completely stationary retina that it would stimulate only one cone at a time. This cannot be done. Consequently, data like those in Figure 4.5 always represent the activity of many receptors. Figure 4.8 is for foveal cones, presumably averaging all three types of cones. Since there are no rods in the center of the fovea, this function is virtually uncontaminated by the spectral sensitivity of rods. It is very difficult, however, to do the converse experiment on rods without some cones being involved as well. While the center of the fovea is rod-free, no part of the retina is cone-free, even though the frequency of cones does become progressively less as one samples farther into the periphery. It is possible to do this experiment by first adapting the cones to high-intensity light, and then testing the rod spectral sensitivity function with low-intensity light that would be below the cone threshold. The adapting light should be put into the eye through the center of the pupil, which maximizes the probability of its being absorbed by cones, but the spectral sensitivity function of the rods should be measured with light put in near the edge of the pupil, making it more difficult to be absorbed by cones. It is under such circumstances that the rod spectral sensitivity function can be measured.

Figure 4.9 represents the results of such measurements. It shows that the rods also have a spectral sensitivity function that covers the entire visible spectrum, but that their greatest sensitivity is to wavelengths shorter than

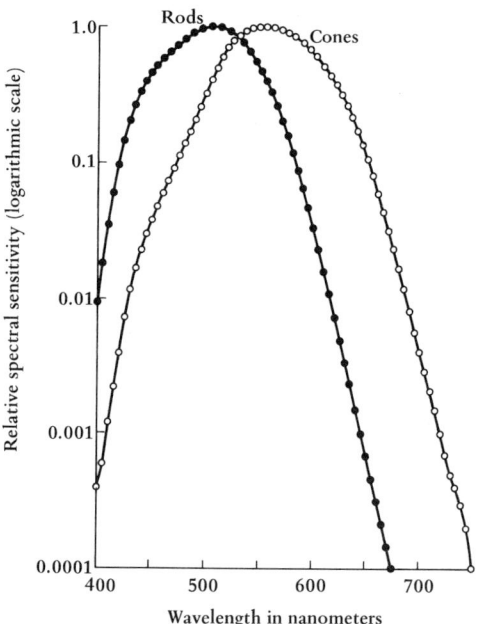

FIGURE 4.9 Spectral luminosity functions for cone and rod portions of the retina.

that of the cones. The entire function is shifted to the shorter end of the spectrum by about 50 nanometers.

This says that the probability that a photon will be absorbed by a rod is also a function of the wavelength of that photon. But we know that rods are not involved in color perception per se, because there is only one kind of rod receptor with respect to its spectral sensitivity function. This tells us that rods will respond to spectral differences only by registering differences in intensity, but not in saturation or hue.

One way of observing the difference between the rod function and the average cone function is to see what happens to the perception of the brightness of colors with rods and with cones. Purkinje (1825) first reported this effect, and it is named after him. Pick two wavelengths that look equally bright when viewed with cones, say a 500-nanometer (blue-green) light, and a 620-nanometer (red-orange) light. These both have a 40 percent relative spectral sensitivity in Figure 4.9 for the cone function. If the overall luminance is lowered, so that the brightness discriminations are now being made by the rods, the 500-nanometer light looks much brighter, relative to the longer wavelength light. Purkinje noticed this with flowers. In bright daylight a red and a blue flower might appear equally bright, but at twilight, although both now look less bright, the blue ones seem much brighter than the red.

We have already noted that the matching procedure will not separate out the individual cone functions. How can we be sure that separate and different cone functions exist? One technique is to study retinas supposedly similar to humans', remove individual rods and cones, isolate their photopigments, and examine the amount of light they absorb at different wavelengths. This has been done with rods, since there are many more of them and each one has a lot of photopigment in it. The absorption spectrum of the photopigments of rods measured in this way is very similar to the psychophysical spectral sensitivity function for rods shown in Figure 4.9. But this technique has not been useful with cones for practical reasons, so we have no comparable data for the different types of cones.

A second procedure was designed by Rushton (1958). He projected two small spots of light of differing wavelengths on nearby areas of the fovea. Some of the wavelengths were absorbed, thereby exciting those cones. More of the light passed through the cones and was absorbed by the inside dark lining at the back of the eye. But some was reflected from the back of the eye and passed back out of the front of the eye. Rushton measured the wavelength of reflected light, and by comparing it to the wavelength of the incident light, he could determine which wavelengths were being absorbed. Then he adapted the photopigments with an intense light of a narrow band of wavelengths. This bleached the photopigments so that they now absorbed fewer photons. Rushton compared the difference in relative absorption of each wavelength before and after bleaching the photopigments with different wavelengths. With this procedure he was able to isolate two cone functions, one with a maximum absorption for light in the long-wavelength end, and one in the medium-wavelength region. He did not locate a third cone type, but his procedure was not appropriate to finding cones maximally sensitive to the short wavelengths, so his failure to find these types was not surprising. Even so, his results were the first concrete evidence that there are two separable cone types.

A third procedure is microspectrophotometry, which examines the absorption spectrum of a very small number of cones measured in monkey and human eyes that have been removed for reasons other than retinal disease. This technique has proved itself sensitive enough to show three separable cone types. The absorption of different wavelengths is measured before and after the cones are adapted to intense monochromatic light. The difference between the absorption of each wavelength before and after the bleaching of the photopigment by the intense light provides a measure of the sensitivity of the photopigment itself. Figure 4.10, taken from Wald and Brown (1965) shows the three cone functions with their peak sensitivities at about 450, 530, and 570 nanometers. When measurements were made on individual cones by this procedure it was shown that each cone has only a single sensitivity function and hence probably contains only one photopigment. Thus we can identify the three receptor processes with three different types of cones, again, loosely speaking, red, green, and blue cones.

We have already described how mixing only three wavelengths is sufficient to match any wavelength. From this, many theorists, beginning with Helmholtz, argue that if the retina has just three different receptor systems, each maximally sensitive to a different region of the spectrum, then we should be capable of perceiving all colors. This is a trichromatic or a component theory of color perception. If all colors can be made by mixing only three, and if we have only three types of cones and the outputs of those can be sent independently to the cortex, then combining these outputs should provide suf-

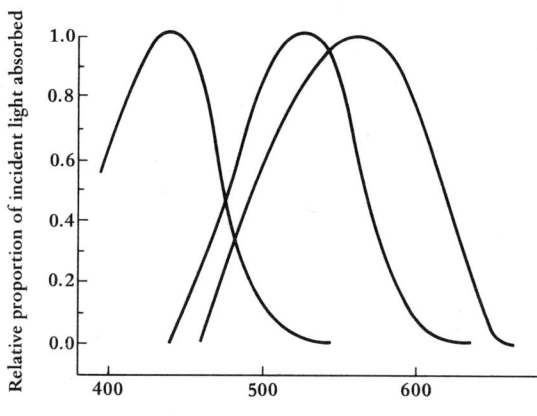

FIGURE 4.10   Spectral absorption functions for three types of cones (from Wald and Brown, 1965).

ficient coding to permit us to distinguish and see all of the different colors in the spectrum. The search for these three cone types has been a major interest of many visual scientists. The facts concerning the three receptor processes have turned out almost exactly as the trichromatic theory would predict even though at the time this idea was first proposed virtually nothing was known about the structure or anatomy of the retina.

COLOR CODING BEYOND THE RECEPTORS

The previous discussion has shown how Boynton's third prerequisite is met by describing three types of cones, each with a different spectral sensitivity function. Boynton's fourth prerequisite concerns how the outputs of these three receptor systems are coded and transmitted to the cortex.

The early versions of the trichromatic theories of color had assumed that the three receptor outputs were transmitted to the brain separately, and then combined to yield the different color experiences in roughly the same way that lights of different wavelengths can be mixed. This was seen as a very parsimonious transmission and coding system, in that all colors could be based on only three receptors and their combinations would follow rules that had already been demonstrated to work for mixing lights.

Young had recognized that having a sensory channel for each different wavelength was implausible, inefficient, and suffered on some logical grounds as well. Thus, he suggested that some type of rather broad-band tuning should be involved. Helmholtz in 1867 (see 1962), who followed this logic, did not speculate about the output of the three types of receptor systems he assumed were present, although by implication he was suggesting that their outputs must have been transmitted separately to the cortex.

However, such a system of independent pathways from each type of cone to the cortex is unlikely, since we now know that these pathways show substantial inhibition effects among them. Actually Hering in 1870 (see 1964) suggested a coding scheme based on inhibition, even though he had no direct evidence of such inhibitory processes. However he noted several perceptual effects of color coding that suggested an opponent rather than a component coding. Specifically, he suggested that there were three pairs of coded representations which acted in opposition. With respect to color, he saw one pair as a red-green opponent system, and a second as a yellow-blue opponent system. A third was a black-white opponent system, primarily to specify brightness and saturation. Figure 4.11 illustrates the model Hering had in mind for coding processes.

The model suggests that the wavelengths corresponding to red and green are coded as opposites and not as combinations. Thus, the red-green system receives inputs from the red cones and the green cones (it also gets a little from the blue cones to account for purple). If the red input predominates, then the output of the red-green opponent system is positive, indicated by an increase

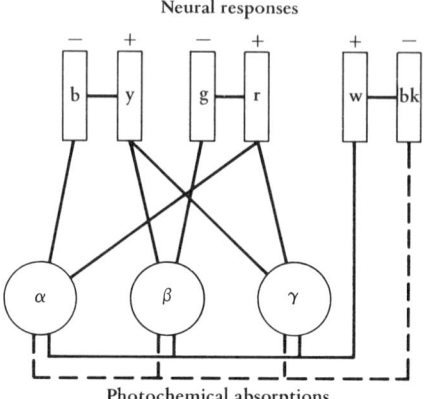

Neural responses

Photochemical absorptions

FIGURE 4.11 Opponent color coding model based on Hering's proposals (from Hurvich and Jameson, 1957).

in its frequency of firing over the spontaneous level of activity, while it is negative if the green input is greater. Hence, the coding of reds and greens is handled by one system, and presumably this occurs immediately after the initial receptor processes. Similarly, yellow and blue are opponent outputs of another system whose inputs are all the receptor processes. Again, yellow is signaled by an increase in excitation and comes from a predominance of long wavelengths stimulating the three receptors, while blue is signaled by a decrease in excitation of the system in a comparable form.

There were several kinds of data that suggested an opponent coding process. The appearance of color suggests some concern about simple color mixing. Yellow appears to be as unique a hue as red, green, or blue, yet the component system would argue that yellow is always a mixture of red and green. Further, you cannot have a perception of something that is both red and green in the same place at the same time, nor yellow and blue at the same time. This would suggest some opposition between these pairs. Color afterimages, to be discussed below, involve opponent color arrangements—green is seen after looking at red, blue after looking at yellow, and so forth. The effect of overall luminance changes suggests a pairing of opposites, since as the level of illumination increases above the scotopic range, first only the reds and greens appear while blue and yellow objects are still perceived as achromatic. Only at higher levels of illumination do the blues and yellows appear. This differential would be difficult to explain by simple chromatic conceptions.

Hurvich and Jameson measured the spectral sensitivity functions for the two opponent color processes, as shown in Figure 4.12. We will first examine what these functions tell us about the appearance of colors, and then indicate how they are derived. Each of the two functions dip above and below a zero level in the relative visual response scale. The zero level corresponds to the spontaneous neural activity of the coded system, presumably a pathway to the cortex. When the red-green function is above zero, the output signals that

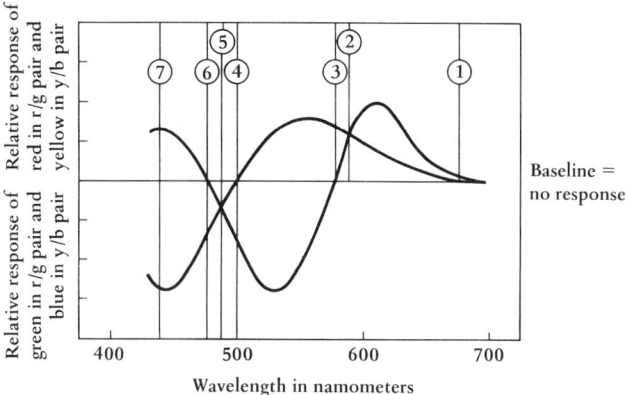

FIGURE 4.12   Theoretical spectral sensitivity functions for the two opponent color processes, one for red-green and the other for yellow-blue (from Hurvich and Jameson, 1957).

the predominant wavelengths are long, so that red is seen. When the output is negative a green hue is signaled. Similarly for yellow and blue. These codes represent the sign and the amount of output from the two opponent systems.

These can be illustrated in more detail by looking at specific wavelengths that are numbered in Figure 4.12. Wavelength 1 produces a positive response from the red-green system and a much smaller positive response from the yellow-blue system, yielding a primarily red hue. Since the sensitivity of the yellow-blue system is lower at this wavelength, a more saturated red is best obtained with moderate to low intensities. Which hue will be seen will be a function of the ratio of the heights of the two curves. Wavelengths above 600 nanometers all look equally red, since the ratios of the red to the yellow remain constant beyond that wavelength. As wavelength decreases below 600 nanometers, both the red and the yellow functions increase. While the red curve increases more, the ratio of red to yellow is decreasing, so that the hue becomes yellower with respect to red.

At wavelength 2, the red and yellow systems are equal and the best orange is seen. At wavelength 3 the red-green function is at zero, and only a pure yellow is seen. As the wavelength shortens more, the negative values on the red-green system signal green outputs now, so that we see yellow-green combinations. At wavelength 4 the yellow-blue function has reached zero and we see a green, without any yellow or blue in it. Wavelength 5 yields a green-blue combination, and wavelength 6 is a pure blue since the red-green function is again at zero. At wavelength 7 the red-green has become positive again, so that red and blue combine to be perceived as purple.

Thus, Figure 4.12 provides a description of how variation in wavelength will lead to appropriate changes in the hues that we see. These functions were psychophysically determined following the assumptions of the opponent system. If a perceiver is shown a particular short wavelength that is perceived as blue, it should be possible to add yellow of a particular wavelength to it until the blueness completely disappears without at the same time looking yellow. This locates the zero point between the balance of yellow and blue. The amount of that particular yellow that was added to that particular blue will provide a measure of the relative blue response of the yellow-blue system for that wavelength of blue. This process can then be repeated for all values along the spectrum for both yellow-blue and red-green. The results of such measurements generated Figure 4.12 (Hurvich and Jameson, 1957).

Neural Evidence for Opponent Coding Processes

When Hering proposed his opponent coding system he had no neurophysiological evidence of opponent or inhibitory processes. None of the evidence up to that time about the three-receptor mechanism suggested any interaction among the outputs of the three cones. If there is no interaction, then how could the opponent processes function? In the 1930s the first discoveries of lateral inhibition among adjacent neural units provided the first hint of the mechanism. In the 1950s the first concentric receptive field structures of the ganglion

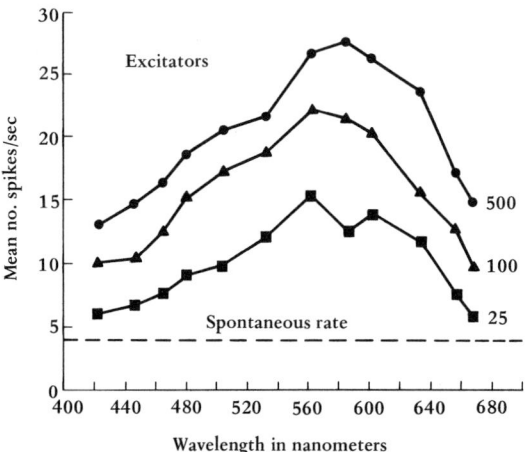

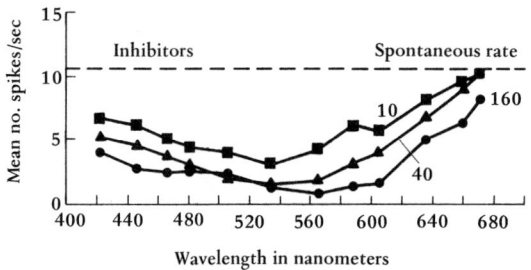

FIGURE 4.13 Responses from lateral geniculate cells in the monkey to varying wavelengths of light showing evidence for nonopponent coding of color information (from DeValois, Abromov, and Jacobs, 1966).

cell level were described. These reports led Hurvich and Jameson in 1957 to postulate such mechanisms as the basis of opponent color coding.

It was not until the early 1960s that DeValois reported direct evidence of opponent color coding in the nervous system. For example, DeValois, Abromov, and Jacobs (1966) reported microelectrode recordings from single cells of the lateral geniculate nucleus. They diffusely illuminated the eye with monochromatic light, and studied the output of different lateral genicul-ate cells. They found two types of cells, one which they classified as a non-opponent cell, and one as an opponent cell. The nonopponent cells behaved as one would expect intensity detectors to respond. Two examples of the frequency of firing rates are shown in Figure 4.13.

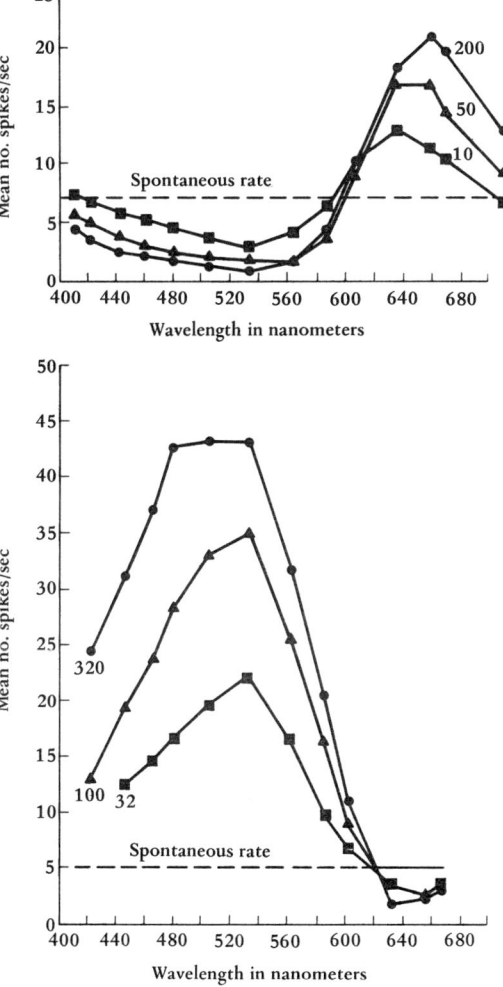

FIGURE 4.14   Responses from lateral geniculate cells in the monkey to varying wavelengths of light showing evidence for opponent coding of color information (from DeValois, Abromov, and Jacobs, 1966).

The more interesting data are from the opponent cells which increase their rates of firing above their spontaneous levels for some wavelengths and decrease them for others. Figure 4.14 shows two examples. The first shows a positive response to long wavelengths (that is, an increase from the spontaneous level), and a negative response to short wavelengths. The other example is roughly the reverse.

Further evidence has been reported since DeValois's pioneering work, all of which suggests that at the receptor level there are three different types of cones, but that above that level the output of the cones has been combined via inhibitory networks that act in opposition. Thus when investigating the color-perception system at the level of the receptors themselves, as with adapting lights or measures of light absorption and reflection, we will find evidence of a component process. But when we investigate higher levels of the system, as when we ask perceivers how colors appear, then we are dealing primarily with opponent processes. Not all of the details of the interaction among the receptors and the coding systems are worked out; many problems still remain to be explained. But it appears that both of these processes are present, with components being coded as opponents.

COLOR AS A UNIQUE PERCEPTUAL EXPERIENCE

Boynton's last prerequisite for color perception is that sensory information be transmitted to the cortex and associated with unique perceptual experiences. There is as yet little evidence on how this requirement is met, and research is just at the beginning stages. Attempts to find and study the terminus of color-coding pathways in the cortex have not been particularly successful. There are hints of cortical receptive field organizations for color perception, perhaps similar to those for several dimensions of form and motion. It is probable that the opponent color coding found in the lateral geniculate body is continued to the cortex, but it has not been located. In short, the evidence to date is not adequate to differentiate brain activity correlated with color as distinct from intensity perception. Until we have evidence on the transmission and representation in the cortex, it is not possible to tell whether one can study their linkages with unique perceptual experience.

We will turn now to several phenomena of color perception to round out our discussion. These will include the effects of adaptation on the color-receptor systems, the induction of color by other colors, color constancy, and color-defective vision.

THE ADAPTATION OF COLOR PERCEPTION

Chapter 2 discussed light and dark adaptation to white light, considered without regard to its wavelength. How does that picture change when the adaptation is to light of specific wavelengths? We can list several expectations concerning adaptation of rods and of cones.

In general, stimulating any receptor intensively with a large number of photons will both excite the receptor and reduce its sensitivity to continuing or subsequent stimulation. Figure 2.18 showed both a very transient, dramatic initial loss in sensitivity, and a less extensive but steady-state effect of a stable reduction in sensitivity proportional to the number of photons incident to the receptor. We indicated in our discussion of the mechanism of light adaptation that the transient effect must be neural in character and probably is of an inhibitory nature, since the photochemical changes in the receptor caused by adaptation are not fast enough to account for the rapid transients.

On the other hand, the loss in sensitivity to more prolonged intense light stimulation, such as would be normally encountered in bright sunlight, is due to the bleaching of the visual pigment in each molecule of the receptor. When the pigment of the receptor has been unstimulated for some time, it is in an unbleached state and is capable of absorbing photons of the appropriate wavelength. As it is bleached, the pigment becomes transparent and the photons pass through it without being absorbed, and thereby, without exciting the receptor. Very intense light applied for several minutes can nearly completely bleach all of the photopigment in a receptor, rendering it virtually incapable of responding immediately thereafter.

Figure 2.19 plotted the increase in sensitivity after the adapting stimulus is turned off. This function is identical to the regeneration of the photopigments observed in a test tube in the laboratory, so that we can be quite confident that it is the bleaching and regeneration of the photopigment which accounts for the nontransient effect of dark and light adaptation.

Rod Adaptation

Only one type of rod photopigment exists and we know that it responds differentially to monochromatic light as a function of wavelength (Figure 4.9). Hence, we should expect to find greater adaptation in rods to those wavelengths to which the rods are maximally sensitive. Thus a 650-nanometer (red) light should have relatively little impact on rods at all, cause little bleaching, and it should not lower the rod's sensitivity either to white light or to any other particular wavelength. We have already observed that light adaptation can be attenuated in rods with the use of red goggles to preserve sensitivity at night. On the other hand a 500-nanometer (blue-green) light, to which rods are maximally sensitive, should produce very large adaptation effects, even at a moderate intensity.

Cone Adaptation

The above expectations apply to the cones as well, except that with three different types of cones, each with a different spectral sensitivity function, the effects of adaptation are more dramatic. In fact, such experiments provide further evidence for the three component systems of receptors.

The three spectral sensitivity functions of Figure 4.10 can be used to predict the differential absorption of photons by the three types of cones to any particular adapting wavelength. If we present 600-nanometer (red) light we would expect it to lower the sensitivity of the red cones greatly, the green cones somewhat, and the blue cones little. If this is true, then we have momentarily changed the relative heights of the three spectral sensitivity functions, though we will not have changed their shapes. This means that for a perceiver to match a 600-nanometer (red) and a 550-nanometer (green) light in brightness following a 600-nanometer adapting light, he will need to put in much more long-wave light than medium-wave light. As the impact of the adaptation wears off, the relative amount of long to medium wavelengths needed for equality will gradually reduce over the time that dark adaptation takes for cones, until it reaches the ratio that existed before the adaptation occurred.

When the adapting light is white light, containing all wavelengths, then all three cone systems will be affected in roughly equal proportions and the relative heights of their spectral sensitivity functions will not be changed. Thus no shift in sensation over the spectrum will occur after white adapting light.

Since virtually all experiments with selective wavelength adaptation have found evidence consistent with these expectations, such data are very supportive of the component receptor processes made up of three different types of cones.

COLOR CONTRAST

There is another class of phenomena that illustrates changes in sensitivity as a function of concurrent stimulation. We shall consider these contrast-induction processes in much more detail in the next chapter. There we will show that differences among luminances falling on different parts of the visual field are still capable of inducing perceptual changes. Thus a gray square against a white background looks darker than when it is seen against a black background. This is called simultaneous brightness contrast. The explanation that will be offered for this involves lateral inhibitory effects of the adjacent light and dark areas.

We can look at the same type of task with stimuli that differ in wavelength rather than in intensity. A gray square on a red background looks greenish, but when viewed against a green background it looks red. On a yellow background it looks blue, and on a blue background it looks yellow.

How can these effects be explained? They are not examples of adaptation, because there is no bleaching of receptors at these lower intensity levels; moreover, there are no more red receptors being stimulated by the gray square when the gray square is seen next to a red background than next to any other background. There will be some long wavelengths in the gray, but these will not be different for different backgrounds. So it looks very much as if the background is providing some lateral inhibition onto the gray area just as it does for brightness contrast, except that here it appears that the inhibition is specific to particular cone types. Thus, stimulated red cones in the background inhibit nearby red cones from the gray area, but not green or blue cones.

This is exactly the kind of process that an opponent color-coding system would produce. It suggests that the outputs of receptors, rather than being transmitted independently to the cortex, seem to be able to inhibit each other reciprocally. Thus in every case the color seen when gray is induced on a chromatic background is the complement of the background, as would be predicted from Figure 4.12.

In the above examples of simultaneous color contrast, the background induced the complementary color onto a gray area seen against it. Comparable effects can easily be demonstrated for successive color contrast. If you stare at a green patch for a few seconds and then shift your eyes to a gray surface, the gray surface will take on a reddish hue. The explanation for these effects is based on the same mechanisms as for simultaneous contrast.

COLOR CONSTANCY

In Chapter 5 we will show that the perceived brightness of an object seen against a particular background does not change when the level of illumination on the object and surround is changed. This phenomenon is known as brightness constancy. Color constancy is an analogous phenomenon since the perceived hue of a surface does not change even if the wavelengths of the illumination on the surfaces change. As with brightness constancy, it is critical that the change in illumination occur over the background as well as over the surface being judged.

Color constancy is an important property of the visual system. It permits a stability of attribution of characteristics to the surfaces in the visual world, even though there are substantial changes in the light reaching the eye from those surfaces. Thus color constancy permits us to perceive the spectral reflectance distribution of a surface (and therefore, perceive the color of the surface) even under conditions in which the illumination on that surface changes in its spectral composition.

In Chapter 5 we will develop a general explanation for brightness constancy based on ideas of Cornsweet (1970). These can be directly applied to color constancy as well. Since that analysis requires some development, we will postpone discussion of the mechanisms of color constancy until that section of Chapter 5.

DEFECTIVE COLOR PERCEPTION

There are two general types of defective color perception. The first is represented by a group of perceivers who are missing one, two, or all three of the different cone receptors responsible for color perception. If a normal perceiver can match any wavelength of light by mixing different combinations of three wavelengths, then someone who is missing one type of cone would need only two wavelengths to be able to match any other wavelength. The color perception of such perceivers is called dichromatic.

Perceivers who are missing two or all three cone systems are called monochromats, since they will match a particular wavelength with only one other, by simply adjusting its intensity. Monochromats may have all of their cones functioning normally, except that each has the same spectral sensitivity function. But some monochromats have no cones at all, so that in addition to having monochromatic color perception, they also have poor visual acuity, poor central vision, and all of the other defects that would be associated with the absence of cones.

The second general class of defective color perception, and by far the largest is composed of people called anomalous trichromats. Being trichromats, they need, just like a normal person, to mix three different wavelengths to match any particular wavelength. What is anomalous is that their mixtures may deviate from normal in several respects. They may act as if the spectral sensitivity functions of one of the cone types had been shifted along the spectrum. The largest class is composed of trichromats whose green functions are anomalous. When given a spectral orange and asked to match it with a mixture of three wavelengths, these perceivers will add much more green to the mixture than would a person with normal color vision.

SUMMARY

The perception of color has been defined as any noticeable difference between two parts of a visual field that is not due to variation in their space, time, or intensity. We have distinguished five prerequisites that the visual system must meet in order for perceivers to notice or perceive color.

In the first, there must be variation in the wavelength of the light from sources that are illuminating the eye and the visual world. We showed the ways in which light was composed of different wavelengths, how these could be separated and combined, and why there had to be two or more available for color perception to occur.

The second prerequisite specifies that there must be variation in the spectral reflectance of surfaces in the visual world. If all surfaces reflected the same wavelength, no differential stimulation would reach the eye, and no perception of color would be possible.

With the introduction of these two prerequisites, we discussed the descriptions of colors, especially as a result of mixing lights of different wavelengths. We distinguished three sets of dimensions of color, each in terms of its physical variables and its psychological appearance. Thus, the luminance of light can be varied, and this can produce changes in its psychological brightness. Second, the dominance of one wavelength over all others can be varied, and this will produce changes in the hue. Finally, the amount of white light that is present can be varied, and this will produce changes in the saturation of the color.

The third prerequisite for color perception is the need for two or more receptor systems that are differentially receptive to variations in wavelength. We presented psychophysical, photochemical, and electrophysiological evidence for the existence of three such systems in the human visual system, corresponding to three different types of cones, each maximally sensitive to different parts of the visible spectrum.

The fourth prerequisite concerns how the outputs of these three receptor systems are coded and transmitted to the cortex. Current evidence shows that most of the coding is by opponent processes, so that red and green are coded as opposites, as are yellow and blue. Such coding depends on inhibitory processes after the receptor level.

The last prerequisite focuses on how the cortex attaches separate or unique color experiences to these coded representations of wavelengths differences. Although we know that this must occur, we have virtually no evidence yet on the details of the processes.

In the last section of the chapter, we briefly considered the adaptation of color perception, color contrast and constancy, and defective color perception. Each of these topics was presented primarily as a way to show how the principles of color perception developed during the chapter are applied to specific phenomena, and conversely, how these phenomena can help up learn more about the basic principles of color perception.

Readings

In addition to Boynton's excellent chapter, several textbooks on color perception are available. Le Grand (1957) is the best, but is now getting out of date. Several chapters in Graham's handbook (1965) are useful, but difficult, as are those in the Jameson and Hurvich handbook (1972). Cornsweet covers much of the color coding systems. Wyszecki and Stiles (1967) give a detailed and advanced coverage.

5
psychophysical measurement and parameters

INTRODUCTION

In the preceding chapters we have seen how light enters the eye, how the receptors in the eye transduce photons into neural impulses, and how the network of neurons further encodes information and transmits it through the central nervous system. In this chapter we will examine simple psychological or experiential aspects of perception and their relationship to the physical characteristics of the stimulus.

Physical properties of light and the objects that reflect light can be measured using the instruments of physics. While it is tempting to associate the physical values of stimulation with their psychological counterparts, this relationship is rarely if ever simple. For example, doubling the number of photons in a light source does not make it appear twice as bright. If simple, linear relationships cannot be assumed, then the specific functions must be determined experimentally. To do so, we must first measure the physical variation and then measure the perceptions that result from these physical variations, a very difficult and complex task. This will produce functional relationships between the physical and the psychological domains.

The difficulty in making these measurements comes from the need to ask the perceiver questions about his experience. Each of us can describe how bright a light appears, or how red it is, or how beautiful a sunset is. But those descriptions are not precise because they reflect differences in the kinds of words we prefer to use, the care with which we attend to our experiences, our memories of past perceptions, and what we think the listener wants to hear. Thus the primary task of psychological measurement in the study of perception is to eliminate these biases in the descriptions of our experience. This problem is the core of much of the study of perception and, therefore we shall focus on it first in this chapter.

Classical psychophysics is that area of psychology which attempts to determine the functional relationship between a perceived or subjective magnitude and a physical magnitude. The most frequent form of psychophysical functions studied deals with the relationship between perceived magnitude and stimulus intensity, such as perceived brightness as a function of the intensity of light. We have implied that the specification of physical dimensions of stimulation is relatively straightforward. This is not always the case, and as we will see in several places in this book, the search for the physical dimensions has been more complex than that for the psychological concomitants with which they are correlated. The perception of beauty is one example.

One of the major advances provided by the psychophysical methods is the restriction on the responses the perceiver is permitted to use to describe his experience. Modern approaches to psychological measurement require the perceiver to use a carefully restricted set of responses when describing his experience. Thus, instead of asking him to describe what he saw, we can ask him whether two lights appeared to be the same or not. Instead of asking him what a stimulus looked like, we can ask him whether he noticed a change. In these examples, the perceiver is asked to make rather simple discriminations, which by themselves are quite trivial. But we can infer the dimensions of perceptual experience from such relatively simple and restricted responses by following some procedures which govern how we vary the physical dimensions at the same time that we ask for the perceiver's description of what he sees.

The study of classical psychophysics and the development of the psychophysical methods evolved independently of theoretical points of view. Nevertheless, it provided a major area in which the problems of method were worked out—namely, the development of careful and precise means with which to formulate exact, often mathematical statements about mental and physical events. In this sense, classical psychophysics provides a model for all of psychology.

In this chapter, we shall examine two of the three aspects of psychophysical measurement: the methods used to evoke responses indicative of perceived qualities of stimulation, and the techniques by which those perceived qualities are specified.

SENSORY SCALES: CLASSICAL PSYCHOPHYSICS

Types of Scales

Precise description requires measurement and measurement must be made in terms of a dimension or scale to be meaningful. There are four basic types of scales which, loosely speaking, differ in the precision of the possible descriptions. These are the nominal, ordinal, interval, and ratio scales. The nominal scale is one in which the members are simply named or numbered. They are designated as individuals or as members of groups, classes, or categories. The relationship implied among the members or among the groups is equality—each member is equal to every other, but has a different name or number. The numbering of the members of a team and the different teams in a league are examples of nominal scales. Since the members are equal, one could be substituted for another without loss or change in any of the properties of the group.

If inequality is introduced into the relationships among the members, they may be ordered, say, from smallest to largest or from lightest to heaviest. This produces an ordinal scale. The operation for producing an ordered scale of categories or classes is the determination of "greater than" or "less than." Ordinal scales produce increasing monotonic functions, for instance, the scale of "hardness."

If, in addition to order, there is a unit of measurement, then the scale is called an interval scale. Such a scale does not require a zero point. The notion of a unit of measurement only requires that distance measured between equally spaced members within it be consistent. If, in addition to the equality of intervals (units), the scale yields equality of ratios of values, the result is a ratio scale. Such a scale always implies an absolute zero point. Physical dimensions of size or weight are ratio scales.

It should be clear, then, that whether a scale has a zero point and whether it has only equal intervals or equal ratios of intervals will determine what form the functions may take which use the scale. A major task in the study of classical psychophysics has been the attempt to determine whether the psychological world can best be described on an interval scale, or whether we can show that it produces a ratio scale.

Sensory Qualities

Perceptual experiences may differ both qualitatively and quantitatively. Examples of different sensory qualities are hue, brightness, pitch, timbre, and the like. Sensory qualities provide a nominal scale because we merely have a list of names for different perceptual experiences. Within each sensory quality, however, it is possible to measure quantitative differences. In this case, higher-order scales would be desirable.

THE CONCEPT OF THRESHOLD

The concept of threshold has been important to classical psychophysics because it can help to specify both the zero point of the scale of measurement and the size of the units along the scale.

Obtaining a Zero Point: Absolute Threshold

The zero point on a sensory scale is called the absolute threshold. Theoretically, this point is the beginning of perceptual experience. Below this point no awareness of stimulation occurs, and above this point there is always an experience. Since there exist measurable amounts of energy that do not produce responses, it seems reasonable to assume that such a threshold exists. Thus, the classical definition of threshold has been the minimum amount of energy required for a change from no perception to perception. The pattern of responses that would theoretically be produced when a perceiver is instructed to say "yes" when he has a sensation and "no" when he does not is shown in Figure 5.1, where the percentage of "yes" responses is plotted as a function

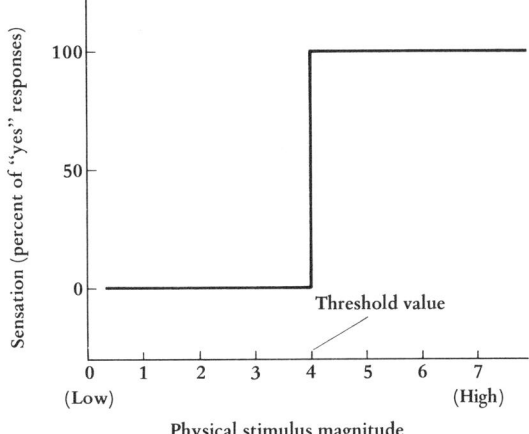

FIGURE 5.1 A theoretical absolute threshold response distribution illustrating sensitivity as a function of stimulus energy under the assumption of a step function change in sensitivity.

of stimulus intensity. This is a step function, with the percentage of "yes" responses going from zero (all "no") to 100 percent (all "yes") at the threshold value. Notice that the threshold is defined in terms of physical stimulus magnitude.

Unfortunately, actual data collected in an experiment designed to determine an absolute threshold never yield a step function. Empirical determinations of sensory thresholds always look like the function in Figure 5.2. This shows a smooth curve, with the percentage of "yes" responses increasing at some rate as a function of stimulus intensity. This function is produced because many variables enter into the processes that determine the sensitivity of the visual system, and therefore, measurements differ from moment to moment. Some of these variables result from the testing situation itself, some from variation within the perceiver, and some from the nature of the task the perceiver thinks is before him. For example, the stimulus energy may vary from trial to trial. The number of photons in a very dim pulse of light fluctuates substantially, even with the most precise stimulating sources. This problem is critical in vision because the eye is such a precise light-detecting instrument. When fluctuation in energy occurs, the values along the abscissa in Figure 5.1 are difficult to repeat exactly from trial to trial. The error produced make the results look like those in Figure 5.2.

In addition to the instability of the stimulus, there are substantial changes that occur in the perceiver which may alter the sensitivity of the visual system being measured. For example, placing the perceiver in the dark for half an hour will raise the sensitivity level of the visual system to its maximum point. However, once the testing has begun each stimulus presentation changes the level of adaptation, thereby causing the eye to lose some of its sensitivity. Thus, if the trials are spaced too closely together, later trials will be testing a less sensitive visual system. Therefore, more energy would be required and

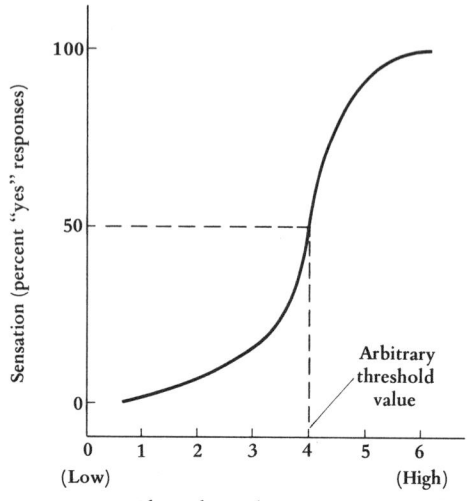

FIGURE 5.2   A more typical absolute threshold response distribution showing a continuous and smooth change in sensitivity as a function of stimulus energy.

this, in turn, would lower the sensitivity still further. Sensitivity may change for other reasons, too. If a perceiver takes a coffee break in the middle of an experiment, the caffeine might have some effect on some threshold systems; if he gets bored or fatigued, that might have some other effects.

Finally, in most threshold experiments the responses are difficult to make. Usually the perceiver has some uncertainty as to whether he saw the stimulus. Whenever decisions are difficult, variables other than the energy in the stimulus begin to play a disproportionately large part. For example, if the perceiver is very confident of his judgmental abilities, then he may tend to say he sees the stimulus even when he does not. Conversely, if he feels that he should never say "yes" unless he is absolutely certain, then he will tend to withhold his reports of seeing, and it will appear to the experimenter as if he is very insensitive. Thus, the perceiver's bias in his willingness to make a positive report may enter into the measurement itself.

All of these variables are present in any threshold experiment. They all interact and in many ways are impossible to assess. Usually, they are combined in unpredictable ways and, from the experimenter's point of view, create error. Their combined impact is that the empirical threshold functions obtained always look like that in Figure 5.2 rather than Figure 5.1. This second function shows clearly that the perceiver will sometimes say "yes" to relatively low amounts of energy and sometimes will say "no" to relatively high amounts. Since the experimenter sees only the pattern of responses, he must accept this curve as a measurement of the threshold and base his definition on it. Consequently, the theoretical definition of threshold given earlier must be different from its empirical definition, for the latter must take into account the statistical property of the responses.

Thus, the empirical threshold determination does not yield a single point which can be identified directly with the theoretical threshold. For measurement purposes, some value must arbitrarily be selected to represent this value. This is usually the 50-percent point, the value of stimulus intensity for which the perceiver responded "yes" half of the time and "no" half of the time.

Figure 5.3 presents the hypothetical results of two threshold experiments, labeled steep and shallow. Both of them yield the same threshold, defined as the point at which the perceiver says he can detect the stimulus 50 percent of the time. However, they differ sharply in their steepness. The situation which generated the steep function gives a much more precise estimate of the threshold than that of the shallow function, since the range of stimuli over which the perceiver changes his response is much narrower. For the steep function, energy values just slightly less than threshold yield a "no" response 100 percent of the time, and for energy values just slightly above threshold the perceiver says "yes" 100 percent of the time. Other things being equal, one should prefer a psychophysical method and measuring situation that produces steep as compared to shallow functions.

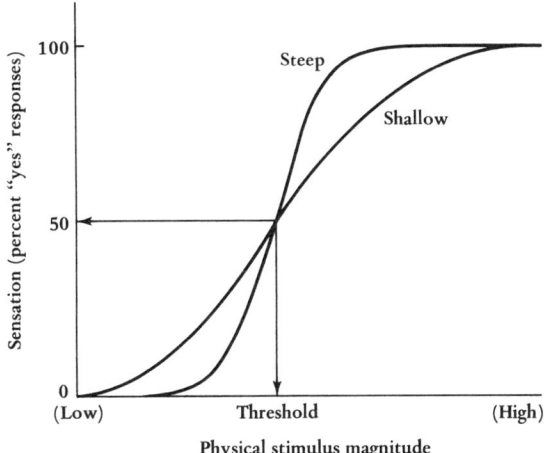

FIGURE 5.3   Hypothetical absolute threshold response functions under two conditions: one which produces rapid changes in sensitivity as stimulus energy is varied, and another which yields slow changes. The threshold is the same in both functions.

This is not the only criterion, however. In some circumstances, one might also like to have a method which gave indices of the lowest possible threshold. Thus, in Figure 5.4 the two functions have the same slope and consequently are presumably sensitive to the same amounts of error, but the low curve indicates a more sensitive system. Consequently, a second criterion for evaluating threshold procedures would be in terms of their ability to indicate maximal sensitivity.

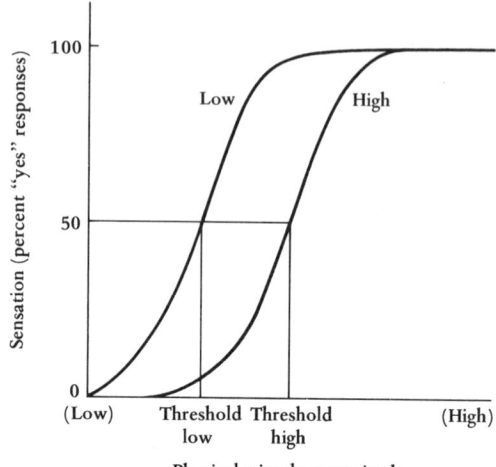

FIGURE 5.4 Hypothetical absolute threshold response functions under two conditions which differ in the amount of stimulus energy needed to define the threshold value.

Obtaining a Unit: Differential Threshold

To continue with the construction of a sensory scale, once the origin or zero point has been determined, we need a unit of measurement. Theoretically this unit should be the smallest amount of change in stimulating energy which can be perceived as a change in perception. Therefore, in a sense, this is a special case of absolute threshold determination and it is called a difference or discrimination threshold. The unit is often called a just noticeable difference, or a jnd.

Although we will examine some experiments and results on difference thresholds for brightness later in this chapter, a brief preview may be helpful here. If we wish to determine, for any luminance of a background, how much additional light has to be added in order to be noticed, this is a jnd experiment. The arrangement will be similar to the absolute threshold experiment, except that the perceiver will be asked whether he can see the increment that has been added to the background—can he notice the difference? The data can be plotted as the percentage "yes" responses as a function of the size of the increment. The difference threshold will be the point at which the perceiver says "yes" 50 percent of the time. That magnitude of the increment will be the size of the jnd.

The experimental task could be arranged in other ways as well. For example, the perceiver could be presented with two lights and asked which one is brighter. The left might be designated as a standard, and the right one could be set at the same or at a different intensity. The perceiver's responses of whether the variable is brighter than the standard could be plotted against the intensity of the variable, as in Figure 5.5.

These procedures provide an estimate of the size of the jnd for one

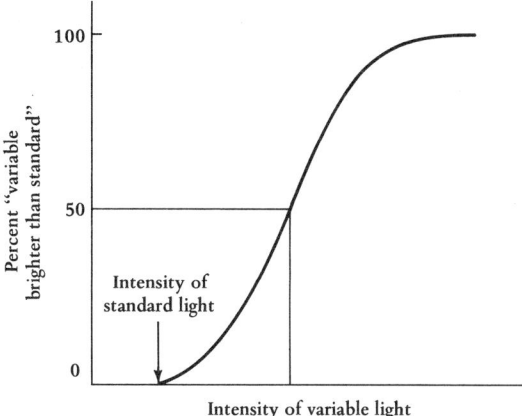

FIGURE 5.5 Hypothetical difference threshold response function for the judgment of whether the standard light or the variable light is brighter when the variable is always equal or greater in intensity to the standard.

magnitude of the standard or background. To determine the scale of psychological magnitude, the jnd will have to be measured at a number of values of the standard. If these jnd's, determined empirically, are roughly equal, then we can say that the intervals of the scale of sensation are equal. This is an empirical question, since there is no reason why the intervals should be constant over the entire stimulus scale.

These procedures were developed by Fechner (1860) and form the basis for discriminability scales of psychological magnitudes. After we examine Fechner's approach, we will consider very briefly two recent procedures which rest on different assumptions about the structure of psychological dimensions.

The fundamental assumption of discriminability scales is that some minimal increment of perceptual magnitude exists, below which differences in perception are not discriminable. The method usually used to determine the value of such units is some type of comparative unidimensional judgment. Discriminability scales require the assumption of an absolute threshold as a zero point and measure jnd units from there. The scale characteristics are those of an interval scale and usually take the form of a logarithmic function where sensation varies with the logarithm of the intensity of the stimulus ($S = K \log I$). This function is plotted in Figure 5.6. For scales of this form, small changes in stimulus magnitude at low intensities produce large changes in sensation, whereas they produce small changes in sensation at high intensity levels.

Another way to visualize this relationship is to plot the jnd as a function of the logarithmic transform of luminance (see Figure 5.7). This function is linear. The dashed lines in this figure show that empirical measurements of this relationship depart from Fechner's law at the extremes, but fit well for most of the scale.

Two other types of scales of magnitude have been used with some success. We will briefly describe them, without commenting on the theoretical models underlying them.

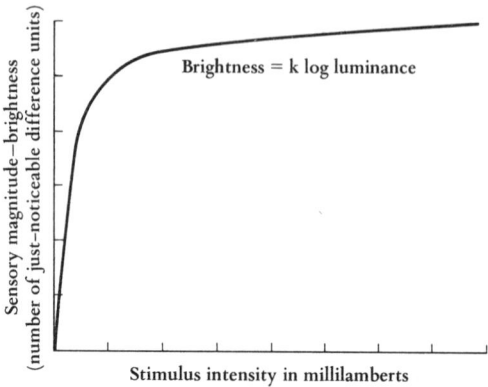

FIGURE 5.6 A discriminability scale showing perceived brightness as a function of the intensity of the stimulus. This function relates just-discriminable difference brightness units.

Category or partition scales are determined by identifying the extremes of the scales and dividing the stimuli among some arbitrary number of subdivisions or categories, such that the intervals are equal. Thus, once again it is assumed that the increments of sensation are equal, but this time the increments are not associated with the jnd. It is not clear whether these scales require the assumption of the absolute threshold as a zero point, but it is frequently assumed. The unit of the scale is the equal-appearing interval. Category judgments usually produce an interval scale.

Magnitude scales are based on direct estimations of the magnitude of sensation associated with different values of stimulation. A typical magnitude estimation experiment might ask perceivers to rate the magnitude of their sensory experience by assigning it a numerical value between one and ten. The absolute threshold is also assumed to be the zero point of these scales. The

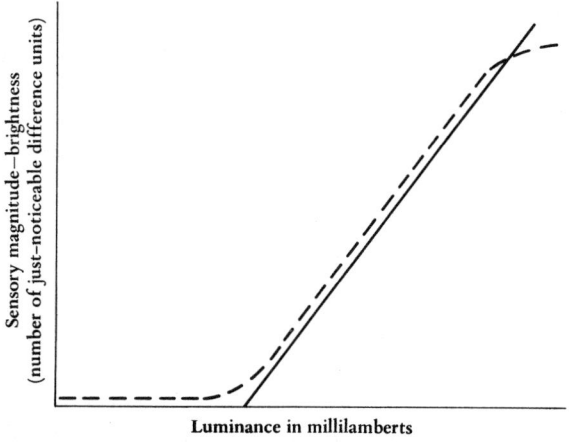

FIGURE 5.7 A discriminability scale relating the jnd to the logarithm of the intensity scale.

unit of this scale is the ratio of jnds rather than the jnds themselves. The resulting function has the form $S = K I^n$, called a "power," or "exponential" function, since the value of sensation is given by the value of stimulus intensity raised to some power (n). The exponent of I is nearly always constant for a given modality.

Figure 5.8 shows sensory magnitude plotted as a function of the physical magnitude of stimulation for three different modalities—brightness, electric

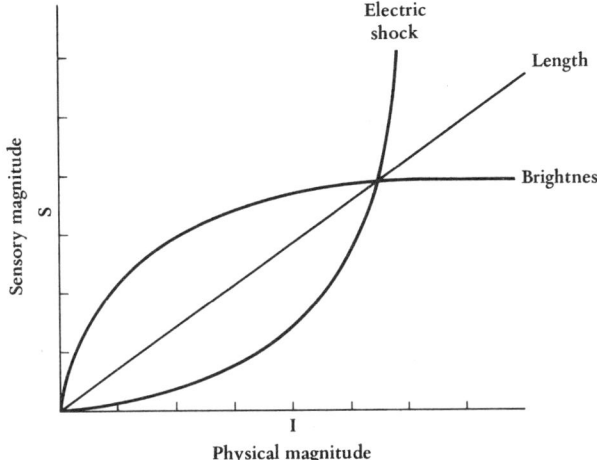

FIGURE 5.8 Sensory magnitude estimation functions for electric shock, length, and light intensity.

shock, and length. Since the exponents are different, the curves have very different shapes. If the function is transformed into its logarithmic form, then the exponent is the slope of the line representing the relationship between log S and log I. This relationship is shown in Figure 5.9 for the same three sensory modalities.

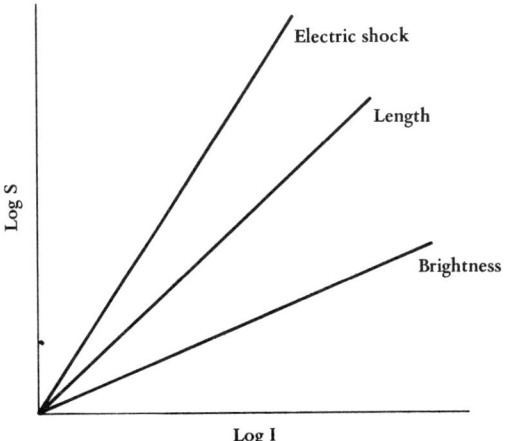

FIGURE 5.9 Sensory magnitude estimation function for shock, length, and light intensity, when energy and the responses are plotted on logarithm scales.

THE PSYCHOPHYSICAL METHODS

Since careful measurement is necessary in both the physical and the mental domains in order to write precise functions, the early psychophysicists developed methods that could yield some precision. Four principal methods are used today: the methods of adjustment, of limits, of constant-stimuli, and the staircase method. There are a number of variations of each of these. With the exception of the staircase method, all of these were devised and utilized by Fechner before 1860.

The method of adjustment is often considered the simplest. In this method, the perceiver adjusts the energy in the stimulus, changing it until he can see it. For example, he might have a knob that controls the output of the light source. A trial would begin with the knob set at a very low level, and the perceiver would turn it until he could see the light. The experimenter would then record the setting on the knob, reset it to zero, and ask the perceiver to do it again. This might continue for a number of trials. When the settings of the knob are plotted as a frequency distribution, this will usually yield data like that in Figure 5.10. If these data are replotted as a cumulative function, they look like Figure 5.2.

Usually in such an experiment, the knob would also initially be set sometimes at very high values, and the perceiver would turn it until he could no longer see the light. This occasionally gives a slightly different estimate and in such cases these trials are averaged together with the adjustment going in the opposite direction.

The method of limits is very much like adjustment, except that the experimenter does the adjusting, and he does it in separate trials rather than continuously. Here he presents a separate pulse of light to the perceiver at a

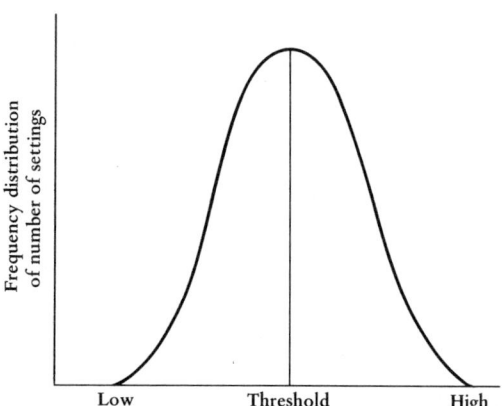

FIGURE 5.10 Hypothetical distribution of detection responses using a method of adjustment procedure.

very low energy level, and asks him whether he saw it. He then increases the energy slightly, and gives another pulse. He continues this procedure until the perceiver says he saw it. The experimenter then records the amount of energy on the trial in which the perceiver changed from "no" to "yes." The sequence is repeated, starting again at some low level. These values are also usually normally distributed, as in Figure 5.10.

As with the method of adjustment, the experimenter might also start at higher values and decrease the energy until the perceiver says he can no longer see it. The method of limits is probably the most generally used procedure. A major problem is that the perceiver always knows the next trial will have more energy in it than the preceding trial. Consequently, his knowledge about the repetition procedure may interact very strongly with the responses that he makes (see Haber and Hershenson, 1965, for a discussion). It is for this reason that the next method is often used.

The method of constant stimuli is just like the method of limits, except that the sequence of individual presentations is randomized. First, the experimenter decides which energy values he will use. Then on the first trial he will select one from this set at random, present it to the perceiver, and note whether it was seen or not. On the next presentation, another energy value will be selected at random. In this way the perceiver cannot predict the sequence of pulses. For each one, the experimenter notes whether the pulse was seen or not. With this procedure, he can plot his data directly in the form shown in Figure 5.2. This method takes a long time and many trials, usually many more than the methods of limits or adjustment. On the other hand, the data are usually more stable, and not open to the same types of criticism.

The staircase method is a different type of refinement of the method of limits. It attempts to take account of the fact that over most of the range of presentations, the perceiver's responses are uninformative. If we are looking for the threshold value, we should concentrate most of our trials right around the 50-percent point, and not give very many trials out at the extremes of the function, since we are not interested in those values. The staircase method does this. The standard procedure is to start at some low value and on each trial increase the energy, and ask the perceiver whether he saw it. This is continued until the perceiver says he sees it. Whenever he says he sees the light, the energy is decreased by one unit. If he still says he sees it, it is decreased more, until he stops saying he sees it; then it is increased again. If one continues to adjust the stimulus specifically in terms of the perceiver's responses, then all of the data collection will be around the point at which he is changing from "I see it" to "I don't see it." This sequence of trials is continued until the perceiver has developed a relatively uniform rhythm. The threshold now would be defined as the average of the energies needed to get him to change from "no" to "yes," and from "yes" to "no." Figure 5.11 illustrates the typical threshold curves obtained by this method. One can also run the sequence starting at a high value and moving down. Typically, these curves overlap when threshold is found.

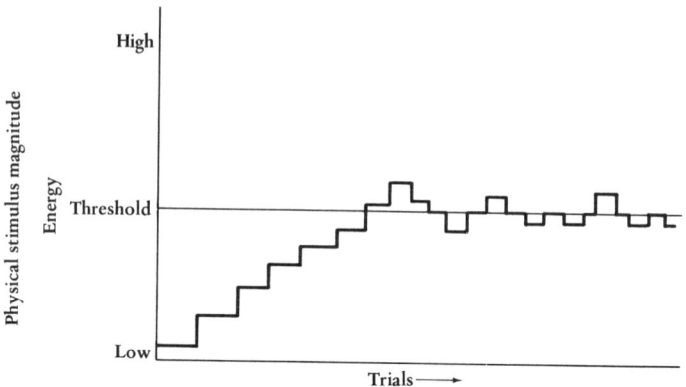

FIGURE 5.11 Hypothetical distribution of detection responses using a staircase psychophysical method.

RESPONSE INDICATORS

Up to now, we have been considering the perceiver's verbal report of seeing or not seeing the stimulus. While this yes-no procedure is the most popular one, it has certain drawbacks that have led to other procedures. Its major disadvantage is its very great sensitivity to changes in the perceiver's willingness to respond "yes" or "no." He can say "no" either because he did not see the stimulus, or because he is not particularly confident about his response even though he may have seen it. Likewise, he may say "yes" either because he did see it, or because he wants to appear to have very sensitive perception. While occasionally the perceiver is aware of his bias in making decisions, it may affect his responses without the perceiver being aware of it.

Blackwell (1953) argued very convincingly that the forced-choice response was often a better one than the yes-no response for making psychophysical measurements. While the psychophysical procedures remain the same with forced-choice response, the arrangements of the experimental task and the rules governing the perceiver's response are slightly altered. For example, instead of presenting a single light in a known position in the visual field and asking the perceiver whether he saw it, the experimenter now tells him that a light will sometimes come on the right side and sometimes on the left side of straight ahead. The perceiver is not asked to tell us whether he saw it, but simply to say on which side it appeared. If he truly cannot see anything, then his chances of reporting the location correctly should be 50-50. As soon as his responses are significantly above 50 percent, then we know that he must be seeing something of the stimulus. This procedure is called forced-choice since the perceiver is always forced to say "yes."

On logical grounds, the forced-choice procedure is not biased by the perceiver's criteria or confidence. No matter how uncertain he is as to whether he saw the light or not, he should still report the spatial location in which he thinks it was most likely to have occurred. He may think he is guessing wildly, but to whatever degree he has some stimulus information, he presumably will use it. Blackwell has shown in a number of experiments that thresholds tested with forced-choice procedures generally yield lower threshold curves and ones that are steeper (that is, less variable). Hence in both respects, they better meet criteria for measuring the sensitivity of the visual system.

SIGNAL-DETECTION THEORY—
AN ALTERNATIVE TO THRESHOLDS

Blackwell's forced-choice procedure has gone a long way toward controlling the perceiver's decision variables in threshold measurements. The signal-detection approach has attacked the concept of the threshold directly, while at the same time providing a different way to specify the sensitivity of a sensory system. Signal-detection theorists view the threshold experiment as primarily one in which perceivers have to make difficult decisions. When one is straining to "notice" a stimulus, particularly one of small magnitude, it is clear that there are two components to the process: the actual sensitivity of the receptor system to the particular properties of the stimulus; and the decision process as to whether a stimulus change actually occurred or not. The decision process is important because there is always noise inherent in any detection situation. Some of the noise is internal, related to the spontaneous activity level of the various neural processes. Some of it is external—variation in signal strength, light from other sources, and so forth. The internal sources are probably the more critical ones, particularly at very low energy levels. How can a perceiver tell whether the excitation he is observing is a result of the stimulus superimposed on noise, or whether it was a result of noise alone? The inherent uncertainty that all perceivers feel in making responses in absolute threshold detection experiments reflect these two components.

What does the perceiver do when he is uncertain? It is obvious that some behave very cautiously, while others take risks. Figure 5.4 can be viewed as an example of what would happen in threshold data to identical stimuli with a risk-taking and a cautious perceiver. Although the stimulus magnitudes are the same, the "risky" perceiver appears to have a lower threshold. Since all that has been changed is his willingness to take a risk, it is inappropriate to say that he has a lower sensitivity, and yet equating threshold with the frequency of saying "yes" implies just that. Thus, it is clear that one can bias threshold data by changing the perceiver's willingness to say "yes."

One way to control this is to insert blank stimuli into the experiment so that the perceiver can never be sure on any given trial whether the stimulus had been presented or whether there was just noise. In this way, the perceiver cannot be "correct" with his eyes shut, as would be possible in a typical threshold experiment with simply a yes-no response and no blank trials.

Figure 5.12 shows the possible outcomes with blanks inserted in the ex-

Stimulus

	Present	Absent
Yes	Hit	False alarm
No	Miss	Correct reject

Response

FIGURE 5.12   A matrix which provides a classification of the four possible outcomes as a function of whether a stimulus or a blank was presented, and of whether the perceiver responded with a yes or no.

periment. On some percentage of the trials, usually 50 percent, the signal is presented, while on others it is absent. The perceiver could say either "yes, I see it," or "no, I do not." Typical threshold curves show the percent correct response, plotted on the ordinate when the signal is present. This is equivalent to the "hit rate" in signal-detection theory. If blanks are presented, the perceiver will be giving a "false-alarm" response if he says "yes" when the signal is absent. High sensitivity is shown by a perceiver whose "yes" responses produce primarily hits and very few false alarms, and whose "no" responses are primarily correct rejects, and rarely misses. Hence, the ratio of hits to false alarms would be a measure of the perceiver's sensitivity.

Decision theorists have proposed some statistical techniques of data treatment to provide precise and independent estimates of the perceiver's sensitivity and his willingness to guess. Imagine that a perceiver is observing a screen on which he expects stimuli to be presented. First consider circumstances in which the trials are blanks. Even in this case, the perceiver's visual nervous system will be spontaneously active. This may be considered "noise" in the system. On each trial there will be a certain magnitude of excitation that will differ from trial to trial. Since it is due to noise alone, it should be random and therefore will be normally distributed over trials as shown in the left-hand portion of Figure 5.13. The right-hand portion would be the distribution of excitation that would result from those trials in which a signal was embedded in the noise. Since the signal produces some excitations of its own which will be added to the noise excitation, the distribution of signal plus noise would be shifted to the right. However, if the signal itself is weak relative to the noise, then the two distributions would overlap substantially. As the excitation contributed from the signal increased relative to the noise, then the signal-plus-noise distribution would be shifted further to the right with less overlap.

On any given trial in an experiment, the perceiver merely has an observation of excitation. He cannot tell whether it was a sample from the noise distribution alone, or from the signal plus noise. Yet he must make a response of either "yes" or "no." In terms of decision theory, it is assumed that the

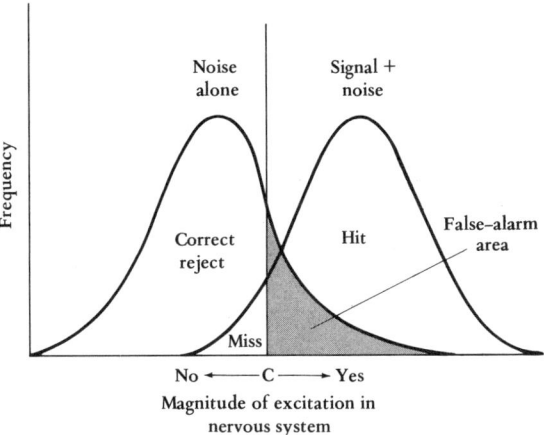

FIGURE 5.13 Hypothetical frequency distributions of excitation as a function of whether the event originated from noise alone or from a signal embedded in noise.

perceiver sets a criterion for his response, saying in effect that if the amount of excitation exceeds some critical value, then he will say "yes," and if it does not exceed that value, he will say "no." If the perceiver is very cautious, then he will demand a substantial magnitude of excitation before he says "yes," and the criterion line (drawn in Figure 5.13 as a vertical line) will be shifted to the right. If he is willing to take risks, then he will say "yes" even with little excitation, and the criterion line will be shifted to the left. The shaded portion of the noise curve to the right of the criterion line is labeled the false-alarm area. If the excitation arose from noise alone, but the perceiver said "yes," this would produce a false alarm, the probability of which is given by that shaded area. The area of the signal-plus-noise curve to the right of the criterion line will give the hit rate, the probability that the perceiver said "yes" when the signal had actually been presented.

Imagine now a perceiver who is more cautious. He will shift the criterion to the right, saying "yes" less often. In other words, he will be demanding greater excitation before he says "yes." This will reduce the false-alarm area but will also reduce the hit area.

These distributions are hypothetical. The perceiver, of course, cannot tell on any trial whether the excitation arose from noise or signal plus noise. On the other hand, visualizing these hypothetical distributions, we can analyze the two principal parameters relevant to detection situations—the sensitivity of the perceiver and his criterion. The sensitivity is given by the degree of separation of the two distributions. Hence, if the distributions are very far apart, there must be a large magnitude of signal relative to the noise. This parameter may be used in defining sensitivity. If the signal-plus-noise distribution virtually overlaps the noise-only distribution, then the sensitivity is minimal. The perceiver's criterion is shown by the location of the criterion line.

He can shift it to very cautious or very risky positions quite independent of his sensitivity.

In any particular experiment in which there are signals and blanks and in which the perceiver says "yes" or "no," we can empirically determine the hit rate and the false-alarm rate. Tables of probabilities associated with the normal curve can be used to determine the separation of the two distributions, as well as the location along the abscissa of the criterion line from these two probabilities. The separation of the two distributions is given in standard deviation units with the mean of the noise curve defined as zero. Hence, a sensitivity of 1.0 (usually defined as d') implies that the mean of the signal-plus-noise distribution is shifted one standard deviation to the right of the noise distribution.

The criterion is defined in terms of the ratio of the heights of the noise curve and the signal-plus-noise curve at the point at which it is located. A criterion of 1.0 would be at the point where the two curves crossed. A very high criterion would mean that the ordinate of the signal-plus-noise curve at the criterion line is much higher than the ordinate of the noise-alone curve. A perceiver taking risks would have a criterion value approaching zero, and the cutoff would be shifted well to the left.

Sensitivity should be reflected primarily by the intensity of the stimulus. Thus, holding other factors constant, as one increases the stimulus strength, the separation of the two distributions should increase. Further, holding stimulus intensity constant, changing the adaptation state of the perceiver should increase his sensitivity, and shift the two distributions apart. Independent of those changes, instructing the perceiver to be very cautious or risky should shift the location of the criterion, without shifting the location of the two distributions. Hence, from any experiment in which a hit rate and a false-alarm rate are available, we can arrive at a sensitivity measure and a criterion measure.

We have already indicated that signal-detection theory provides two measures in a detection experiment. In terms of the statistical properties of the derivation of decision theory, these two parameters are independent, and hence, an experimenter can manipulate the perceiver's confidence without changing his sensitivity, or change signal intensity or the perceiver's sensitivity without changing his confidence. Thus, signal-detection theory offers a means of providing information about the perceiver's sensitivity without its being confounded with his level of confidence.

But the impact appears to be more than methodological. The theory calls into question the concept of threshold as a point or range below which a response will not occur, and above which it will occur. In this view, the perceiver can always gain more information by saying "yes" if he relaxes his criterion. Thus, the basic concept of threshold is discarded as being misleading. While many researchers working in vision have acknowledged the importance of this criticism, they have nevertheless retained the use of the concept of threshold. In fact, as we shall see throughout this book, it is a major dependent variable in perception research.

THE PERCEPTION OF BRIGHTNESS

The first half of this chapter has been abstract and methodological, concerned more with measurement per se than with the things being measured. In the second half we now turn to two topics of central psychophysical interest: the determinants of perception of brightness and the determinants of visual acuity.

At the most primitive level, we will consider the visual system's response to light intensity: What is the lower limit on sensitivity; how much change in intensity is needed to be noticed; what are the effects of area of the light, its duration, or its retinal location on sensitivity; what are the effects on sensitivity to one light when there is another contrasting area of light nearby; and finally, how stable are our judgments of the brightness of objects under changing conditions of illumination?

Brightness is a term which describes our visual experience, the effects of stimulus intensity on the visual system. As we indicated previously, brightness and energy generally covary, but not perfectly. We shall see a number of reasons why not.

Minimum Sensitivity

The absolute threshold for light intensity estimated by Hecht, Shlaer, and Pirrene in 1942 suggested that a rod receptor under maximal sensitivity (remaining in the dark for half an hour prior to the test) with light at about 500 nanometers wavelength, requires the absorption of only one photon to produce a response. Further, the observer is capable of saying "yes" when no more than five to fifteen rods have each absorbed a single photon. Under these circumstances, the visual system is the most sensitive measuring instrument for light energy known.

In the Hecht et al. experiment, the perceiver will not be able to respond if only five to fifteen photons are incident to the eye. The minimum energy needed for an above-threshold response under these most optimal conditions is about 100 photons, which is a luminance of about 10^{-6} millilamberts. However, most of these photons never reach nor are absorbed by the receptors. Some are reflected off the cornea and never actually enter the eye. Many are absorbed by the cornea, the lens, other ocular media, the blood vessels, and the nervous tissue that lie in front of the receptors. Some photons that make it through all of this are scattered inside the eye and land on areas without receptors, or fall between receptors, so that they are not absorbed by the photopigments.

Hecht et al. made assumptions about the effects of each of these losses, and this led them to conclude that if 100 photons are put into the eye, only between five and fifteen actually are absorbed by rods. Given statistical consideration regarding the number and distribution of rods, and of the molecules of photopigment within each rod, those calculations suggest that between five and fifteen rods each absorb one photon at the absolute threshold for vision.

It is important to note that only one photon need be absorbed to set off a photochemical reaction in a single receptor, and that fifteen or fewer rods need react in order to produce a perceptable experience of stimulation.

These values are with all conditions arranged to capitalize on the greatest possible sensitivity of the visual system. But we can still talk about the absolute threshold as the minimum amount of energy needed to produce a response, even when conditions are less than optimal. In fact, we might find that the absolute threshold for intensity is one millilambert (one million times more than 10^{-6} millilamberts) for an eye that has been in daylight just before the test, or for a test stimulus that is red, or very small, or very brief. Many of the graphs in this and later chapters will plot absolute threshold data in which the threshold will be considerably higher than 10^{-6} millilamberts. Thus, it is critical to specify precisely the adaptation state of the eye and the stimulating condition when talking about thresholds.

Sensitivity to Change in Intensity

In practical circumstances, we rarely are required to make perceptual judgments at or near our absolute threshold. In the more common situations, we either respond directly to changes in intensity, or take changes in intensity into account when evaluating other characteristics of perception. Studies of difference thresholds are attempts to measure this type of performance by determining how small a change in intensity can be noticed.

Figure 5.14 illustrates two procedures for the presentation of stimuli in

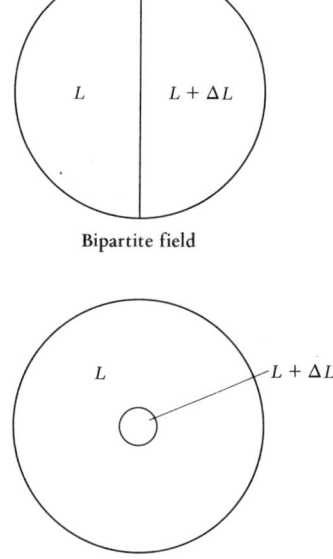

Bipartite field

Increment spot

FIGURE 5.14 A bipartite field and an increment spot procedure used for the determination of a difference threshold.

order to determine a difference threshold. With a bipartite field, one side will be at luminance L, and the other side at luminance L plus some additional amount, usually labeled ΔL (pronounced delta L). With the increment-spot procedure, the full field will be at luminance L, with the center spot at luminance $L + \Delta L$. It should be obvious that if $L = 0$, either of these would be experiments to determine the absolute threshold. Usually in such experiments the diameter of the large field will be on the order of a degree or two, with the increment spot being only a fraction of a degree.

A number of experiments have examined the minimal magnitude of ΔL needed for the perceiver to be able to say that he perceives a difference. From our earlier discussion, we know that the value of ΔL which results in the perception of a difference will depend on the value of L. This relationship is illustrated in Figure 5.15 for nine adapting levels. At every level of L, however, a difference threshold curve is generated, representing the empirical determination of the jnd. If the background L is dim, not much light has to be added to be seen as different. If the background is bright, then ΔL is larger.

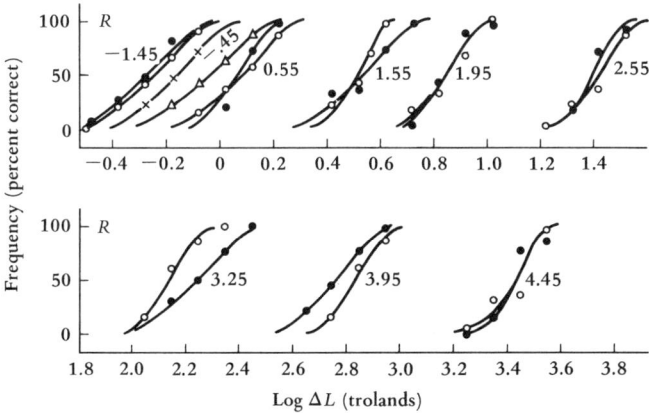

FIGURE 5.15 The frequency of positive responses as a function of the increment in retinal illuminance for nine adapting levels (from Mueller, 1951).

These curves do not represent the sensitivity of a perceiver directly. To determine sensitivity to change, the starting illumination must be taken into account. Therefore sensitivity to change is measured in terms of the ratio $\Delta L/L$, known as the Weber fraction. If this ratio is constant as L changes ($\Delta L/L = K$), then we say that the perceiver's sensitivity is constant. In the visual system, the Weber fraction is not constant, as Figure 5.16 shows. When the background illuminance is low, then a relatively large change in luminance is needed to be noticed. Thus, when the light is one-thousandth of a millilambert (10^{-3}), ΔL has to be ten times larger or smaller (a 1000-percent change) before it will be noticed as different. At a normal reading level of around 10 millilamberts, a 10-percent change can be noticed, or 1 millilambert change out of 10. At very high light levels a 1-percent change in luminance is

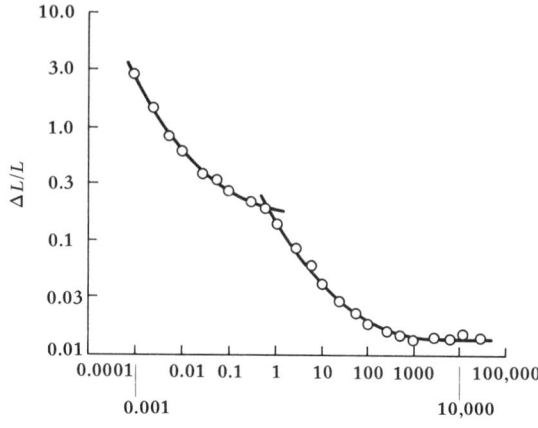

FIGURE 5.16 Brightness discrimination as a function of retinal illuminance (from Hecht, Peskin, and Patt, 1938).

detectable. Hence, brightness changes are difficult to notice in dim illumination. But by the time the light level is fairly high, we can notice even a 1-percent change, which is a very small amount.

Notice the two components in Figure 5.16. The component for the lower luminance levels on the left, reflects the operations of the rod receptors, and suggests that the rod's sensitivity to change in intensity of light is relatively poor. The cones begin to operate at about 1 millilambert, and they become very sensitive as luminance increases. Given the distributions of cones and rods in the retina, we should expect to find the highest sensitivity to brightness discrimination in the fovea. Thus, the peripheral rods are most sensitive to minimal amounts of light, and the fovea is most sensitive to changes in light intensity.

Effect of Retinal Location, Area of Light, and Duration of Light on Sensitivity

We should expect that since the rods are the most sensitive to low illumination, absolute thresholds should be lowest in the periphery. Figure 5.17 shows a threshold curve as a function of retinal position. There is over a twentyfold increase in the amount of energy needed to reach threshold of a test spot to the fovea, as compared to one less than 10 degrees in the periphery, with little change in threshold beyond 10 degrees.

If the distribution or density of rod receptors were the only determinant of this function, then Figure 5.17 should correspond closely to the distributions shown in Figure 2.16. The agreement is not very close, or we should have found that the threshold would be lowest at 16 degrees and rise as the test spot is moved in either direction. Thus, retinal location of sensitivity is not due simply to the number of receptors. The distribution of bipolar, ganglion,

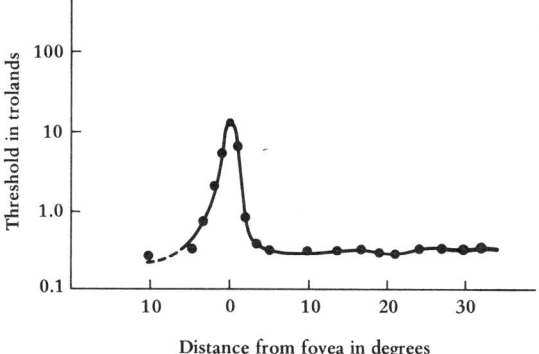

FIGURE 5.17 Absolute threshold sensitivity as a function of the retinal location of the test stimulus (from Crozier and Holway, 1939).

amacrine and horizontal cells also changes unevenly over the retinal surface. The important point to note is that sensitivity to dim light reaches its maximum off center. Thus, to see a dim star at night, do not look directly at it, but rather off to one side of it.

Figure 5.18 shows the luminance of light required so as to be just at threshold as a function of the size of a spot of light for both foveal and peripheral presentations. Since these are linear functions, there is an inverse relation between area and luminance thresholds—small areas have higher thresholds than larger areas. The effect is much stronger in the periphery than in the fovea. This should be expected from the relatively greater effect of summation of interconnections of receptors in the periphery. Because these are straight-line functions, one can talk about a specific reciprocity between area and luminance, implying a direct trade-off between area and luminance. Thus, as area is increased, a corresponding decrease in luminance can maintain the same threshold level. This relationship (area × luminance = constant) is known as Ricco's law. It holds only for small areas up to a degree or so in the periphery. Ricco's law is probably due to the pooling or summation of receptors in the periphery. Since Ricco's law breaks down beyond 1.5 degrees, this sug-

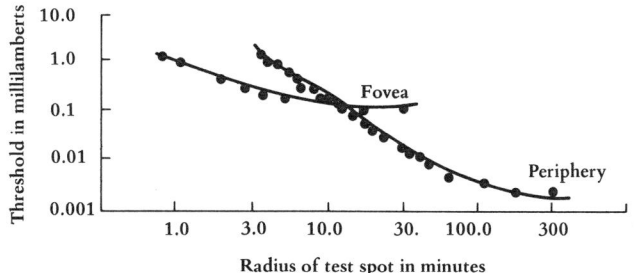

FIGURE 5.18 Absolute threshold sensitivity as a function of the size of the test stimulus for both foveal and peripheral presentations (from Graham and Bartlett, 1939).

gests the limit to the area over which different receptors summate onto the same bipolar and ganglion cells. For difference threshold, ΔL also decreases as area increases. Hence, a small luminance change will be noticed in a large target as compared to a small target. Again, one would appeal to the same type of summation mechanism to explain this result.

The effect of duration of target on sensitivity will be discussed along with other temporal parameters of sensitivity in Chapter 6. Suffice it to say in the present context that a reciprocity is found between duration and luminance for the absolute threshold (known as Bloch's law). Thus, a brief, intense pulse of light at threshold will be equivalent to one that is longer and dimmer. This reciprocity for the absolute threshold breaks down when duration exceeds about 100 milliseconds. A sufficiently dim pulse cannot be made visible simply by leaving it on longer and longer.

For light well above threshold, it would seem reasonable to expect that brief pulses would not appear as bright as longer ones. This expectation is generally supported except for one interesting situation. Figure 5.19 shows the increase in apparent brightness of pulses for two light intensities as a function of the duration of the pulse. As we can see, the apparent brightness of dim fields rises slowly to a maximum during the first half-second or so. However, the apparent brightness of highly illuminated fields rises very rapidly over the first 100 milliseconds and then returns to a somewhat lower level at which it remains. The latter function is known as the Broca-Sulzer effect after its discoverers. It is puzzling because it represents a condition in which a brief pulse appears brighter than a longer one (see Boynton, 1961).

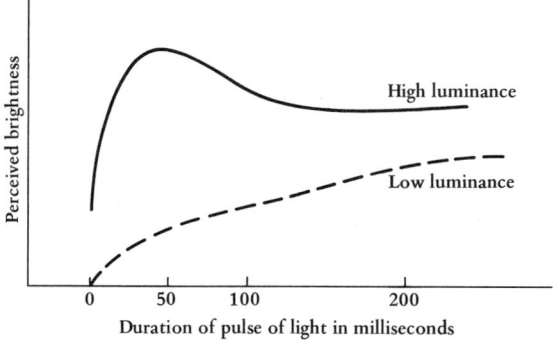

FIGURE 5.19 Hypothetical functions relating the changes in apparent brightness for two different luminance values as a result of changes in exposure durations—the Broca-Sulzer effect.

BRIGHTNESS CONTRAST

Although we have mentioned contrast in the preceding chapter on color, we will discuss it here in more depth. It illustrates one of the basic factors in the perception of brightness, especially to show how lateral inhibition is involved in the coding of brightness.

FIGURE 5.20 An example of simultaneous brightness contrast when looking at a gray square seen against backgrounds that differ in reflectance.

Contrast refers to the affects on the appearance of an object by neighboring objects. Brightness contrast refers to the fact that the brightness of a surface will be in part a function of the intensity of the background against which it is viewed. Thus, a piece of white paper viewed under fixed illumination will appear brighter if placed next to a dark surface than if it is seen against a bright background. Figure 5.20 shows an example of brightness contrast when one views a gray square against backgrounds of differing reflectances. Although the gray squares are all of equal reflectance, their brightness appears to differ substantially.

Figure 5.21 shows a typical stimulus configuration for a brightness contrast experiment (Heinemann, 1955). The test disk and the larger background disk are each set to some luminance value. The perceiver then must adjust the

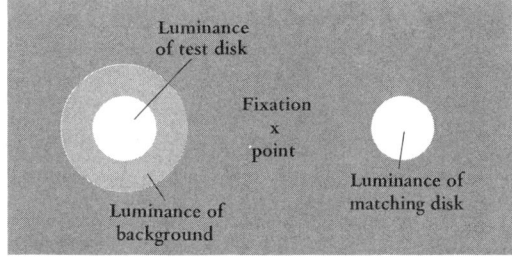

FIGURE 5.21 A typical stimulus configuration used by Heinemann in his experiments on brightness contrast (from Heinemann, 1955).

luminance of the matching disk until he judges it to be equal to the test disk in brightness. If the apparent brightness is uninfluenced by the background, then the matching disk should always be set equal to the test disk, regardless of the background value. Figure 5.22 shows the results plotted in log luminance values for a condition in which the test disk is approximately 10 millilamberts and the background field is varied from 0 to 100 millilamberts. When the background is zero, then the two disks appear equally bright when their physical intensities are equal (except for small and unimportant constant errors of measurement). As the background disk is increased in intensity, little change is found in the apparent brightness of the test disk. As the intensity of the background begins to approach that of the test disk, a dramatic drop in the brightness of the test disk occurs. Near the value at which the test and background disks are equally intense, the test appears to be black. That is, the perceiver sets the matching disk to zero to match the brightness of the test disk.

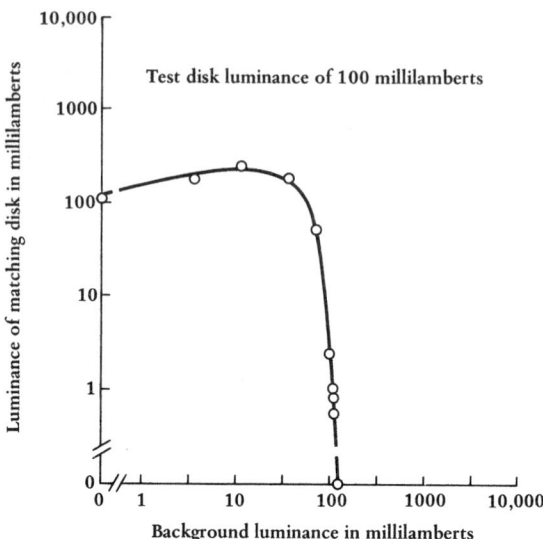

FIGURE 5.22   Changes in apparent brightness of a disk as a function of varying illuminance of its background (data taken from Heinemann, 1955).

The explanation for this effect currently favored (see Cornsweet, 1970) involves lateral inhibition processes. When the background luminance is minimal then the brightness of the test disk will be proportional to the number of photons absorbed by the receptors on which the disk falls, and the amount of lateral inhibition among the neural units to which these receptors are connected. If some nearby receptors are now stimulated by the background disk, this has no impact on the output of the receptors under the test disk, but it will increase the amount of inhibition on the next level of neural units connected to those receptors. The net effect is to reduce the overall output from that part of the retina, causing it to be perceived as less bright.

We have offered the same explanation in the previous chapter to account for color contrast. The only added requirement there was that rather than inhibition occurring between all neural units, it was necessary to assume that the output of long-wavelength cones can inhibit only the output of other long-wavelength cones. Hence, a gray square on a red background looks less red— that is, more green.

BRIGHTNESS CONSTANCY

The brightness of an object or a surface will appear to be constant even with substantial changes in the amount of light illuminating the surface. White paper looks white and black paper looks black both when seen under indoor lighting and outside in strong sunlight. For example, white paper might reflect 90 percent of the light, while black only 10 percent. If the inside illumination is ten units, then the luminances are nine and one unit, respectively, for the two papers. Outside, the sunlight might be three log units more intense, so that the luminance is 9000 and 1000 units, respectively. Thus, the black paper outside reflects much more light than the white paper inside, and yet it will still look darker.

There have been several arrangements used to demonstrate brightness constancy. In general, the perceiver is given a standard gray paper viewed under normal room illumination, and a graded series of comparison gray papers viewed under the same illumination. His task is to pick out the comparison gray that matches the standard gray in brightness. The critical tests occur when the illumination on the standard gray is changed (keeping the illumination on the comparison grays constant) so that the amount of luminance reflected from the standard now is different. For example, suppose a standard reflects 80 percent of the light incident to it, and the room illumination on it is 100 units, thereby producing a luminance of 80 units. If the luminance on each of the comparisons is also 100 units, the perceiver will select a gray producing 80 units of luminance. But if the room lights are now cut in half on the standard, the standard will only have a luminance of 40 units and the comparison chosen, still seen with 100 units of illumination, should be the one with a reflectance of 40 percent, not 80 percent. And yet perceivers will still choose the comparison that reflects 80 percent as equal in brightness to the standard even though in physical terms it has doubled in luminance. Brightness constancy is shown because the perceiver has matched the reflectances of surfaces, not the actual luminances received from the surfaces.

How could a perceiver know something about the reflectances of surfaces? Only from prior familiarity with the actual reflectances or a knowledge of the actual illumination (which, when compared to the luminances received at the retina, will yield the reflectance). But in a reasonable sense neither of these need be an available source of information. Constancy need not depend in any way on past experience or familiarity with the surfaces being judged, nor with knowledge about the actual illumination levels used in the experiment.

However, there is an important source of information about the impact of the change in luminance introduced by changing the room lighting that will give the perceiver information about the reflectance of the standard as a constant, even when the illumination on it changes. When illumination on the standard is changed, it is also changed on the background against which the standard is seen. Thus, if the standard gray reflects 80 percent of the 100 units of illumination that fall on it, and the gray is seen against a dark background that reflects only 10 percent of those 100 units, then the retina receives 80 and 10 units of luminance, respectively. Now if the illumination is dropped to 50 units, the luminances will be 40 and 5 units for the gray and its background, respectively. Whenever the ratios of the luminances remain constant (80/10 = 40/5), brightness constancy will be found. Thus, the constant ratio supplies information to the perceiver that the reflectance of the standard gray did not change, only the amount of light that fell on it.

Cornsweet (1970), among others, offers a lateral inhibition interpretation of why equal ratios produce brightness constancy. First he reviews evidence that the output of receptors is probably a logarithmic function of the intensity of inputs. Such a transformation means that when the overall illumination is increased, the effect of such a change is to add an equal amount of excitation to all parts affected by the illumination change. Further, except for very large increases, the output of the log transformation is not affected much. The second part of Cornsweet's explanation is that the transformed output then undergoes lateral inhibition. But we have already seen that except for very large changes, adding an equal increment of light to an entire scene has little impact on the brightness of the scene because the increase in inhibition cancels out the increase in excitation, as long as the increase is the same over all parts. Since equal ratios lead to equal additions, via the log transform, the brightness of the surface should not change much when light is added to it. Again, it is important that the light is added to all of the scene, not just to the standard being judged. Otherwise the inhibition will not be equal and a brightness difference will be produced.

For the last topic of this chapter, we will shift somewhat from the effects of intensity on the visual system to the effects of intensity discontinuities—what is usually referred to as visual acuity.

VISUAL ACUITY

Up to this point, we have been considering the eye and retina primarily as a device for collecting light. We will now look at it as a device for discriminating details of pattern. Although we can talk about objects on surfaces bounded by edges and located at varying distances from the perceiver, this information, acquired with physical measuring instruments, is a description of the physical object out in space. The retinal projection has no objects, only distributions of luminances—distributions that have discontinuities or inhomogeneities that result from the differences in the reflections of photons to the eye from the surfaces and objects in space. We will consider the relationship between the physical characteristics of objects in space and the distributions in the retinal projection in much greater detail in the last section of this book when we take up the perception of space. In this section we will narrow our attention to the simple level of analysis—how good is the visual system at detecting the presence of a luminance gradient on the retina, and what variables seem to account for this ability?

Knowing what we already do about the structure of the neural networks of the retina, the periphery should be relatively poor for this purpose. While the density of all receptors increases out to about 16 degrees, we know that the interconnection between receptors and their neural pathways increases much more rapidly. Clearly, in the periphery, the convergence of rods onto bipolars and bipolars onto ganglions should result in relatively poor pattern discriminability. Hence, the fovea should show the highest sensitivity to small detail. But the sensitivity of the cone receptors in the fovea to low intensity is poor, so acuity should be good only under photopic conditions.

Acuity Tasks and Measurement

Visual acuity is given by the smallest visual angle of detail that can be discriminated. Most adults are familiar with the clinical eye test (the Snellen chart) for measuring recognition acuity. This assesses our ability to recognize and name a letter by being able to see the widths of the lines. Our ability to resolve the fine detail determines whether we can recognize the letter.

A number of different tasks have been used for measuring visual acuity. Figure 5.23 illustrates four of these. Detection tasks generally present a line

Detection   Recognition   Resolution   Localization

FIGURE 5.23   Illustration of targets used in four different types of acuity tasks.

several degrees in length and attempt to find how narrow the line can be made and yet still be visible. This provides the finest index of visual acuity, generally about one-half second of arc, or roughly one-fiftieth the width of a foveal cone. This is equivalent to a telephone wire viewed at a distance of about two kilometers, or a telephone pole at over 100 kilometers. The localization task involves being able to tell whether a line is continuous or whether it has a sideways displacement. Minimum acuity is about two seconds of arc. This measure is particularly useful in binocular displacement between the two eyes for determining stereoscopic depth perception. The third task, involving resolution, uses line gratings. The perceiver's task is to determine whether the lines are horizontal or vertical. If the lines themselves are too narrow or too close together, the grating simply appears gray without any orientation. Generally, the finest resolution found with line gratings is about thirty seconds of arc, making this test only one-sixtieth as sensitive as detection measures. Finally, recognition acuity is the type measured with an eye chart. Minimal acuity reaches thirty seconds of arc.

Because of the widespread use and importance of detection and recognition tasks, we will consider these two tests in somewhat greater detail. Detection acuity tasks are equivalent to a brightness discrimination. For example, when a dark wire is presented against an intense field, asking a perceiver if he can see the wire is equivalent to asking him whether he noticed a dark bar against the brighter background. Helmholtz (1850) thought detection acuity resulted from having a row of unstimulated cones amid adjacent stimulated cones. Hence, the lower limit of detection acuity should be given by the density of the retinal mosaic. Since cones, even in the densest part of the fovea, are nearly one-half minute of arc from center to center, the visual acuity of one-half second of arc for detection acuity is nearly fifty times finer than the limit placed by the retinal mosaic. Thus, Helmholtz's explanation for the lower limit of acuity is too conservative.

Helmholtz's notion of detection acuity paid no regard to various kinds of optical distortions imposed upon details being focused on the retina. A point, a thin bar, or a wire will produce an image that is spread out on the retina to a size greater than its visual angle. This image will subtend a minimum of about thirty seconds of arc, and its contrast against the background will be reduced. If there were no line, the luminance over that portion of the retina would be uniform. If the reflectance of the line is only a few percent, then relative to the background only a small number of photons would fall on the receptors under the line in the retinal projection. But rather than a sharp luminance discontinuity produced by the line, nearly as many photons fall on receptors under the line as from the background, and the effect of the width of the luminance decrease is far wider than the actual visual angle of the line. This concept of a line-spread, or a point-spread function is illustrated in Figure 5.24. It shows that a bar one-half minute wide (just slightly wider than one cone) will spread out over five or six cones on the retina and produce a brightness differential against the background of only about 30 percent at its center. This means that the bar, by not being sharply focused, will not be as dark. Even so, such a bar is easily detected. A bar one-half second wide produces less than a 5-percent brightness difference along a row of cones, as compared to its neighbors.

If you refer back to Figure 5.16, you can see the threshold sensitivity of the visual system to an intensity difference. If the luminance of the background is high, a perceiver can detect the presence of a discontinuity of only 1 percent from that of the background. Hence, the point-spread function must have a

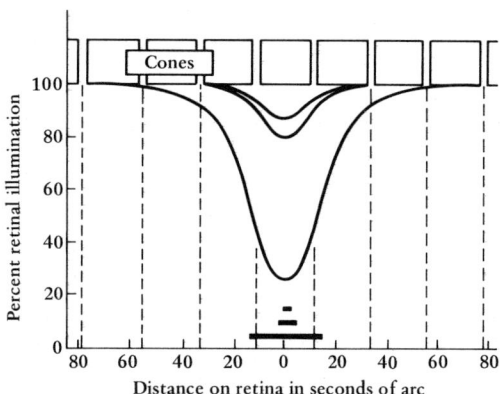

FIGURE 5.24 The spread of retinal illuminance produced by three different widths of a black line seen against an intense background, illustrating a line-spread function (from Hecht and Mintz, 1939).

dip of only 1 percent in it for us to detect that a discontinuity exists. So Helmholtz is right in the sense that the retinal mosaic is relevant, but it is not simply that a row of cones is stimulated and adjacent rows are not. Rather, it turns out that detection visual acuity is limited by the intensity difference thresholds of the eye.

Recognition acuity is usually measured by the standard clinical eye charts used to assess the need for eyeglasses. It is not nearly as sensitive a test as detection, but it is much easier to administer and standardize, and is probably more relevant for the practical uses of visual acuity. Recognition acuity applies a standard of a line one minute of arc, seen at twenty feet. This standard represents slightly poorer acuity than the very best (one-half minute of arc), but for clinical purposes it is quite adequate. Acuity then is specified by comparing the ratio of the standard distance (twenty feet) needed to see the lines of a letter to the distance the lines have to be to be one minute wide and recognizable. Hence, a very good acuity of 20/10 says that a line would be at ten feet distance to be one minute of arc, or would be about one-half minute at twenty feet. This acuity is often stated as 2.0, or 200 percent. An acuity of 20/40 (or 50 percent) says that for you to see the line, it would have to be one minute at forty feet, or two minutes at twenty feet. One is usually defined as legally blind with an acuity of about 5 percent, or 20/400. If your acuity is 20/20, then you have a resolution of one minute of arc. Knowing your visual acuity given by this ratio will permit you to compute your resolution in visual angle. An acuity of 20/10 is about the lower limit for recognition acuity in human observers.

Determinants and Limits of Visual Acuity

A number of factors which limit visual acuity have been identified, some of which are more important than others. Keep in mind that some of these factors determine visual acuity at any given moment in time, whereas others affect individual differences in acuity.

Optical focus is the major determinant of the individual differences, and why some of us have good acuity and others poor. This is primarily what the eye chart attempts to determine, and except in special circumstances, correcting the optical focus with additional lenses placed in front of the cornea will represent an improvement.

It is clear that there would be no further improvement if we had a finer retinal mosaic, and in fact, our mosaic could be somewhat coarser without any loss of acuity. In any event, the density of the mosaic is not a determinant of individual differences.

Getting more light into the eye with a larger pupil opening should improve acuity given the photopic nature of acuity. But there is a very low limit—about one millimeter—over which improvement in acuity occurs. This limit is presumably due to the increased light which is balanced by further optical errors that occur from a larger pupil opening. In any event, the normal operating range of two to five millimeters is beyond the limit with which this effect occurs. Thus, only under laboratory conditions can we demonstrate an effect of pupil size on acuity.

Light intensity is another variable. In starlight (about 10^{-4} millilamberts) one can see the page of a book, but not whether it has letters or is blank. One can discern that there are letters on a page in moonlight (.01 millilamberts), but one cannot read those letters unless there are about 10 millilamberts. Figure 5.25 shows acuity as a function of luminance levels. There is relatively little change in acuity over the rod or scotopic range of luminance levels, since not much acuity perception is possible with so little light. Only when the cones begin to function is there any improvement in acuity, and then this improvement is dramatic.

Exposure duration shows a reciprocity with luminance which we will discuss in more detail in Chapter 6. In general, for most acuity tasks, one good look of up to 100 milliseconds duration is sufficient. Longer exposure times are not helpful. If luminance is very high, then the good look can be of shorter duration.

The same type of reciprocity is found between area and acuity as between exposure duration and luminance and acuity. The limit is rather small, but within that limit, increasing the area of presentation of the pattern improves acuity.

Eye movements affect acuity in two opposite directions. If the eye moves during the fixation of an acuity target, then it might blur the retinal projection, thereby lowering the acuity. Conversely, if a luminance discontinuity that is produced by an edge moves back and forth over several cones, it should help

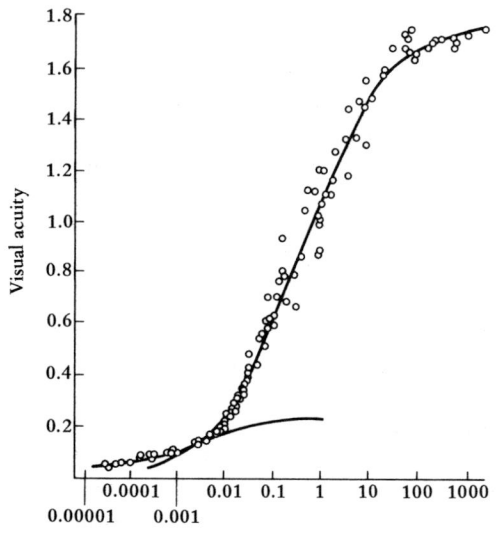

Luminance in millilamberts

FIGURE 5.25   Visual acuity as a function of luminance (from Hecht, 1934).

to sharpen the discontinuity, thereby increasing the chances of detecting it. Keesey (1960) stabilized the eye relative to acuity targets, to prevent slight movements of the retina with respect to the edges of the targets. She found that there was little change in visual acuity as compared to nonstabilized targets. Hence, it appeared that these two effects might have canceled each other. There is some other evidence with stabilized images that acuity for very brief presentations under stabilized conditions is higher, which suggests that the optical blur effect might be of some concern.

The location on the retina of the acuity target is also important. Figure 3.8 already showed the loss of acuity with even small eccentricities from the center of the fovea. This function undoubtedly reflects the fall-off in cone density (Riggs, 1965), but probably because the central foveal cones enjoy more one-to-one connections to the neural cells supporting them. Further, this function probably reflects the $\Delta L/L$ function (Figure 5.16) which reaches its maximum in the center of the fovea. In any event, when considering the eye as relatively stationary, and taking only a single glance at the stimulus, acuity is substantial only in the very center of the visual field of view.

In this discussion of visual acuity, we have made no reference to the receptive field coding processes previously mentioned in Chapter 3. We need to do so here because there is an apparent contradiction between these two discussions. In this chapter, we have noted that the limits of acuity, especially detection acuity, depend primarily on the limits of brightness discrimination, given the quality of optical focus possible on the retina. Although we did not specify the locus of this discrimination, nothing has been said to imply that this discrimination could not be mediated at the receptor level.

However, in Chapter 3 we noted that the ganglion level of the retina (and beyond) appears to be organized into a receptive field structure in which the outputs of receptors interact, especially in a mutually inhibitory manner. One of the most important outcomes of this interaction is to accentuate and sharpen any luminance discontinuities that are present on the retina. It does this by coding the discontinuity as a feature, for example, as an edge, or a bar, of a given orientation, and so forth, and the presence of this feature is transmitted toward the cortex in a much more parsimonious fashion than as the outcome of millions of receptors or even thousands of ganglion cells.

Therefore, although the psychophysical studies of visual acuity may still be quite appropriate, the level of interpretation may have to be modified according to our more recent knowledge of lateral inhibitory coding processes in the retina.

SUMMARY

This chapter has first introduced some principles of psychophysics that describe the functional relationship between a perceived magnitude and the physical magnitude that gave rise to that perception. Such functions are usually difficult to develop, in part because we have trouble measuring the physical magnitude (for example, differences in beauty), and especially because of difficulty in interpreting the responses made by the perceiver that describe his perceptual experience. Psychophysical measurement specifies a number of different procedures for the presentation of stimulation and elicitation of responses. We tried to show some of the effects of these differences, and a few of the reasons why one would be used rather than another. This included discussion of the concept of a threshold, as stimulus magnitude below which no perceptual response occurs and above which one always occurs, and how that concept has to be broadened to include the error inherent in each threshold measurement. Signal detection theory was briefly discussed, both as a methodological improvement and as an alternative conceptualization to the concept of threshold.

The second half of the chapter examined four specific psychophysical topics—the relation of intensity of light to the detection threshold and to its perceived brightness; the effect of surrounding or contrasting light on the perceived brightness of a surface; the constancy of the brightness of a surface even with changes in illumination; and the detectibility of discontinuities in luminance as a basis for visual acuity. All four of these topics were shown to be concerned with the determinants of brightness. In addition, the explanations of the psychophysical relationships all rested, in varying degrees, on lateral inhibitory processes.

Readings

One of the best discussions of psychophysical measurement is by Galenter (1962). Torgerson (1963) has a complete discussion of scaling. Corso (1967) has an excellent discussion of the threshold concept and the psychophysical methods. We have already mentioned Blackwell's 1953 monograph, which covers many of the problems of threshold measurement, method, and indicators. Signal-detection theory is presented by Green and Swets (1966) and Nachmias (1972), with an excellent discussion of many applications, especially in juxtaposition with more traditional threshold notions. The best presentation of current work on the perception of brightness is by Hurvich and Jameson (1966), along with Cornsweet's excellent coverage. A more recent chapter on simultaneous contrast is by Heinemann (1972). Riggs (1965) has a fine detailed chapter on visual acuity, with a more advanced one by Westheimer (1972).

6
temporal factors in visual perception

INTRODUCTION

This chapter covers the basic time-keeping functions of the visual system. While vision is often considered a spatial sense, four important reasons require that we pay attention to its temporal properties as well.

First, most visual stimuli are modulated in time—they do not occur in an instant and then are gone forever. Rather, most events have a duration—a temporal extent. Further, they occur in succession—we are able to separate them into distinct events, and can usually tell which came first, which second, and so forth. Since the environment has a temporal dimension, the visual system must be able to represent and respond to it.

Second, a temporal modulation is imposed upon the stimuli by the movement of our eyes over the environment, including stationary objects. As a consequence of these movements, the brain is presented with information that varies with time. This variation is important for some kinds of perception.

Third, the study of temporal factors is important because perception itself takes time. It does not occur instantaneously with the onset of stimulation. Some stages of perception occur rapidly, while others are relatively slow. To know how perception of temporal events takes place, we must understand how long it takes each part of the visual system to respond.

Finally, temporal processing is important because the visual system is easily overloaded with both spatial and temporal information. Since over 100 million receptors are capable of responding at rates of many hundreds of times per second, the brain cannot come close to handling this bombardment of information. Therefore, in addition to the need for the reduction of spatial information, temporal coding of information must occur in order to make perceptual processing manageable. Several of these temporal resolution mechanisms were mentioned in Chapter 3, and others will be discussed here.

As a first step in understanding temporal factors, consider how long it takes for the various neural events that we have described in the previous chapters to occur. Although it is not possible to make precise time measurements at all of the various functional levels of the visual system in man, the picture is fairly complete. Light energy travels instantaneously for all practical purposes from sources to the receptor surface of the eye. When the eye is dark adapted, the latency of the onset of receptor activity is effectively instantaneous, with a graded response to the light being produced within a few hun-

119

dred microseconds of the onset of the pulse. Not only does this initial response begin extremely fast, but the output of a receptor will follow a flickering stimulus at rates over several hundred cycles per second. Thus, at the receptor stage the eye is capable of very fine temporal resolution.

On the other hand, the temporal information reaching the brain is quite different. Using either electrodes placed on the scalp, or microelectrodes located in selected cortical cells of area 17 to measure the response of the visual system, it is clear that this fine temporal resolution has all but disappeared. Not only does 50 to 150 milliseconds elapse between receptor stimulation and area 17 excitation, but the resolution of temporally separate impulses of light requires the pulses to be spaced between 10 and 100 milliseconds apart, depending upon the state of light adaptation. This is at least a hundred-fold loss of temporal resolution.

We know that most of this elapsed time occurs in the retina. For example, Woodworth (1938) reported that electrical stimulation of the ganglion cells produces a cortical response in only a few milliseconds in cats and in rabbits. Although we do not have direct measures of transmission time through the cortex, we do have some indirect evidence. For example, the simple reaction-time task, in which a perceiver must press a key as soon as he notices the onset of a light in a known location, yields data on the speed of transmission of information from receptor to fingertip. The fastest motor reaction time of a finger press to light onset is about 150 milliseconds. This high speed is found, however, only with very intense lights, and is much slower otherwise. The time needed for an efferent nerve impulse to leave the motor cortex and travel to the fingers is about 10 to 15 milliseconds, with another 30 milliseconds or so needed to move the key with the finger (Woodworth, 1938). Adding all of these times together leaves about 100 milliseconds of reaction time for events occurring on the retina and virtually none for those in the cortex.

As an aside, if the reaction time involves a choice (press the right finger if the right light comes on, and the left finger for the left light) then another 200 milliseconds or so is added to the total reaction time. Presumably all of this addition involves cortical handling of the localization and decision processes.

In this chapter we will examine a number of temporal tasks, those involving both the perception of time and the time of perception. Unfortunately, because of the coding processes, the analyses of these two aspects are generally inseparable. We will first examine several different lines of work on how the coding of time interacts with nontemporal processing, especially intensity and temporally contiguous events. Then we will look at a number of aspects of how long it takes perceptual events to occur, and how the processing of time is carried out.

One brief note on terminology: In order to differentiate physical from psychological variables, we need to separate the duration of the visual stimulus from its temporal appearance. To do so we will refer to the physical duration of brief stimulation as pulses of light, and we will use the term flash to refer to its perceptual consequences. Thus, brief pulses usually appear as brief flashes.

TEMPORAL SUMMATION AND TEMPORAL INTEGRATION

We have already noted in Chapter 5 that time and luminance were reciprocally related to visual acuity. The acuity obtainable from a short, intense pulse is equivalent to that of a long, dim pulse within specified limits. This reciprocity is generally true for threshold sensitivity and superthreshold brightness judgments as well. For example, suppose that a perceiver is asked to set a briefly pulsed spot of light so that he can just see it. What will happen if the pulse is made longer or briefer? Below about 100 milliseconds of exposure duration, there is a trade off between the duration of the pulse of light and the intensity of that pulse (Bloch's law). Figure 6.1 shows two traditional ways of plotting these effects, both of which illustrate that below a critical duration, in this case about 100 milliseconds, the degree to which intensity (I) and duration (T) contribute to the total energy in the light pulse is irrelevant as long as the simple product is held constant ($I \times T = K$).

The reciprocity specified in Bloch's law breaks down if the duration of a pulse is too long. The upper limit of the reciprocity is called the critical duration—the duration beyond which adding more time ceases to have any effect. Thus a very dim light may never become visible, no matter how long it is left on. The magnitude of the critical duration depends on a number of variables. For reciprocity at absolute threshold of a spot of light seen against a black background (that is, under scotopic conditions), the critical duration is about 100 milliseconds. Under photopic conditions—somewhat more relevant to the normal functioning of the visual system—the critical duration is less, more on the order of 20 milliseconds. On the other hand, when the task is a form discrimination based on acuity, such as being able to tell the orientation of a small gap in a circle (Kahneman, 1966), then time and intensity are reciprocally related for durations as long as several hundred milliseconds. Therefore, it is important to keep the nature of the task in mind when defining the value of the critical duration as an upper limit on the time over which reciprocity holds.

Bloch's law suggests that energy is integrated somewhere in the visual system—that intensity is averaged over time. This process is called temporal

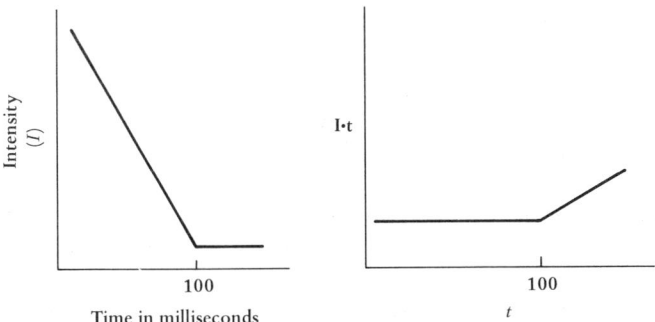

FIGURE 6.1 Two ways of illustrating Bloch's law showing the range over which time and intensity are reciprocally related.

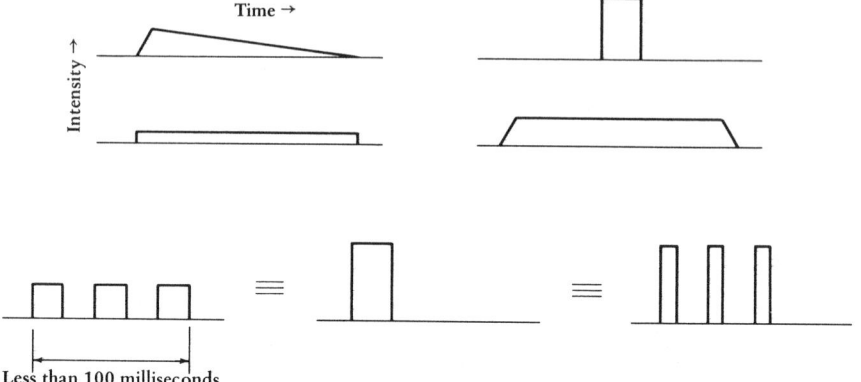

FIGURE 6.2   The top part illustrates that at threshold, the distribution of energy over time is irrelevant, as long as the duration does not exceed the critical duration. The bottom part illustrates temporal integration, in which the integration of time and intensity can encompass separate pulses as long as the total time does not exceed the critical duration.

summation. Bloch's law states that the temporal composition of the pulse is irrelevant, as long as the simple product with luminance is constant. For example, the response of the visual system to each of the pulses shown in the upper part of Figure 6.2 will be the same (Long, 1951; Davey, 1952; Boynton and Seigfried, 1962).

So far we have referred only to presentations of a single pulse. It might be expected that if time and intensity can be averaged, the number of pulses given would not matter as long as all of them occurred within the critical duration. This in fact has been shown to be the case, and is called temporal integration. As long as the offset of the last pulse occurs in less than the critical duration from the onset of the first pulse, the response will be a function of the total energy averaged over all of the pulses. See the bottom of Figure 6.2 for some examples of equivalent stimuli.

These summation and integration processes obviously obscure much of the temporal specificity of stimulation. As we observed in Chapter 3, such summative effects might be useful to aid responding under scotopic conditions. Thus when light intensity is very low, any strategy which allows intensity to be integrated over longer periods of time will improve the chances of detecting the presence of that energy. But the price paid for this is loss of temporal specificity. The visual system does not record whether the pulse is long and dim, or brief and intense, or whether it is one long, dim pulse, or several briefer but more intense ones.

We also observed in Chapter 3 that although this is a useful trade-off at scotopic levels, the same trade-off is found at photopic levels as well. In this sense, then, the visual system never achieves the precision of temporal resolution that it does in spatial resolution. The critical duration does shrink from about 100 to 20 milliseconds, but even 20 milliseconds means that temporal resolution is not very precise.

Where in the visual system does the temporal integration occur? Boynton (1961) has suggested that given the precision of this reciprocity relationship, one might be tempted to look for the integration at the very first stage, in the receptors themselves. However, Boynton offers three arguments to show that integration in the receptors is impossible, and that it must be a neural process occurring beyond the receptors. First, the receptors begin their response very quickly and can continue to respond to closely spaced pulses. Based on the rate at which rhodopsin changes when exposed to very brief pulses (Wulff, Adams, Linschitz, and Abrahamson, 1958), Boynton suggests that even within the critical duration the speed of reaction of a photoreceptor should be fast enough to allow two separate photochemical events to occur. If this does occur, then the receptor cannot be integrating over time.

Second, at threshold the chances that two or more photons will hit the same receptor are negligible. Thus a receptor is capable of responding to the absorption of a single photon by only one of its millions of molecules of photopigment. If two or more photons never hit the same receptor at scotopic levels, then the receptor cannot be integrating over time.

Finally, temporal integration is just as effective if the two pulses fall on nearby receptors as it is when they fall on the same one. For all of these reasons, integration must occur beyond the receptor stage, since there is more than one receptor involved. At the receptor level there appears to be little if any integration over time at all.

To show this more dramatically, Boynton, Sturr, and Ikeda (1961) demonstrated in the same experiment both good and poor temporal resolution. They presented a train of pulses at a rate of thirty-three per second, so that each pulse was on for 16 milliseconds with a 16-millisecond dark interval between each pulse. At this rate, under the conditions they used, the pulses appeared fused—the perceiver saw them as one continuous light, not a rapidly flickering one. The perceiver was told that periodically a 1-millisecond test pulse of light would be presented against this phenomenally fused background, and his task was to detect it. The intensity needed to make the test pulse just visible—that is, to keep it at threshold—was varied. They found (see Figure 6.3) that if the test pulse occurred during one of the 16-millisecond dark intervals it could be substantially dimmer and still be detected, than if it occurred during one of the 16 millisecond pulses. Hence, even though the perceiver could not perceive the flicker, the increment threshold was dependent upon these very small differences. This also implies that the fusion of a rapidly flickering light occurs higher in the visual nervous system than the processing of increment thresholds.

The experiment by Boynton, Sturr, and Ikeda does not tell us where in the visual system temporal summation and integration occur. Boynton's arguments suggest that it is not at the receptor level. This experiment makes that even more certain, since if it were how could the temporal precision noted in the increment threshold values ever be subsequently obtained? Thus integration must be neural, but is it at the bipolar or ganglion levels, or in the lateral geniculate nucleus, or the cortex? We as yet do not know for sure.

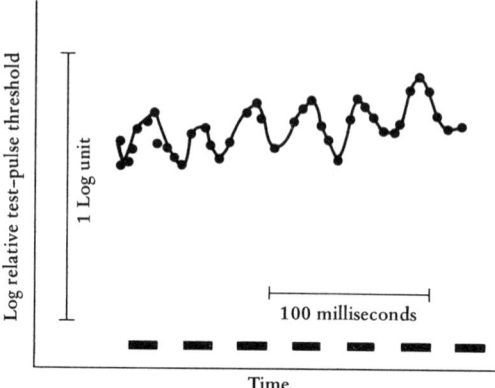

FIGURE 6.3   Changes in the test-pulse threshold as a function of presentation relative to the cycle of a thirty cycles per second flickering light (adapted from Boynton, Sturr, and Ikeda, 1961).

The temporal integration we have already considered used two or more pulses of light of the same size, presented to the same area of the retina. As we see, their separateness is often lost. But what happens when the size and location do not precisely overlap? Here we will see a different type of interaction of profound importance for temporal processing.

VISUAL MASKING PHENOMENA

Because the visual system does not keep careful track of time to the same degree at all levels, it is possible to show temporal interactions among stimuli that do not overlap in time. The most striking of these is called backward masking—backward because the stimulus arriving second acts "backwards" in time to affect one which has already come and gone. Several types of such backward effects have been studied (see Kahneman, 1968, for a general review). A large literature exists on masking by light, where the masking stimulus—usually a large intense pulse—is preceded by a smaller dimmer target pulse whose presence is to be detected. There has also been a large amount of research on spatial interactions involving temporal parameters. This is called metacontrast, and refers to arrangements of stimuli which have adjacent contours. We will also consider a third category, in which the masking stimulus is a visual noise pattern, usually a random collection of line segments. Unfortunately, the phenomena underlying these three arrangements are not altogether similar, and their explanations often have little in common.

Masking by Light

Kandel (1958; see Boynton, 1961) showed the effect of masking by light within the context of the loss of sensitivity due to light adaptation. If the dark-adapted eye is suddenly flooded with light it loses sensitivity, requiring an increment in the test pulse to be increasingly more intense for it to be noticed. Kandel presented a small test pulse at various intervals before and after dark adaptation was ended by a large and intense presentation. While it is well known (see Chapter 5) that the test pulse would have to be more intense if presented after dark adaptation ended, he showed that the effect acted backwards up to 100 milliseconds. Figure 2.19 showed the intensity needed for the test spot to be just at threshold as a function of the time relations to the end of dark adaptation.

Crawford (1947) had first studied the effect of masking by light. He thought this type of masking was caused by the shorter latency of the more intense and larger masking pulse, which traveled faster to the central nervous system than did the smaller and weaker test pulse. Crawford referred to this as neural overtaking. We reported evidence earlier in this chapter to show some basis for Crawford's assumption of a differential latency, for example, simple reaction time is increased substantially if the light is not intense. However, a difference in latency of 100 milliseconds between intense and dim pulses is quite unlikely.

Boynton (1961) has argued against a simple overtaking explanation, and suggested that masking by light may be related to the massive on-discharges caused by the masking stimulus. Figure 2.19 illustrates the on-discharges to which Boynton refers. At the onset of a large and intense masking stimulus a dramatic increase in threshold occurs, lasting only about one-tenth of a second, after which the sensitivity gradually returns to a stable level. (That is, until the masking light is turned off, when another on-discharge may occur.) We already reviewed electrophysiological evidence in Chapter 3 that these discharges are due to the lateral inhibitory processes and the receptive field organization of the retina. Thus, the onset or the offset of a light produces a signal, but not its steady-state component.

Boynton suggested that when the adaptation level is low the amount of the on-discharge produced by the masking stimulus will be especially large. Relatively little inhibition would be present so that the temporal discontinuity would be especially emphasized. Although the test stimulus also produces an on-response, the masking stimulus coming somewhat later overwhelms the visual system, preventing the response from the weaker test stimulus from being treated as a separate event. To demonstrate this, Boynton suggested the counterintuitive prediction that if the overall level of adaptation was raised, the massive on-response to the masking stimulus would be reduced, which in turn would reduce the masking effect, and *lower* the test stimulus threshold. Thus, if the effect of the masking stimulus could be reduced, even though the higher adaptation levels would reduce the overall sensitivity of the retina, the on-discharge produced by the masking stimulus would now not be able to overwhelm the test pulse, and the latter would be seen. Boynton tested this prediction at several levels of adaptation, and found the effect he predicted.

Schiller (1968) provided some physiological evidence for Boynton's proposal. He made single-cell recordings in the lateral geniculate nucleus in cats, and showed that the response from the test stimulus is entirely obliterated by the much larger response from the masking stimulus, when the masking stimulus precedes or follows the test stimulus. Donchin (1967) has also shown that the response to the test stimulus is missing from recordings taken from the retinal end of the optic nerve in kittens. Thus, the locus of the masking appears to be the interactions in the retina.

Boynton's argument, based on massive on-responses, is directed primarily at explaining the large overshoot in thresholds coincident with the masking pulse onset. That these on-responses appear to act backward is explained by the poor temporal resolution of the visual system. Somehow the weak test pulse and the intense masking pulse are temporally fused whenever they are within 100 milliseconds of each other, so that the separate identity of each is lost. Naturally the largest one is all that is seen.

One procedure that is frequently employed to determine whether an effect is retinal or cortical is to see whether it can be produced across the two eyes as easily as within one eye alone. If an effect is entirely retinal, due to interaction at the receptor level or among the neurons in the retina, then simultaneous events in the other eye should neither diminish nor increase the effect. One of the most important uses of this procedure occurs in the research on masking. The research results reported so far have been monoptic—all stimuli have been presented to one eye, with the other eye usually covered. A number of masking experiments have included a condition in which both eyes are adapted to the same level and then the test pulse is presented to one eye and the masking light to the other eye. This procedure is called dichoptic presentation. The general finding has been of a small, or often negligible amount of masking. To the extent that masking by light is minimal dichoptically, such masking can be attributed to processes in the retina and not to events that occur after the signals from each eye reach the cortex.

Although the main thrusts of Boynton's explanation of masking by light (based on on-discharges) does fit most of the data, no completely satisfactory theory of visual masking by light has yet been elaborated. All of the theories presently in the running are based upon the recognition that events existing only briefly in time have consequences in the visual system that last much longer. Thus, events that do not physically overlap can easily be perceptually contemporaneous. We will return to this later when we consider how psychological time is demarcated.

Although most of the work with masking by light has used homogeneous presentations for the test stimulus, such masking can also be demonstrated when the test field consists of luminance discontinuities. Thus a patterned stimulus might be a dark bar seen against a lighted background. The luminance and the duration of this pattern can be adjusted so that a perceiver can just report the presence of the line (or correctly identify its orientation). When the line presentation is followed, either immediately or after some brief delay, by a homogeneous masking field, this recognition threshold is elevated. This is caused by a reduction in the effective contrast of the line against its background, thereby making it more difficult to detect.

Contrast between two adjacent areas is defined as the ratio of the luminances of light being reflected from the two areas to the eye. Thus, if the retinal projection of the line has a luminance of 10 millilamberts and the background against which the line is seen has a luminance of 100 millilamberts, then the contrast ratio is one to ten. This could arise, for example, if the illuminance was 200 millilamberts and the black ink of the line had a reflectance of 5 percent and the background had a reflectance of 50 percent.

What happens to the effective contrast if after the presentation of the line, a homogeneous lighted field is presented, covering the area on the retinal projection where the line had been? Given the properties of temporal integration, the energy from the presentation containing the line will be integrated with the energy from the blank field following it, as long as it follows soon thereafter. This will change the contrast substantially. For simplicity, let us set the masking pulse luminance also at 100 millilamberts, so that it is as intense as the background against which the line is seen. Now the total amount of light falling on the area where the line was is 10 millilamberts from the line, plus 100 millilamberts from the second pulse, or a total of 110 millilamberts. For the rest of the field the total energy is 100 millilamberts from the first pulse and 100 from the second, making a total of 200 millilamberts. But now the contrast is no longer one to ten, but rather, less than one to two. This means that the line will be closer in intensity to that of its background, and hence far less discriminable. The more intense the masking pulse is, the greater will be the reduction in contrast.

This analysis, advanced in greatest detail by Eriksen (1966), nicely accounts for the masking by light of luminance discontinuities in a previously presented visual field. Eriksen refers to this as luminance summation, which leads to contrast reduction.

Notice that if the masking is done by projecting more light onto the scene, which is then reflected to the eye, there will be no contrast reduction. Since the contrast ratio is determined in this example by the reflectances of the line against its background, that ratio will be unchanged regardless of the amount of illumination falling on the scene. Masking occurs not because the added light from the mask fell on the scene, but because it fell on the same parts of the eye as the scene did, but from a different light source.

In terms of instrumentation, masking experiments require at least two separate light sources, each of which can be projected into the eye without affecting the other source. In the type of task being described, a device called a tachistoscope is often used. A two-channel tachistoscope is illustrated in Figure 6.4. Both of the channels can project light into the eye. At the back of channel 1 is a surface being illuminated by the light source. The light is reflected from the surface toward the eye. In its path is a beam splitter oriented so that the light traveling from channel 1 passes through it to the eye. Thus, with channel 1 alone, the luminance and the duration of the presentation can be varied by adjusting the light output from the lamps.

Channel 2 is similar in all respects except that the beam splitter is oriented

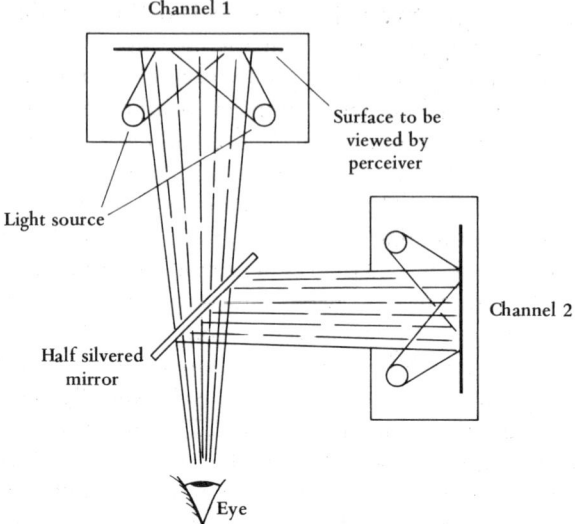

FIGURE 6.4   A schematic representation of a two-channel mirror tachistoscope.

such that it reflects the light hitting it at 90 degrees so that it too goes into the eye. Additional beam splitters could be inserted into the light path, allowing more channels to be added.

Referring back to the contrast of a line against a white background that would be projected from channel 1, no contrast reduction would occur if the illumination coming from the lamps in channel 1 is increased, since the contrast ratio is left unchanged. However, if light is added from channel 2, either during the presentation of that of channel 1, or anytime thereafter up to the time of the critical duration, then the effective contrast in the retinal projection will be reduced. It is for this reason that the contrast of a slide shown on a screen with a slide projector is reduced if the room lights are left on. Although the contrast ratios in the slide itself are unchanged, the added light is veiling the entire screen, adding equal amounts to the intense and dim areas, thereby reducing the contrast ratios between them. If the room lights are intense enough all contrast from the slide can be lost.

Masking by Adjacent Contours—Metacontrast

Although the topic of metacontrast is often included under masking by light, the effects are sufficiently dissimilar that they deserve separation, especially because of the spatial component involved (Kahneman, 1968; Lefton, 1972). The effects are similar in that a second stimulus appears to act backward to distort the perception of an earlier one. But visual masking by light as discussed in the previous section does not work well when the luminances or sizes are nearly equal, and it does not work much at all when the pulses do not overlap spatially on the retina. Further, the masking by light appears to be primarily retinal. Metacontrast, on the other hand, usually works with both stimuli at the same luminance and of the same general size. More important, it is dependent upon a precise spatial relationship, not one of overlap but of close adjacency of contours. Figure 6.5 shows several types of patterns used to study metacontrast.

Werner (1935) showed that if a briefly presented small disk is followed after about 50 milliseconds by a ring just circumscribing it, the perceiver is either unable to see the disk or he describes it as being much dimmer and with indistinct contours. This is still a backward masking effect, in that the aftercoming ring interferes with the perception of the earlier disk, but now the effect is spatial as well, in that as the inner circle of the ring becomes larger in relation to the outer edge of the disk, the masking effect decreases. Werner stressed that a spatial continuity is needed, arguing that contours take time to develop perceptually and that the ring interferes with this development. We will return to this argument in more detail in Chapter 8.

This basic phenomenon of metacontrast has been demonstrated many times with different kinds of stimuli. Thus in addition to a ring and disk, it can be shown with a square as a test stimulus, and two flanking squares as the masking stimulus. With an interstimulus interval of between 50 and 100 milliseconds between the offset of the test stimulus and the onset of the flanking masking stimulus, the test square is usually reported to be phenomenally absent (Fehrer and Raab, 1962). Letters or other simple visual forms have also been used as test stimuli, with a ring circumscribing one or more of the letters used as a masking stimulus (for example, Weisstein, 1966).

Alpern (1953) has reported the most detailed data for pulses of rectangu-

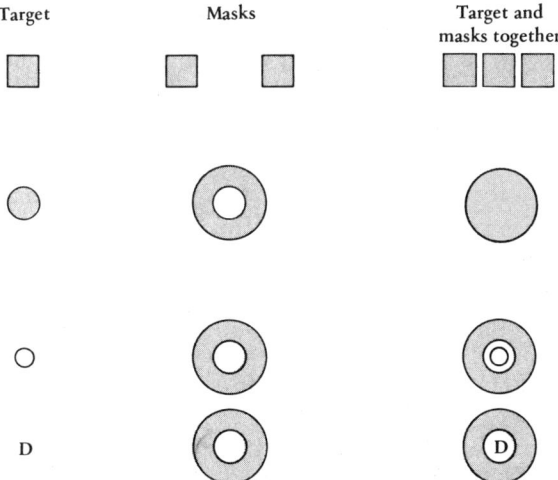

FIGURE 6.5 Examples of several sets of targets used in different types of metacontrast experiments.

lar patches of luminance. He found that the amount of masking (as measured by the reduction in the brightness of the center patch) increases with the luminance of the mask. Further, the interstimulus interval for the maximum masking increases with the luminance of the mask. Thus, as the effectiveness of the mask increases with its luminance, it can be delayed later in time than the center patch and still be effective. Masking is maximal when the borders of the mask are contiguous with the borders of the center square. The border contiguity appears to be crucial for masking since the masking effect drops off sharply as spatial separation increases.

Fehrer and Raab (1962) used a reaction-time measure in a metacontrast experiment. Alpern (1953) had already shown that the brightness of the center patch was reduced substantially by the subsequent arrival of the two flanking patches. We have already mentioned that reaction time is substantially increased as the luminance of a stimulus is lowered. Fehrer and Raab asked whether the reaction time to a center square would be longer if it was made darker by metacontrast. They measured reaction time for the center square presented alone and for the center square followed by the flanking squares at delays of 0, 10, 25, 50, and 75 milliseconds. They found that the reaction time to the center square was not affected by the addition of the flanking stimuli, even though the flanking squares decrease the brightness of the center square. They concluded, therefore, that the perceiver's phenomenal experience, as reflected in his verbal reports of presence or absence or in his judgment of brightness of the center square, was not reflected in reaction time. They suggested, rather, that reaction time is determined only by the stimulus characteristics of the first pulse of light.

In a follow-up experiment by Fehrer and Biederman (1962) the same apparatus was arranged so that the brief extinction of an otherwise constantly illuminated center square could be masked by the onset of the flanking squares. Reaction time was measured to the center square alone, to the flanking squares alone, and to the combination of the two. The verbal reports of the perceivers show that they were able to judge the presence of the darkening of the center square when it was presented alone, and the accuracy of verbal report improved with an increase in interstimulus interval. Most important, however, was the fact that at interstimulus intervals of 30 and 50 milliseconds, the reaction time detected the presence of the first event accurately even though the verbal report was not accurate. This suggests that the reaction-time response was initiated by an event whose presence was not suspected. Fehrer and Biederman concluded that reaction time is determined by brief changes in energy and that later events determine phenomenal experience. Thus, metacontrast affects the appearance of the stimuli but not the detection of presence or absence.

Metacontrast effects are almost always found to be as large dichoptically as monoptically. Thus, unlike masking by light, all of the effect with metacontrast seems to be cortical. This implies that the appearance of this stimulus requires cortical processing. On the other hand, the reaction-time response to the onset of a stimulus appears to be initiated by information coming from the eye without complex analysis in the cortex.

Werner felt that metacontrast illustrated processes underlying the development of contours in the visual system. Thus, a second stimulus interfered with contour development in the first if it occurred during the critical time for that development. If it came too soon or too late it had no effect. His argument is supported by the necesssity for closely aligned contours, by the evidence that the effects are central and not retinal, and by the temporal pattern of metacontrast.

Since spatial adjacency is so critical, it appears that some kind of lateral inhibition effect must be involved in metacontrast, even though it is not the simpler types of retinal effects between adjacent receptors. Lefton (1972) has reviewed the arguments and evidence for an inhibition explanation to metacontrast. While the evidence is quite supportive, no single or general explanation for metacontrast is yet available, although some detailed models have been described (see especially Weisstein, 1966, 1972). It is obvious that temporal processes are involved in both, but not in any simple way.

Masking by Visual Noise

The third type of masking involves the temporal interaction between a stimulus pulse containing a pattern followed by a stimulus pulse containing a random pattern of lines and squiggles. Such random patterns of line segments are referred to as visual noise (Sperling, 1963). A pattern of this sort may cover the entire visual field, being much larger than the test pulse to be detected or recognized, or it may only cover specific areas of the visual field. When the masking pattern just covers the area over which the test pulse falls, it is still not considered simple metacontrast because it overlays the entire test presentation rather than only surrounding it. Usually the average luminances of the test and masking fields are equated so that the effects of masking by light and by visual noise can be separated. Masking by pattern has proved very useful as an operation to study more complex information-processing tasks that we also consider in the next section of the book.

When discussing masking by light, we noted that the perceptibility of a patterned stimulus was reduced when it was masked by light. A comparable effect might be expected when the mask is patterned. Thus the background part of the visual noise field reflects light, and this light summates with that from the pattern, thereby reducing its contrast. However, the masking by light effect can be controlled by using an adaptation field before and after the pattern presentation. Thus, if the perceiver first sees a homogeneous background field of, say, 100 millilamberts, which is briefly turned off just when the pattern field is presented, also with background luminance of 100 millilamberts, then the effective contrast ratio of any pattern will be reduced by the veiling light added over the entire retinal projection. Let us say that the adaptation field (channel 2) is on for several minutes, and then goes off for 10 milliseconds during which a field containing a line (channel 1) is presented, after which the adaptation field returns. This sequence is illustrated in the top two lines of Figure 6.6. Using a three-channel tachistoscope, in which channel 2 and channel 3 are both set to deliver 100 millilamberts of luminance, it should not matter which one follows channel 1, nor even if channels 2 and 3 are alternated.

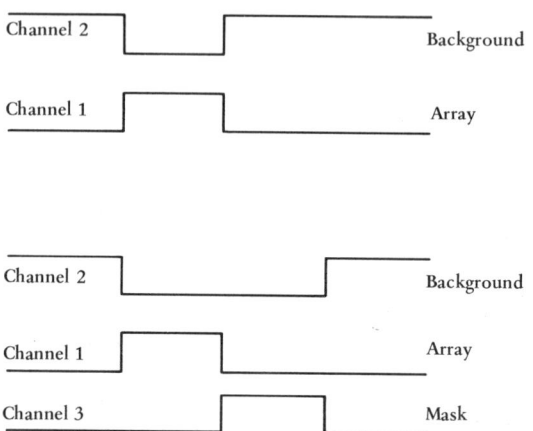

FIGURE 6.6 Schematic representation of the temporal sequence of a background and a letter array presentation in a two-channel tachistoscope (top), and with the addition of a masking pulse immediately following the array using a three-channel tachistoscope (bottom).

A test of the effects of visual noise asks whether a visual noise field in channel 3, with the same background luminance as a blank field in channel 2, will produce more masking than will channel 2. Such a test is illustrated in the bottom three lines of Figure 6.6. Virtually every experiment done in this way has shown that the masking effect is much greater from visual noise on a lighted background than from the lighted background alone (Lefton, 1972). Hence the masking by visual noise must be more than simply creating luminance summation which leads to contrast reduction. There must be some impact of the additional contours being imposed upon the retinal projection of the patterned stimulus.

Sperling (1963) explained the visual noise masking effect in terms of disruption of the representation of the luminance discontinuities after it reached the cortex. He suggested that the representation of the second patterned stimulus interferes with that from the previous one, either replacing it, combining with it, or in some way rendering it ineffective. Thus, until the arrival of the second pattern, the central representation of the first one would be available for processing or information extraction.

Sperling based his argument on an experiment in which a test stimulus containing an array of letters was followed by a visual noise presentation after varying interstimulus intervals. Figure 6.7 contains his results. Sperling found that for each 10 milliseconds that the visual noise was delayed beyond the onset of the test stimulus, the perceiver could report one more letter. This suggested to Sperling that the visual noise was controlling the time that the test stimulus was available for processing, but not the adequacy of the test stimulus representation itself. This effect has been replicated by a number of other experimenters under a wide range of experimental conditions.

Sperling's interpretation of visual noise has been challenged by a number of other investigators, especially Kinsbourne and Warrington (1962) and Eriksen (1966). Their argument is that the neural response to the visual noise summates with that from the test stimulus, degrading the primary visual representation. In other words, they wish to treat the explanation for masking with visual noise as similar to those for backward masking by intense pulses of light. In this view if the visual noise mask and the test stimulus are always combined, then the test stimulus is never available for processing in an unde-graded form. Thus visual noise would be controlling the quality of the visual representation and not simply the amount of time the perceiver has to process it.

Several recent experiments and arguments have come to Sperling's support. For example, when visual noise follows the test stimulus by about 10 to 25 milliseconds, the perceiver reports that he could see the elements of the test stimulus clearly, but did not have enough time to recognize the content (Sperling, 1963; Liss, 1968; Haber and Standing, 1968). Haber and Standing (1968) showed that there were conditions in which the perceiver said he saw the letters in the presentation with substantial clarity, but not for long enough to identify them. This would not be likely if the visual noise simply degraded the contrast of the letters against the background.

If Sperling is correct that the visual noise determines the time available

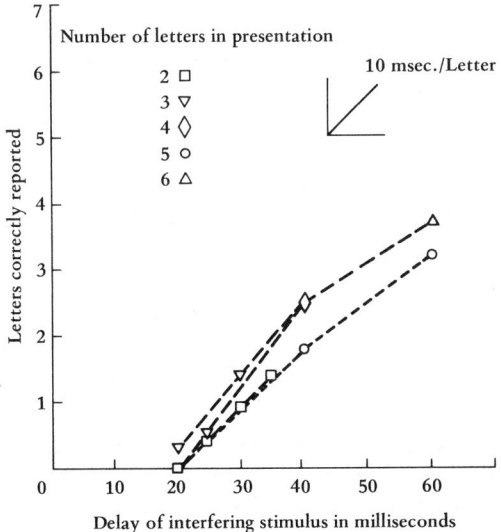

FIGURE 6.7   The number of letters correctly reported as a function of the delay between the onset of the letters and the onset of a visual noise field (from Sperling, 1963).

for processing the content of the test stimulus, then visual noise represents a powerful tool to study the temporal characteristics of visual perception. Several such examples will be discussed in Chapters 7, 10, and 11.

The choice of visual noise as a masking stimulus has probably been fortuitous, given our present knowledge of the receptive field organization of the retina. What is likely to be happening is that contours in the mask are creating visual features of sufficient similarity to those in the test stimulus that when they are presented in close spatial and temporal contiguity the perceiver can no longer tell which features came from which stimulus. Specific evidence for this will have to await further research, in which constructed masks are made to "fit" the test stimulus, in a way that rings fit disks and squares flank squares (see Haber, 1970a).

We have now considered several aspects of how coding of temporal information changes the perception of nontemporal aspects of stimulation. Now we will turn to several topics that involve the perception of events that are varying in time, in which the critical factors concern how we are able (or unable) to perceive the distribution of events over time.

THE DURATION OF THE PRESENT

We have seen that a spot of light or a thin line, no matter how small, is spread out on the retina to about 30 seconds of arc, even though we can resolve a line one-half second of arc wide. Does the same kind of thing happen with the dimension of time as it does for size? Is there such a thing as a point source in time, one that is visible, but that has no temporal extent? What is the apparent duration of a brief pulse of light? How long is the shortest instant of visual time?

There are several ways to approach these questions. For example, Efron (1967) presented a pair of very brief pulses, each of 1 millisecond duration, separated in space and time so that the perceiver could easily tell they were different events. On successive trials, one of the pulses was varied in duration while the other was held constant. The perceiver was asked to judge whether the two pulses appeared equal or different in duration. Only when one of them reached 60 milliseconds or more did perceivers begin to report that they were different in duration. Therefore, Efron argued that the minimum duration of a stimulus that has temporal extent is around 60 milliseconds.

In another study Efron presented two pulses of light to the same retinal area, the first a red pulse of 30 milliseconds, and the second a green pulse of 30 milliseconds, with no interval of time between them. The perceiver reported seeing yellow, just as if the two lights were contiguous in time. If the times were shortened, the report of yellow continued. However, if the total combined exposure time exceeded 60 to 70 milliseconds, then the perceiver reported yellow and, in addition, either green or red, depending upon which of the two lights came second. If the presentation was 30 milliseconds of red followed by 30 of green followed by 30 of red, the perceiver reported seeing yellow followed by red. However, 30 milliseconds of red followed by 30 of green followed by 30 of red followed by 30 of green looks like a longer yellow flash. Again, Efron concluded that between 60 to 70 milliseconds was the minimum unit of time. Similar results were obtained with dichoptic presentations, suggesting that this temporal minimum was determined centrally.

There is a long history to the belief that brief pulses produce a persisting visual representation which seems to last longer than the physical energy. We will discuss three recent studies that illustrate some aspects of the measurement of persistence and point out its relevance to topics to be covered in the next section. In one of these tasks, Haber and Standing (1969) alternated two display fields. One contained an outlined form drawn on a white background, and was presented for about 10 milliseconds. The other was a blank white field of variable duration. By changing the duration of the blank field, the time from the offset of the form to its onset in the next cycle could be systematically varied. The perceiver viewed a sequence of about ten cycles and judged whether the form had completely faded away before it reappeared (see Figure 6.8). The duration of the blank field needed to find such a persistence threshold was about 250 milliseconds. That is, it appeared as if the visual persistence of the brief intense pulse was about 250 milliseconds. When the background was reduced by two log units, persistence was increased only a few milliseconds. When the blank field was turned off altogether, however, persistence increased to about 400 milliseconds.

A dichoptic presentation was also used in which pulses of the form were presented to alternate eyes. If the persistence judgment is based entirely on retinal events, then each eye would need to receive a pulse every 250 milliseconds, thereby requiring a 125-millisecond dichoptic presentation rate. However, the dichoptic procedure produced no differences—the rate was still 250 milliseconds, suggesting that the persistence was occuring after information from the two eyes had been combined.

In another experiment, Haber and Nathanson (1968) showed a perceiver an outline drawing of a form. An opaque surface with a narrow vertical slit one-eighth of an inch wide cut into it was placed in front of the form. The

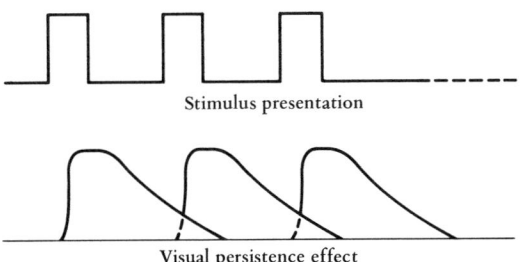

Stimulus presentation

Visual persistence effect

FIGURE 6.8 Schematic representation of a hypothetical persistence resulting from repeated stimulus presentations (from Haber and Standing, 1969).

only part of the drawing that the perceiver could see was what was visible through the slit. The slit was moved back and forth over the drawing. If the perceiver attempted to hold a steady fixation, the moving slit effectively painted the drawing across the retina. Thus, instead of all of the drawing coming on at one time, it was spread out in time so that first one end, then the middle, then the other end, was presented. The slit passed back and forth over the figure in this way. The minimum rate of movement (specified as the time the slit exposed one end of the form until it reached that point again on the next cycle) for which the perceiver said that he could see all of the form simultaneously averaged about 240 milliseconds. This speed was independent of the familiarity of the forms or the perceiver's experience in the task.

In a third study, Haber and Standing (1970) used a different technique to the same end. The perceiver saw a form presented for a brief duration, and at the same time he heard a brief click. This pairing was repeated every few seconds. The perceiver was asked whether the onsets of the pulsed form and the click appeared to be simultaneous. (See the top of Figure 6.9 for the procedure.) If he judged that they were not simultaneous, then before the next pairing was presented, he could adjust, by turning a knob, the relative asynchrony of the visual and auditory onsets. This process was continued over as many cycles as the perceiver needed until he was satisfied that he had their onsets synchronized. The experimenter noted the physical asynchrony between the visual and auditory stimulus that the perceiver judged to be simultaneous.

The perceiver was then asked to perform the same task and judgment, setting the click simultaneous with the offset of the visual presentation. That physical asynchrony was also noted. The difference in time between the two click settings was used as a measure of the apparent duration of a light pulse. Thus, the perceiver has provided an estimate, based upon his settings of an auditory marker, of when he perceived the visual pulse to begin, and when he perceived it to end. The difference between these two settings is thus the apparent duration of the pulse.

The bottom of Figure 6.9 presents the results, in which the interclick interval is plotted against the physical duration of the pulse. Values along the diagonal would indicate that the perceiver judged the apparent duration to be equal to the physical duration, while values above the diagonal suggest that there is some perceived persistence beyond the physical offset of the pulse of light. The results show that for brief pulses, those less than about 100 milliseconds, with a light-adapted eye, the apparent duration was judged to be nearly 200 milliseconds more than the physical duration. As soon as the pulse itself is several hundred milliseconds, additional persistence is negligible. When the eye was dark adapted, persistence was about 400 milliseconds, but again only for brief pulses. Thus it appears that only brief pulses produce significant visual persistence.

We have already mentioned Sperling's interpretation of the effects of visual noise. One aspect of that interpretation was that the arrival of visual noise terminates the persistence or representation of the stimulus. He had

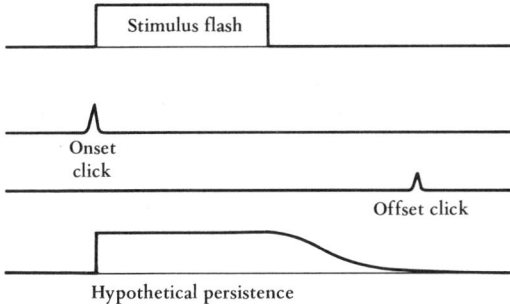

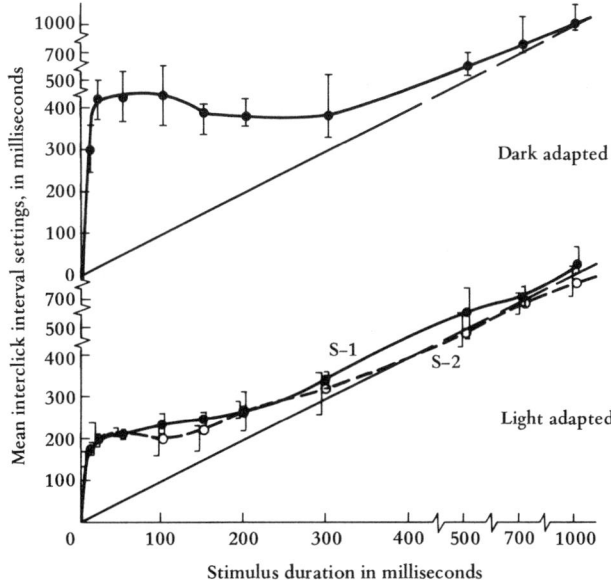

FIGURE 6.9 Schematic representation of the presentation sequence of a light pulse with a click heard near its onset or near its offset (top), and the resulting mean interclick interval as a function of exposure duration of the pulse in both a light and dark adapted condition (from Haber and Standing, 1970).

reported a provisional experiment to test this (Sperling, 1967), but Haber and Standing (1970) added a condition to their pulse-click study to provide a detailed exploration of Sperling's predictions. In that condition, a visual noise mask always followed the visual stimulus. The perceiver was still instructed to adjust the click first so that it was simultaneous with the onset of the pulse, and then with the offset of the pulse. The results of this condition were consistent with the assumption that the arrival of visual noise terminates the apparent duration of the stimulus if the stimulus and the noise overlap in time, and it terminates the persistence of the stimulus if that persistence has not already ended.

For example, a 10-millisecond pulse has a persistence of about 200 milliseconds (see Figure 6.9). If visual noise comes at any time less than 200 milliseconds after the pulse onset, the interclick interval is set equal to the time between the pulse onset and the visual noise onset. If the visual noise comes any time after 200 milliseconds, the interclick interval always equals 200 milliseconds. As another example, a 150-millisecond pulse has an additional persistence of about 100 milliseconds. If the visual noise arrives at any time less than 250 milliseconds after the pulse onset, the interclick interval equals the time between the pulse onset and the visual noise onset. If the visual noise is delayed more than 250 milliseconds, the interclick interval is equal to 250 milliseconds regardless of how much longer the visual noise is delayed. Thus, strong support is found for Sperling's assumption that visual noise will control the temporal characteristics of a test stimulus, over and above the effects it might have on its contrast.

The results of these three experiments provide some consistency on estimates of visual persistence—the apparent duration of brief visual presentations. The magnitude of persistence in these and some other studies centered around one-quarter of a second. Efron's estimates are much shorter, usually somewhat less than one-tenth of a second. However, in none of the experiments have any precise criteria for persistence been imposed upon perceivers as they make their judgments. In the three studies by Haber, the perceiver was asked to give a perceptual report based upon the slightest noticeable appearance of stimulus persistence. This criterion would probably tend to produce relatively long estimates. The variation within perceivers over the different trials and between perceivers was relatively low, so that they were consistent in their judgments. Efron appears to have asked his perceivers to use a more restrictive criterion. This would tend to produce a lower, though equally reliable estimate.

Although the experiments on the apparent duration of brief visual pulses tell us something about the processing of temporal information of visual stimulation, they have turned out to be important as components of more complex tasks. Specifically, if brief visual presentations outlast their physical termination, then it should be possible for perceivers to use that extra time in order to extract information about contours, patterns, and meanings from the presentations. We will consider evidence for this in some detail in the next several chapters.

PERCEPTION OF SIMULTANEITY AND TEMPORAL ORDER

If two stimuli are presented in different modalities or in different locations in the same modality, so that they are spatially clearly discriminable, how far apart do they have to be in time for the perceiver to tell that they were not presented simultaneously? At that time, can he also tell which of the two came first? From what we have seen already, if the perception of simultaneity and temporal order were to require only very peripheral information, then a slight asynchrony in time should be immediately obvious to the perceiver. However, as it turns out in vision, relatively large differences are needed before a perceiver can reliably perceive two stimuli as nonsimultaneous, and even larger differences are needed before he can tell for sure which one came first.

Schmidt and Kristofferson (1963) presented two pairs of stimuli, made up of a click and a pulse of light. In one pair their offsets were physically simultaneous. In the other the click ended earlier than the pulse by an amount which was varied from trial to trial. For each trial the perceiver had to indicate in which pair the stimuli had nonsimultaneous offsets. Figure 6.10 shows their results. If the asynchrony of offsets is less than about 10 milliseconds, they both appeared simultaneous. From 10 to 60 milliseconds separation, performance increased in accuracy until by 60 milliseconds the perceiver could always tell which pair had nonsimultaneous offsets. While the particular values change slightly with changes in intensity or other stimulus parameters, Schmidt and Kristofferson's data are generally representative for the simultaneity discrimination problem. The results are changed little when both stimuli are visual.

Apparent simultaneity judgment illustrates some of the losses in temporal resolution in the visual system. Ten to 60 milliseconds uncertainty may not seem like much error. The auditory system, however, has a temporal resolution for asynchronies in time of arrival of sounds to the two ears on the order of

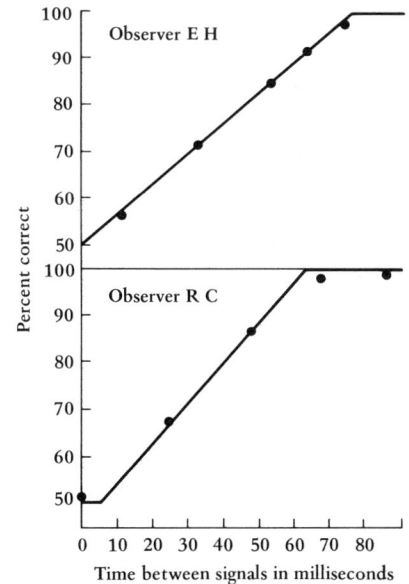

FIGURE 6.10 Percentage of trials in which the variable pair rather than the standard pair was judged to be more successive as a function of the time interval between the offset of a light pulse and a tone (from Schmidt and Kristofferson, 1963).

millionths of a second. These are routinely used for spatial localization of the sound source. However, although time is measured in somewhat coarser units in vision, it is incorrect to say that time is imprecisely recorded.

Hirsh and Sherrick (1961) argue that the discrimination of order should require even more time than the judgment of simultaneity, suggesting that for some intervals of time, one may be able to judge that two stimuli were asynchronous, without knowing which was first. This interval, they suggest, should be about 20 milliseconds.

TEMPORAL NUMEROSITY

If there is temporal summation in the visual system, or any other kind of process which limits the temporal discrimination of inputs to the senses, then the number of closely timed events that can be differentiated should also be limited. When events are presented at a rate of no more than five or six per second, perceivers have little trouble in perceiving and counting the number. Problems develop when the rate is faster. If a chain of pulses of 10 milliseconds duration each is presented at varying rates—10, 15, 25, or 30 per second—the number of flashes reported increases at a slower rate than the number presented. Further, the perceived rate appears to level off at about six to eight pulses per second (Cheatham and White, 1952; Forsyth and Chapanis, 1958).

Harter and White (1967) measured the evoked cortical potential with a scalp recording, and found that it corresponded to the perceived number of flashes, not the actual number of pulses. Hence the loss of information on number had occurred before the information reached the cortex. To support this, White, Cheatham, and Armington (1953) showed via recording of electrical activity at the retina that the stimuli were being followed at a rate of up to forty per second. Therefore, the loss has to be between the retina and the cortex.

THE PERCEPTION OF FLICKER

Experiments considered in the previous section asked the perceiver to count the number of flashes in the presentation of a rapidly pulsed or flickering light. There has been a much longer history of research on the perception of flicker in which the dependent variable is the rate of presentation at which the pulses become indistinguishable, that is, the rate at which the flickering light appears to be fused or continuous. This rate, often called the critical flicker frequency, represents the limit of temporal resolution of the visual system to temporally varying light.

A basic question concerns the rates at which the visual system can perceive that a flickering light is flickering, rather than looking continuous. In flicker experiments the stimulus frequently consists of a pulse of light of a given duration and luminance which is pulsed over and over again with the off-time between each pulse equal to the duration of the pulse. Such a temporal wave form might resemble the top row in Figure 6.11. We can specify the frequency of the light as the number of on-off cycles per second. The intensity or amplitude of the flicker is the difference between the peak luminance and the average luminance of the wave form. Often in early work the luminance of the lowest part was zero, so that the light was being flickered on and off, although it might be some value other than zero. The average luminance would be the average of the light and dark intensities.

The perceiver is asked to look at this objectively flickering light and indicate whether he sees it as flickering or continuous. Other things being equal, better temporal resolution would imply that the light would have to be flickering at a higher rate before the perceiver would be unable to notice its flicker. In this sense, the higher the threshold for fusion, measured as the rate of flicker for which the perceiver says the flicker is just barely noticeable, the greater the perceiver's sensitivity to this type of temporal resolution.

Using this paradigm, a number of findings have been verified. The most important ones concern the effects of luminance on temporal sensitivity. The perceiver has greater temporal sensitivity as the luminance of the flicker is increased. This effect might be expected from the finding that relates the critical duration in temporal integration to luminance. When the luminance is

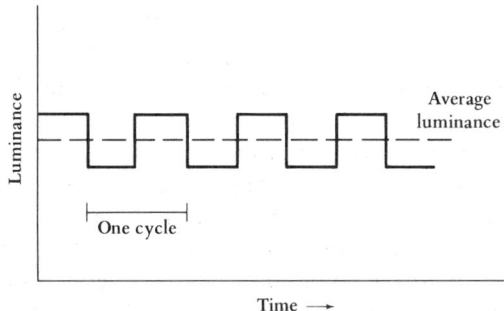

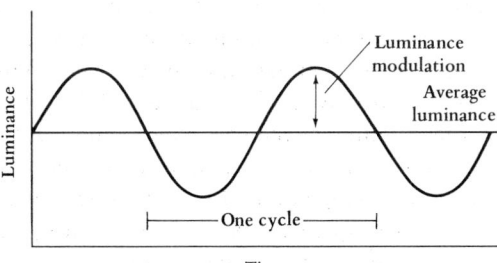

FIGURE 6.11 Two examples of wave forms used in studies of flicker perception. The top shows a square wave and the bottom a sine wave.

very low, as in scotopic conditions, the critical duration approaches 100 milliseconds, but can drop to as low as 1/100 of a second under very high light levels. With a critical duration of 1/100 second, two pulses would be integrated only if they occurred within 1/100 second of each other. This would suggest an upper limit on fusion of 100 cycles per second. At the other extreme under scotopic conditions, as with a very low average luminance level in an otherwise dark-adapted eye, two lights would be integrated if they came within one-tenth of a second of each other, so that even ten pulses per second should fuse.

It should be noted that the relation of the critical duration to the critical flicker frequency is a relative one. If you find the critical duration at which two pulses will fuse, presenting more than two may produce some flicker. This is probably because of changes that occur in adaptation during the course of observing a flickering light. For example, if you are dark adapted and then look at a flickering square wave of light, such as in the top of Figure 6.11, you will gradually become light adapted to the average luminance level of a flickering light. A reliable finding is that the temporal resolution of the visual system goes up with light adaptation (Lythgoe and Tansley, 1929) so that higher levels of flicker are needed to achieve fusion with light adaptation. Given this effect, as more cycles of a flickering light are observed, it will produce some light adaptation, thereby increasing visual sensitivity. Thus, two pulses might be seen as fused, a third just barely, but by the fourth or fifth some perceptible flicker is noticeable.

Kelly (1961) varied the frequency of the flicker, its average luminance, and the luminance amplitude—the luminance difference between the average and the peaks in a flicker discrimination experiment. (See the bottom wave form on Figure 6.11. The difference between the shapes of the two wave forms in this figure will be discussed below.) The perceiver was shown a flickering field of a given frequency and average luminance and asked to adjust the luminance modulation until the flicker was just barely perceptible. Figure 6.12 presents his results for six different average luminance levels.

Consider the top function, based upon a very low average luminance of only .06 trolands. If the frequency of flicker is low, only two cycles per second, then the luminance modulation has to be .01 troland, or about a 15-percent change for the flicker to be just noticeable. If the flicker rate exceeds ten cycles per second, then the luminance modulation must be larger. It cannot exceed .06 trolands, which is the average luminance, or else when the flickering light would be turned off entirely, its luminance will drop below zero. This means that at this average luminance the perceiver cannot find any luminance modulation that will let him see flicker above about ten cycles per second. This implies that when the average luminance is very low, the visual system is most sensitive to temporal frequencies below about ten cycles per second. Above ten cycles per second sensitivity drops off rapidly.

Now consider the function obtained at the very high average luminance values. The greatest temporal sensitivity is found between ten and thirty cycles

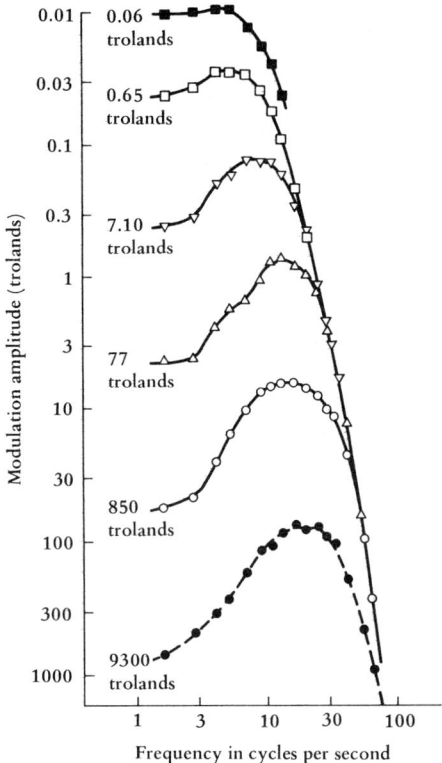

FIGURE 6.12 Modulation amplitude in trolands needed to keep a flickering light of different frequencies at flicker fusion threshold, for six different average luminance levels (from Kelly, 1961).

per second, that is, the least amount of luminance modulation is needed in order for the perceiver to notice the flicker at these rates. If the flicker rate is increased above thirty cycles per second then the luminance modulation must be increased sharply, and by sixty cycles per second no amount of luminance modulation will enable the perceiver to notice the flicker.

Thus, except at very low average luminance values, we are most sensitive to flicker between ten and thirty cycles per second, with a rapid falloff in sensitivity above or below these rates of change. This falloff in temporal sensitivity is found in the spatial domain as well, in which the visual system is most sensitive to spatial frequencies of about six cycles per degree and loses sensitivity for finer and coarser frequencies. This has been shown by Campbell and Green (1965) and Davidson (1968), and is illustrated in Figure 6.13, taken from Cornsweet (1970).

We have already mentioned that Bloch's law should help to specify the upper limit of temporal resolution. Two pulses that are within the critical duration will be fused and seen as one event. Further, the greater the dark adaptation of the eye, which implies for flicker that the average luminance

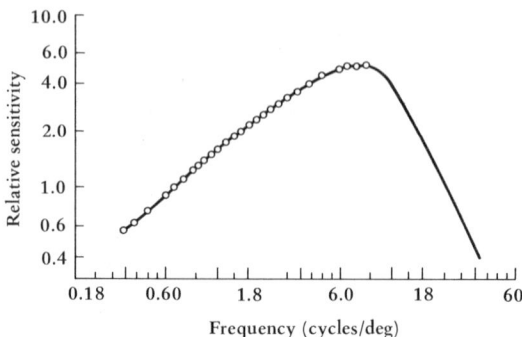

FIGURE 6.13 The relative sensitivity of the human visual system to varying spatial frequencies (data of Davidson, 1968, reprinted from Cornsweet, 1970).

is low, the larger the critical duration and therefore, the lower the temporal sensitivity to high frequencies. This is seen in Kelly's data, in that the peak of each of the functions is shifted to the left as average luminance is reduced.

But what does it mean to say that the sensitivity to low frequency temporal variation is also poor? Kelly's lowest frequency was two cycles per second. What would be expected from even lower rates? If the flickering light is spatially homogeneous and very large, so as to preclude any spatial frequencies at the edges, then we should expect that sensitivity would approach zero as temporal frequency approaches zero. Thus the ability to detect that a light is slowly changing in intensity should be very poor. We briefly indicated in Chapter 3 that sensory coding mechanisms have little means to signal steady states of excitation falling on the receptors. We will discuss this process in some detail in Chapter 8 when we consider the effects of stabilized retinal projections, a procedure to remove low temporal frequencies. As we will see there, the temporal sensitivity of the visual system becomes increasingly poorer as the rate of change in intensity over time approaches zero.

In this discussion we have skimmed over one distinction that is quite important. Kelly's experiments used sinusoidally varying intensity, as shown in the bottom part of Figure 6.11, not a square wave as shown in the top. As we observed in Chapter 3 with spatial frequencies, any wave form can be described as a combination of sine waves of different frequencies and amplitudes. Specifically, a square wave is composed of a sine wave of the same frequency and then sine waves of three times, five times, seven times, . . . , frequencies of the fundamental, each with an amplitude of one-third, one-fifth, one-seventh, of the square wave, and so on. Temporal frequencies can be described in this same type of Fourier analysis. Knowing this we can predict what Kelly's results would have been had he modulated his light as a square wave rather than as a sine wave. With a relatively high frequency of a square wave, say, twenty cycles per second, the sensitivity to the fundamental sine wave would be high, as shown in Kelly's data. The higher frequency sine waves composing the square wave would be at 60, 100, 140, . . . , cycles per second, and these are virtually unnoticed in that there is no sensitivity to these frequencies. Thus, square-wave and sine-wave modulation should yield exactly the same data in the middle and high frequency range.

The story is a bit different at the low frequency end. If the square wave is at a frequency of, say, two cycles per second, then it will be composed of sine waves of 2, 6, 10, 14, 18, . . . , cycles per second, to all of which the visual system is sensitive. Hence, the sensitivity of a square wave at two cycles per second should be higher than that to a sine wave of the same frequency because the square wave has in it temporal frequencies at these higher levels to which the visual system is very sensitive. These predictions have all been verified. This can be seen in terms of the sensory coding mechanisms as well. If a sharp luminance discontinuity in the retinal projection is moved over a few receptors on the retina, it will produce a larger change in the receptive field outputs than when a gradual luminance discontinuity is shifted. It is in this sense, then, that we can be more sensitive to square waves of low temporal frequencies than sine waves of low temporal frequencies.

There are many other aspects to the perception of flickering light. This brief treatment hopefully should indicate some of the basic principles and show how they are anchored in other characteristics of the processing of temporally varying information. This analysis also should indicate some of the value in attending to the temporal as well as spatial frequencies contained in the stimulus, rather than simply considering the number of cycles per second.

THE PERCEPTUAL MOMENT HYPOTHESIS

Stroud (1956) presented a novel and intriguing proposal designed to explain many of the temporal phenomena considered in this chapter. While it has by no means been proved, it has sufficient merit and usefulness for us to consider it in some detail.

Stroud argued that at some point before the information reached the cortex temporal events were quantized into temporal units of about 100 milliseconds. In this way time would be represented discretely, and not as a continuous variable. William James (1890) had argued that time had to be psychologically continuous or else we would lose information about the order of events. However, as we have already seen, if the events are close enough together in time we cannot tell their order from the temporal sequence alone. Stroud made this explicit: Two or more events which fall within the same quantum of time (often called a time frame or a perceptual moment) cannot be discriminated with respect to order. They can be told apart or discriminated in other ways if their locations are different, or color or size or orientation varies, but not which one came first. If there are no other cues to discriminate separateness, then the events will be seen as simultaneous. All of the energy which falls

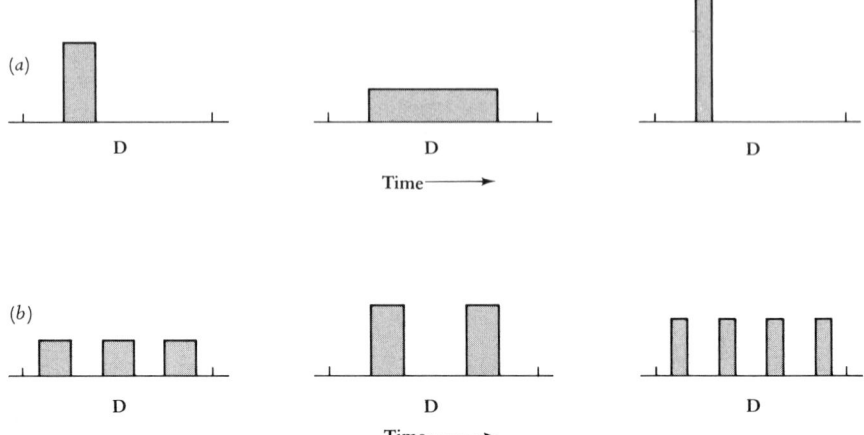

FIGURE 6.14   Several examples of Stroud's perceptual moment hypothesis.

entirely within one time frame will be integrated over time, and its output will be proportional to this total energy, regardless of its actual temporal distribution. Figure 6.14 illustrates schematically what Stroud had in mind.

Consider first the simplest case, in which the onset of the pulse coincides with the beginning of one of the time frames. Since, within each time frame, time ceases to be a variable, it is clear why Bloch's law should hold, at least under scotopic conditions. All of the time frames in row (a) should produce the same output. Only when the pulse duration is greater than the size of the frame (remember the critical duration of 100 milliseconds for scotopic presentations) should the $I \times T = K$ relationship break down.

Row (b) of Figure 6.14 shows how temporal integration is handled by the hypothesis. Since temporal discrimination between the events is lost within the time frame, the output of each time frame in these examples is the same.

These are somewhat idealized cases. If the duration of the pulse is very short, especially in relation to the size of the frame, then the probability of the pulse falling entirely within a single frame, rather than straddling over two frames, is quite large. However, as the duration of the pulse approaches the size of the frame, the chances that part of the pulse will fall in two frames increases. When this happens, then time again will be relevant and Bloch's law and temporal integration will break down. Hence Stroud expected that actual data concerning Bloch's law would look like Figure 6.15, in that the fit to two straight line segments would be rather poor around the critical duration. The same should be true for temporal integration. Hence the perceptual-moment hypothesis predicts complete integration over time, except for an error given by the probability of the events straddling more than one time frame.

While the extension of this hypothesis is fairly straightforward, several more examples might be useful. Masking by light of one pulse by a later one

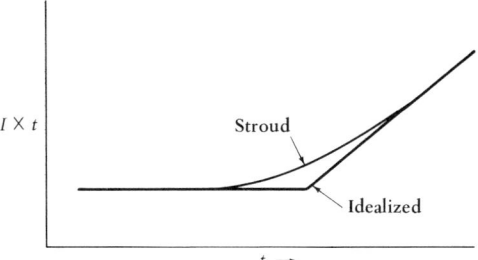

FIGURE 6.15   Stroud's prediction of data concerning Bloch's law.

occurs because the two pulses fall within the same time interval. Although the pulses may be discriminable on the basis of size, location, or shape, the energy of the two is integrated. Since the second is so much more intense as well as larger, the contribution of the first pulse is negligible on the average, and is undetectable. It is to this type of mechanism that Boynton (1961) appealed to explain masking by light. The masking stimulus can act backward in time on the test pulse, not because it gets to the cortex faster, but because the two fall within the same time frame and are integrated. If the time-frame width is 100 milliseconds, then the greatest range of backward masking by light should be 100 milliseconds, as already noted.

Continuous apparent motion will also be expected if the separate pulses fall in the same time frames. Even with motion pictures at sixteen presentations per second or faster, enough presentations will fall within each time frame so that continuity will be maintained. A similar argument holds for the perception of fused continuous light from a flickering source, as long as the pulse rate is greater than the size of the frame. Boynton's (1961) experiment on the increment threshold imposed upon a fused flickering light suggests that the increment pulse is detected before the excitation from the train of pulses is fed into the time frame.

Metacontrast can rest partially on this mechanism, at least to the degree to which metacontrast and backward masking by light are similar. However, the perceptual-moment hypothesis is not designed to explain the spatial interference among contours that is observed in metacontrast phenomena.

Temporal numerosity studies show that although the perceiver can estimate quite easily how many stimuli are presented in a burst when the rate is less than six or seven per second, he consistently underestimates faster rates. Further, the losses seem to occur in a step function as if the perceiver does not separate those stimuli that all fall within a frame, but can differentiate only those that straddle or fall in different frames.

Apparent simultaneity fits the perceptual-moment hypothesis quite closely. In fact, much of the work on simultaneity has been carried out within the context of this hypothesis. Again, the principle is that two events will be seen as simultaneous if they both fall within the same frame, but they will be judged as successive when in different frames. As the separation approaches the frame size, sometimes they will both be in one frame or sometimes they will straddle two, so that the same probabilistic nature should be found as for temporal summation. Kristofferson (1967) has carried out a number of studies on the perceptual moment, most of which concern simultaneity judgments. In addition to the study of temporal order already discussed, he measured reaction times to a light which could come in one of two locations. On the assumption that the information transmission does not begin until the end of the frame, and that the light could arrive at any time during the frame, the variability of reaction times would be a measure of the width of the frame. Figure 6.16 shows his results, which closely support his reasoning. Notice, however, that by extrapolation the results of Fehrer and Biederman (1962) suggest that the reaction-time response is initiated before the stimulus is framed, rather than after as Kristofferson assumes. The contradiction remains to be clarified.

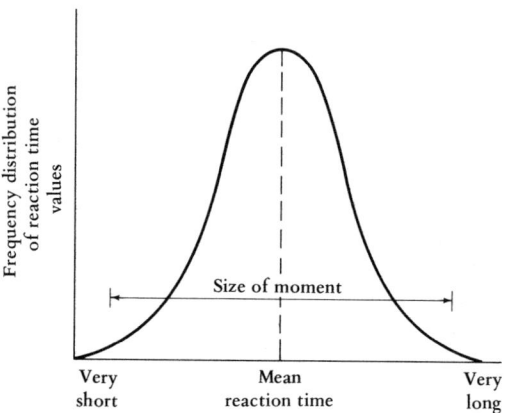

FIGURE 6.16   Hypothetical frequency distribution of reaction times to the onset of a light pulse.

Kristofferson (1967) and others have suggested that the alpha rhythm of about ten cycles per second might be the generator of the timing for the frame. Kristofferson found that the half-cycle of about 50 milliseconds corresponded closely with his findings. More important, he finds that individual differences in alpha rhythm correlate with individual differences in the estimates of the time-frame size derived from his experiments. Thus this analogy is suggestive, although the neurophysiological evidence needed to relate the two mechanisms is still lacking.

While the hypothesis of a perceptual temporal moment appears to be very useful, it suffers as yet from at least four defects. First, we have little neurophysiological evidence to support its existence, nor do we know much about the level of the visual system at which the inputs are framed. Some timing sequences are generated in the central nervous system, but except for Kristofferson's correlation with the alpha rhythm, nothing seems particularly useful.

The second problem concerns the triggering of the frame. One possibility is that the time frames are free running, triggered by some central process quite independent of the occurrence of stimulation. If this is the case, then the arrival of any stimulus is uncorrelated with where in the time frame it will fall. This assumption is used in the analyses shown in Figures 6.15 and 6.16. It is also the assumption used in looking for correlations between the size of the temporal moment and the alpha rhythm. On the other hand, it is possible that the timing sequence can be restarted by the onset of a stimulus presentation, especially if that presentation is substantially different from adaptation level or noticeable in other respects. This might permit much more precise timing in some circumstances, although it will lose temporal precision in others. The problem with a triggered-frame onset is that it implies that there would have to be many different rates since we are often bombarded with a multiplicity of stimuli that are themselves unsynchronized.

A third problem is whether all temporal events are framed before leaving the retina. It seems reasonable that they are (for example, see Harter and White's work on numerosity), but then how can we explain Boynton's flicker study or the Fehrer metacontrast experiment? Each shows that precise time information is available even when the phenomenal characteristics of the stimulus suggest that precise timing is lost. But how did that precise time information get out of the retina without being framed?

The fourth deficit is more complex. The size of the time frame does not appear to be a constant, since it has been shown to vary with a wide range of parameters. For example, the adaptation level, the area of the pulse, and other manipulations will affect the critical duration in tests of Bloch's law. For a flickering light, fusion occurs at a lower rate when the light is presented to the fovea than when it is in the periphery.

There is no need, of course, for the size of the time frame to be invariant over all stimulating conditions. In fact, following some of the implications from Chapter 3 on coding strategies, several reasonable predictions about variable time frames can be advanced. Most of this reasoning stems from Boynton's speculations (1961, 1972) on the relative specialization of the visual system to maximize spatial information at the expense of temporal resolution. Under low scotopic conditions the task of the visual system is to collect light, doing so at the expense of optimal resolution in time and space. The same may be true for temporal order. With a long time frame, more photons can be collected into the frame before the information is transmitted to the cortex and the processing of the next frame begins. High photopic conditions present the opposite condition. Here the visual system must somehow reduce the powerful effects of overwhelming numbers of incident photons. Mechanisms of adaptation, including bleaching and other processes, accomplish this to a considerable extent. But now it is not necessary to integrate over as long a time to get a good sample of what is coming in, nor over so large a spatial extent either. Inhibitory mechanisms that do not operate under the low scotopic conditions come into play. Now an area which previously served only to integrate light can respond to it in a complex but useful way in order to enhance edges and pattern. Similarly, there is no need to wait as long as before to terminate one time frame and start the next. The time frames could be even shorter than they are, but this could be accomplished only by using up some of the available processing capacity, especially at the optic nerve bottleneck. This capacity is much more importantly used to transmit spatial information.

Thus, this interpretation suggests that the quantization of time is one of a number of coding mechanisms which are used to specialize the visual system for the various tasks it needs to perform. But there are still problems to be faced in developing a coherent theory of temporal aspects of perception. The perceptual moment hypothesis needs substantial further work before it can be shown to be useful. At present, it has a heuristic value far outstripping the actual support it has received in the laboratory.

SUMMARY

Since perceptual processing takes some time to complete, and since most visual stimulation has a temporal dimension to it, we have included a number of topics concerning temporal factors in visual perception in this chapter.

Temporal summation and integration refer to findings that the visual system integrates the energy in light over brief periods of time. During those time periods, temporal information is lost, in order that spatial information can be maximized. When the amount of light is high, then the critical duration over which integration occurs is quite brief—on the order of 10 milliseconds or less, so that some temporal precision is available. The integration does not occur at the receptor level, but does seem to be accomplished in the retina.

Because of the temporal properties in visual processing, it is expected that visual stimuli that do not physically overlap in time could still interact and interfere with each other. Three varieties of visual masking phenomena are discussed in some detail. In masking by light, a large intense light coming after a small brief test pulse can raise the threshold of the test pulse, even when the former is delayed up to 100 milliseconds. Several not entirely satisfactory explanations are offered to account for this backward masking by light, with our choice leaning toward one based on poor temporal resolution. In meta-contrast, the backward effect seems to be caused, not by a more intense masking stimulus, but by the presence of adjacent contours, which in some way, connected with lateral inhibitory processes, interferes with the development of previously presented contours. In the third type of masking, using visual noise as the masking stimulus, the effect seems to be one in which the amount of time available for processing the test stimulus is restricted by the after-coming visual noise mask.

The next topic concerned how long brief visual presentations last or persist in the visual system. For a pulse of light to have any temporal extent at all it has to be at least 60 milliseconds in duration. In addition, no matter how briefly a pulse lasts, it has a visual persistence of nearly one quarter second—that is, it has some coding or representation in the visual nervous system which remains for up to that time. It will be shown in the next section of the book how useful this persistence is for information extraction.

Because of the poor temporal resolution, it is difficult to tell whether or not two nearly contiguous pulses of light are simultaneous in time. It is even more difficult to tell which one came first unless their asynchronies are substantial. Further, it is difficult to count or perceive precisely the number of separate pulses that had been presented when the rate exceeds five or so per second.

The perception of flickering stimuli was considered within the context of some of the principles already developed. Since temporal resolution improves with luminance, the separate pulses in a flickering light are detected more easily when the intensity level is higher. But it was also noted that the visual system is differentially sensitive to different rates or frequencies of flickering light, depending on the average luminance of the light. These differences are important in our understanding of the sensitivity to temporal variation in stimulation, and seem to be related to similar spatial variations in sensitivity.

The last part of the chapter examined the perceptual moment hypothesis of Stroud as an attempt to describe a number of different aspects of temporal resolution. His notion that processing is framed into temporal packages, so that within each frame temporal sequence and identity is lost, is a powerful device, even though several problems still remain to be explained.

This chapter concludes Section One of our book. Although it does not begin to cover all of the basic sensory, physiological, and psychophysical properties of the visual system, it should provide enough of these to permit us to examine more complex perceptual tasks. Section Two will consider various aspects of information extraction—form, search, attention, recognition, and meaningfulness.

Readings

Since temporal factors usually are given some coverage in most handbooks on visual perception, many of the sources previously listed will be useful here, too. Specifically, several excellent chapters on temporal factors are found in Rosenblith (1961), Graham (1965), Kling and Riggs (1971), and especially Jameson and Hurvich (1972). This latter handbook contains chapters by Boynton on temporal integration and masking, Weisstein on metacontrast, and Kelly on flicker. Fraisse's book (1963) on the perception of time includes much material not normally covered in a chapter like the present one.

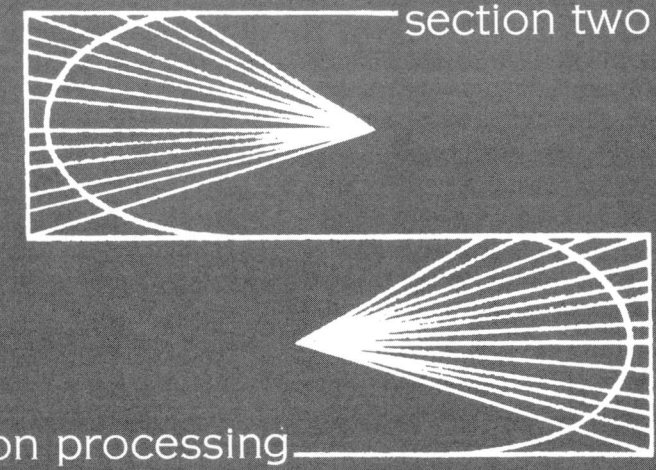

section two

erception as information processing

In the first section of this book we have been concerned with the impact of light on the visual system, but without attending much to any consequences of that impact, other than as it initiates transmission of information from the photoreceptors through the retina to the cortex. Thus we focused on light as energy and on the visual nervous system as it transduces that energy and follows various coding strategies to transform and transmit it. We also looked at the dimensions of light that yield the experience of color, and the basic psychophysical measurements, as well as temporal factors in perception. In each of these chapters we paid little attention to possible organizations or meanings that the surfaces and objects reflecting light to the eye might have for the perceiver. In one sense we need not have worried about meaningfulness of the visual world yet, because for virtually all of the phenomena discussed in these chapters we would not have changed the selection of stimuli, the psychophysical procedures, nor the interpretation of results. In fact, in spite of valiant efforts to demonstrate the contrary, these phenomena do not seem to be influenced by any meaningfulness that the perceiver might impart to the sources of light radiation or reflection. In this sense, some theorists have referred to these phenomena as sensory as distinct from the perceptual ones to be found in the rest of the book. This distinction, however, has not been a very useful one and has caused more trouble than it has been worth, unless one merely wants to use it to designate basic properties and processes as compared to more complex ones.

In the second section of the book, we will not only begin to contend with organization and meaning, but also with their extraction from the information available to the perceiver. This will represent an important change of focus, away from definitions of stimulation entirely in terms of photons, wavelengths, and milliseconds to those of structure, organization, meaningfulness, and information content. This does not mean that the objects defined as to their meaning are not also specified in terms of their luminance or duration. They must be in order to describe the experimental circumstances precisely. But it means that such specification does not constitute the major interest of the experiment. Thus we will make fewer references to the energy or wavelength of the light reaching the eye, and we will be less concerned with the details of retinal processing or neural transmission. As such, these are the basic building blocks for the remainder of the book. We will never be far from the basics, although usually we will assume them rather than explicitly redescribe them.

This will inevitably make the rest of the book appear less rigorous or scientific because we do not anchor all of our stimulus specifications back to energy in the light, nor are our perceptual responses anchored simply in terms of detection. There is some truth to this appearance. We cannot be as precise in our definitions of organization or in meaning as we are in photons or wavelength. Much imprecision arises in this manner. Equally as important, the perceptual experiences to be described are far more complex, and although we often can learn much about them from simple detection or same-different responses, such are usually inadequate to discover what we need to know.

There are five chapters in this middle section of our coverage of visual perception. The first of these provides a general framework for our analysis of organization and meaningfulness. It is a model or a way of thinking about perception that has come to be called an information-processing analysis. Chapter 7 describes this approach, and provides several examples of its application. The remaining chapters then select different aspects to focus on in more detail. Chapter 8 looks at the perception of form as organization, Chapter 9 discusses visual search, and Chapter 10 is concerned with selective processes in perception. Finally, Chapter 11 explores the processes that occur in recognition and familiarity.

information processing of visual stimulation

INTRODUCTION

This chapter begins a new section of this book—a shift to problems that contain a cognitive as well as a perceptual component. Naturally, much of our new interest will be with meaningful stimuli—how we perceive and come to understand letters, words, and sentences as conveyors of meaning. But we shall also be interested in pictures and scenes as representations of meaning. The concepts to be developed and elaborated in the remaining chapters may be applied to many of the problems discussed previously, although we have not done so explicitly. Nevertheless, we trust that the continuity between these sections will become apparent as we develop the principles of information processing.

THE NATURE OF INFORMATION-PROCESSING ANALYSES

This section will describe the assumptions and some of the concepts used in the information-processing approach to the study of perception. Information-processing approaches are usually applied to the study of human perceptual and cognitive activities. They are especially useful in studying how we experience the perceptual world, how we recognize objects, how we remember, and how we speak and understand language.

The information-processing approach to the study of perception did not arise as a reaction against other viewpoints. Rather, it was a reflection of new conceptualizations and methods applied to the study of perception. Along the way, however, some conflicts with older approaches have developed. For example, as perceivers, we usually express a naïve realism when describing our perceptual experience—we feel that what we see is a mirror of the stimulus. Moreover, this realism implies that seeing occurs automatically, immediately upon the onset of stimulation, and that it terminates with the offset of stimulation. These assumptions are clearly unwarranted (see Neisser, 1967), and the demonstration of their falsity has provided the foundation for developing the information-processing explanations for perception and cognition.

Assumptions

The major assumption of an information-processing approach is that perception is not an immediate outcome of stimulation, but is the result of processing over time. Neither the perceiver's visual experience nor his overt responses are immediate results of stimulation. They are consequences of processes, or a sequence of processes, each of which takes a finite amount of time. Therefore, in studying a complex perceptual task such as visual recognition, this time interval may be divided into a number of stages or processes, corresponding to a series of transformations of the information in internal representations of the stimulus.

An information-processing approach also assumes that experimental operations could be devised to examine the contents of the representation of the stimulus information at every point in the sequence. Comparing the samples over time with the original stimulus projection provides the basis for inferences about the nature of the processing involved. The total time from stimulus onset to the occurrence of a response can be divided into intervals, each characterized by a different operation. Each process can be assigned a duration (at least theoretically) during which its characteristic operation is performed. The various juxtapositions of processes can be represented by a flow diagram, in which blocks are used to represent the processes occurring at different intervals. Each block is then labeled according to its operation. The blocks are connected to suggest the order in which the operations are performed. This approach makes explicit the operations, stages, or processes that occur in the time between stimulation and the observed response. It is the identification of the processes, along with the determination of their position and impact in the sequence, which provides the major task for information-processing theorists.

The processes are usually thought to be limited in the amount of information that they can hold or process in a given period of time. The magnitude of this limitation must be determined empirically and must be considered for each operation separately. Thus there are some circumstances in which only a few items can be processed at one time, while in other circumstances, the amount of information processed may be limitless. For example, Luria (1968) has reported tests on a person with an apparently limitless memory.

Capacity limitation usually leads to selectivity—not all information can be processed to the same degree within the time available for such processing. One of the major characteristics of information-processing analyses is to specify the determinants and mechanisms that account for selectivity. These will be discussed in detail in Chapter 10.

Storage or Memory

Information may be deposited and retained at various stages along the way in the sequence of processing. This property of an operation is called storage or memory. Frequently, different types of storage will be separated according to their relative durations, as for example short-term or long-term memory. We will ask many questions about the nature of the contents of different storages. Since the retinal projection of the light itself cannot get "into" the organism, a representation of it, which we call information, is the content that we will describe in our theories. When this information is stored, we will want to know its relation to the information in the retinal projection of the stimulus. Is it in the same form, or has it been transformed? Is it coded in some way? We will also ask about the nature of the storage. Is everything preserved in its original form or does the information decay slowly over time? Is it possible for information to be removed from this storage, and if so, how?

Processes

The essence of the information-processing approach is that operations may be applied to information which transform it in various ways as it is used by the perceiver. The identification of some of these operations have already been suggested. For information to be in a certain place such as a store, it will require a process to put it there (read-in), and one to take it out again (read-out). One read-out process, called scanning, is a systematic procedure of going from one portion of an information field to the next, and then to the next, and so forth. When a field is scanned, each item is treated in turn, that is, serially. An alternative procedure, called parallel processing, would be to process all the items at once, rather than one at a time. Notice that these processes refer to internal representations and are not to be equated with a visual-search procedure involving eye movements (see Chapter 9).

Read-in and read-out processes represent transfer of information from one place to another, usually between separate storage points. These transfer processes can treat information randomly, or arbitrarily, or according to some predetermined pattern of transfer. Frequently these processes involve the loss of information in transmission. Transfer may also involve coding processes which preserve a portion of the information in a more efficient form. We shall see many instances of the operation of these processes.

Information

The approach just described is sometimes confused with Information Theory, a statistical specification and measurement of information in a stimulus and in responses (Attneave, 1959; Garner, 1962). This approach grew out of the early attempts to define and measure stimulation—a notoriously difficult task. Notice that even in this book on perception, we have not offered a formal definition of a stimulus, although there are many definitions by example. Part of the reason for confusion of the two approaches is that they have a common ancestry and frequently have been practiced by the same investigators (see Haber, 1973, for a general review).

Information was initially defined by Shannon (1948) very specifically as the amount of uncertainty reduction in a particular communication channel. This quantity could be calculated and was independent of the particular content of the uncertainty being reduced, that is, independent of the content of the stimuli, the responses, and the particular communication channel involved. This definition of information was applied to psychology in all areas in which psychological tasks were viewed as reducing uncertainty between stimuli and responses.

Initially heralded as a major breakthrough, the promise of information measurement as applied to perceptual stimuli has not been fulfilled. Since it turned out to be relatively easy to calculate the amount of information contained in a stimulus or in a response, widespread use was made of this metric. But when the amount of information in stimuli and responses was correlated with reasonable dependent variables, the relationships were negligible by and large. The amount of information in a pattern did not always correlate with ratings of complexity, simplicity, or similarity to other patterns, nor more importantly did it usually predict recognition, recall, speed of perception, threshold, or a number of other measures. Thus, the failure of information measurement in perception was empirical rather than theoretical. There are exceptions to this generalization in the literature, but in substance the metric failed to provide a useful description of form as a visual stimulus, and of recognition as a response. See Corcoran (1971) for a more recent review of this failure. The success with judgmental tasks has been much better (see Garner, 1962), probably because the amount of information is computed over a number of different stimuli or the number of possible outcomes in a particular task. These situations are probably closer to the original application Shannon had in mind.

The failure of Information-Theory measurement has been most dramatic when the meaningfulness of the material is a component of stimulation. Miller (1956) rejected the definition of information measured in "bits" and substituted a much more pragmatic concept of "chunks." He found an impressive amount of data from various sources which suggested a limit to immediate memory of about seven items, plus or minus two. This held broadly when the items were unrelated. However, as soon as a perceiver recognized that the items could be related—as when letters spell words—then the limit expanded rapidly. To illustrate with a slight exaggeration, the limit of perceptual processing should be seven unrelated line segments, or seven unrelated letters if the line segments can be organized into letters, or seven unrelated words if the letters can be organized into words, or seven unrelated simple sentences if the words are organized semantically or syntactically, or seven ideas, or seven cosmic thoughts, and so forth. While it may be possible in theory to carry out an uncertainty-reduction analysis on each of these levels, it seems quite unlikely that they would be equivalent, and it has not proved very amenable to do so in practice. Rather, Miller suggested that the unit of information ought to be the subjective units being employed by the perceiver in the particular task. Thus, if letters are presented that spell words, then the response unit is words.

Thus, the refinement in definition offered by uncertainty reduction has had to be replaced by sophistication in experimental design, as well as a substantial amount of intuition. Rarely is information defined per se. Rather it simply refers to that aspect of the content of the stimulus that the experimenter is interested in studying or manipulating. It is probably the feeling of most theorists working in these areas that to be more precise at this time will go beyond our theoretical capacities and our ability to measure what we have defined.

Thus, by using a less precise term, we are able to speak more generally and to relate processes to one another which might otherwise be thought unrelated. In this sense, therefore, information is even less definable than stimulus. We do know that light impinges upon a perceiver, and we do know that something is processed and that we may label it information. It is part of the task of this approach to learn how to specify these terms more precisely.

A MODEL FOR PERCEPTUAL INFORMATION-PROCESSING TASKS

A number of information-processing models have been proposed to account for many different psychological tasks (Sperling, 1963, 1967; Atkinson and Shiffrin, 1968; Norman, 1970; Neisser, 1967; Broadbent, 1958, 1971; Posner, 1969). A somewhat generalized version is presented below which owes much to the models suggested by these authors and others. It is an illustration of models of perceptual tasks and also provides a general framework within which the perceptual literature may be discussed. Research findings in the area of perceptual and cognitive functioning are changing the science so rapidly that any model is likely to need revision frequently. The model presented in Figure 7.1 illustrates many of the general characteristics of information-processing models—stages, processes, storages, channels, and the interdependence of elements. While we will not be able to discuss all of the details relevant to such a model of processing in perceptual tasks, there is some agreement about this general characterization, and we will review some of this evidence.

The overall model may be divided into three parts: the luminance discontinuities in the light projected over the retinal surface at any instant in time; the overt observable response made by the perceiver; and the nonobservable processes which form the heart of the model. Most models omit the first two parts, assuming that the distinction between observable and nonobservable phenomena is somehow to be understood. The model presented here makes explicit the difference between the retinal projection and the immediate internal representation of it. It also differentiates, at the other end, between the internal mental organization necessary to produce overt responses and the responses themselves.

The general shape of the model has some intuitive base, but it now also derives from substantial empirical evidence. We will review some of it here

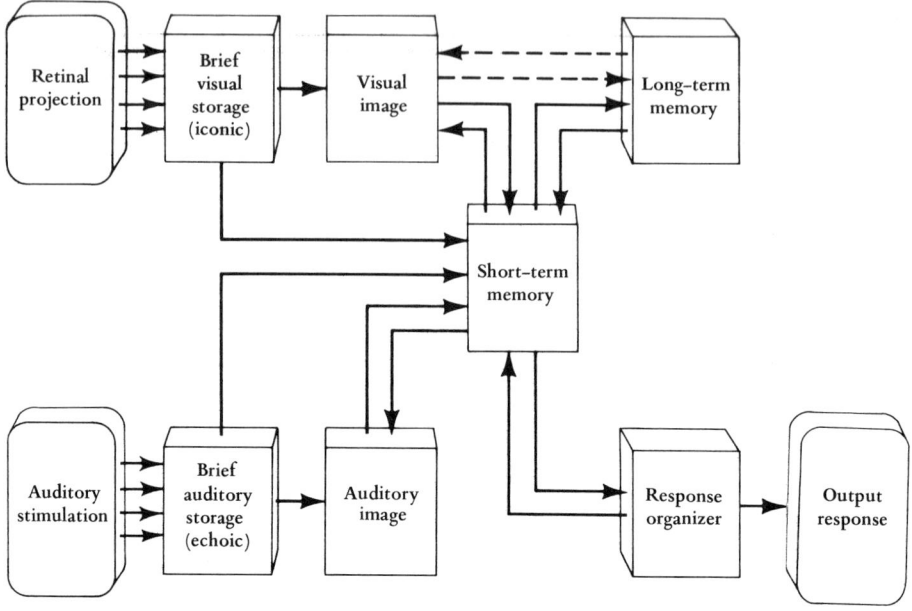

FIGURE 7.1   An information-processing model illustrating the more important stages, storages, processes, and channels.

and in the remaining chapters of this section. If we start by analyzing what should (or, in some cases, must) occur to stimulus information to produce a relevant response, certain components of the model almost seem logically necessary. For example, the information defined by the luminance distribution in the retinal projection must be internally represented in some way. Therefore, any model would have to include this first storage. Second, it is clear that the overt responses require some prior programming and organization. Therefore, this fact must also be taken into account. Frequently a substantial delay occurs between the first representation and the organization and production of a response. This would suggest that the information must be kept in some kind of storage for a period of time. The model suggested in Figure 7.1 will take these considerations into account, while modifying them in accordance with recent experimental findings.

Brief Visual or Iconic Storage

In the first stage, the information from the light impinging upon the retina is represented internally, presumably in some central locus. The visual features that are the outputs of the receptive field organization of the cortex are prime candidates for the content of this representation. If the receptive field organization is the proper model for this information extraction, then we should show many arrows from the physical stimulus to the brief visual storage indicating that this analysis of features is a parallel process. This would reflect a simultaneous coding of a large number of visual features from all parts of the retina.

Another view of this representation of the stimulus is simply to note that the stimulus information is coded "visually." This is the sense that Sperling (1960) implied by labeling this first stage visual information store, and what Neisser (1967) had in mind when he called it iconic storage. The names visual information store, icon or iconic storage, and brief visual storage will be used interchangeably in the following chapters.

It is very tempting to assume that visual features defined according to the research reported in Chapter 3 are the first central representation of information from the luminance discontinuities contained in the retinal projection. We feel this temptation, but also feel somewhat cautious. As we noted at the end of Chapter 3, the search for visual features is by no means over, and it is possible that the more interesting features are yet to be discovered and mapped. Thus, any model based on today's features may be greatly distorted by future findings. In addition, the dramatic discoveries of the past decade concerning the functional organization of coding in the visual system suggests that more is yet to come, and a premature commitment to one system may prevent flexibility later. Uttal (1971) has raised some theoretical, as contrasted to these more practical, reasons for not yielding to this temptation. In any event, we feel we have to keep an open mind about the content of this first stage of visual storage.

The content of the iconic store is clearly related to the periodicity of saccadic eye movements. During the fixation time between saccades—a minimum of 250 milliseconds—the visual representations could be registered. When a saccadic movement occurs, the representations from the previous fixation are lost, due either to rapid decay during the eye fixation or to the suppression of visual sensitivity during the movement. (See Chapter 9 for a more detailed discussion of saccadic eye movements.) It is also possible that the new representation which arises from the new fixation erases the previous one. If the duration of exposure of the visual field is less than 250 milliseconds, then the persistence mechanisms discussed in Chapter 6 extend the duration of this brief visual storage to about 250 milliseconds. The quality of this representation deteriorates over this time and has essentially faded away after one-quarter of a second.

Thus, in any perceptual task, the perceiver has little more than one-quarter of a second in which to process the content of this initial visual representation so that the information can be transferred to a somewhat more stable or permanent storage. Whether the contents of the icon itself, before further processing has occurred, are affected by meaning, organization, or familiarity with the stimulus material remains a topic for research. These questions will be discussed in Chapter 11.

Visual Image Representation

Two directions are indicated in Figure 7.1 for the processing sequence beyond the icon. It is expected that normally both channels are used in parallel. The upper one, shown in Figure 7.1 refers to the construction of a visual image representation that occurs soon after the onset of visual stimulation. This sequence says that stimulation is represented in a visual image—the conscious awareness of the experience of perceiving. Many perceptual theorists identify such a process as occurring after the original iconic storage and it is represented in our flow diagram in that position. It may be thought of as a constructed representation based on the content of the icon, or it may not be separable from the iconic processes. This too is a problem for research and will be considered again in Chapters 8 and 11. If the representation is constructed, we would expect that it is integrated over time. Successive saccades introduce visual components which are combined with previous ones to build up an integrated image or picture. Such an image is by no means photographic, but rather follows the rules of perceptual organization (see Chapter 8).

The question of the duration of the visual image is also complex. If the visual image is a construction of the visual world, it will contain more than the representations of the current fixation. Instead, the entire visual scene will be represented in the image since our eyes continually change fixation over the scene. In this sense, then, the visual image will represent the entire visual world, not just that part seen with sharpest clarity in the center during the particular fixation. Since the visual image can be different from the specific content in the brief visual storage, the image may not be constrained at all by the one-quarter second duration of the iconic storage. If after a visual construction has been established, the stimulus is removed, and the visual field is blank, it is possible that the visual image could persist. This would be especially true if it can be refreshed from short-term memory. Of course, from that source the content of the image might be regularized as a function of the name coding that created it.

Short-Term Memory

The second component into which visual information is transferred is called short-term memory. This sequence represents the encoding of the visual information into linguistic or conceptual representations which may occur either in parallel with the construction of a visual image or in series with it. The sequence might function as follows: When the stimulus is letters the visual representations of the letters may be rapidly scanned in the icon so that they can be coded into the letter names. As we shall see, however, if the letters spell a familiar word, not all of the letters may need to be scanned separately. Rather only a few may be named, which along with word shape and length may be sufficient to derive the name of the word for storage in short-term memory.

There is a substantial amount of evidence that the short-term memory representation is in the form of an acoustic code. The perceiver might literally name internally the letters when presented individually, or the phonemes comprising the word as he scans them and transfers them from iconic storage to short-term memory. There may be a similar sequence for processing auditory stimuli. The acoustic signal would be held briefly in an "echoic" (rather than iconic) storage while its basic acoustic features are processed and encoded into phonemes which would then be held in the short-term memory.

Short-term memory is not a permanent storage. Since it can store an auditory code (for example, letter and word names) it would require a duration sufficient to retain information until it could be encoded and stored in long-term memory, or used in an immediate response. For example, suppose you look up a telephone number and then need thirty seconds before you can use it by dialing the number. You cannot look at the telephone book during this time, but you are able to retain the information—the number has been residing in short-term memory. You may notice, moreover, that you are rehearsing it by saying the number to yourself over and over. A number of investigators have suggested that rehearsal of the auditory code is an essential feature of this type of storage. Without constant rehearsal, parts or all of the information may be lost. Thus rehearsal permits the information to be retained until it can be transferred to long-term storage, or used and forgotten. The duration of short-term memory is very much longer than that of the initial iconic storage. It certainly lasts several seconds without rehearsal, and may be much longer when rehearsal is used.

Long-Term Memory

The longest lasting information store is called long-term memory, with persistence measurable in decades. We will not say much about the properties of long-term memory in this book. Nevertheless, this system cannot be ignored since its activities and contents will affect both the contents of earlier stages and of the types of transfers between them. Briefly, we should note that the content of long-term memory may be images, or letters, or words, but is most likely to be some type of semantic representation that contains meaningful structure. Some of the properties of this system will be discussed as they relate specifically to a perceptual problem or task under analysis in subsequent chapters.

Output Processes

The last box in Figure 7.1 concerns the outputs from the perceptual information-processing system. A spoken response requires a motor program to operate the articulatory apparatus. Written or pointing responses, or other behavioral indices reflecting perceptual activity also require programs for their operation. Thus, this box represents many possible avenues for output from the system, all of which are organized in some way.

Notice that the model provides no outputs from any other components of this information-processing system. There can be none from the visual image representation because there is no way that others can see our visual images. Nor is any output indicated from long-term memory, for the model assumes that the contents of memory would first have to be translated into words or actions. Finally, no output is shown directly from the iconic storage. These assumptions of this model clearly require empirical evidence. Some already have strong support, but others do not. We shall discuss several of these further in subsequent chapters.

Interconnections

The interconnections between the processes in Figure 7.1 are specified by arrows that suggest the direction of action and influence. Thus, arrows in both directions mean not only that information can flow in both directions, but that each process can influence the other. In general, the arrows represent the possible sequences for the processing of information. Thus not only does the ordering of the processes supply conceptual hypotheses to be validated by research, but the arrows also suggest experimental problems.

The inputs to the iconic storage are shown in parallel. Thus all of the information about the luminance discontinuities that is extracted from the retina is assumed to arrive at the same time. It is possible that future research may discover some latency differences between the detectors of different kinds of features or over different parts of the retina, but at present the assumption of parallel and simultaneous entry into the icon seems reasonable.

The two exits from the icon are assumed to be parallel and independent, although the possibility that they are serial is not disproved yet. Thus, there can be simultaneous naming of items represented in the icon along with a construction of their visual image representation. These are both information-extraction processes. It is supposed that the visual image construction always occurs, but the naming may occur only if the names are available. The contents of short-term memory (often influenced by long-term memory) may affect these two extraction processes. Hence, naming should occur faster if the material is familiar. Likewise, although we can construct a visual representation without prior experience with the stimulus pattern, such familiarity might be capable of changing the visual image representation.

The arrows between the visual and short-term memory representations suggest that both can affect the other and both can be used to generate the other. Thus from the name we can generate a visual image representation, even in the absence of concurrent visual stimulation. Similarly, we can name and describe our visual images even if we did not name the components when we initially processed them from the icon.

Long-term memory is reciprocally connected to short-term memory. Thus, the names of the components in the stimulus can be stored more permanently either as literal names, as when we rehearse and memorize a poem, or more typically as ideas or concepts. To retrieve these concepts later from long-term memory, names as words would have to be regenerated. But these will be paraphrases of the original text or representation, since the original itself was not stored. Notice also that visual image representations might be translated into long-term storage as concepts or ideas. It is not clear whether one can generate an image of stimulation directly from long-term memory, or whether one first has to go back through short-term memory—hence the dotted lines.

The various stages (icon, visual image, short-term memory, long-term memory, articulation) can have substages within them. For example, the content of short-term memory can be maintained longer if it is rehearsed. This must be some form of repetition of the content, and must be conveyed by a self-feedback loop. It is possible that visual constructions can be rehearsed or refreshed internally without further inputs from the icon or short-term memory.

This completes our brief review of the principle components of an information-processing model for perceptual tasks. While we cannot consider all of the processes in detail in this book, the remainder of this chapter will focus on the experimental evidence for the existence of the early stages and processes —the iconic storage, the auditory-coded short-term memory, and the visual image. It will become clear in these sections that the sequence and positions of the processes are of great importance to our understanding of the processes themselves. This will also be true in Chapters 10 and 11 where we will consider the more complicated problems of attention and the role of memory or past experience in perceptual tasks.

We noted earlier that the model proposed here bears close resemblance to those proposed by other investigators. However, these authors have not given prominence to the visual image representation, except for some speculation about the "locus" of consciousness (Sperling, 1967; Posner and Keele, 1970). This may be because they have been concerned almost exclusively with linguistic information and not with the perception of scenes, objects, and pictures. Or it may be because of the old behaviorist strictures against using the term consciousness or even acknowledging its existence. Whatever the reason, there is an attempt to reintroduce this problem into psychology by many of those using the information-processing approach, and the inclusion of a visual image box represents the reassertion of that concept.

ICONIC STORAGE

The evidence for the existence of a brief visual or iconic storage comes from two principle sources: direct measurements of visual persistence and indirect measurement of information content as ascertained with partial report procedures. Virtually all of the work has been done with linguistic material, so that we must be aware of the possibility that the processes proposed may be limited to this type of information.

Visual Persistence Studies

One aspect of the procedure for measuring iconic storage was reviewed in some detail in Chapter 6. There we discussed the apparent duration of a brief visual stimulus as a measure of how long a brief pulse appeared to persist before it faded out. Several different procedures produced estimates of about 250 milliseconds for this duration. When perceivers had to space repeated pulses so that each just followed on the tail of the previous pulse as it disappeared, they inserted about 250 milliseconds between the pulses (Haber and Standing, 1969). If a visual form was painted across the retina by sweeping a narrow slit in an otherwise opaque surface over a stationary form, perceivers report that they can see all of the form simultaneously only when the slit traversed it within one-quarter of a second. If the sweep rate was slower, one part of the form had already faded from view while the other end was still being painted on (Haber and Nathanson, 1968; Haber and Standing, 1969). Finally, when perceivers set clicks to occur simultaneously with the onset and offset of brief light pulses, the clicks were set nearly 250 milliseconds apart, even when the pulses were only 10 milliseconds in duration (Haber and Standing, 1970).

In the last study it was also noted in Chapter 6 that visual persistence was shorter for longer pulses. In fact, the data suggested that visual storage from brief pulses lasted up to one-quarter of a second after the pulse ended, but that longer pulses had less persistence. This suggests that the icon lasts about one-quarter of a second, either from a continual representation of the stimulus as it remains on view, or as a persistence after the stimulus ends. Knowing what we do about the rate at which the eye changes fixation, there should be little usefulness in saving visual information in storage beyond one-quarter of a second.

Partial-Report Studies

Sperling (1960) used a partial-report procedure to assess the amount of information present in the initial representation of the visual display. He exposed displays containing twelve letters, four letters in each of three rows for brief durations (see Figure 7.2). When asked to name all twelve letters, perceivers could rarely report more than about four—the capacity of the span of immediate memory for visually presented items (Miller, 1956). This finding by itself could indicate that all of the letters in the array were not available in the initial representation, or conversely, that all the letters were represented intern-

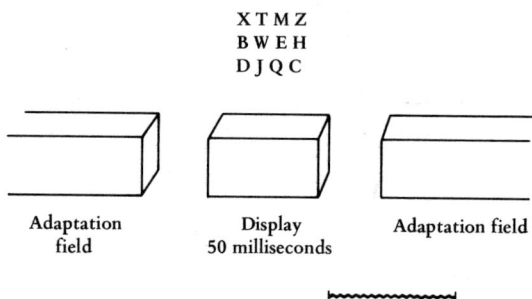

FIGURE 7.2 Schematic representation of the stimulus sequence in the Sperling (1960) poststimulus indicator experiment.

ally but there was insufficient time to name and rehearse all of them before the representation decayed.

The partial-report procedure is designed to permit a choice between these two alternatives. In this condition, the perceiver is required to report only one of the three rows. After the visual presentation terminates, the perceiver is told which row to report by the pitch of a tone—high, medium, or low pitched —to indicate that the perceiver should report the top, middle, or bottom row, respectively. The tone occurred either coincident with the offset of the presentation of the letter display or after varying interstimulus intervals up to several seconds.

The report of letters was very good when the tone followed the visual presentation immediately, or by less than about one-quarter of a second. Since the perceiver did not know which row was to be reported until the display had ended, he must have been able to store all of the information from the display (that is, all twelve letters), until the indicator sounded. The number of letters available as a function of delay of the tone indicator is shown in Figure 7.3. The shaded area represents that duration during which information from the stimulus was available after stimulation had terminated. Since the function levels out after about one-quarter second, Sperling argued that this was the duration of the iconic storage. This type of evidence also shows rather convincingly that the limitation on report noted by Miller, of about a half-dozen items, could not be an input limitation. It appears as if all of the information in the retinal projection is available in this iconic storage, since the perceiver can extract whichever part is asked for. The limitation must occur after that point in time, probably in the poor retention during short-term memory after the items had been processed from a visual to an acoustic representaton.

There have been a number of other replications of variations on the

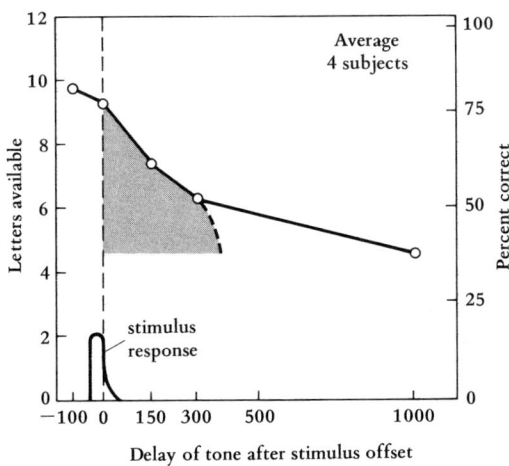

FIGURE 7.3 Number of letters correctly reported as a function of the delay of the poststimulus indicator (from Sperling, 1960).

partial-report procedure, all of which find evidence for some type of iconic storage of visually presented information. Almost invariably the duration of this storage is placed at about one-quarter of a second.

What Is Stored in Iconic Storage?

We already suggested that visual features are a good candidate for the content of iconic storage, but that it is too early to commit a model to that position. But we can still ask this question in several other ways. For example, if it would be possible to prevent further processing beyond the iconic storage, one could ask what a perceiver could report of the visual field from the content of this iconic storage alone. The principal procedure for producing this situation is to have visual noise (see Chapter 6) follow the stimulus presentation. Thus it should be possible to let the information reach the cortex but somehow destroy it before it can be processed into names or into images. Liss (1968) and Haber and Standing (1968) independently reported experiments designed to examine the content of the iconic storage. They both showed that if a visual noise mask follows hard on the heels of a display, perceivers report a visual impression of the display, but are not able to note any of its characteristics. Moreover, nothing remains of this representation after the mask arrives. If the mask is delayed a bit, then the perceivers report seeing the display long enough to describe its general layout, or to name some of the items.

We have considered the assumptions underlying this use of visual noise in the previous chapters. In this context, the two experiments suggest that the visual noise prevents the naming of the items held in iconic storage. It does permit enough of the visual image to develop so that the perceiver can at least rate the contrast of the lines against the background, but it does not remain on view long enough for him to use that image to extract the names of the forms displayed in it, or to construct those names directly. These results suggest that the build-up of a visual image begins prior to or faster than naming the items.

As we noted earlier, much of the research on information processing has used stimuli that could be coded linguistically. We know much less about the time course of processing pictures or scenes. The input to the icon should be in the same format, so at this level it should not matter what the ultimate nature of the representation will be, nor the nature of the intervening processes. But we are lacking the evidence. This model also suggests that at the level of the icon, no effect of familiarity, meaningfulness, or past experience should be apparent. The initial representations, be they visual features or something else, are defined by the sensory coding mechanisms exclusively.

INFORMATION EXTRACTION FROM THE ICON

Virtually all of our evidence about the processing of visual features concerns the route into short-term memory. Again, we have little detailed experimentation on the specific route of the visual image representation. Many questions on information extraction of linguistic material have been explored: How fast does it occur? Is there a spatial ordering to the processing, such as left to right, as in reading? Is one item processed at a time, or can several be worked on in parallel? Are items that can be grouped into familiar larger units, such as letters that spell familiar words, processed any faster than unfamiliar items? We will briefly comment here on three aspects of information extraction— the rate of processing, duration of processing, and effects of familiarity on processing. Each of these will be considered in greater detail in the next four chapters.

Rate of Processing

If information is processed sequentially, then it should take a fixed amount of time to process similar items. The more time available for processing, the greater the number of items that could be processed. If this description is accurate, then an experiment could be devised to measure the rate of processing —the amount of time necessary to process one item. Sperling (1963) attempted to do this by presenting a display of from two to six letters and asking the perceiver to name all of the letters in the display. Immediately following the presentation, a visual noise field was presented to terminate the icon. Sperling reasoned that, at the time of arrival of the visual noise, only those letters already transferred from the icon into short-term memory should be available for report. Those not yet processed would be irretrievably lost. Figure 6.12 already presented Sperling's results. As the duration of the display was increased, thereby providing more time to process the content of the icon, the perceiver could report more letters. The rate of extraction was about one letter per 10 milliseconds of processing time. Since Sperling found that the curves for the two-, three-, four-, five-, and six-letter arrays all overlapped, he proposed that the letters were processed serially. Thus, the perceiver scans the visual representations, naming the first letter, then the next, and so on until he has named all of the items or run out of time. A parallel process, on the other hand, in which the perceiver attends to several or all of the letters at once, should have found that more letters are reportable per unit time for larger as compared to smaller sized displays. Sperling's data, as far as it goes, is more consistent with an item-by-item processing.

A number of other studies have examined the rate of processing using this general procedure, and have tended to find evidence of processing rates around 10 milliseconds per item or less. It is important to note that this manipulation—following the display by a visual noise mask—is designed specifically to assess information extraction from the iconic storage. Thus it would be expected to show very fast rates of processing, much faster than rates based on processing of information within short-term memory, for example. We will examine some of the research on these latter processes in Chapters 10 and 11.

Direction of Processing

We have already noted evidence for item-by-item processing in Sperling's (1963) experiment. It might be expected that if a perceiver processes the items one by one, he might do so in a consistent direction. Since these are letters, a left-to-right sequence based on reading habits might be expected in this task as well. When Sperling replicated his experiment in 1967, he found a consistent left-to-right superiority. When a perceiver did not have enough time to report all of the items correctly, he was always better in reporting the left-hand as compared to the right-hand letters. These data suggest that the perceiver encodes the letter names following an internal left-to-right scan of the icon. Thus the visually coded, spatially stored initial representation is transformed into a linguistically coded, sequentially stored temporal representation. At a rate of one name per 10 milliseconds or less, all of the linguistic information that is needed in an experimental visual display can usually be extracted in less than one fixation.

But there is evidence from Sperling's experiment as well as from those of others to suggest that this interpretation is too simple. This can be illustrated by one result from Sperling (1967). Figure 7.4 shows a condition in which a five-letter display had been presented. Notice that the accuracy of reporting each of the five letter positions increased as processing time increased. Also, the perceiver appears to begin to process left-hand letters before right-hand ones. But notice that the curves for right-hand letters begin to rise from the baseline before the curves for the left-hand ones have reached maximum, suggesting that the perceiver is processing some aspect of the right-hand letters while he is still continuing to process the left-hand ones. This suggests either some type of parallel processing, transferring more than one letter at a time, or a breakdown in a consistent left-to-right order.

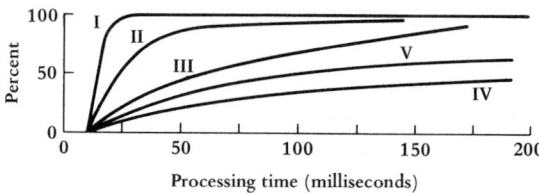

FIGURE 7.4   Percentage of letters reported from each of five letter positions as a function of processing time, as determined by the delay of the visual noise making field (from Sperling, 1967).

Effect of Familiarity on Information Extraction

If the perceiver scans the visual representations of each letter, processes them in some manner into the name as he transfers them into short-term memory, can he do this faster if the items are more familiar? A familiarity effect might manifest itself by faster scanning per item, made possible by the sequential redundancies among the more familiar letter sequences. This might mean that the perceiver does not need to spend as much time processing an item if he could predict it from the results of processing a previous item. Several experiments have reported data consistent with this prediction, and we will review them in Chapter 11.

On the other hand, it is possible that with more familiar sequences some type of parallel processing occurs in which several items are processed together. Unfortunately most of the research to date on these questions has used nonmeaningful linguistic materials which differed in sequential redundancy. When actual words are used, better evidence for parallel processing might be found, and there is already some hint of this in the literature. Again, we will consider this in later chapters.

We have only mentioned three components of information extraction from iconic storage, and then only very briefly. Our purpose at this point has been to illustrate the processes and show that they are amenable to manipulation, rather than to provide specific answers about their function.

INTEGRATION OF SUCCESSIVE FIXATIONS— THE VISUAL IMAGE REPRESENTATION

The previous section has briefly considered information processing of linguistic information from the iconic storage into short-term memory. That processing channel will usually be used for all stimulation that has nameable components, especially if the content is printed language. But this channel represents only part of our information-extraction processes—it is not concerned with the construction of an organized visual representation of the world around us.

Under typical circumstances the eye remains fixated for little more than one-fourth of a second, and then rapidly moves to a new fixation. The vast majority of such movements will be to nearby locations on the same scene or picture. Yet we do not perceive a kaleidoscope of shifting and displaced images. Instead the visual world is seen as a stable structure which our eyes sample. This integration uses the information available in each fixation but it probably is not limited to that. It is likely that it can be combined with the information from previous fixations, and expectancies based on information from past fixations, and in some cases from past experience predating the current stimulus before the eyes.

Hochberg (1968, 1970) has pressed a distinction between the information available in a single glance or fixation and the integration of that information from successive glances. He has suggested that most of our constructions of visual space cannot be completely specified from a single glance alone. The initial visual representations are not available for a large area, so that unless the perceiver is some distance from the scene he would only have local depth information around the center of fixation to guide him in his organization of the scene. Further, within a single glance a high level of visual acuity is available for only a narrow area centered on the fovea. In order to see the world clearly in all locations, we must construct an image representation that takes information from several fixations. Hence, only with several fixations of a scene can a detailed construction be made. Moreover, much of our information about depth depends upon a change in the viewer's eye or head position. For this reason as well, construction of the visual world would be greatly facilitated by multiple fixations.

Unfortunately, in many perceptual experiments conducted in the laboratory, the perceiver has only enough time for one fixation. Therefore it is often difficult to distinguish the properties of the iconic storage from those in the visual image. We know we can construct an image from a single glance, since we can see something of a scene which is illuminated so briefly that a second fixation is not possible. But such scenes have very fuzzy edges with sharp clarity only in the center. It is likely that good sharpness extends farther from the center in our image than our visual acuity would predict, especially when we have some expectations about what is in the scene to guide our constructions of our image.

There is little evidence to guide our thinking on how these integrations and constructions take place. In fact, with the exception of Gibson and Hochberg and a few others, little attention has been paid to how such processes occur at all.

SUMMARY

This chapter has introduced our section on perception as information-processing. It is intended as an overview, and to provide a way of thinking about perceptual processes that goes well beyond the specifications exemplified in the first section of the book.

Information-processing is characterized by its focus on how the information of the luminance discontinuities contained in the retinal projection are transformed into different forms of representations or codes, visual codes, auditorily represented linguistic codes, and semantic codes. In this sense, we are able to see, to hear, and to understand the visual stimulation reaching our eyes. This way of thinking makes it clear that several stages or processes are involved, and that in no sense can perceptual processing be considered immediate or instantaneous. Further, the result of each process must be stored or temporarily maintained, so that the information-processing sequence can be subdivided into stages, stores, and processes—each with its own sequences, time constants, and interactions.

These were illustrated in a generalized model, whose discussion formed the middle part of the chapter. In the last part, some evidence is briefly reviewed concerning the existence of a brief visual or iconic storage as the first central store of information, drawn from studies on persistence, on partial reports, and on visual noise masking. This was then used to examine several aspects of the extraction of information from the iconic storage, particularly work on the rate of processing items of linguistic information, the duration of storage of the iconic, image, and short-term stores, and the effect of familiarity of material on those processes and rates.

Finally, we briefly mentioned some of the properties of the visual image representation, as the other coded output from iconic storage. Special note was made of the integrative properties of this representation, since there has to be some way for us to see a panoramic view of the visual world around us, uninterrupted by eye movements and unaffected by the momentary unevenness of clarity over the visual field in each single glance.

Readings

Although this is a relatively new area in perception, a number of general discussions are available for further study. Haber (1973) has written a brief general introduction to information-processing approaches in perception. His collection of readings (Haber, 1969) on a variety of topics in this area provide a wide range of research and theoretical articles. Some other general models of information-processing tasks are developed and discussed in Broadbent (1971), Norman (1970), Moray (1970), and Neisser (1967), as well as in some of the more specific references given in the chapter. Leibovic (1969) provides a link to some of the visual nervous system components of these more complex processes.

8

figural synthesis—the perception of form

INTRODUCTION

We have seen in Chapter 3 how the neural organization in the retina seems to be designed to provide information about the presence of discontinuities in the optical projection on the retina. Properties of some of these discontinuities appear to be coded directly by the receptive field organization of the visual system and represented in the cortex by the activity of single cells. Using this analysis as a foundation, we will turn in this chapter to the question of how processing continues from retinal stimulation to produce an organized perception of form. We will first consider how contours are indispensible for form perception by examining the effects of homogeneous stimulation (Ganzfelds) and stabilized visual images. We will then turn to figure-ground segregation, the initial stage in the synthesis of form. Finally, we will examine what is meant by perceptual organization and the Gestalt laws of organization, and we will review some attempts to treat these laws quantitatively.

The questions being raised in this chapter are fundamental to an understanding of the organization of perception. Unfortunately, one of the side effects of the advances in psychophysical research has been the greatly diminished interest with "how things look." The precision gained in measurement and interpretability by limiting the perceiver's responses—reporting only whether or not a signal is perceived, or which signal is brighter—is gained at the expense of detailed descriptions of the stimulus as it appeared to the perceiver. Consequently, our theories and our research in perception have tended to ignore these problems, often simply treating the perceiver as a decision maker without any perceptual experiences at all. In most theories of perception, the conscious experience of the perceiver is not considered to be a source of information to the perceiver, or useful to the theorists.

An information-processing approach does not in itself demand attention to the perceived qualities of the visual world. In fact, many of the models of information processing have no components that are concerned with the way things look. The model described in the previous chapter (see Figure 7.1) does contain one component explicitly for this purpose—the visual image representation. It is only with such a representation that the perceiver would ever "see" the visual world. In fact, given only the acoustically coded short-term memory of most models, we would end up "hearing" the visual world, but never being able to have an integrated visualization of it.

This chapter begins the discussion of some of the perceived attributes of the information in the retinal projection. Our focus will be narrow at first, attending primarily to the factors that account for the perception of form. In later chapters we will broaden this to the perception of objects and surfaces extending away from us—the perception of the visual world.

THE ROLE OF INHOMOGENEITY IN THE PERCEPTION OF FORM

The earlier chapters have shown how luminance discontinuities in the retinal projection are transduced into neural information which reflects these discontinuities. It seems reasonable that the presence of borders, edges, and contours in the stimulus would be the minimal information necessary for pattern perception since they could provide the building blocks for the perception of stable segregated portions of the field as figures and objects. Investigations concerning this problem have focused on the perceptual effects of homogeneous stimulation in a Ganzfeld and studies of stabilized retinal projections.

Ganzfeld Research

Completely homogeneous stimulus fields, called Ganzfelds, are difficult to produce. The most comprehensive work has been described by Metzger (1930). He was concerned with the perceptual consequences of observing a homogeneous surface—one containing no luminance discontinuities at all. Although his apparatus produced such homogeneities, it was moderately complex. In a much simpler, though less precise experiment, Hochberg, Triebel, and Seaman (1951) had perceivers wear caps over their eyes made out of halves of ping-pong balls. Light was focused on the eyecaps and red and green filters were used to obtain color stimulation. Perceivers reported their visual sensations in a number of different situations. Under continuous red-light stimulation, they reported seeing a surfaceless field, sometimes described as "a fog of color," followed by total disappearance of color within three minutes. They then reported seeing a black or dark gray field sometimes containing "hallucinatory shapes" and also sometimes containing what has been called a "flight of colors." The perceivers in this experiment reported that they believed they ceased to see color because the illumination had been changed.

To determine whether the effect is peripheral or central, Hochberg et al. exposed only one eye and asked the perceiver to describe his perceptual experience as given by his unexposed eye. For example, the perceiver's left eye would be exposed to red light until the color disappeared, and then both eyes were illuminated by red light. Most viewers reported seeing red after this sequence of stimulation. Two of them said they saw red in both eyes, but three of them reported seeing red in the right (unadapted) eye alone. The fact that the adaptation occurred predominantly in one eye suggests that the adaptive processes are peripheral rather than central.

The introduction of inhomogeneity into these stimuli further altered the perceptual experience. If, after the disappearance of color, a shadow is introduced over the eyecap by moving a finger vertically onto the central portion of the eyecap, the perceivers report seeing a black shadow with a color halo around it on the background. These halos quickly disappear with removal of the finger. If perceivers are asked to move their eyes briskly back and forth from left to right, half of them report the reappearance of the color, and half report a quickly fading flash of color. If the light is interrupted for a two-second period, nearly all perceivers report seeing complementary colors. The reestablishment of the stimulation yielded a flash of color. Thus, stimulation by a homogeneous chromatic visual field leads to the loss of the perception of color. Inhomogeneity or change in the stimulus field appear to be crucial for the maintenance of the visual experience.

Cohen (1957) explored the changes in perceptual experience as a function of alteration in the textured and spatial characteristics of the Ganzfeld in a series of experiments in which the stimulus field was more controlled. The appratus employed two one-meter diameter spheres which were joined together. Their inner walls were highly reflecting and showed no visible texture to the eye (see Figure 8.1). A hole in one sphere allowed monocular vision perpendicular to the plane of the aperture between the spheres. Therefore a viewer could see partially into both of the spheres. Two projectors were used to control the illumination, one for each Ganzfeld. When the Ganzfelds were equal in luminance, a homogeneous luminance distribution was presented to the eye. This resulted in the perception of a homogeneous field, that is, the aperture between them ceased to exist in the perceiver's experience. They reported seeing a foglike field, close at hand, but extending for an indefinite distance in front of them. The perceivers felt as if they were immersed in a fog. Given three minutes of adaptation, five of the sixteen perceivers even reported complete cessation of all visual experience, that is, not even the experience of blackness.

When the two spheres differed in luminance, perceivers then reported seeing a simple inhomogeneity in an otherwise uniform field. This tended to re-

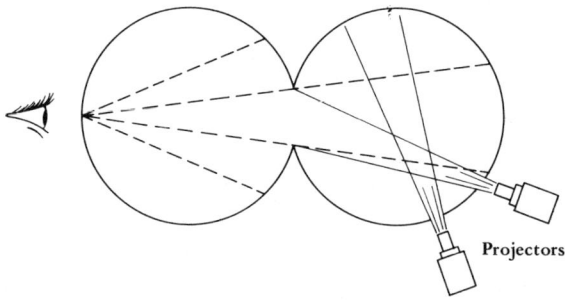

FIGURE 8.1 Schematic representation of the arrangement of two spheres used by Cohen (1957) to produce a Ganzfeld.

duce the density of the fog and increase its distance. For larger inhomogeneities, the aperture is seen as a figure on a background (see below). The appearance of a surface is related to the definiteness of figure-ground segregation, which is, in turn, related to the sharpness of boundaries. Chromatic gradients alone produced an indefinite figure; intensity gradients produced definite segregation of figure-ground, with the disappearance of the fog.

Cohen concluded that spatial inhomogeneity and temporal change are crucial for the maintenance of even minimal perceptual experience. Inhomogeneity in a field created figures and grounds and stabilized the colors and the distances of the backgrounds. Thus figures depended upon inhomogeneity in the stimulating environment and, as will be seen below, the presence of a figure was essential for the maintenance of the ground from which it emerged.

Cohen (1957) also reported that electrical activitiy (EEG) recorded from over the visual cortex seems to exhibit patterns typical of the cessation of visual stimulation at about the same time the perceiver describes a fading of color and the emergence of foglike experience. This finding, taken in conjunction with the Hochberg et al. report of minimal dichoptic effects, suggests that the Ganzfeld produces its impact primarily as a result of retinal processes. Although the receptors undoubtedly continue to signal the presence of photons hitting them, this information probably is lost by the ganglion cell level, so that the retina ceases to signal the cortex about the presence of stimulation when that stimulation is uniform. This is to be expected, given the bias against responding to steady-state information (see Chapter 3).

Although it might be thought that Ganzfelds do not exist in nature, all of us are equipped with two of them—our eyelids. Closing our eyelids reduces pattern stimulation but still permits intensity and wavelength stimulation to reach the retina. No matter how intense these are, however, the neural excitation leaving the retina should be reduced within a few minutes. Thus, not only do the lids cut out pattern stimulation, but probably result in a cessation of all effective stimulation.

Stabilized Retinal Projections

In Chapter 5 we described the effects of small eye movements, such as tremors, drifts, and microsaccades, on visual acuity. We have also referred to the impact of these movements on sensitivity to low temporal frequency flicker. In both contexts, we have implied that such movements would be very useful in the enhancement of sensitivity of the visual system. But it was not until the early 1950s that the technology became available to show this effect (Riggs, Ratliff, Cornsweet, and Cornsweet, 1953; Ditchburn and Ginsburg, 1952). Two principal mechanical procedures have been used to study stabilized images. In the first, a contact lens is fitted over the cornea. A stalk attached to the lens holds a miniature projector (see the right portion of Figure 8.2). Since the contact lens, stalk, and projector will move with the eye, the image projected onto the retina will not shift over the retina as the eye moves. If the contact lens is carefully fitted, stabilization capable of eliminating the effect of drifts and

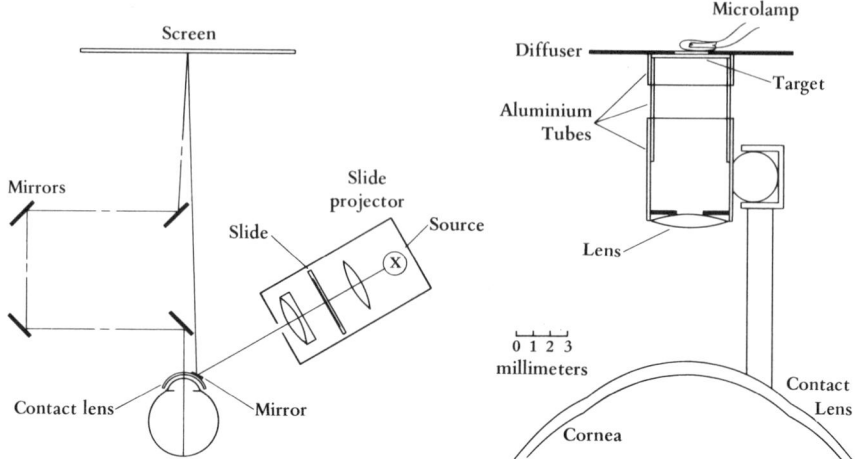

FIGURE 8.2 Two techniques used to produce a stabilized retinal projection. The right panel illustrates the apparatus used by Pritchard (1961), and the left one used by Riggs, Ratliff, Cornsweet, and Cornsweet (1953).

microsaccades is possible. The left side of Figure 8.2 shows a second procedure, in which a mirror attached to the contact lens reflects projected light from an external source in such a way that it moves exactly in the amount that the eye moves, thereby producing a stabilized projection.

Of course, there has always been a procedure which requires no attachment to the eye at all, but it is not as useful in many circumstances. If a bright pulse of light is presented to a dark-adapted eye, an afterimage is created that will persist for up to several minutes. Since this afterimage persists because of the adaptation changes in a particular set of receptors over which the projection fell, this is another example of a stabilized projection. Hence, it should be the most precise method, but it is useful only with intense stimuli relative to the adaptation state of the eye. Further, as we will note below, it does not necessarily produce a perfectly stabilized projection.

Heckenmuller (1965) has reviewed the procedures, results, and interpretations of the vast majority of stabilized visual image research. We will discuss a few of the most important effects. A general loss of perception of color and form occurs as soon as a stabilized projection is presented, usually within seconds, as long as the precision of the stabilization is within about one minute of arc—no more than about three cones. Obviously, as fading progresses acuity for detail is lost, even though before fading began details may be seen with normal or even supernormal acuity (see Chapter 5). Most of the fading occurs in a hazy fashion—a fog comes over the field, beginning in the periphery and then moving centrally. The haze may have a periodic reappearance, as in some kinds of afterimages. The farther a stabilized contour falls in the periphery of the retina the faster it fades. The presence of peripheral contours will speed up the whole process of fading. If only the center of a field is stabilized, the unstabilized peripheral contours will continue to be seen and will dictate what is seen in the center after the center contours have faded. This may help explain why we normally see the centers of large homogeneous fields, rather than having them fade out. The peripheral contours fill in the centers.

The fading of forms is more complicated, since the fading also appears to be related to the integration of the form. Figure 8.3 provides several examples in which a form decomposed into component parts (Pritchard, 1961). These results have been replicated with a number of variations to control for response bias. If they are accepted at their face value, they pose a great complication for the explanation of stabilized retinal projections, as well as with the locus of the perception of form. If they can be shown to be artifacts of measurement or of response, then some parsimony can be maintained. We will discuss these attempts below.

The general pattern of results (except for the form simplification and meaningfulness) provides very strong support for the thesis that variation in stimulation on the retina is needed for perception to occur. The stabilized visual image procedure removes temporal variation. When the identical pattern remains in the same location on the retina, perception fails rather quickly. It can be reinstated by movement, by flickering the stimulus in time, or by changing its luminance, even while keeping it stabilized in space.

The interpretation of the effects suggests that the disappearance is due to the relative paucity of retinal receptive fields that respond under steady-state conditions. Most receptive field organizations require that either the retinal projection change in its luminance discontinuities, or that the projection shifts its position relative to the receptors in that receptive field. When both of these are prevented, as when the projection is stabilized, then the receptive field can-

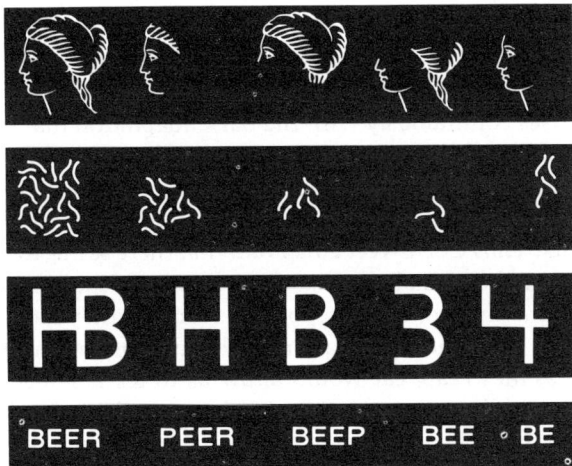

FIGURE 8.3   Several examples based upon perceivers' reports of the ways in which forms decomposed into simpler patterns during viewing under conditions of stabilized retinal projections (from Stabilized images on the retina by R. M. Pritchard. Copyright © 1961 by Scientific American, Inc. All rights reserved).

not signal the presence of the projection and its output is indistinguishable from that produced from a homogeneous projection on the retina.

We briefly mentioned the periodic reappearance of the perceived form, or a simpler component of it. Both of these are usually linked, in that the simplification occurs upon reappearance. The reappearance has puzzled researchers, although the general interpretation has been that it is due to some slippage of the contact lenses over the cornea, which of course will lead to some loss of stabilization, and consequent movement of the retinal projection relative to the retina (Cornsweet, 1966). Pritchard (1966) and others have argued, however, that the reappearance is not due to slippage, but rather reflects, a central component in form perception. They argue that, for example, the reappearance of forms in the "stabilized" afterimages cannot be due to slippage. Therefore why should it be attributed to slippage in other experiments?

However, Cornsweet (1970) notes that slippage will not only explain the reappearance, but also the form meaningfulness and simplifications ascribed to the forms. In this way we can preserve a receptive field interpretation without having to invoke central factors. If a contact lens slips it will do so in only one direction, and for only a given amount. When this happens all luminance discontinuities in the projection perpendicular to the direction of slippage will now be capable of producing a change in the receptive field outputs over which they project. But discontinuities parallel to the direction of slippage will not produce any change unless the amount of slippage is substantial. This means that reappearance will be only for a subset of all possible luminance discontinuities in the pattern, a subset which shares some common features, such as lines parallel to one another rather than at various other angles. In this way those aspects that reappear after slippage will be both simpler (in the sense of having fewer components than the original) as well as more organized or meaningful.

Cornsweet (1970) also suggests that afterimages may reappear from time to time for similar reasons. They are not perfectly stabilized in that their intensity decreases continuously with the dark adaptation that follows the offset of the light that produced the afterimage. The afterimages also spread somewhat over the retina with time (Brindley, 1963) and are sensitive to small changes in blood supply which could be produced by pressure changes due to eye or lid movements. Thus Cornsweet concludes that there seems to be no reason at present to reject the retinal slippage hypothesis for the reappearance effects, as well as for the changes in the reports of forms as they fade and reappear.

There is one other implication to this interpretation—that the changes in the forms as they reappear would allow us to learn something about the processing of visual features in the visual system (Pritchard, 1961; McKinney, 1963; McFarland, 1973). Thus, if the last component to fade or the component to reappear most often is a straight line, then this would imply that lines are a basic component or a visual feature. The slippage explanation calls this interpretation into question, since it suggests that the content of the reappearance will be a function of the direction of slippage of the contact lens and the direction of components in the retinal projection that were displaced when the slippage occurred. Thus, in this interpretation, the reappearance changes in these studies can tell us nothing about basic features. The order in which components fade might be useful for this purpose as long as it was not due to inaccuracies in the stabilization itself.

A similar critique can be made of studies of fading induced by prolonged viewing of nonstabilized patterns. Both McKinney (1963) and McFarland (1973) have reported that such perceptions also fade and reappear, with the reappearances becoming simpler in form. It is easy to induce such fading with blurred edges and low contrast between the high and low luminance values in the pattern. Even when the projection of the form is not stabilized on the retina, the gradual changes at the edges and the small overall changes due to the small contrast differences mean that minimal eye movements cannot produce much change at the output of the retinal receptive fields. Cornsweet (1969) demonstrated this by showing that targets with the blurred edges faded out and reappeared while sharp-edged ones did not.

Given these explanations, it would seem unreasonable to assume that the pattern of fading and reappearance, even in the absence of stabilization, reflects basic visual features. Rather, it probably reflects the pattern of eye movements which occur during the fixation upon the pattern. With primarily horizontal drifts and microsaccades, vertical components will reappear more than will horizontal ones. If the movements are vertical, just the reverse should occur. When the movements are random, then any pattern in the reappearance can be noticed, especially if a long enough sample in time is taken.

In conclusion, then, the explanation of stabilized retinal projections based upon coding mechanisms sensitive to changes rather than to steady-state stimulation may be taken as evidence of the need for constant change in order to produce stability in perception. In addition to processing luminance discontinuities, lateral inhibitory mechanisms of the retinal coding systems actually enhance such discontinuities so that they stand out even more than they would in physical measurements. The presence of such enhancement can be considered further evidence of the need for luminance discontinuities to provide stable perception of form.

So far, this has not carried us very far into the perception of form. Assuming that there are luminance discontinuities that are enhanced by lateral inhibition and small eye movements, what are the perceptual consequences? The first that we will consider concerns figure-ground segregation.

FIGURE-GROUND SEGREGATION

If a perceiver naïvely attends to his perceptual experience, he describes that experience as one of objects seen on surfaces or as figures against background. This phenomenal appearance occurs regardless of the complexity or simplicity of the stimulation in the retinal projection. It is considered so basic that this segregation has usually been taken as the starting point of organized perception. Thus, any inhomogeneity in the retinal projection leads to a perceptual segregation of the field into one part called a figure and another part called a ground. These parts are usually separated by a contour which may be said to divide figure from ground, although the contour seems to belong to the figure. Generally, only one of two homogeneous parts of a field may be seen as the figure and the other as the ground; it is the rare case where both would be experienced as figure on ground. Thus, figure-ground segregation may be said to be immediate and self-evident.

The features of figure-ground organization were first studied by Rubin (1921); see Figure 8.4. He noted that the figure has form or shape, whereas the ground is formless. The ground may have form properties but those properties are weaker and less definite. Thus the figure has thinglike qualities whereas the ground appears uniform. The figure appears to be nearer than the ground, and the ground appears to be extended unbroken behind the figure, even though all of the ground cannot be seen. The figure is more easily identified; its color is more impressive; it is more easily connected with meaning, feeling, and esthetic values. The reason camouflage works is that it breaks down the figure-ground relationships which carry the meaning.

In his neurological theory of perceptual and psychological development, Hebb (1949) noted three aspects of figure-ground segregation: a primitive, sensorially determined unity; a nonsensory unity, affected by experience; and the identity of a perceived figure, affected by experience. By primitive unity Hebb meant that segregation from the background which is seen as a direct product of the pattern of sensory excitation and the coding strategies of the visual nervous system. It is an area of homogeneous color and intensity within a sharp boundary which is seen as one, unified, and distinct from its surroundings. As Hebb points out, this segregation is necessary and inevitable for perception.

The nonsensory figure was viewed as one in which the boundaries of a figure are not determined by luminosity discontinuities in the visual field. For

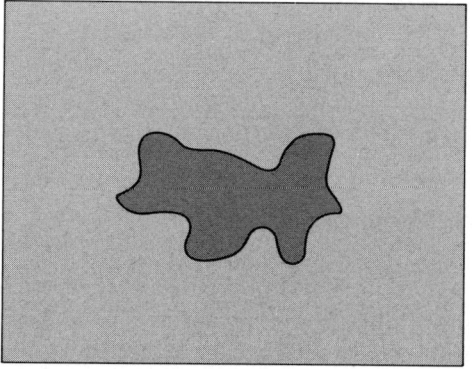

FIGURE 8.4   An example of figure-ground segregation.

Hebb this occurred whenever a perceiver responded selectively to a limited portion of a homogeneous area in the visual field. Hebb's example was that of looking at the middle part of a rope as distinct from the rest of it when one is interested in tying a knot; or when one perceives a foreground in an unbroken landscape. In these cases, no sensory or physical delimitation of figure from ground could be made, and yet there is a segregation of sorts in perceptual experience.

For Hebb the wife-and-mother-in-law reversible figure illustrated a combination of sensory and nonsensory figures (see Figure 8.5). Clearly the figural outlines are sensory in nature. Nevertheless, perceptual organization is controlled by experience and expectation, which involves nonsensory organization. A similar case may be made for looking through a microscope to read neurological sections of brain tissue. Here perceptual organizations are made only after experience with the objects. In some figure-ground organization there is an inevitable component determined by the stimulus structure; in other cases, organization also requires prolonged experience. Thus the properties of nonsensory figures may be affected by experience and other nonsensory factors. In this sense they are not inevitable or necessary for perception.

The third aspect of figural organization which Hebb described is identity. This represents the properties of association or memory inherent in perception. For example, a figure is seen immediately as similar to some figures and dissimilar to others; it falls at once into certain categories and not into others. Thus, identity may be thought of as spontaneous association, since it may occur on the first exposure to an object. An object with identity or thingness is capable of being associated readily with other objects or with some action. A figure which does not possess identity is recalled with great difficulty, or not at all, and may not be recognized or named easily. Moreover, identity is a matter of degree; it depends to a large extent on past experience. Identity can be ob-

FIGURE 8.5   The wife-and-mother-in-law reversible figure (from Boring, 1930).

served to grow, as in situations which have been described by Gibson (1969): the tea taster learning to discriminate taste, or the researcher learning to discriminate among chimpanzees. First, all chimps appear to look alike, and to have similar features, but later one can select among them and call each by name.

Figure-ground unity may not be a primitive and primary process, however. Unless we are quite distant from the figure-ground pattern, a perceiver will not be able to see all of the figure clearly in a single glance. Instead, he will make a number of eye movements to explore the pattern visually. Can there be a primitive segregation of figure from ground if it takes several eye movements to achieve it? Hochberg (1968, 1971a, 1971b) suggests that, in viewing large figures, figure-ground segregation may not result in the perception of a unified figure until the information in several glances has been combined and integrated. The information in each glance would be stored until integration could be achieved. Further, the content in the first glance may determine the direction of the eye movement to get the second glance. In addition, eye movements have to be programmed prior to their execution. Thus a decision, probably based on information seen in peripheral vision (see Chapter 9), is made about where to look next. This determines what information will be brought into foveal view. This pattern of information acquisition suggests a derived segregation of figure from ground as a result of successive views of the stimulus pattern. The process does not in itself imply a learned activity, but it certainly cannot be primitive in the sense of an automatic outcome of the structure of the stimulus pattern.

Figure 8.6 provides an illustration of some of these points. The "impossible figures" show how the function of a contour changes when one looks from one place to another in the pattern. The stimulus components of organization and depth are not specified by the entire configuration, but only by specific fea-

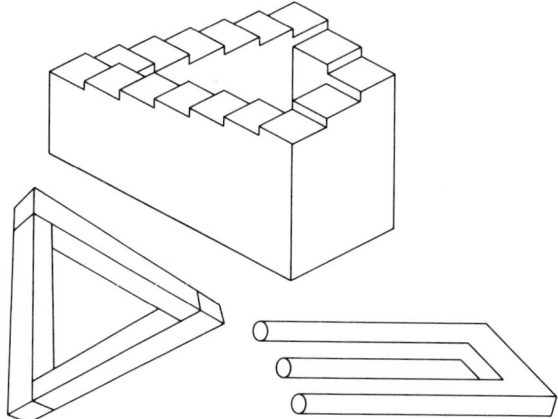

FIGURE 8.6 Several examples of two-dimensional drawings of impossible three-dimensional forms.

tures—local depth cues—which exert their control over small regions. However, form perception must result from an integration of these separate glances into an abstract structure, a construction of what Hochberg calls a schematic map.

Some interesting support for this notion comes from King (1971), who has developed a computer simulation of figure-ground segregation. The program organizes any pattern of two-dimensional line-drawing elements into figures against backgrounds, including properties of "in front of." His program does not have to know the shapes beforehand, nor have any prior experience with the figures, to be able to resolve discontinuities in the two-dimensional visual field into separate figures. It arrives at virtually the same figures that human perceivers describe when shown the same patterns. The principal component of King's model is a shifting center of attention or eye position. If the first look is centered near a discontinuity, this "edge" is tried out as part of the figure. If not, the center of attention shifts until it maps out the contours and interprets them from successive looks.

Hochberg has emphasized this distinction between what is registered in a single glance or fixation and what is represented or integrated from successive glances. He is not arguing that figure-ground segregation cannot occur within a single glance, but rather that in many circumstances perceptual organization, including figures against backgrounds, must depend on the information picked up from several glances. In this sense, figure-ground segregation cannot be primitive, as Hebb thought.

We will see the impact of Hochberg's distinction in nearly every one of the remaining chapters. It is central to visual search (Chapter 9), to selection and recognition (Chapters 10 and 11), and especially to the perception of space (Chapters 12 through 15).

We have already considered one other aspect of this in the previous chapter on information-processing models. There we noted that the visual image representation must be more than a representation of the luminance discontinuities contained in the current fixation of the eye. Rather, it has to be an integration of the information from several fixations, in just the way Hochberg argues that the accumulation of information from successive glances is needed to segregate figure from ground.

Although a segregation of figure from ground, as Rubin described it, represents a perceptual organization, it is only the very first of far more complex aspects of the perception of form.

FIGURAL ORGANIZATION

The visual field is perceived as organized into objects with relative positions. The features are seen as grouped in some way, with some seen as going together while others are perceived as part of larger structures. This superordinate organization seems to take place spontaneously. According to Gestalt theory, the tendency for any two elements in the visual field to be grouped into larger units depends upon certain "relations" between them, and it is these relations that became codified into the Gestalt laws.

While the Gestalt theorists first asked this question over sixty years ago, we are still posing it today: How can we account for the organization of perception? The cortex receives information about luminance discontinuities, which may be represented as discrete visual features. How are these combined into one particular organization rather than some other one? What are the rules?

Gestalt Organizational Laws

The Gestaltists proposed a number of laws of organization which describe perception as the result of the organizational processes of the brain and the relationships among the elements making up the stimulus. More precisely, they argued that the perceived organization arose from the impact of these elements on the representational processes within the nervous system, which the Gestalt psychologists saw as made up of field forces. This neurological model has fallen by the wayside, but their guiding principles are still central to our understanding of form perception.

Figure 8.7 illustrates the major organizational laws of Gestalt theory (Koffka, 1935). These include the laws of proximity, similarity, continuity, common fate, and closure. The law of proximity says that some groups are

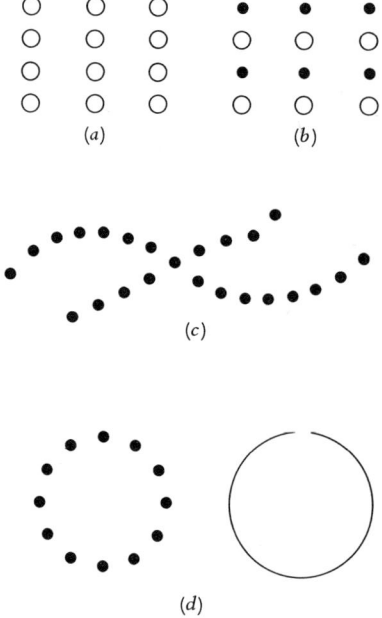

FIGURE 8.7   A number of examples of Gestalt laws of perceptual organization.

formed from elements which are either spatially or temporally closer to one another. Thus, in part (*a*) of Figure 8.7 we see three vertical arrays of dots because the vertical spacing is smaller than the horizontal. The law of similarity says that some groups are formed from elements that are more similar to one another. Thus, in part (*b*) of Figure 8.7 we see horizontal rows because, even though the elements are equally spaced, the elements in the horizontal rows are similar while those in the vertical rows are not. The law of good continuation says that a vector of a set of elements will determine the direction of the next element. This can be seen in part (*c*) where there is a particular direction in which the next element would be considered "good" and other directions would not be considered "good." The law of closure says that parts of a figure not present will be filled in to complete the figure. This is seen in part (*d*). This law is similar to good continuation, although it adds the property of filling in. It also suggests why we can denote a continuous line by closely spaced dots as in part (*c*) of the figure. The law of common fate says that objects which move or change together are seen as a unit or with a common fate. The law reflects the great power of relative movement as an organizing force to perception, as we will see in Chapter 14. The laws of continuation, closure, and common fate are often grouped together as laws of good figure, or the Pragnanz principle (Koffka, 1935).

All of these laws predict that certain perceptions will occur rather than others. For example, in the top of Figure 8.8 we may organize the lines in a number of different ways, only one of which satisfies the Gestalt laws. Thus, while other organizations are logically possible, we usually see it as it is shown in the middle of Figure 8.8.

The problem with the conception of good figure and with the other laws is that there are no adequate means for specifying the variables which underlie the organizations predicted by the laws. Thus, the laws appear to be descriptions of perception rather than laws of perception. Nevertheless, it is quite clear that the laws work in an intuitive sense and they appear to have rather direct practical applications, as in their use in the construction of camouflage or embedded figures.

In one of the exceptions to the lack of evidence, Beck (for example,

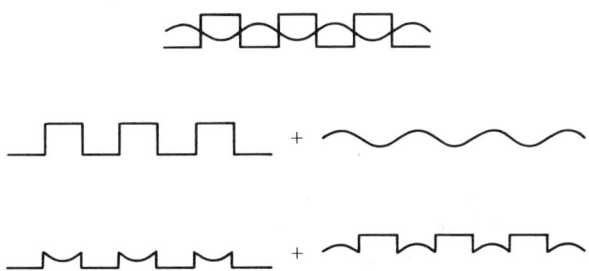

FIGURE 8.8   An example of the organizational properties of a pattern. Of several logically possible perceptual organizations, only one is actually seen.

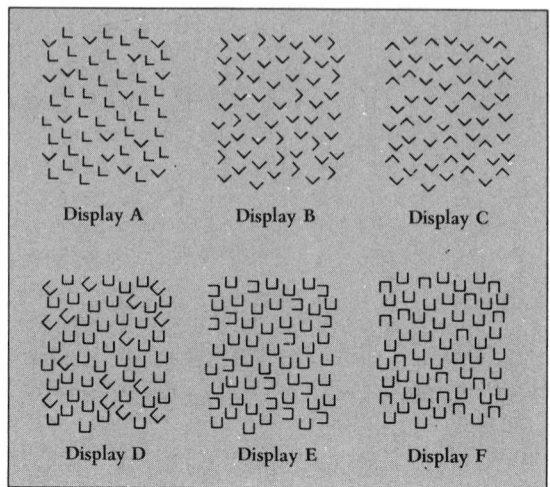

FIGURE 8.9   An example of a stimulus display to study the role of form similarity (from Beck, 1972).

1967, 1972) has been pursuing an important program of research on some of the determinants of perceptual groupings, especially those concerning the similarity among elements. He has used relatively simple shapes, such as those shown in Figure 8.9. If the perceiver is asked to count the number of V shapes in the top panels, or the U shapes in the bottom, any process that facilitated the organization of Vs or Us as different from the rotated shapes should speed up the counting process. Beck has shown that speed of counting, and by assumption therefore grouping, is fastest on the left and slowest on the right for the displays in Figure 8.9. This would imply that organization is a function of similarity of the slopes of the line elements.

Beck has also argued that this property of slope difference is picked up in peripheral as well as central vision, as a function of the discrimination of stimulus differences prior to a narrowing of attention. This makes perceptual grouping primarily an acuity task—being able to notice differences throughout the visual field that will help organize the forms. Anything that will increase peripheral acuity will help in this organization. Apparently slope differences among the constituted elements are more easily noticed than the overall orientation of the forms, for example.

In one test of this Beck (1972) presented in one condition four forms, one at each of the corners of an imaginary square about 5 degrees on a side. One of the forms was different, and the perceiver had to locate and describe the odd one. As would be expected, the perceiver was best at this when the odd one differed in slope from the other three. Here the perceiver must direct his attention to each of the forms, and he has no way of knowing the location of the odd one. In another condition, only one form was presented, which might be at any one of the four locations. No differences in accuracy of describing the form were found. Beck argues that in this case the luminance discontinuities direct the attention to the form, since there is nothing elsewhere in the visual field. Thus, no further segregation processes are needed, and no difficulty is encountered in naming the form.

Thus, Beck argues that grouping occurs over the entire retina to the extent that there are differences in the stimulus elements which can be noticed before any detailed analysis of them is carried out. We will notice this distinction between peripheral location of figures and a central identification of them again in the next chapter, since it plays a critical role in visual search processes, not unlike what Beck is describing.

Perhaps the greater contribution of the Gestalt psychologists was in their isolation of a unit of analysis. The name Gestalt comes from the notion of the Whole, that which is given by the relations of the elements. In this sense, the whole has unique properties of its own, ones that are not merely given by the sum of the properties of the elements. Moreover, frequently the properties of the whole have no relationship to those of the parts and cannot be predicted from them (and vice versa). For example, in Figure 8.10 the four round black dots have no squareness in them, yet together—and in a certain relationship to one another—they make a square. Similarly, the fact that the units making the square may be triangles or circles does not change the squareness. Thus, it is the patterns or relations of the parts which contribute the essential quality of the whole. The crucial test of a Gestalt quality, therefore, is transposition—replacing the elements with other elements while retaining the quality of the whole. If transposition is successful, the relationships are independent of the elements. The example of the square is a transposition in the spatial domain. In the temporal domain a melody can be transposed into a key in which all notes are changed although the melody remains the same.

FIGURE 8.10 An example of transposition in which the elements of a pattern can be interchanged without affecting the whole.

Informational Aspects of Figures

In recent years it has become clear that our understanding of the perception of figures could not progress past the descriptive Gestalt laws without quantification of some aspect of figures. Attneave (1954) provided such an analysis by applying the techniques of Information Theory (see Chapter 7) to figures in order to understand their stimulus qualities. To do this, Attneave considers perception as an information-handling or processing system, noting that much information perceived by the organism is redundant; that sensory events are interdependent in space and time. Thus, if we know the state of a number of receptors at some point in time, we can make better than chance inferences about higher states and subsequent states.

Attneave first noted in his analysis of figures that the stimulation from objects in the field is highly redundant. By this he means that portions of the field are highly predictable from other portions of the field. We have already considered this property at the sensory level in Chapter 3. In this present context, Attneave illustrates this point by the following experiment. Suppose a picture containing a black ink bottle on the corner of a brown desk in front of a white background is divided up into a very large number of cells (see Figure 8.11). And suppose a perceiver is asked to start at any cell, note its color, and then to guess the color of the next unit. In some sense the task is like describing the picture in a temporal sequence and, therefore, is similar to scanning process. If the perceiver's error score is significantly less than chance, this implies that his responses can take into account the redundancies among the picture elements.

The simplest way to understand the task is to follow a typical perceiver as he performs. He starts in the lower left-hand corner and guesses whether each cell is white, brown, or black. First he may go across the bottom row, then up to the next row. We can keep track of the errors he makes. The first guess in the lower left-hand corner will, or course, be chance since he does not know what color to start with. But then when he guesses white and finds out it is correct, he will probably continue to guess white until he hits the first brown cell. After an initial error or two, he will continue to say brown and be correct. Now he may assume that the second row is similar to the first. The response pattern will be similar except that the original white errors will disappear.

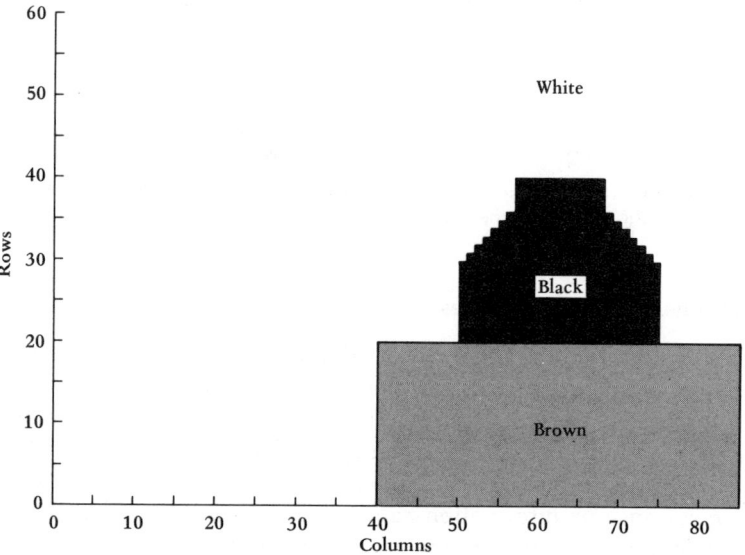

FIGURE 8.11   An example of redundancy in pictures (from Attneave, 1954).

What we will find is that errors will pile up only in the first two rows and that gradually the perceiver will be correct for the white-brown transition until he hits the corner of the desk, and then he will begin to make errors again.

According to Attneave, this shows that redundancy results both from an area of homogeneous color or brightness, and from a contour of homogeneous direction or slope. Thus, one may suggest that information or uncertainty is concentrated along contours—regions where color changes abruptly, and at those points in the contour at which its own direction changes most rapidly—at angles or peaks of curvature. Objects which are similar in contour but unlike in other ways may nevertheless appear remarkably similar. This may be related to a Gestalt quality. This is brought out by the fact that artists can sketch the essence of a thing with a very few lines.

To demonstrate this point, Attneave asked perceivers to represent a figure with changing contours by using ten dots only. This is illustrated in Figure 8.12. He found that most points were placed on regions where the contour differed most from a straight line, that is, the concentration of information was at points where the contour changes were most rapid. In this way we can

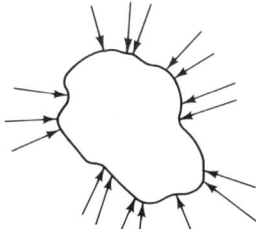

FIGURE 8.12   The high information location of an irregular form as defined by where perceivers specify defining points (from Attneave, 1954).

represent common objects by first indicating points at which contours change direction, and secondly connecting appropriate ones with a straight line. This minimal representation can be seen in another way by examining Figure 8.13.

Let us return to Figure 8.11, and to the bottle on the corner of the desk, and continue to follow the perceiver. He will make some errors at the edge of the ink bottle but will soon learn the pattern. This suggests that there is redundancy in the pattern also. The step pattern is symmetrical, so that the right contour is predictable from the left contour by simple reversal. Thus, the perceiver will cease to make errors on the right-hand side, given his knowledge of the left-hand side. This is another type of redundancy. Many of the Gestalt principles of perceptual organization pertain essentially to the distribution of information in the picture. For example, a "good" figure is a figure with a high degree of internal redundancy. Any given part is predictable from previously seen parts. The grouping laws, such as similarity, good continuation, proximity, and common fate all refer to arrangements of elements that reduce uncer-

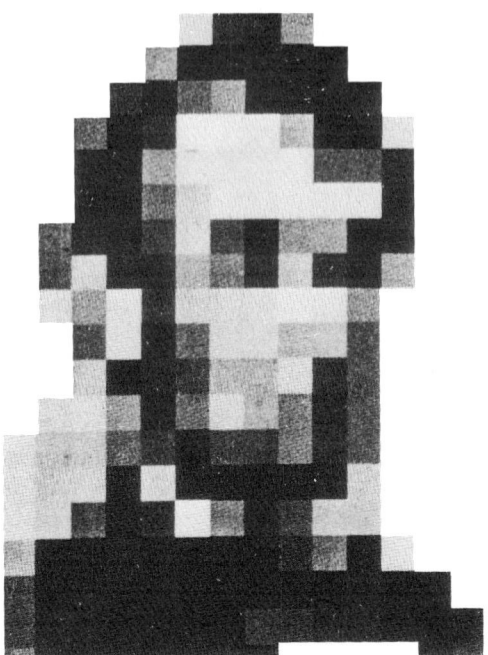

FIGURE 8.13   A computer-constructed picture, using only squares of different shading to represent a familiar face. If you have trouble recognizing it, hold it back, or defocus your gaze somewhat. If you still cannot recognize him, solve the anagram NNLLCIO (courtesy of Bell Telephone Laboratories).

tainty. In this sense, the perceptual system groups those portions of the input which share the same information. As a general statement, one may say that any source of physical invariance constitutes a source of redundancy for an organism capable of abstracting the invariance and utilizing it properly.

A related approach is taken by Hochberg and McAlister (1953). They suggested that figural goodness may be inversely proportional to the amount of information necessary to describe or specify a figure. This implies that perception or organization of a stimulus array is related to its information content. Further, of all possible organizations, the most probable perceptual result is one which involves the least amount of information, that is, the greatest redundancy. Figure 8.14 is seen as two overlapping rectangles in this formulation, because less information is required to specify that organization than when it is seen as five odd shapes. For example, to specify two rectangles, one needs eight line segments and points of intersection; eight angles and angles of intersection, or two line segments plus regularity, plus the angle of interconnection and the point of intersection. To specify it as five figures, one needs sixteen different line segments and sixteen angles.

In order to test these notions Hochberg and McAlister performed an experiment in which perceivers were shown the four outline drawings in Figure

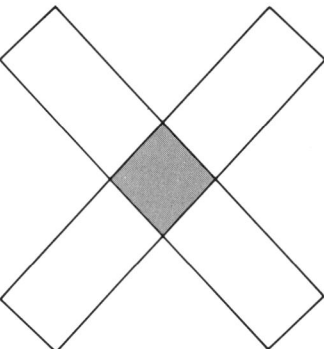

FIGURE 8.14   An example of how figural information may determine which of several possible organizations will be perceived (from Hochberg and McAlister, 1953).

8.15. They viewed each of the figures separately, and while they watched, signal tones were presented at random intervals. The perceivers had to rate at each tone whether the figure was seen as more two-dimensional or more three-dimensional. The figures which were most symmetrical (for example, Z in Figure 8.15) were seen least often as three-dimensional patterns. This suggests once again that the perceptual system organizes simple figures according to their information content and distribution.

      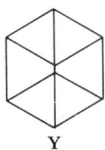   

W   X   Y   Z

FIGURE 8.15   Stimulus forms that would be seen as two- or three-dimensional figures (from Hochberg and McAlister, 1953).

Hochberg has recently carried this analysis further. Neither his earlier work nor that of Attneave provides any quantification of the Gestalt laws into statements which will predict perceptual organization from physical measurements of the stimulus. Since the most important of the Gestalt laws is that of Pragnanz, Hochberg followed upon the work of Kopfermann (1930) in developing what he called a minimum principle—of two possible organizations, the one seen will be the simpler one.

In one application, Hochberg and Brooks (1960) attempted to predict the perceptual outcomes for some simple line drawings (see Figure 8.16)—would they be seen as two-dimensional or three-dimensional? A group of perceivers first looked at a number of figures and rated whether they appeared more two-dimensional or more three-dimensional. Hochberg and Brooks then examined a number of physical measures of these drawings, such as the number of lines, angles, discontinuities, crossings, inside corners, and so on. In this way, they

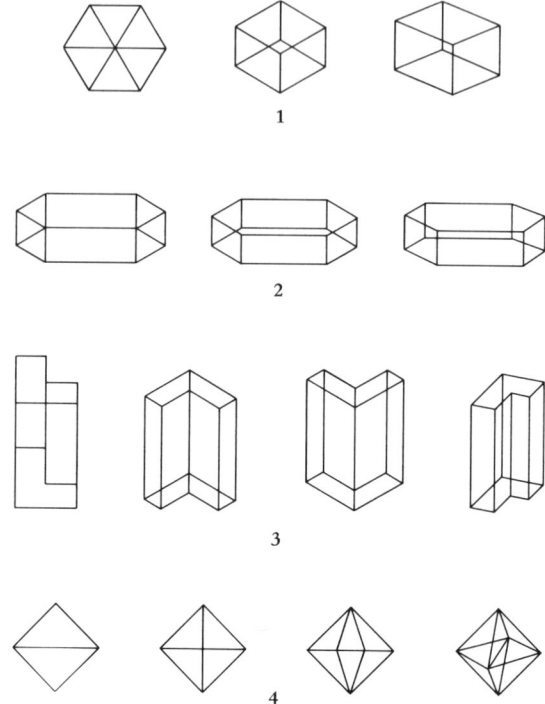

FIGURE 8.16   Examples of stimulus forms that can be seen as two- or as three-dimensional figures (from Hochberg and Brooks, 1960).

found a good fit between the perceivers' reports and a formula which took account of combinations of number of angles, lines, and discontinuities. Thus empirically, as the complexity of a two-dimensional picture increased, it was more likely to be seen as a three-dimensional rather than a two-dimensional picture. To demonstrate that this was not simply a post hoc analysis, they then showed a new set of pictures to a new set of perceivers and used their formula to predict the perceived organization. Figure 8.17 shows their results with the new set of pictures, which clearly supports their interpretation. It is not clear whether this procedure will work with any set of stimuli, nor how to generalize the formula to nonline drawings. But within the confines of this study the result is quite impressive.

Microgenetic Development of Contours

While our discussions in Chapter 6 on temporal processes make it quite likely that all perceptual events take time to occur, relatively little work has been done on the phenomenological characteristics of these temporal events. In their microgenetic theory, Werner and Wapner (1952) argued that contours should take time to be perceived, and that this development can be observed.

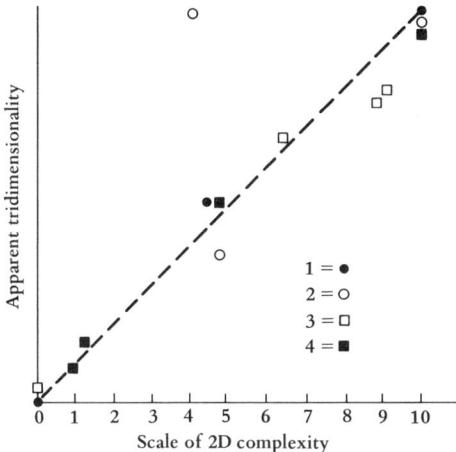

FIGURE 8.17 Perceived three dimensionality as a function of the simplicity of the two-dimensional representations (data taken from Hochberg and Brooks, 1960).

The development can be interrupted if other contours are presented at about the same time. Several interesting experiments demonstrate this.

Cheatham (1952) tried to determine how long it takes a stimulus to be perceived, and how the contours develop during that time. He presented a stimulus field which contained either a circle, a triangle, a square, or a diamond for 100 milliseconds, followed by a large masking field, presented some time later, also for 100 milliseconds. The response measured was transition points between three zones of phenomenal development. The first was the time for the perceiver to report the change from a simple brightening in the central part of the field to the appearance of the first part of a contour. This latency measured how long it took from the onset of the stimulus to the first inkling of contour that the perceiver could discriminate. The second was the latency of the change from a partial or incomplete contour to a complete or total contour (the figural development time). The results show that latency and development time are inversely related to the luminance of the first stimulus field. Latency did not vary for the initial appearance of contour as a function of the shape of the stimulus, but it was important for the development of complete contour—the circle and the square were more rapidly perceived than the triangle or diamond. Phenomenologically the perceivers reported that the sides of figures appeared before the angles and that hue was not perceived until the complete contour was formed. This is a simple demonstration of the sequence of events in the perception of simple forms, and supports the assumption that perceptual processes take time.

Simple interactions in this sense have also been shown for figural stimuli such as a disk and annulus (see Chapter 6). If a black disk is presented in a white field for approximately 25 milliseconds followed by a black ring which surrounds the disk at various interstimulus intervals, most perceivers report that, for some critical interstimulus interval, the annulus has a light center rather than a dark center. In explaining this phenomenon Werner (1935) suggested that the perception of an object takes a finite time to develop, and that, if the contour cannot be formed during that time, then the figure will not be perceived. If in the above situation the process of forming the contour of the disk has been identified with the inception of the whole process of constructing the ring, it is used in the latter process. Therefore the inner contour is usurped, so to speak, by the annulus. Consequently, the center of the annulus is identified with the background and seen as white. Werner uses the notion of contour development to explain why the maximum masking occurs with a delay of about 50 milliseconds rather than with simultaneous presentation of disk and annulus. If the annulus comes at the same time as the disk, the inner contour does not develop at all and the entire area is black. Thus there must be some development in order for interference to occur. If the annulus comes first, the contour can develop and the disk cannot interfere with it.

THE REPRESENTATION OF FORM

Sutherland (1974) has suggested a list of facts that any successful understanding of form perception must encompass. While we will not review or add documentation to all the facts and details, consideration of some of these items is quite useful to maintain perspective about the goals of this chapter. Specifically, Sutherland is interested in explaining what types of central representations of objects in the environment are created and maintained. Thus, he is asking the same types of questions as those posed in the previous chapter, except for the narrower focus on form and pattern.

Properties of the Perception of Form

The first fact suggested by Sutherland concerns the invariance of perception over retinal position. A representation cannot entirely be anchored in the specific retinal location over which it was first registered. We can easily recognize a form as familiar regardless of the part of the retina it covers now or covered in a previous presentation. The only limitation is the acuity of the retinal region. The important point is that a theory or model of form perception should not be specific to the retinal location on which the form is presented (see Hochberg, 1971, pp. 449–451, for a discussion of this point).

The second fact concerns invariance over size. Most pattern recognition tasks do not depend on specific object size or retinal size. Human beings and animals usually give the same response to a form regardless of its size. This is not to say that we cannot learn an absolute size discrimination, but we rarely need to. As we will see in the next section, we are very sensitive to relative size, and have little difficulty discriminating between the sizes of two objects or patterns, but the actual sizes themselves are irrelevant. Thus, a model of form perception cannot restrict representations of form to specific sizes or be anchored in the sizes of the retinal image.

The same comments apply to brightness and to color as to size. We can distinguish absolute color and brightness, but we rarely do. Occasionally we have some difficulty in recognizing negatives of black and white or color photographs, although it is not clear where this loss in invariance occurs.

There are a number of stimulus transformations which are treated as equivalent. For example, octopuses (Sutherland, 1962) and young children (Liberman, et al., 1971) have great difficulty discriminating between left-right reversals of form. Thus for these perceivers, such transformations must be seen and organized as equivalent. Nearly all beginning readers have some difficulty because they reverse letters and even the order of letter sequences. This behavior disappears in most children by eight or nine years of age. Most animals, children, and adults can discriminate between up-down reversals. Turning a form upside-down rarely leaves it equivalent even though a mirror image transformation does.

We have already considered that there has to be some representational device to capitalize on redundancy, symmetry, and other types of predictability in patterns and forms. In Chapter 3 we showed how the visual system has evolved sensory coding processes which accomplish this to some extent, and in this chapter we have seen some illustrations of such processes at much higher levels. Thus the representation of form must be at least partially structured by rules that govern predictability, so that all the elements in a pattern do not have to be represented independently. In this sense, predictability rules are stored as part of the representation.

Another fact presented by Sutherland concerned individuation and category membership. Differentiation is a major component of perceptual learning. For example, there is substantial evidence that wine tasters can differentiate hundreds and perhaps even thousands of varieties of wine. This skill is learned since, to the novice, most wines are indistinguishable. Eleanor Gibson (1969) has provided a comprehensive discussion of this aspect of perceptual learning. Many perceptual tasks show large practice effects in which the perceiver becomes progressively better in discriminating the characteristics of the stimuli from other stimuli, from backgrounds, or from noise.

There may also be more complex aspects to this type of learning. For example, deGroot (1965) gave chess players a brief look at a chess game in progress and asked them to remember the location of each of the pieces on the board. Chess masters could do this easily even with twenty to twenty-five pieces, but chess novices could place only six to eight pieces correctly. A master must have had a set of rules that he had learned that permitted him to maintain a representation in memory made up of many more elements than in the immediate memory span. When the pieces are placed on the board at random, that is, not as a result of a sequence of realistic moves, then neither the master or the novice can remember more than six to eight positions. Thus the two perceivers did not differ in their familiarity with chess pieces but with the organization of the pieces into patterns. The master has rules that must be part of his representation of the board that he had only briefly glimpsed. Further, he can identify viewed complex stimuli only because he has learned parts of the representation beforehand and had it ready when perception occurred.

The last fact we will consider concerns segmentation. We have already discussed figure-ground organization as a segmentation process and the Gestalt laws as descriptions of organization. These laws presently are not broad enough to account for all of the organization in perception, however. Stimulation is messy in the sense that the two-dimensional patterns on the retina have many features that overlap, are mixed up, and are interrelated. Not all of them go together even when they overlap or touch. Thus when two lines cross, it is not clear whether they should be structured as the two lines of the "X", as one line passing in front of another—each part of a different figure, as two "v"s touching at their points, and so forth. How these patterns are segmented will determine what is seen and, probably even more important, what is remembered and later recognized.

Models of Form Perception

Sutherland's list is by no means exhaustive although it does cover the principal aspects of pattern recognition which must be encompassed by any theory or model. None of the theories or models to date are particularly successful in meeting these demands. We will consider three very general models—a template model, a visual feature model, and a constructive model. It is beyond the scope of this book to examine these theories in detail, but we do want to point out a few salient features of each. Corcoran (1971) has a more detailed discussion.

The template model of pattern perception assumes that the representations of patterns are structurally identical to the stimulus patterns. Recognition consists of matching the representation of present stimulation to stored templates to find the one that is the closest match. Neisser (1967) discusses several versions of this model and presents some empirical and logical objections to it. This model fares rather poorly in handling the requirements of Sutherland's list. Invariances over retinal position, size, brightness, and color are all very difficult to retain with templates and the equivalences present difficulty as well. Since templates must be matched in "canonical" form, that is, in one particular scale and orientation, an initial normalization process is an essential feature of a template model. It is even more difficult for template models to deal with segmentation, learned differentiation, and redundancy coding. All of these suggest that perception involves a more active process than template matching.

Visual feature models have grown in popularity (see, for example, the work of Eleanor Gibson, 1969), almost as a reaction to the failure of template models. Feature models describe perception as an analytic process. The visual representation of a form or pattern is analyzed into features which are then stored, possibly even in a list form. As we develop perceptually, these feature lists become larger and larger as a result of our increasing ability to make discriminations. The features of new incoming stimulation are then compared with this stored list on the basis of its features. A match occurs when there is a close correspondence between the features of the new stimulus and those of a particular list.

This type of model has been applied successfully in the analysis of the distinctive features of phonemes (for example, Chomsky and Halle, 1969). Gibson has extended the analysis to the visual recognition of letters of the alphabet. She suggests that all letters can be described in terms of twelve features (for example, vertical line segments, horizontal line segments, closed loops, and so forth). For recognition to occur, a stimulus letter is analyzed as to its features, and this list is checked against the feature list for all twenty-six letters until the best match is found. Although here the analysis is an a priori one, and not empirical, there has been some empirical support as well.

The visual feature model is able to account for more of Sutherland's requirements although serious problems remain. Specifically, what is missing from most feature models is the description of relationships among features. For the feature list system to be useful, the number of different features must be finite. It is critical, therefore, that information about the relationships between features be coded and retained, and somehow used in later processing.

Constructive models, the third alternative, also grew out of the failures of the template model. The constructive model might best be understood as a feature model with relationships included. But more important than the simple addition of relations of features, constructive models usually describe perception and the recognition of pattern as more active processes. In general, constructive theorists (for example, Neisser, 1967; Hochberg, 1968, 1970; Kolers, 1970, 1972) propose that the perceiver first forms an abstract representation of the stimulus pattern, guided by the organizational properties in the stimulus. The perceiver then makes hypotheses based on expectations about what the stimulus might be. The hypotheses take into account the rules of similarity, redundancy, and probability which the perceiver has formed in past experience. In the construction process, one particular pattern of segmentation might be tried and rejected when it results in an inconsistent, incomplete, or improbable representation. Then other hypotheses or constructions would be tried until one is found which matches most of the incoming information. The one that works best will be the abstract construction that is stored as a representation of the stimulus. The invariances and equivalences may now be explained on the basis of the evolution of the nervous system or learning over the life span of the organism. Perceptual learning would be the addition of specific details to the construction so that slight variations of categorical representations can be differentiated.

None of these models has been totally successful and, at this point, none can be eliminated. Our discussion should serve to emphasize the tasks remaining before we can say that we understand the perception of form.

SUMMARY

This chapter continued our information-processing analysis into the problem of the perception of form. We first considered some evidence for the need to have inhomogeneities in stimulation as a prerequisite for form or pattern to be perceived. In the absence of luminance or temporal discontinuities, perception quickly fails. To show this, we look first at some research with homogeneous fields, called Ganzfelds, and then at work with stabilized visual projections on the retina. In both cases, the analyses showed that perception ceases, due most likely to a failure of coding in the retina itself.

Given that some inhomogeneity is necessary, we then turned to the most basic organization that occurs—a segregation of these inhomogeneities into figures seen against backgrounds. We noted several meanings implied in this segregation, and discussed in some detail arguments that such segregations normally do not occur in a single glance but are the result of integrations of several fixations over different parts of the figure or scene. This topic served as an introduction to consideration of figural organization, especially the Gestalt laws of relationships among elements of figures. A number of laws were illustrated, and one line of research by Beck on the law of similarity is discussed in some detail.

We noted that the Gestalt laws were not sufficient for a complete understanding of form perception. To further illustrate this, we explored several attempts to use informational descriptions of organization; especially by Attneave and by Hochberg. These focused upon the development of measures of redundancy or simplicity—arguing first that information is concentrated on contours, edges, and changes, and second, that what will be seen will be the simplest organization of all those possible from the elements present in the scene.

The chapter closed with a more formal consideration of some of the facts of pattern recognition that must be covered by a successful model of the perception of form. These facts were used then to look briefly at three different views, a template, a feature, and a construction model. Although none of these are entirely sufficient to account for most aspects of form perception, they represent most of the avenues of current thinking.

Readings

The most complete source book on the perception of form is by Zusne (1970). Hochberg (1971a, 1971b) covers a vast range of topics on form and pattern. The original presentation of the Gestalt laws is by Koffka (1935) and has not been improved upon in nearly forty years, although Hochberg (1973) has an excellent discussion. A few more specialized books have appeared recently. Corcoran (1971) has an excellent introduction to pattern recognition research, and Kolers and Eden (1968), as well as Dodwell (1971), have collected some important, although usually advanced, research and theoretical articles on this topic. Neisser (1967) has one of the best analyses of the models of pattern recognition.

chapter
9
selection in visual search

INTRODUCTION

The selectivity of perception has been recognized since the beginning of experimental psychology. The obvious fact of its existence, however, has not made its explanation easier. Part of the difficulty has been the wide range of phenomena that show some sort of selectivity, and part has been caused by the assumption that, for selectivity to occur, all stimuli would first have to be identified, and the unwanted ones discarded without intruding into awareness. This assumption has caused more theoretical trouble than any other in perception because it implies a mechanism which acts as a censor in selecting what will enter consciousness and what will not.

The very nature of selectivity implies information loss. We have already observed that information loss occurs through transduction and recording of stimulation as it is communicated through the visual system. At every step of the way, beginning with the earliest receptor processes, some aspects of stimulation are transmitted at the expense of others. Those selected are represented in a new form—sometimes enhanced—but often in such a way that recovery of the prior form is impossible. This is accompanied by an irreversible loss of information not present in the new representation.

Because selectivity has broad meaning, it must be understood in different ways depending on the particular information involved, and the particular processes and tasks which provide the context. We have already examined those aspects involved in the establishment of a representation of visual stimulation both in terms of its spatial properties (Chapters 2 and 3) and its temporal properties (Chapter 6). This chapter will focus on the direction and control of the movements of our eyes to locate stimuli of potential interest. In the next two chapters, we will discuss selectivity within a single fixation, and the recognition of objects and features within and across fixations. All of these topics are so intertwined that it is difficult to provide explanations for one without referring to the others. For example, if we are searching the environment, our eyes follow one pattern of movements; if we are searching a list for a letter or a word, they follow a different pattern; and if we are scanning a page for meaning, they follow still another pattern. Thus, the movement between fixations is not independent of the information taken in during the fixations—these two aspects of selectivity are closely intertwined.

CONCEPTION OF VISUAL SEARCH PROCESSES

The movements of our eyes and head provide a mechanism for gross selection among visual stimuli. Clearly the position of the eyes at any point in time will determine the pattern of stimulation on the two retinal projections and, therefore, the stimuli which are potential objects of interest. In the natural environment, we want to look *at* what we are looking *for*. Thus, the variables which underlie visual search are major determinants of selection in normal perception.

A number of different visual search tasks have been intensively studied. In one task, perceivers are asked to search for a target in a large, sometimes cluttered field, a task much like looking for a face in a crowd. Frequently the search is for only one or two targets with little or no concern for nontarget objects. This task requires the selection of one stimulus while ignoring others. An interesting variant of this task is performed by the proofreader who must search for errors in spelling as well as erroneous words embedded in a background of continuous correct text. The proofreader's goal is to search for error, not to read for meaning. The task changes when meaning is involved, for example, when trying to find your name in a newspaper article.

These tasks are quite different from reading, our most common visual search task. Reading can be understood as a search for meaning in which we not only need to locate many more targets, but at the same time construct an integrated story. In this sense, the target is the story, not the letters or the words they spell. But to "find" the story, some of the letters and some of the words have to be identified. Obviously, the determinants of this type of search are much more complex than for the reconnaissance task. Looking at pictures is another task, one that may be similar to reading when conceived in terms of search.

Several common threads run through each of the search tasks mentioned above. The most important is the distinction between what is in foveal as compared to peripheral vision at any given instant. The objects in central vision can be identified in detail, permitting the perceiver to determine whether it is the target being sought. But since that determination usually will be negative (otherwise the search ends), the perceiver will have to shift his gaze to another part of the visual field. Presumably he decides where to look next largely on the basis of information available in peripheral vision. This information cannot be in fine detail because pattern acuity has dropped 50 percent for an object located only 1 degree from the center of the fovea and, for one 8 degrees from the center, it is only 15 percent of maximum (Riggs, 1965). But different kinds of information can be utilized besides fine detail. For example, an object in motion is important information and may draw an eye movement, even when that moving object is seen substantially far out in the periphery, and the object itself cannot be identified. We shall see later how other stimulus dimensions can be noticed even when they occur well into the periphery.

Thus, there appear to be two components to the search process occurring at roughly the same time—an identification process of the parts of the retinal projection falling on the fovea, and a decision process concerning the direction of the next eye movement, based on information from the periphery. Can these two tasks be performed at the same time? Do they interfere with one another? How far into the periphery can information be and still be useful? How do we sort out the vast amount of peripheral information available at any given moment?

One view relating these two different processes has been proposed by Neisser (1967). He suggested that objects could not be identified visually until they were segmented—that is, until the entire visual field was divided into figures on backgrounds (see Chapter 8). Neisser called this segmentation a "preattentive" process, suggesting that it is global and wholistic, while subsequent processes may focus on specific aspects of figures for further analysis. Presumably the preattentive processes would be spatially parallel so that the entire visual field could be processed simultaneously. These processes would be used primarily to direct focal attention but they would also be important in directing or guiding immediate bodily motions such as orienting responses and locomotion. For example, walking or driving an automobile frequently does not require detailed attention to the visual world around us. Instead, we respond to some objects directly, without recognition. It is this type of process to which Beck (1972) referred in his analysis of figural organization based upon similarity (see Chapter 8).

When an important aspect of the environment is segmented, then focal attention can occur, either by a shift in a position of the eyes or by a narrowing of attention. Focal attention operates on the important aspects of the field segregated by the preattentive processes. It is focused because attention is concentrated on only one aspect of stimulus information at a time. As a consequence, analyses may be performed, or figures may be constructed using the information previously extracted. The constructions may result in identification (for example, it is a circle), in description of the attributes (it is green and edible), or even in a negative statement (it is not an apple).

Preattentive processes serve to isolate and locate objects in the visual field. There is no further specification of the properties of such objects beyond that given by the visual features themselves. Thus, one region of the field might be segregated according to color (one might be green and another red), but not according to shape (for example, not one a square and the other a circle). The latter discrimination requires further processing beyond what the preattentive mechanisms alone can provide. Thus, Neisser's distinction between preattentive and focal attention is a useful heuristic device. It permits us to be more explicit in separating some of the control function of eye movements from the identification components of target search. We shall consider some further evidence of this distinction throughout the next few chapters, but more research still needs to be focused on the conceptualization of search processes.

VISUAL ACUITY DURING EYE MOVEMENTS

In considering visual search, we are primarily concerned with the movements which reposition the eyes. In Chapter 2, we mentioned the various eye-movement systems, their controlling processes, and the stimuli which give rise to them. Head and body movements may also cause displacements of the eyes with respect to the visual world around us, independent of eye movements or in addition to them. Of the various types of eye movements noted in Chapter 2, saccadic movements, and to a lesser extent pursuit movements, are the ones most relevant to the problem of visual search.

The typical stimulus for a saccadic movement is a sudden displacement of an object in the visual field. The eye will then shift to a new position that projects the object onto the fovea again. This is most probable when the object had been the center of fixation, so that its projection had fallen on the fovea, but a saccade may also be initiated if a nonfixated object is suddenly displaced. Saccadic eye movements can also be considered voluntary since an observer can initiate them when he wishes to look at some other part of a stationary visual field. This is the typical pattern in visual search. It is more difficult to study the temporal characteristics of the voluntary saccades, since we have no way of knowing when the command to begin such a movement is initiated.

The latency and speed of saccadic eye movements can be studied precisely (see Alpern, 1962, 1971) by moving the fixation point and noting subsequent changes. The latency of movement is quite long — about 180 to 250 milliseconds will elaspe between stimulus displacement and the initation of an eye movement. However, if the perceiver has prior knowledge of the time and direction of the shift, he can start his movement somewhat faster. The estimate of one-fifth of a second is probably more representative of real life. Once initiated, the movement itself is very fast. For example, only about one-tenth of a second is needed for a 40-degree movement (400 degrees per second). Velocities are faster for larger movements, approaching 1000 degrees per second for a 90-degree shift. The movement time for a return sweep after reading a line of print is about 50 milliseconds, and is relatively independent of the length of the line.

Saccadic eye movements are ballistic movements — like those of bullets or rockets — in that their path and distance are completely determined prior to the actual motion. Just as the path of a bullet is specified by the direction in which the gun is pointing and the initial force of the propelling charge, the path of a saccadic movement is determined by a program which issues efferent commands to the muscles to move the eyes to a new fixation. Thus, once programmed, a saccadic eye movement will proceed to its destination unchanged, even if new visual information is added after the programming but before the movement starts.

This fact has been demonstrated by Westheimer (1954). He had a viewer fixate a spot. This spot was then moved to a new location and then returned to its original position after 40 milliseconds. If the eye movements were not ballistic, the return information could have been utilized, and the eye would simply remain where it was. However, Westheimer found that the eye moved to the new location 200 milliseconds after the light had begun to move even though, by this time, the light had returned to its original position and had been there for 160 milliseconds. The eye remained at the new location for another 200 milliseconds (the latency of the next eye movement), and then returned to the original position.

Pursuit movements are those involved in tracking moving objects in order to maintain a stable retinal projection of that object. Pursuit movements require that there be a moving object in the visual field, or that the head or body be in motion. Figure 9.1 illustrates pursuit motion for four different speeds of moving objects, shown from the time an object begins to move. The 200 millisecond latency is for the initial saccade. Then the eye matches the velocity of the moving object and can track it smoothly, as long as the velocity of the object's motion is not high. Pursuit movements are distinguished from saccadic movements by their slower speed and by their smoothness. It is likely that a completely different control system underlies the two types of movements. Occasionally, pursuit movements are combined with saccades as when an error in pursuit occurs. Then, a rapid movement may be made to correct the position.

While the eye is in motion, it seems reasonable to expect some limitation of vision. During the actual movement itself, there should be some blur due to

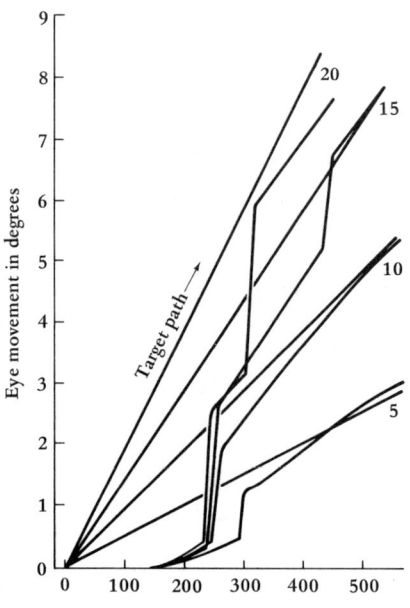

FIGURE 9.1 Displacement of the position of the eye pursuit movements as a function of time for four different speeds of moving objects (from Robinson, 1965).

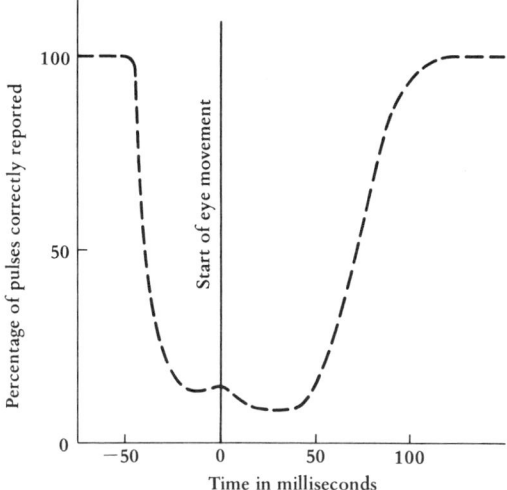

FIGURE 9.2   Percent of light pulses detected as a function of the time of their occurrence in relation to the occurrence of a concomitant saccadic eye movement (from Latour, 1962).

smearing of the retinal projection at the very high rate of motion. Latour (1962) studied the percent of light pulses that were seen at various times before, during, and after a saccadic eye movement. The test pulse occurred midway between two fixation lights which were oscillating irregularly. The perceiver was instructed to switch his eyes back and forth between the fixation lights when they changed. Figure 9.2 shows Latour's results. Experiments by Volkmann(1962) and Volkmann, Schick, and Riggs (1968) confirm this pattern. Perception is not totally blanked out during a movement, but sensitivity is reduced substantially, not only during the movement itself, but for 50 milliseconds before the movement begins to about 50 milliseconds after the eye is settled in the new position. The greatest suppression occurs during the actual movement time itself. But because suppression occurs before and after the movement itself, it cannot be caused simply by retinal blur.

While little is known of the mechanism that controls this suppression, it is functional in that it minimizes the perception of blur during the movement. But it is important to note that we are not blind during movements. Volkmann's (1962) data show a threshold rise during movements of little more than one-half log unit of luminance under the worst circumstances. This is not a great change, considering the total range of sensitivity of the visual system—but enough, perhaps, to reduce blur below annoyance. The change is probably enough, however, to reduce the sensitivity to details that pass across the retina as the eye moves. This is further evidence of the ballistic nature of the movement. Once planned, the eye movement cannot be changed, and for the 100 milliseconds before, during, and after the movement, the chances of noticing new information or fine detail is sharply reduced. This can also be taken as evidence of interference between the directing and the identifying aspects of search, since the chances are reduced that the perceiver will be able to identify targets passed over during an eye movement.

When the eye is pursuing a moving target, the stationary visual world is being blurred across the retina while the moving target is kept on the fovea. Mackworth and Kaplan (1962) studied the situation in which a perceiver was asked to track a target moving across a screen at velocities of between 0 and 120 degrees per second (the zero-degree condition is for a stationary eye). An acuity pattern was pulsed in the center of the screen, just when the target passed beneath it. Figure 9.3 shows their results. When the stationary acuity pattern was intense and on for 100 milliseconds, acuity was not reduced, no matter how fast the eye was pursuing the moving target. As the acuity pattern became dimmer, its stripes had to be increased in width to be seen, and the effect was more pronounced for vertical stripes (which are smeared with high speeds) than for horizontal stripes (which merely look longer). Although target velocities up to 120 degress per second were used in this study, the eyes are unable to track them perfectly at those high speeds.

When the energy in the acuity target was held constant, but its duration and intensity were varied reciprocally, different effects were found (but not shown in Figure 9.3). In a control condition with a stationary target and no movement of the eyes, perfect reciprocity was found. When the eyes are moving and the target is dim (less than 0.01 millilamberts) but long (100 milliseconds), increasing the velocity of pursuit took its toll of acuity, especially for vertical stripes. However, when the target was intense but very brief (0.001

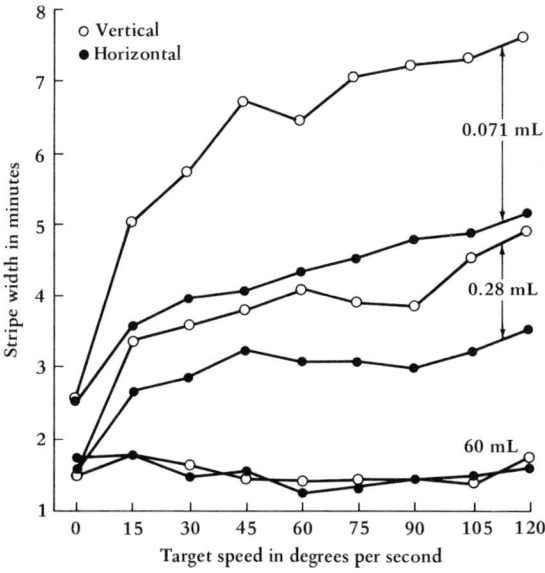

FIGURE 9.3   Minimum width of stripes of an acuity target that could be resolved when the eye was attempting to pursue a target moving at various speeds as a function of different luminances and orientations of the acuity target (from Mackworth and Kaplan, 1962).

milliseconds), there was virtually no effect of the velocity of pursuit movements, nor of the orientation of the pattern. This finding is to be expected, since, even at the highest velocity, a pulse that brief would not be smeared.

In summary, there is some suppression of vision just before, during, and just after a saccadic eye movement. This would seem to be designed to reduce the perception of blur and other distortions of patterns that might occur at the very high velocities encountered with saccadic movements. On the other hand, there is little loss of acuity of stationary objects seen during pursuit movements, except under impoverished conditions of viewing. This also is to be expected, given the much slower velocities normally used for pursuit movements, and the much longer durations over which they occur. The fact that the visual world remains relatively stable and discriminable even when our eyes are moving is an important phenomenon. We shall have something more to say about it in Chapter 14 when we discuss the perception of motion.

ATTENTIONAL FIELDS

Mackworth (1965) has measured the size of the field of attention by placing several targets in various parts of the periphery and asking observers to indicate whether or not all the targets were the same. For example, he pulsed three letters for 100 milliseconds, one on the center of fixation and the other two flanking it equidistant on either side. His results are shown in Figure 9.4. Accuracy was virtually perfect, even when the two flanking letters were as much as 10 degress apart. Performance deteriorated sharply, however, when fourteen irrelevant letters were added on the line, or twenty other lines of seventeen letters each were added. When all three targets to be matched were roughly within the fovea, accuracy of matching dropped from 99 percent when

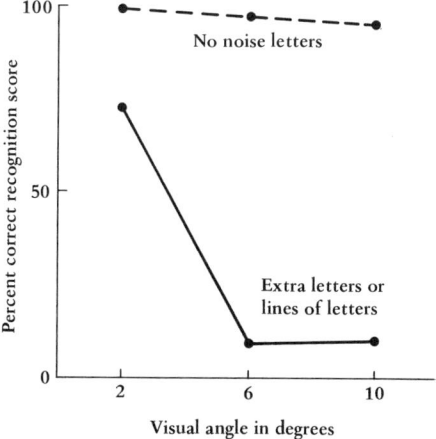

FIGURE 9.4   Percent of correct matches between central and peripheral letters as a function of visual angle and the presence of noise letters (data taken from Mackworth, 1965).

no other targets were present, to about 70 percent with the addition of a line or page of irrelevant letters. As soon as the targets were extrafoveal (more than 3 degrees apart), accuracy dropped from over 95 percent to about 10 percent. The difference between a line and a whole page of unwanted letters was not large.

In a second condition, Mackworth showed that adding unwanted targets outside the targets was far worse than between the target and the center (see Figure 9.5). Comparing this with the previous condition shows that adding only two unwanted letters drops accuracy from 99 to about 80 percent. However, if they are placed outside of the targets, accuracy drops to nearly 40 percent.

FIGURE 9.5 Percent of correct matches between central and peripheral letters as a function of whether two noise letters were inside or outside the peripheral letter (data taken from Mackworth, 1965).

			Recognition Display Width	
DISPLAY ARRANGEMENT			6°	10°
RN	N	NS	43	41
NT	N	ZN	79	81

Mackworth interpreted these results in terms of the size of the useful visual field—the area surrounding the fixation point from which information can be briefly stored and processed during a fixation. Too much information causes this field to constrict so as to prevent overloading the visual processing system. Adding visual noise or unwanted signals can narrow this useful field of view, creating what Mackworth calls tunnel vision—a priority given to targets in the fovea. There is even some loss in foveal recognition. In Chapter 11 we will consider the order in which information is processed and suggest that this probably takes place in a left-to-right or outside-to-inside direction. Mackworth's result concerning the impact of the location of unwanted targets supports this view.

Obviously, information supplied by the periphery of the retina is of great importance in normal perception. How easy is it to detect such stimuli? How quickly can we respond to stimuli which appear in the peripheral retina? Is the response a function of direction of regard, the number of signals present, the amount of practice, or the expectations of the perceiver? The greatest amount of work on these questions has been carried out by Sanders, and most of it is reported in his 1963 monograph. In these experiments, generally two signals appear, one straight ahead and the other off to the right. The perceiver is usually required to press a telegraph key as quickly as he can to indicate the presence of one, both, or some combination of the two signals. Response latencies (reaction times) may then be compared for the different responses.

Sanders distinguished between three different types of attentional fields. The display field includes central and peripheral vision of the display as seen during a single glance without any change in fixation. The eye field includes all that can be seen with saccadic eye movements. The head field has, in addition to the display and eye fields, the field of vision exposed by head movements. In one series of experiments, Sanders mapped the relative sizes of these fields. A perceiver was presented with two patterns, each of which was a column of either four or five lights. He had to press one of four response keys to indicate whether the two stimuli had both contained four lights, or both five, or the left one four and the right one five, or vice versa. He had to respond as quickly as possible but, of course, to do so, he had to view both stimuli. He was told to fixate the position where the left-hand stimulus would appear. The right-hand stimulus was from 19 degrees to 94 degrees to the right. Both stimuli appeared simultaneously.

Figure 9.6 shows that, when the head and eyes are both free to move, two discontinuities in performance occur, one when the patterns are around 30 degrees apart, and the other at about 80 degrees apart. When the perceiver's head was fixed so that no head movements were possible, his performance fell off rapidly for the larger display angles (81 to 94 degrees).

Sanders suggested that the two dips correspond to the break points between the display and eye fields, and the eye and head fields, respectively. Thus, with relatively large and simple stimuli, peripheral vision is adequate out to about 30 degrees and eye movements extend the visual field out to about 80 degrees. This means that beyond 30 degrees the eye must move, and beyond 80 degrees the head must move.

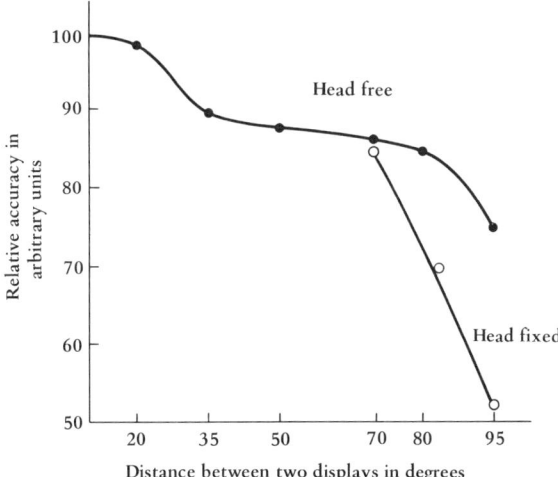

FIGURE 9.6   Accuracy in reporting the number of lights in two columns as a function of the distance between them, when the head is free to move and when it is fixed (from Sanders, 1963).

This point is strengthened in another study in which the perceiver was told either to remain fixated on the left stimulus or to move his eyes between them. Figure 9.7 shows that when no eye movement is permitted, peripheral vision ends at about 30 degrees. Even before this, reaction time increases exponentially as the visual angle increases from 0 degrees. When the perceiver is permitted to move his eyes, his reaction time is constant out to about 90 degrees, after which it increases rapidly. Notice that even for small angles this condition is slightly slower, suggesting that the perceiver's strategies must be different in some way when he knows he can move his eyes.

Sanders notes further that these values are dependent on the complexity of the stimuli. The dot task that he used has many cues and does not need acute resolution of fine detail. Although letters are nearly impossible to read at 5 degrees when pulsed briefly (Woodrow, 1938), large block letters displayed for 1500 milliseconds could be discriminated at 30 degrees (Geer and Moraal, 1962).

Sanders reports a further series of studies in which he recorded eye movements and head movements during similar reaction-time tasks. He showed that these decrements in performance seen in Figure 9.6 were not due to the time needed to move the eyes or the head. Those times were a linear function of the distance moved. Consequently, the discontinuity in performance must be due to some selective processes. His hypothesis was that within the display field, that is, a single glance, both stimuli are attended to and processed simultaneously, allowing a more rapid transmission and subsequent processing of the information. Outside of the display field, two separate selective acts are needed, and the drop in performance reflects this additional time for the second selective act that is being added. Sanders believes there are actually three stages. In the first, from about 0 degrees to 25 degrees, both stimuli can be adequately discriminated simultaneously without an eye movement. Thus, although the perceiver fixates the left one, he can see enough of the visual features of the right one at the same time to be able to make the discrimination

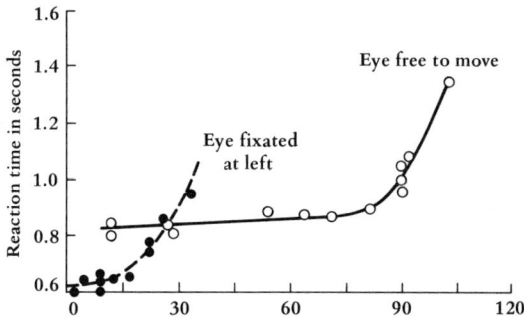

FIGURE 9.7 Choice reaction time to two stimuli varying in their separation as a function of whether the perceiver is permitted to move his eyes (from Sanders, 1963).

and organize the response. His response is slowed down as the display size approaches 25 degrees, which might imply a loss in confidence about the right stimulus, or that it takes longer to process a degraded stimulus.

Once the right-hand stimulus is outside of the display field, its features are no longer adequate to lead to a decision and response. However, Sanders believes that the perceiver still can get enough information about it to form a hypothesis which can then be tested after an eye movement. Since the perceiver has a hypothesis, less information should be needed for confirmation than if he knows nothing about the right-hand stimulus. Thus, the time to process the right stimulus should be less than that to process a new stimulus altogether. As the angle approaches 80 degrees, however, even the partial information to form a hypothesis is inadequate and an entirely separate processing is needed. Therefore another increment of time is added causing the second drop in performance around 80 to 90 degrees.

Sanders verified these predictions in several specific instances. For example, a perceiver was asked to attend and respond to the left stimulus and then to the right one, giving two separate responses. If he can process the right-hand stimulus while fixating on the left, as he should be able to do for small angles, then reaction time to the right should be much shorter than to the left. As the angle increases, forcing him to use two selective acts, the ratio of the two reaction times should decrease until, by the time the eye field is exceeded (that is, around 80 degrees or so), the ratio of the two reaction times should be unity. Sanders found this result, even after he subtracted the eye-movement time from the reaction time to the right-hand stimulus. Since this subtraction process runs counter to his prediction, his test is conservative and still supports his interpretation.

We will not have many occasions to consider research using visual angles as wide as those employed by Sanders. But it is important to realize that the same processes normally applicable to single glances and to those using little of the periphery apply equally well to most of the retina. Further, they are generalizable even when eye and head movements occur to extend the range of vision.

Although peripheral information is used to determine the next fixation, the target presently being fixated is also being analyzed. Thus, two tasks are being performed simultaneously. Is this a division of attention or are the two tasks performed independently? If this does represent a division of attention, does one task interfere with the other? While Sanders did not study interference per se, he clearly showed that the central and peripheral tasks interacted—at least in his experimental situation. When the fixated signal and the peripheral signal were both within the eye field—and especially when they were both within the display field—the time needed to respond to the first signal was increased slightly over that needed when only a single signal was presented and no peripheral processing was needed.

Sanders's theory of selective acts can be reinterpreted in terms of preattentive processes which operate simultaneously over large areas of the retina.

Within the display field preattentive processes are capable of locating and segregating all figures and of testing global characteristics. The perceivers in Sanders's experiments only needed information about the height or brightness of the stimulus to tell the difference between four or five lights. When the visual angle between the objects in the field surpasses the limits of the pre-attentive processes, the spatially parallel nature of the processing will be lost and an eye movement will be needed to complete testing. One of Sanders's most important findings is that even out to 80 degrees in the periphery, some information is available. This information will reduce the amount of time needed to process the stimulus when it is directly fixated after an eye move-ment. Thus, preattentive processes appear to operate over wide reaches of the peripheral retina. Once a slower head movement becomes necessary, then the preattentive processes have clearly lost their spatially parallel character and two separate glances are needed.

Sanders's notion of selective acts illustrates another interaction between control and identification processes in search. When single targets are not too far into the periphery, it appears that some identification can occur, even while the eye is being directed to move toward them.

SEARCHING FOR FORMS

Visual search as a reconnaissance task has received attention both as a theo-retical problem and with respect to specific applied tasks. Much of the concern has been with the factors that control the position of the next fixation. For example, Williams (1966, 1967) has reported data which suggest that observers use peripheral information to select the position of the next fixation. He pre-sented relatively large fields of nearly 40 degrees containing 100 geometric shapes, each of which was in one of five colors, one of four sizes, and could be one of five shapes (see Figure 9.8 for a schematic example). There was a two-digit number in the center of each form. The observer's task was to find the form with a particular number. Trials differed according to the amount of information supplied to the observer about the dimensions and values of the form containing the number—sometimes he was told only the number, and sometimes the specific object containing the number was described. The position and direction of each eye movement was recorded.

When no information other than the number was given, there was no tendency to fixate one type of target more than any other. When information was given about a single one of the three dimensions, only color information biased fixation choice. This was shown by a strong tendency to fixate only on the color indicated, permitting search times to drop by nearly 80 percent when the perceiver knew the color of the target. This was less true for size and held only when the size was either largest or smallest. Shape information was rarely used to determine fixation choices. When two dimensions were com-bined, (for example, the number being sought is in a red circle figure) the per-

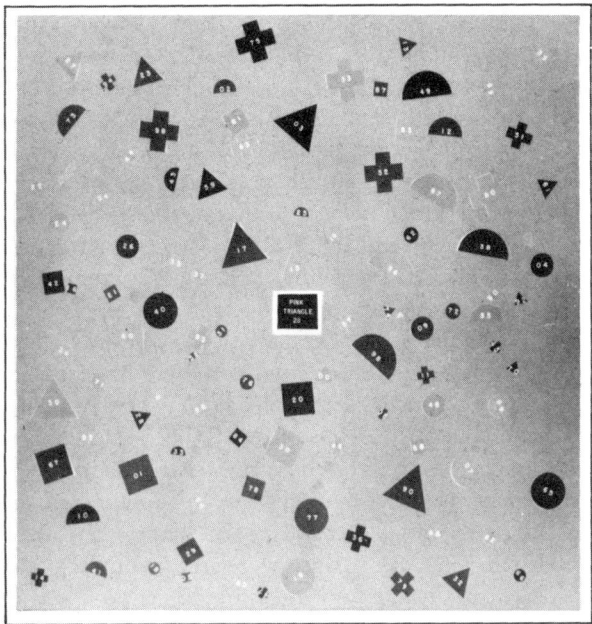

FIGURE 9.8 A schematic representation of a stimulus display used by Williams in his study of visual search (1966).

centages of fixations were primarily determined by those of the most powerful cue alone. Hence combining color with shape did not increase the fixations on the particular shapes.

Williams's data show that the observers used extrafoveal information to select the object of the next fixation. Search patterns are not random unless the observer has no information about the target. Further, Williams showed that some of the cues are far more important or useful than others.

It is not surprising that shape was not used to select the next fixation point since differences among the targets were small and would have required a fair degree of resolution. The extrafoveal information available to the viewer probably could not be used to distinguish among them. Moreover, it is possible that even if the shapes were more distinguishable, perceivers still would not use that information in search. If the information from the periphery is based only upon visual features preattentively segmented and organized, specific shape information would not be available. But orientation, movement, and color would be available since, even in the periphery, these could be specified by single feature analyzers. It is possible that reconnaissance might be a device for testing the usefulness of particular visual features in guiding visual search.

Boynton and his co-workers have studied the psychophysical parameters of visual search tasks by evaluating the impact of a large number of variables on the speed of search and on the probability of a successful search. One of their major conclusions is that any variable which reduces visual acuity will reduce the likelihood of locating a target by visual information alone. For example, Boynton and Boss (1971) investigated possible trade-offs between luminance, contrast, and size of target. Such trade-offs are available within limits, but, for example, if contrast is too low, no increase in luminance or target size will permit successful search among targets seen in peripheral vision. The target will have to be centrally fixated first, and only then might it be identified (assuming that foveal acuity is adequate).

Boynton, Ellworth, and Palmer (1958) recorded eye movements during search under a variety of conditions. Of special interest is a subsidiary analysis. They selected two perceivers, one who was very proficient at finding targets, and one who was quite poor at it. The better one had an average duration of fixation of 200 milliseconds, compared with over 330 for the poorer. The better perceiver also made much larger sweeps between fixations, covering nearly 2½ degrees, compared to 1½ degrees for the poorer. These differences may reflect better strategies for search or differential acuity. The better perceiver did have better acuity, and he might therefore have needed less fixation time to recognize an item. His better peripheral acuity may permit him to sample information further into the periphery, thereby allowing larger saccadic movements. In this sense, the subjects in Williams's experiment may not have been able to use shape information because peripheral acuity for those shapes was not adequate. Boynton has shown in a number of studies that if peripheral acuity is high enough, the shape of the target does appear to stand out, even when viewed peripherally.

We have already mentioned the impact of the number of background items in the peripheral field. Boynton and Bush (1957) varied the number of background curvilinear forms from eight to 256 in a display in which a single rectilinear target was embedded. In general, the accuracy of finding the target decreased with greater numbers of background items. The decrease was nearly a linear function of the logarithm of the number of items.

EYE MOVEMENTS IN READING

Probably the most important search task that literate adults perform occurs when they read. What determines where each fixation will fall on a page of print? The answer is complex, since it involves the entire information-extraction process involved in reading for meaning. Although some of these processes will be considered in more detail in Chapter 11, this section will examine the eye-movement patterns found in normal adult reading.

Typical eye-movement patterns occurring while reading a Shakespearian sonnet are illustrated in Figure 9.9. The reader of the sonnet fixates on nearly every word once, with few regressions or refixations. The last word of each line is fixated longer, a pattern probably unique to poetry, and probably representing time used for gaining understanding of the line or checking the rhyme rather than for perception. Excluding the last fixation on each line, the average number of words per fixation in this example is about 1.2, the average duration

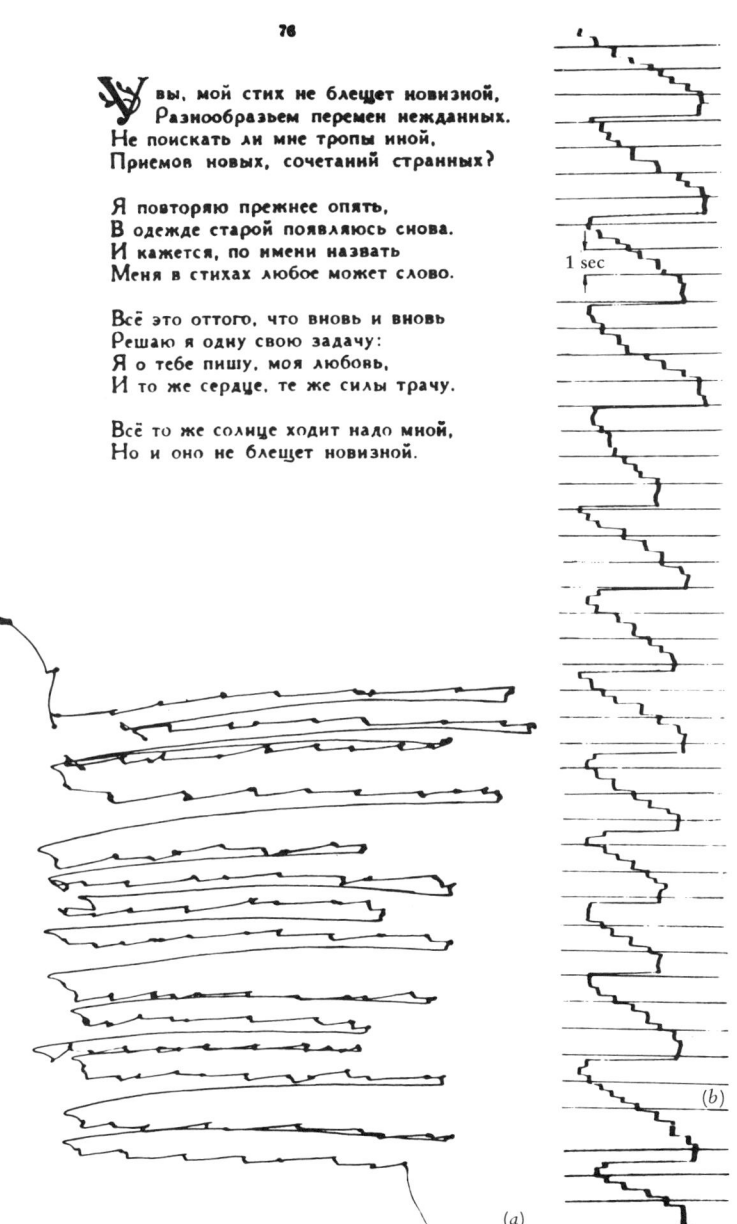

76

Увы, мой стих не блещет новизной,
Разнообразьем перемен нежданных.
Не поискать ли мне тропы иной,
Приемов новых, сочетаний странных?

Я повторяю прежнее опять,
В одежде старой появляюсь снова.
И кажется, по имени назвать
Меня в стихах любое может слово.

Всё это оттого, что вновь и вновь
Решаю я одну свою задачу:
Я о тебе пишу, моя любовь,
И то же сердце, те же силы трачу.

Всё то же солнце ходит надо мной,
Но и оно не блещет новизной.

1 sec

(b)

(a)

FIGURE 9.9   Two different ways to record eye movements made while a perceiver is reading a poem (from Yarbus, 1967).

of fixation is nearly 300 milliseconds and the average time to shift the eyes from one fixation to the next is about 35 milliseconds. These three variables describe the salient characteristics of the pattern of eye movements. They would yield a measure of reading speed of just over 150 words per minute if the extra time on the last word of each line were excluded.

In most reading research, the average duration of fixation is between 250 and 300 milliseconds and the average speed of eye movements is between 25 and 50 milliseconds regardless of reading speed, difficulty of material, or the ability of the reader. Thus, reading speed depends upon how far apart each fixation is in space and time, and not on how long each fixation lasts or how long it takes to move the eyes. The general goal of most speed-reading programs is to have the reader make fewer fixations, thus covering more words per fixation.

Figure 9.10 shows some developmental changes in reading rates. In general, fixations during reading are close together at the beginning of a paragraph, often with one or two regressions or refixations of a word. Apparently once the context of the paragraph is obvious to the reader, he can settle down to a pattern determined by the difficulty or familiarity of the material. Some of

FIGURE 9.10 Reading speeds and number of regressions for readers of various ages (from Buswell, 1922).

School grade	Fixations per line of print	Mean duration of fixation (msec)	Regressive movements per line
I B	18.6	660	5.1
I A	15.5	432	4.0
II	10.7	364	2.3
III	8.9	316	1.8
IV	7.3	268	1.4
V	6.9	252	1.3
VI	7.3	236	1.6
VII	6.8	240	1.5
High school I	7.2	244	1.0
High school II	5.8	248	0.7
High school III	5.5	224	0.7
High school IV	6.4	248	0.7
College	5.9	252	0.5

these changes are accounted for by the substantial drop in the number of regressions as proficiency in reading increases, as shown in Figure 9.10, but Figures 9.9 and 9.11 below for adult readers still contain some regressive movements. Buswell (1922) has shown that adults can regress in up to 50 percent of their movements, such as when they are studying a foreign language grammar text. Taylor (1965) reports that regressive movements make up nearly a quarter of all saccades of first-grade readers, while they are only 15 percent for college students. As Kolers (1972) points out, this drop, while substantial, cannot be used to account for the large increase in reading skill. Further, the presence of such a large number of regressive movements, even in college students, poses a severe problem for any model that describes reading as progressing smoothly from left to right, picking up information from the text in the order in which it is presented. Kolers notes two separate and quite interesting problems in this regard. First we have already seen that a saccadic movement

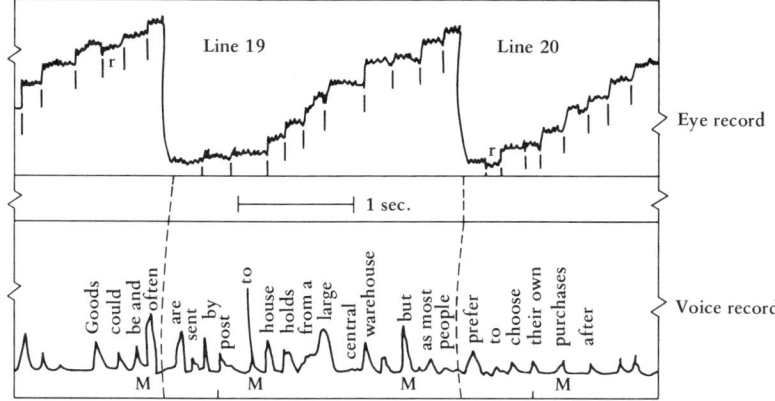

FIGURE 9.11 Simple eye movements and oral reading records showing an eye-voice span (from Morton, 1964).

must be programmed several hundred milliseconds before it occurs. Thus, in most cases, a regressive movement is made on the basis of what happened during a previous fixation, and not based on what is being currently perceived. In this sense, programming of regression, as well as all fixations, is not based upon conscious awareness of difficulty of understanding, but on information not yet in awareness.

Even more important, regressive eye movements present to the reader a sequence of text which can best be described as a word salad. This completely disrupts any linguistically coherent sequence of inputs, and it remains for any model of reading to be compatible with this fact.

While we will consider some of the information-processing aspects of reading in Chapter 11, a few other characteristics of the search properties can be mentioned here. One very interesting measure is the eye-voice span in aural reading—how far the eyes are ahead of the voice. It can be measured either in terms of the number of words or the number of milliseconds. The eye-voice span can be considered an index of the amount of material the reader must perceive, process, and retain from the time his eyes fixate on it until his voice pronounces the words. In this way, the size of the eye-voice span has been used as a measure of ongoing short-term processing and storage.

In one study of reading, Morton (1964) had students read nonsense and meaningful passages which differed in their statistical resemblance to English prose. (The procedure for constructing words or text for different approximations to English is described in Chapter 11.) He recorded the voice of the reader on a tape recorder which was synchronized with an eye-movement recorder. In this way, Morton could tell where the eye was fixating on the line and what word was being uttered at each instant in time. Figure 9.11 shows a typical record. The upper part contains the eye fixations, and the lower part the voice track. Morton found that the duration of fixations was about 240 milliseconds and was constant over different kinds of materials ranging from random words to continuous meaningful text. This was the case even though reading speed increased from just over 80 to nearly 230 words per minute, and the eye-voice span increased from about one to nearly three words. In the latter cases, this represented a span of 640 milliseconds in length.

Geyer (1968) using meaningful texts of varying difficulty, also found fixation time to be constant. His measurement of the eye-voice span ranged from about 800 milliseconds for difficult material to nearly 1200 milliseconds for easy material. Neither Geyer nor Morton could discover any regularities in the pattern of fixations, although Geyer did attempt to examine the kinds of errors readers made. He classified corrected errors into those in which the reader misperceived the word and those in which he merely mispronounced or misspoke his aural response. When misperceptions occurred, the voice usually would stop, the eye would return to the misperceived word and reread the text out to the size of the span. Then the voice would pick up again. When mispronounciations occurred, only the voice would return to the error, the eye retreating enough only to maintain the span. Geyer also noted that when the voice had to pause for punctuation or emphasis, the eye also paused. But, of course, the eye was looking at a word unrelated to the pause, further down the text, and often even on the next line.

Kolers (1970) noted that nearly all attempts to classify fixation choices by the syntactic or semantic context have failed to show any pattern. This is to be expected in terms of the distinction between preattentive and focal attention proposed earlier. Peripheral cues should be used to guide fixations, but only in terms of the physical properties isolated, such as shape and spatial position. We are only beginning to discover the degree to which word shape and word length are available as peripheral cues. The shrinkage of the span and the increase in the number of fixations per line as difficulty of material increases is quite compatible with tunnel-vision effects. This difficulty is not necessarily due to the words themselves being difficult or unfamiliar (see Chapter 11), but rather to the problems in combining information from each fixation.

SEARCHING PICTURES

Although the ways in which we look at or read pictures have not drawn the attention of researchers to the extent that reading textual material has, we already know of some important differences as well as some striking similarities. Research dates back nearly as far as that on text reading, with Buswell (1935) providing extensive data on eye fixations while looking at pictures. More recently, Mackworth has carried out an extensive program with television-recorded eye movements. In Russia, Yarbus (1967) has reported a twenty-year program of research in eye movements, including picture viewing.

As one example, Mackworth and Morandi (1967) measured eye fixation choices while the perceiver examined each of two unfamiliar pictures. He was instructed to choose the one he preferred and therefore had no reason to expect to be asked questions about their content. The stimuli were large (16 degrees) square pictures presented for 10 seconds each. To obtain a measure of the information in each part of the pictures, each picture was cut up into sixty-four squares. A second group of perceivers was asked to rate each little square on informativeness—specifically, how easy it would be to recognize the square on another occasion.

Mackworth and Morandi's findings were quite clear-cut (see Figure 9.12). Fixation choices, which averaged about 300 milliseconds each, were confined primarily to the high-information parts of the picture. Since this was as true within the first two seconds of viewing as within the last two seconds, the viewers did not depend on scanning to find the important parts. Instead, peripheral cues must have been guiding fixation choices from the outset. The authors also found that uniform texture was generally fixated less than contours. However, if the contours were highly predictable and redundant, they did not attract fixations—the eye appeared to be searching for the unusual and irregular.

What is striking about these findings, as well as those of Buswell and Yarbus, is the lack of uniformity in the fixation patterns. There is no broad sweep over the picture, nor any global viewing pattern. Instead, a high concentration of fixations is confined to a few regions, those containing relatively great variation, unpredictability, or a high rate of change. Equally important, the perceiver appears to know where to look before he has completed even a cursory examination of the picture. Thus, peripheral information must be guiding fixation choices to a location of unpredictable or unusual aspects of the picture.

What is even more interesting is the lack of regularity in the order of searching the picture, even in circumstances where the predictability of the fixated parts is impressively high. There does not appear to be any natural

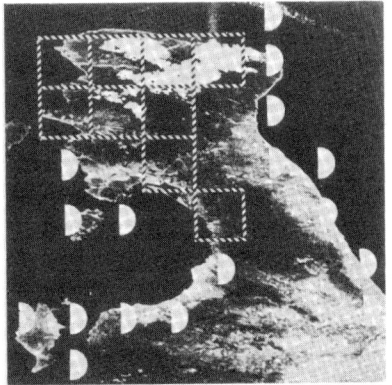

FIGURE 9.12   Eye fixations made while looking at a map picture (from Mackworth and Morandi, 1967).

order of fixations in viewing a picture. As Kolers (1972) noted, it remains for theory to explain how so many different input sequences can be used to arrive at roughly the same perceptual experience.

Yarbus (1967) reported some work in which he varied the instruction to the perceiver. Each condition alerted the viewer that he would be asked different kinds of questions after he looked at the picture for three minutes. Figure 9.13 shows the picture and the eye movements made during the three-minute intervals in each of the instruction conditions. It is clear that the fixation patterns were dramatically altered, both in details and in pattern. It is as if the perceiver concentrated on those parts he expected to use for the task presented to him. In no sense was he stimulus-bound, either in position or sequence of fixations, nor was he response-bound, following some habitual sequence each time.

Recently, Noton and Stark (1971) have argued for a limited specificity of the sequence of fixation choices—what they call a scan path. While they recognize that the sequence of fixations will be largely unpredictable before viewing begins, they argue that part of the memory for a picture comprises information about the sequence actually used. Thus, each fixation yields a view, and what is stored is a sequence of pairings of motor commands and views—the scan path. They predict that when a perceiver is asked to recognize a picture he had only recently seen, the re-creation of the scan path that was used to view the picture initially will be a critical component of the recognition process. While Noton and Stark offer some data in support of this hypothesis, it is difficult to see how perceivers store information on the sequence of their eye fixations. Further, even if this information was stored, it would seem to be a very complex way of coding information. As with regressive eye movements in reading, the order of the movements in picture reading—the sequence of inputs—must be relatively independent of the organization we construct from them.

One other possibility is that the scan-path hypothesis is more appropriately applied to perceptual development. Children's recognition memory might be highly dependent upon the specific sequence of eye movements. The sequences themselves might be stored as part of the memory experience, and familiarity might provide greater freedom of search with less dependence on the sequence of looks. Whiteside (1972) provides some data in support of this hypothesis, although the question is far from settled.

This brief review should make us aware of a curious discrepancy between our eye-movement patterns and our phenomenal experience while looking at pictures. Within less than a second of first viewing a picture, we have the feeling of seeing it all, and all at once, no matter how complex it is. All details may not be clear, and may require further visual exploration, but even during that exploration, the entire picture remains in view no matter where we look, for what purpose, for how long, and in what order. Yet, the eye-movement records show a discontinuous viewing, jumping back and forth, here and there. Hochberg (1970) has described this as an integration of single glances into a schematic map of what we are viewing—in other words, a construction

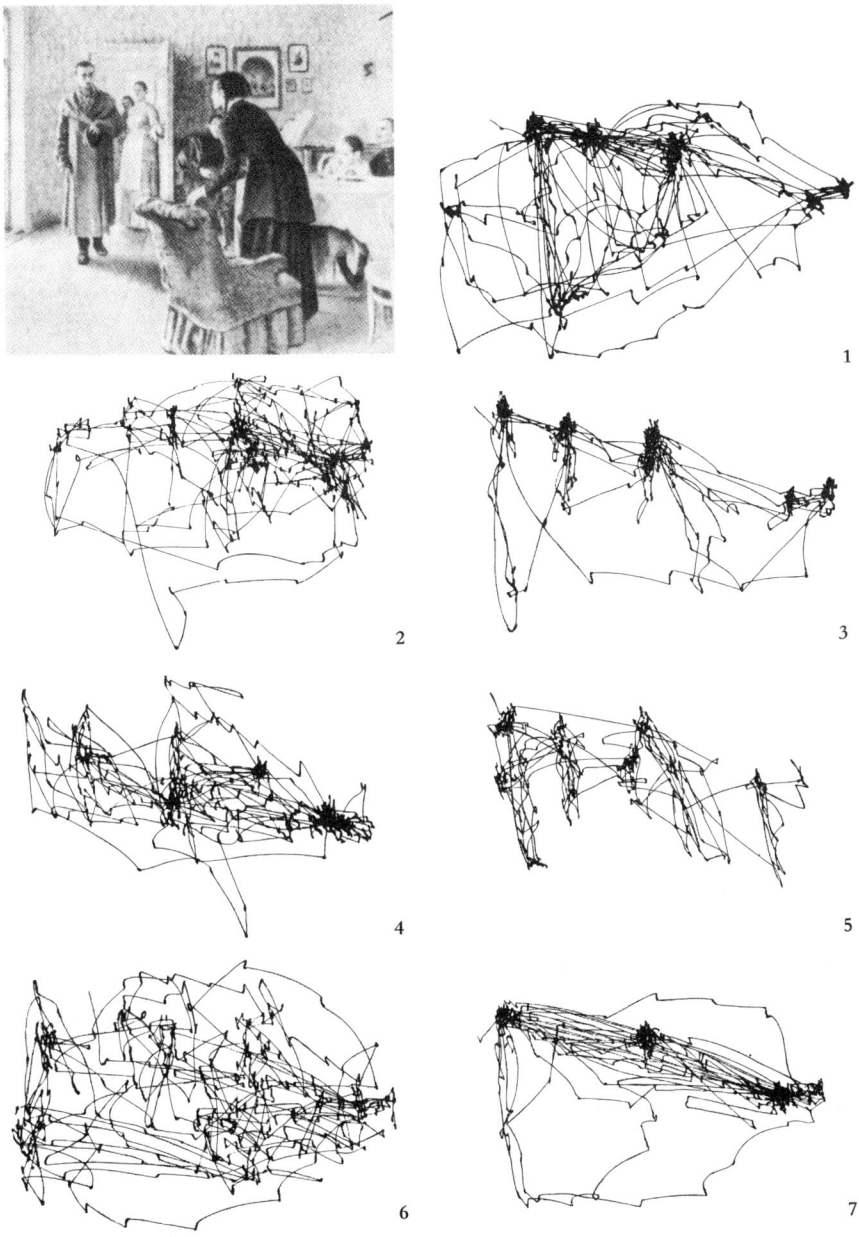

FIGURE 9.13 Different eye-fixation patterns made to the same picture as a function of the instructions to the perceiver (from Yarbus, 1967). (1) Free examination of the picture. Before the subsequent recording sessions, the subject was asked to: (2) estimate the material circumstances of the family in the picture; (3) give the ages of the people; (4) surmise what the family had been doing before the arrival of the "unexpected visitor"; (5) remember the clothes worn by the people; (6) remember the position of the people and objects in the room; (7) estimate how long the "unexpected visitor" had been away from the family.

of perception which rests on a sampling of the visual world, but not determined solely by the content of the samples, nor in any way by the ordering of the sampling. See Chapters 7 and 8 for fuller discussion of this point. We have already seen this in our analysis of reading texts, especially in considering regressive eye fixations. There, too, the sequence seems to be irrelevant. All that is important is getting the necessary samples—enough to construct the full perception. Notice also that even in reading texts we have the phenomenal experience of seeing all of the words on a line, even when we may have fixated only a few of them.

SUMMARY

Visual search is not usually covered in general textbooks on visual perception, even though it represents some of the most important features of selective processes in the extraction of information from visual displays. To illustrate this, a number of different examples of search tasks were briefly mentioned, and used to contrast two different aspects of any search task: peripheral retinal processing to determine where to move the eyes for the next fixation; and foveal identification processing to determine whether or not the object being presented is the target being sought. Neisser's distinction between preattentive and focal attentive processes was used and elaborated to support these two aspects of visual search.

With this as an introduction, we considered some details of saccadic and pursuit eye movements. We noted some research on visual acuity and suppression of perception during eye movements, which showed that the perception of blur was minimized by some loss of sensitivity just before, during, and after the movements. We explored the ballistic character and the relatively long latencies to initiate a saccadic movement, and examined some of the implications that these might have for information processing.

To determine the size of the effective visual field during a simple fixation, several lines of work were considered. The most important was that of Sanders who showed that preattentive processes could be deployed fairly widely, but that at the limit, additional time was needed. The concept of tunnel vision was also used to cover a narrowing of attention when the amount of information in the visual field was increased.

We briefly looked at several studies on searching for forms or objects, both with respect to the sources of information used to select the next fixation, and the limits placed on search by visual acuity.

The last two parts concerned search during reading of text and reading of pictures and scenes. Several eye movement records made during reading were illustrated, so that some of the temporal and spatial variables in reading could be examined. It was shown that the major variable in adult reading is the number of fixations, not their duration nor the speed of eye movements. The importance of regressive eye movements was discussed, especially in light of the need to consider construction of meaning somewhat independent of the order of fixations. Several different lines of work pointed to how peripheral information might be used to direct fixation choices, both with text and with pictures. We closed by again noting that both types of reading must be constructive since some mechanism is needed to integrate a coherent perceived organization across several fixations.

Readings

Most of the topics in this chapter are not treated in relatively unified packages at either the introductory or the advanced and technical level. Many of the ideas of this chapter owe their origins to Neisser (1967), as well as to Yarbus (1967). The latter is probably the most complete source of information about eye movements, even though he concentrates primarily on his own work and that of other Russians. Alpern's three chapters (1962, 1971, 1972) are somewhat more technical, and are concerned with the physiology, neurology, and mechanical and psychophysical components of eye movement processes. Sanders's 1963 monograph is strongly recommended for anyone who wishes to learn more about an elegant program of research and some elegant answers about the effective visual field. Several relevant papers on eye movements in reading are contained in the collection by Young and Lindsley (1970) as well as the paper by Kolers (1972).

chapter
10
selection in perception

INTRODUCTION

The visual world surrounding us at any given moment is of great complexity, composed of a myriad of objects and surfaces, at various distances, of differing qualities, textures, and colors, and with diversity of meaning and importance to us as perceivers. With our eyes open and oriented in a particular direction, the luminance discontinuities produced on the retina from the visual world will be a function entirely of the light-capturing properties of the optics of the eye and the physical parameters of the interaction of the light sources and the scene being illuminated. But what will we perceive and what will we be aware of perceiving in such a scene? Surely only a small part of it—only a few of the objects, and a few of the details. This chapter will examine several aspects of this type of implied selectivity, both with respect to the ways we conceptualize selective processes, and the kinds of evidence we have about the extent of selection in visual perception.

The term attention has often been used to refer to selectivity, although its useful meaning is far broader than just to refer to cover selection tasks. Moray (1970) and Berlyne (1973) each discuss a number of different meanings of attention, only one of which refers explicitly to selection. As an example, attention is often considered in relation to arousal, or the intensity of attention. It is related to what a teacher means when admonishing pupils to "pay attention." Most of the research on the intensive component of attention has been related to the activity of the reticular activating system—a brain structure known to be sensitive to stimulation from all sense modalities. Thus the senses play an important role in the maintenance of a general state of arousal—a drowsy person can be made active by the onset of stimulation; an active person has a difficult time reducing arousal while stimulation is present; and the sharp reduction or cessation of stimulation is one of the clear antecedents of central nervous system deactivation leading to sleep.

As a concept in the field of perception, arousal is directly related to vigilance or prolonged watch-keeping. Vigilance is studied in tasks where a perceiver must remain alert to the possibility of the occurrence of a target, although nothing happens during most of the period of his observation. For example, a radar operator watching for a blip on a radar screen must continue to direct his attention to the screen, and to remain sufficiently alert so that he can notice a change when and if it occurs. Although there has been a great deal of interest in vigilance in perceptual-motor tasks, we shall not be able to consider it here. The reader is referred to Broadbent (1971) for a recent survey and treatment.

We began our discussion of selectivity in perception in the previous chapter, in which we looked at the means by which perceivers decide where to look and for how long. Undoubtedly this is the most important means by which we select one part of the visual world over another part to attend to. In this chapter we shall concentrate more on the selectivity that occurs within each glance or fixation. Such selection implies that some of the luminance discontinuities in the retinal projection are processed or represented as organized figures, objects, or symbols, while others are not. It also implies that the order in which processing takes place may be adjusted by the perceiver, or that the rate at which processing occurs may change as a function of the perceiver or the importance or meaningfulness of the stimulation to him.

Selective processes have been conceptualized in two rather different ways. One proposes that selection occurs by filtering out or blocking some information at some level in the information-processing sequence so that it never reaches the next stage. The other approach focuses on what is processed, rather than what is not, so that the ignored aspects may drop out, even without any active filtering. Broadbent (1958, 1971) and Treisman (for example, 1969) have been the most active proponents of the filtering model, but we shall not use it here. There probably is little fundamental difference other than emphasis, in that few occasions have arisen in which different predictions are made by the two approaches. We shall follow the active processing approach, because it lends itself much better to the general information processing model being followed in this book. Thus, we shall be concerned with the representation, extraction, and transfer of information at each stage, especially with the coding strategies used by the perceiver.

For example, we have already suggested that the initial representations of information are in relatively brief duration iconic storage of large capacity. To preserve it further, it can be transferred to a longer lasting but much smaller capacity short-term memory. If all of the original information cannot be transferred at once, the items extracted and encoded first will have an advantage over those transferred later. Moreover, if the original information is available only for a very brief period of time, once again the information encoded early will have the advantage. By the time the encoding process can be directed to the remaining information, it may only be available in degraded form or it may already be lost irretrievably (Egeth, 1967).

Thus, a number of processing parameters are important in determing the type of selection that would take place. The duration of the brief storage, the rate of extraction and encoding, and the order in which different information is processed would determine the nature of the selective processes. Moreover, it would be very important to determine whether the extraction and encoding of information from this early representation was serial—one item processed at a time—or whether it could be encoded in parallel—a number of items encoded simultaneously.

We suggested in Chapter 7 that the content of the initial storage was not influenced by the meaningfulness or familiarity of the stimulus material, or by any other potential source of selectivity imposed by the perceiver. But is the information extraction process from this initial store by which information is transferred either to a visual image representation or to short-term memory (or both) subject to selective biases? We shall consider in this chapter several rather different lines of research, each of which was initiated originally to provide positive evidence for this question.

VISUAL SEARCH REVISITED

One of the clearest examples of selectivity in the processing of the content of the icon is based on experiments on visual character recognition, especially those by Neisser beginning in 1963. Although these experiments are often called visual search tasks, discussion of this particular line of work was postponed from the previous chapter because the search properties are not as important as what happens during each fixation. A number of experiments using a similar task have been reported (Neisser, 1963; Neisser and Beller, 1965; Neisser and Lazar, 1964; Neisser, Novick, and Lazar, 1963; Neisser and Stoper, 1965). Typically, 50-line lists that contained a target in unpredictable positions (see Figure 10.1) were presented. As soon as the list appeared, the perceivers began to search down the list as rapidly as possible to find the target letter (for example, the letter K in list *a*). They pressed a button as soon as the letter was found. Neisser then computed the processing time per row by dividing the time needed to complete the search by the number of letters in the list. Typical results are shown in Figure 10.2 in which reaction time is plotted as a function of the row of target letter. The function invariably shows a linear increase in search time with target position. The value of the slope is the average processing time per row.

These experiments are classified as search tasks, because the perceiver must move his eyes down the list to find the target letter. However, the major interest is not in these movements, which are highly regularized, but in the time needed to determine if any of the letters seen in the current fixation are the target letter. Neisser assumed that the time taken per row would reflect the complexity of the information extraction processes of the letters on that row. Thus, if the task permitted the perceiver to test specific features of the shapes, without having to name the letters, then processing should be much faster. This improvement in speed could be due to less time being needed for each letter, or to more letters being processed during each fixation. The latter is likely when preattentive processing can be used on separate features prior to any identification.

FIGURE 10.1 Abbreviated examples of lists for visual search tasks. The target letter is K in (a), the absence of Q in (b), and the presence of Z in (c) and (d) (examples taken from Neisser, 1963).

(a)	(b)	(c)	(d)
EHYP	ZVMLBQ	ODUGQR	IVMXEW
SWIQ	HSQJMF	QCDUGO	EWVMIX
UFCJ	ZTJVQR	CQOGRD	EXWMVI
WBYH	RDQTFM	QUGCDR	IXEMWV
OGTX	TQVRSX	URDGQO	VXWEMI
GWVX	MSVRQX	GRUQDO	MXVEWI
TWLN	ZHQBTL	DUZGRO	XVWMEI
XJBU	ZJTQXL	UCGROD	MWXVIE
UDXI	LHQVXM	DQRCGU	VIMEXW
HSFP	FVQHMS	QDOCGU	EXVWIM
XSCQ	MTSDQL	CGUROQ	VWMIEX
SDJU	TZDFQB	OCDURQ	VMWIEX
PODC	QLHBMZ	UOCGQD	XVWMEI
ZVBP	QMXBJD	RGQCOU	WXVEMI
PEVZ	RVZHSQ	GRUDQO	XMEWIV
SLRA	STFMQZ	GODUCQ	MXIVEW
JCEN	RVXSQM	QCURDO	VEWMIX
ZLRD	MQBJFT	DUCOQG	EMVXWI
XBOD	MVZXLQ	CGRDQU	IVWMEX
PHMU	RTBXQH	UDRCOQ	IEVMWX
ZHFK	BLQSZX	GQCORU	WVZMXE
PNJW	QSVFDJ	GOQUCD	XEMIWV
CQXT	FLDVZT	GDQUOC	WXIMEV
GHNR	BQHMDX	URDCGO	EMWIVX
IXYD	BMFDQH	GODRQC	IVEMXW

In a wide range of experiments, Neisser varied many parameters of this task. Looking for the presence of a letter (for example, K in list a) is faster than looking for the absence of a letter that is present in every line but one (for example, looking for the absence of a Q in list b). This suggests that rela-

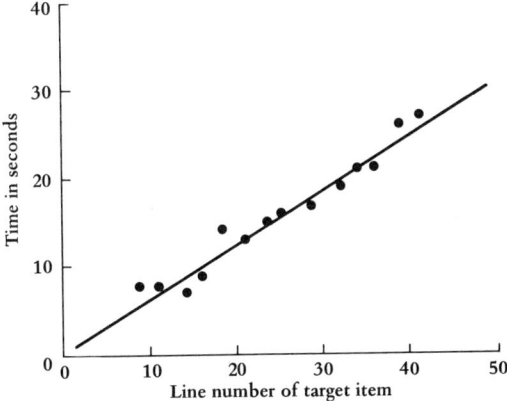

FIGURE 10.2 Typical findings from visual search, showing reaction time as a function of the row in which the target appeared (from Neisser, 1963).

tively little identification of the background letters was needed in list *a*, thus allowing the scan time to be faster. But it took much longer when the target had to be checked on every line as in list *b*. Neisser also found that it was easier to find a Q among a background of angular letters than round letters, and conversely for a Z among round letters (see lists *c* and *d* in Figure 10.1, also Figure 10.3). Thus if the features that differentiate targets from nontargets were easy to discriminate, search was faster than if the targets and nontargets required more complex identification.

Rabbitt (1967) has shown more clearly that perceivers are capable of learning to select features which differentiate targets from nontargets. He had perceivers sort decks of cards into one of two piles, depending upon whether the card contained the letter O or C. The eight background items were either angular (for instance, A, E, F, H, I, K, L) or curved (for instance, B, D, G, J,

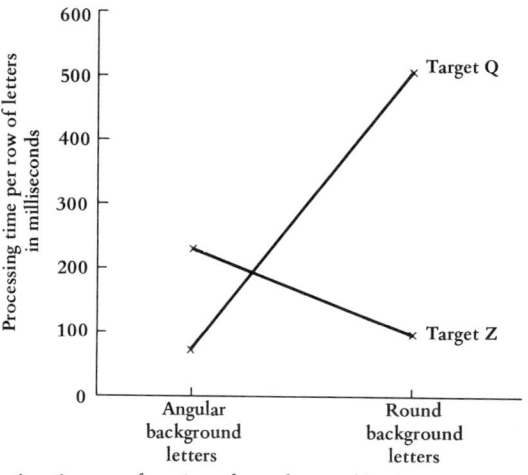

FIGURE 10.3   Reaction time as a function of angularity of background for angular (Z) and round (Q) targets (plotted from data taken from Neisser, 1963).

P, Q, S). One of the angular packs was sorted six times. Then half of the perceivers were switched to another angular pack (for example, with background letters M, N, T, V, W, X, Y, Z,) while the remainder were switched to the curved pack. Sorting time for those transferred to the other angular pack did not change, but it increased by 20 percent for the perceivers who were transferred from angular to curved background items.

Rabbitt interpreted these results to mean that the perceivers had learned to find those features which differentiated the targets from the background items. The effortless transfer from one angular set to another must mean that the perceivers were not learning anything about the names of the items, but only something about their features. When the names were changed but the features held constant, as from one angular pack to another, no loss in performance was noted. But when those features were changed, the discrimination took longer.

Broadbent (1971) has proposed a distinction that might be useful in this context. He suggested that if the perceiver can use a physical feature difference to locate a target, as in the tasks used by Neisser and Rabbitt, then they will do so and improve the speed of processing, because they do not need to make a complete name identification. On the other hand, if there is no feature difference that distinguishes targets from nontargets, then perhaps complete analysis of all dimensions will be made, and the comparison made on the basis of the names of the letters.

There seems to be ample evidence from Neisser's work that the perceiver can find a target without having to identify fully each letter he encounters. After a perceiver had searched through many displays, he could not recognize the nontarget background items in a subsequent recognition test. Certainly, if all of the features had been fully analyzed to the point of identification, the perceiver should be able to remember some of the letters. In fact, perceivers from almost all search tasks of this sort report that the backgrounds looked like a blur—only the targets stood out. Thus not only were the perceivers unable to remember the background items after the experiment, they were apparently not even aware that they were looking at them. Unfortunately this data on subsequent recognition was not obtained in any of the experiments in which the features of the targets and the backgrounds were very similar. Presumably, the perceiver should have remembered more of the background letters there, if he had to identify them.

Neisser (1963) also examined what happens in this task when the perceiver has to look for more than one target at a time. Thus, instead of looking just for a K in list *a* of Figure 10.1, he might have to look for a Q or a K, and respond when he finds an instance of either one. Figure 10.4 shows the results for searches of one, two, or four letters as a function of days of practice. It is clear that without exhaustive practice, perceivers take longer per row when they have to search for more letters. Thus searching for an instance of one of ten letters takes much longer than a single letter, although not ten times as long. The important finding is that after many days of practice on this task, perceivers were able to search down the list at the same speed regardless of how many targets they were looking for. Wattenberger (1970) replicated this result, and showed that it holds regardless of whether the perceiver is permitted to make errors in order to go rapidly or is required to hold errors to a bare minimum. Neisser (1967) also noted that searchers in news-clip agencies can look through the newspapers for the names of clients at search rates of 1000 words per minute for over 100 target names. Of course, we have no idea of how many items they miss.

Several explanations have been offered for the improvement with practice in multiple target search tasks. One possibility is a change from a serial feature by feature processing, in which each feature of each target is examined one at

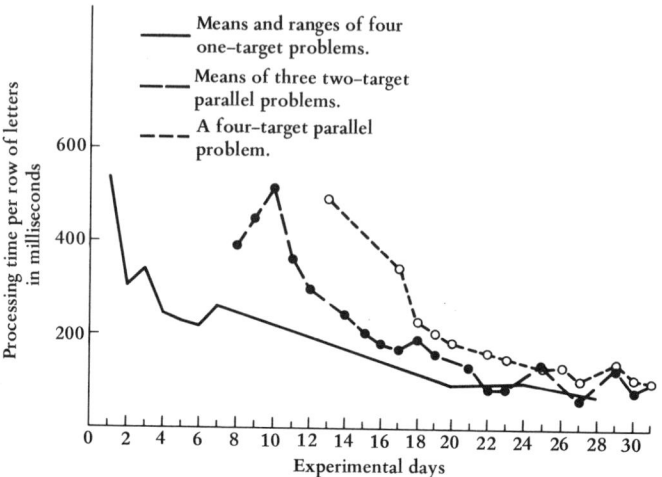

FIGURE 10.4   Reaction time as a function of days of practice when looking for one, two, or four targets (from Neisser, 1963).

a time, to one in which several features or several targets are processed at the same time. This might be due to a change in the strategy of the perceiver or a change in the familiarity of the target items that permits them to be grouped or chunked together into a more meaningful unit, thereby reducing the number of separate items to be processed.

The improvement might also be explained in terms of a reduction in the number of different features that must be processed. Since it is not necessary to analyze all of the features of most letters to tell them apart, the improvement could reflect better discrimination of the critical features used to distinguish targets from nontargets. An unpracticed perceiver might use too many features and therefore be inefficient. Thus, while the perceiver might think he is searching for a particular target, he might actually be looking for certain distinctive features. This possibility could lead to the prediction that perceivers could make correct responses in noting the presence of the target without being able to name it. Neisser noted that many of his perceivers reported this feeling. When they had found one of the target letters in the multiple-letter search tasks, they frequently could not say which one they had found.

At present, these two types of explanations are not well differentiated by experimental tests, although we tend to lean toward the latter interpretation, based upon a reduction in the number of feature tests that are needed. In any event, however this question is ultimately resolved, this entire line of research has provided rather strong evidence that perceivers are capable of extracting information from visual displays without having to perform a complete analysis and identification of the items. Presumably this can occur whenever the task permits the perceiver to capitalize on any feature differences that might be present that will distinguish sought-after items from the irrelevant background material. Thus, in terms of the concepts of this chapter on selection, it *is* possible for perceivers to select some aspects of the visual display without having carried out the processing to its full extent. This follows from Neisser's distinction between preattentive and focal attentive processes, in which target search can be carried out preattentively if the differences between the target and non-target items are sufficiently large and can be emphasized by practice.

INSTRUCTIONAL SET EXPERIMENTS

A second class of tasks that have been used to explore selectivity in the early processing stages involves telling the perceiver, before he reports about what he has just seen, that some part, feature, or character is more important than the other parts. Since this manipulation generally results in a higher accuracy of report for the part emphasized in the instructional set, it suggests that a selective process was initiated. The research on this question has been voluminous, and we shall not attempt to cover very much of it here. Haber offered a general review in 1966, and not much new data has been presented since then to change the conclusions fundamentally, even though we will incorporate the interpretation of this research within the model being pursued in this book (which is not entirely consistent with Haber's earlier review of 1966).

A favorite research procedure spanning over sixty years of work has been to present briefly a number of geometric forms, which could differ in a number of dimensions such as in their shapes, colors, sizes, the number of each type, and so forth. The perceiver would generally be told to report everything that he had been shown, but that one of the dimensions (for example, the colors of each of the objects) was more important so that he should especially attempt to get the various instances of that dimension correct. The instructional set effect occurs whenever the perceiver is more accurate on the dimension emphasized.

One interpretation of this effect has held that the features specifying the emphasized dimension would be represented in iconic storage more vividly. Thus, if colors were made more important, the features specifying the various colors would be stronger or more salient than the features for shape, size, numerosity, and so forth. Stated somewhat more loosely, the colors would stand out. Support for this position has been proposed based on when the instructional set was given to the perceiver. If he does not know what the emphasized dimension is until after the presentation, there would be no way for those features to stand out in the icon—the icon would have decayed away by the time the set was given. Thus, if the set effect occurs only when the set is given prior to the presentation but not afterwards, then an enhancement in the icon would be supported.

The principle alternative explanation has argued that there is no enhancement of features in the icon, following the proposition that the content of the icon cannot be manipulated by familiarity, expectation, meaningfulness, or in this case instructional set. Rather, the facilitation of report of the emphasized dimension occurs because of the way in which the perceiver extracts the information from the icon, and then subsequently organizes and stores that information.

In a series of experiments by Harris and Haber (1963) and Haber (1964a, 1964b) these two types of explanations, plus some variants of each, could be compared. Each study used the same stimuli—pairs of concept cards containing two sets of geometric objects. Thus, one stimulus card might have three green triangles on the left side and two blue squares on the right side. There were three dimensions (color, number, shape) and each could be one of four different instances. That is, the colors on each side were either red, blue, green, or yellow, the shapes on each side were either triangle, square, star, or circle, and there were either one, two, three, or four instances on each side. A stimulus card was presented for one-tenth of a second, and the perceiver had to describe the card completely in his report. The instructional set manipulation was given only before the presentation (no postpresentation comparison was made in these experiments). On some trials, the perceiver was told that all three dimensions (color, number, and shape) were of equal value in their reports. On other trials, they were told they would earn many more points if they correctly reported one of the dimensions. Thus, if the color dimension was emphasized, the perceiver was told he would receive thirty points if he correctly reported the two colors, but only three points respectively, if he correctly named the two shapes or the two numbers. On half of the trials, the perceiver was free to report the dimensions in any order he chose, but on the other half, he had to follow a prescribed order, one that he did not know until after the presentation when he began his report.

The most important manipulation in each of these experiments was the strategy by which the perceivers were trained to encode and remember the stimulus dimensions. Half of the perceivers were trained to use a code which treated the stimulus as two objects, one on the left and one on the right. Thus an "object" code for a particular stimulus might be "one red triangle" (on the left), "three green circles" (on the right). The other half were trained to use a code that specified the stimuli in terms of their separate dimensions. Thus, the same stimulus in the above example might be encoded in a "dimension" code as "red-green; triangle-circle; one-three." Of course, the order in which the three dimensions are described can be varied without any change in the accuracy of the description. There is only one order possible for the object coders—that given by English syntax.

Those perceivers who were trained to use the "dimensions" coding strategy showed a strong instructional set effect, in that when one dimension was emphasized, they were more accurate in reporting that dimension. This was due entirely to a loss in accuracy for the unemphasized dimensions, since the emphasized one was not reported any better than the comparable dimension in conditions in which all dimensions were equal in value. Haber (1964b) showed that the coding strategies differed in the order in which the perceiver encoded the dimension—that is, translated the iconic representation into the words that he had to use to describe what he saw. Thus, it appears as if the encoding takes place from a rapidly fading iconic representation; and parts encoded first are translated relatively accurately, while those aspects left for last are substantially degraded. Since the dimension coders varied the order of encoding as a function of the set instructions given them, they always left the unimportant dimensions for last. The object coders never varied their order of encoding, so no change in performance could be detected, regardless of the instructional set given them.

It is conceivable that these results could be due to order of report and not to order of encoding. If so, then it is not the order in which the dimensions are encoded that is important, but rather some forgetting process after encoding is completed and the information is being maintained in short-term memory during the process of report. The dimension coders were less accurate on the dimension *reported* last, so there probably was some forgetting of those parts of the report given last. This was not true for the object coders, presumably because of the greater predictability of the English syntax order, which helps to preserve memory. But more important, the instructional set was found for the dimension coders even when the order of report was specified and not left up to the perceiver. Hence, an emphasized dimension is reported best even when the perceiver is forced to report it last.

Another comparison in these data is revealing. In each experiment, the overall accuracy shown by the object coders was higher than that of the dimension coders. Thus, not only were the object coders immune to the instructional sets, and to order of report, but they were generally more accurate in their reports for each comparison made. Haber (1964b) argued that this might be due to their use of the highly overlearned English syntax, which permitted them to begin their encoding faster, complete it more rapidly, rehearse it faster, and make fewer errors during its maintenance in memory. He reported some indirect evidence in support of each of these possibilities, all of which would lead to the findings described.

But it is possible that the difference in accuracy between the two coding strategies is due to a more fundamental property of their respective codes. The dimension coders appear to concentrate on one dimension at a time, encode its two instances, which are displaced from each other in space, and then go on to the next dimension, and so forth. The object coders, on the other hand, concentrate on three different dimensions at one time, all in the same spatial location, and then repeat the process on the other side of the stimulus. If one can think of analyzing features represented in the icon (in the same sense as the visual search work of Neisser suggested) through the use of a set of feature detectors, each of which is tuned to the presence of a particular type of feature, then it is a reasonable prediction that two or more different feature detectors might be used simultaneously over the features in the icon, but that any particular detector, such as for color, might have to be used sequentially, looking first for this color, and then for that one, and so forth. Thus, any task that permits the perceiver to use different feature detectors on the icon would be faster than when he has to use the same detectors over and over. The former is permitted by the object coding strategy, while the dimension code forces processing on a pair of instances of the same feature.

Allport (1968, 1971) has suggested this type of hypothesis, and some earlier data by Lappin (1967) is quite consistent with it as well. Lappin examined the extent to which perceivers could divide their attention between and among different dimensions of simple geometric forms. In one condition, a simple circular form could vary in color and size, as well as in the direction of tilt of a line bisecting the circle. In a second condition, three circular forms were presented which could vary in each of the three dimensions. However, in this condition, the instructions were to report the value each had on only one of the three dimensions. In the third condition, three circular forms were presented, but the perceiver was required to describe the first circle using one dimension, the second using another dimension, and the third using the third dimension. Lappin found the first condition to be the easiest and the third to be the hardest. He suggested, therefore, that processing could take place faster for different dimensions of the same form, when the same dimension had to be analyzed over different forms. This would argue that perceivers will be more efficient whenever they can follow an encoding strategy that permits them to use several different feature analyses on each aspect of the stimulus pattern, rather than the same analysis on different aspects. This conclusion obviously needs much more support, but it is consistent with the differences noted and of great potential usefulness in explaining information extraction.

Several conclusions can be drawn from this group of studies on instructional sets. First, there is no evidence that the instructional set affects anything in the content of the icon itself. The emphasized dimension does not appear to stand out or to be more noticeable. Otherwise we should have found that the first dimension encoded was more accurate when it was emphasized than when it was equal in value to the other dimensions. Second, the instructional set effect does seem to be due to the order of processing of the dimensions, the order in which they are encoded from the iconic representation into a form which can be maintained in short-term memory. Because the dimension coders can vary that order of encoding, they are able to show an effect of instructional set. Third, the differences between the two coding strategies may reflect that we can process instances of different features simultaneously but different instances of the same feature only sequentially. In this sense, selective processes can occur both because of the order in which we extract information from a briefly held iconic storage, and because of whether the strategy used permits simultaneous attention to more than one dimension at a time.

It is unfortunate that these experiments on instructional sets generally demand a verbal report. Because of this, the processing sequence almost has to be from the icon to short-term memory, and does not reflect coding of the iconic features into a visual image representation. We know very little about such coding processes, so that it is possible that none of the conclusions just drawn about verbal processing would be applicable. It is our expectation that meaningfulness, and therefore importance generated by instructional sets, would be reflected in the visual images of stimulation. But until the appropriate experiments are undertaken, not much more can be said.

PROCESSING TIME STUDIES

On the assumption that in the kinds of information extraction tasks considered so far in this chapter most processing follows some form of sequential or serial order, interest has focused on the speed with which this processing occurs. Experiments on speed also are useful in providing further evidence on the extraction process itself.

One procedure has been to vary the number of items in a visual display, and either control the amount of time available to process the item or to record the amount of time needed for the perceiver to respond. When a linear increase in information processed with time available is found, this has usually been interpreted as evidence for sequential item by item processing. Although the logic of this argument is by no means perfect, the research is quite important.

We have already described a study by Sperling (1963) in both Chapters 6 and 7 that concerns this type of task. On each trial, an array of letters was briefly presented, followed by a visual noise field to limit the time available for processing the array. The perceiver had to report the letters he could see and remember. These results were presented in Figure 6.7, where the number of letters correctly reported is plotted as a function of delay of the masking field. It is clear that there is a linear increase in the number of items processed as a function of the amount of time available for processing. Sperling estimated this rate to be about 10 milliseconds per item. This would suggest that there is a serial focusing of attention, first on one letter and then on another, and that the limit usually identified with selectivity may be a limit imposed by the amount of time available to encode the information in the iconic storage. Allport (1968) reports virtually the same rate of processing for the items in a digit display.

Sternberg (1966) and Briggs and Blaha (1969) reported comparable results with a high-speed visual scanning task. In these experiments, perceivers were given the name of a single target item and then shown an array of items that may or may not contain the target. The perceiver was required to respond as rapidly as possible to indicate whether the target item was present or absent. Figure 10.5, taken from one condition from Briggs and Blaha, shows reaction times as a function of the number of items in the display. As can be seen, the more items in the display, the more processing time is needed for the response, which suggests a sequential scanning through the icon. When the target item is absent from the array, the perceiver has to examine each of the items before he can respond negatively. Since Sternberg and Briggs and Blaha found that search times were faster for arrays in which the target was present, it appears as if the perceiver terminated his search as soon as he found the target. Thus,

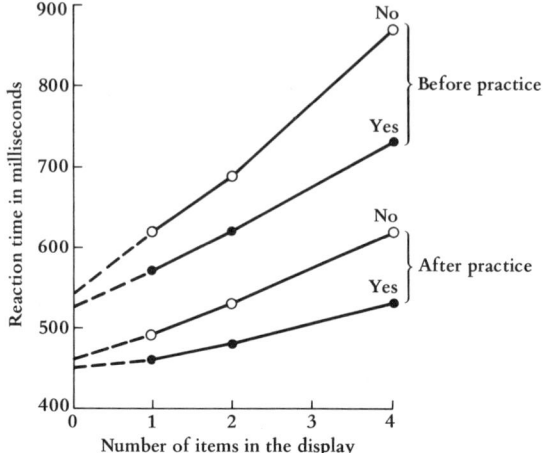

FIGURE 10.5   Reaction time as a function of the number of items in the display when the target was present and when it was absent (plotted from data taken from Briggs and Blaha, 1969).

these studies (and a number of others like them) show a rapid shift in processing time from one item to the next, and a self-terminating process when the target is encountered.

Generally the times found in the high-speed scanning experiments are longer than in the visual noise experiments. This is to be expected, given the processing levels indicated by the manipulations used. The visual noise presentation controls the amount of time that is available to extract information from the icon. Once the features of a letter are extracted, however, no further limitation is imposed on its being named, stored, rehearsed, retrieved, or reported. Thus, this technique taps into the information-processing system at a very early stage. The Sternberg task, on the other hand, measures the time needed to extract information from the icon plus the time to attach a name to the item and compare it with the target being held in short-term memory. Hence the additional time. But in both tasks, the linear relationship between performance and either time or number of items clearly suggests an item by item process. In other words, we select one part of the information represented in the icon to process, and then go on to another part. It seems much more difficult to interpret these results in support of a simultaneous or parallel processing model, in which we are attending to all aspects of the information at the same time. Although such a derivation is logically possible, the pattern of results reviewed in this chapter makes such a derivation intuitively unlikely.

CHARACTER CLASSIFICATION

A series of studies initiated by Posner (beginning with Posner and Mitchell, 1967) have provided another means to examine the representation and processing of visually presented information. The power of the Posner and Mitchell experiments derives from their use of identical stimulus-response combinations to produce differences in response latencies as a function of the different matching instructions. The task used was very simple—the viewers were required to indicate whether a pair of letters were the same or were different by pressing one of two response keys. They were instructed to make their decisions as quickly as they could. Comparisons were made between the response latencies when instructed to match the letters for their physical characteristics (do the two letters look visually the same?), or on the basis of the letter names (do the two letters have the same name, for instance, Bb?), or on the basis of a higher order rule (are the two letters both vowels or not?).

At the simplest level of processing, the match would be based on the physical attributes of the stimulus pair (for example, AA = same; AB = different). At a higher level of processing, the match would be based on the names of the letters so that the stimulus pair "Aa" now would be called "same" instead of "different." The difference between these two tasks is that the physical match could be made solely on the basis of physical attributes of the stimuli and, therefore, without any need to identify the letters based upon labels available in memory. The name match requires some memory contact. A match on the basis of a consonant-vowel rule would be at an even higher level of classification (abstraction) since many letters are vowels and many are consonants.

The response latencies obtained from these conditions support the notion that different levels were involved in responding to the three instructions. The depth of processing needed to respond "same" increased from physical to name to rule match. The same responses based on physical identity were about 75 milliseconds faster than those based on name identity, and this response was about 180 milliseconds faster than the match based on the rule.

These data have been used to argue that when a physical match is permitted by the task demands, then such a match can be made based upon the visual representations alone, without any need to attach names or to carry out any further recognition or identification processing. This presumably occurs in the visual image representation (not in the icon, for as we shall see, the time constants are too long). When the task demands that the items to be classified first be named, then the match must be made on the names, and that would require processing in short-term memory, where the names are available. Presumably, the 75 millisecond latency difference reflects the faster transfer of information from an icon to a visual image than to a short-term memory representation. Several separate lines of evidence support this interpretation.

A number of experiments introduced a time delay between the two stimuli to be matched in an attempt to differentiate processes. On the assumption that a visual representation of the stimulus is available for a limited time, the visual match could be performed only when stimuli are temporally adjacent. If a delay is introduced between the two letters to be matched, the differences in reaction time for the name and physical match should disappear. Figure 10.6 illustrates the differences in reaction time between name and physical identity "same" responses as a function of the time interval between the two successive stimulus letters, measured from the onset of the second letter. This figure represents a composite of several experiments (Posner and Keele, 1967; Posner, Boies, Eichelman, and Taylor, 1969) in which the viewer was presented with a single letter followed by a second letter with the time interval between them varying from zero to two seconds. The two letters could be either physically identical, have only the same name, or be different. The instructions were to respond "same" if the two letters had the same name, otherwise to respond "different." When the second letter was presented immediately after the first, the match appears to have been made on the basis of the visual characterization of the physical stimuli. In this situation, a physical match was about 90 milliseconds faster than a name match, much like the difference reported earlier. As the delay between the two letters was increased to two seconds, the reaction time difference between the visual and the name match declined almost to zero. Since the information about the first letter must have been retained during this interval in order to make the match when the second letter appeared, it is likely that in this situation the initial visual information was encoded into the letter name. When the second letter was presented, it too could be named and then the names compared. Because up to two seconds is required before the match can be made and the visual representation is no

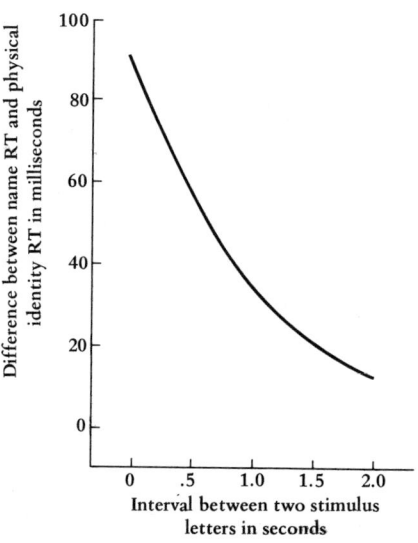

FIGURE 10.6 Difference in reaction time for a name versus a physical match as a function of the time interval between the presentation of the two letters (from Posner and Keele, 1967).

longer available, it seems unlikely that the visual matching is carried out in the icon itself.

Another line of evidence concerns the effects that different kinds of similarity have upon the time needed to classify two characters. If the visual match is made entirely on the basis of a visual representation, then the time needed to make a classification of same or different should not depend on the similarity of the names of the characters, but it might be slowed down if the two forms were visually very similar (for example, an O and Q, or an A and V). On the other hand, if a match requires naming the characters, then visual similarity should not matter, but similar sounding names should delay the classification (as with B and T or E and C). Posner and Taylor (1969) verified these predictions rather precisely. They went on to argue that because visual similarity had no impact on name matches, it is unlikely that the perceiver first created a visual image representation and *then* named the letter. Rather, it appears that the visual image and the short-term memory representation were constructed in parallel. The time difference between them suggests that the visual image representation can be begun, carried out or completed faster than the named representation.

We shall consider one other aspect of the character classification experiment in the next chapter when we examine the effects of familiarity on perceptual recognition. In the present context, the power of the procedure stems from the clear evidence it provides for different levels of processing in the visual system, and that perceivers are able to selectively respond without having made a complete identification of the stimuli.

INTERFERENCE DURING ENCODING

An important aspect of selectivity is being able to ignore irrelevant or unwanted components of stimulation. The visual search tasks considered earlier can be thought of in this way. You can find the target faster if you can learn to ignore and not process the irrelevant background items. But Stroop (1935) developed a more diabolical task with which to study interference among relevant and irrelevant parts of the visual display.

In the Stroop test, a page of up to 100 color patches is presented and a perceiver is instructed to name the colors of the ink as rapidly as possible. Stroop reported that reading speed was reduced over 25 percent if the colored inks were, in fact, the letters that spelled color names. For example, it took longer to name the color red when the red ink spelled the word "blue" than when it was only a rectangular patch of color or if it was letters that spelled a non-color word. Obviously there is interference in naming the colors because the perceiver was reading the word even though it was only necessary to focus on the color. But it was not only because words were also being processed — there is differential interference depending upon the meaning of the words.

For example, Klein (1964) found little interference (loss of speed) when non-color words were used, some interference for color synonyms, and greatest interference for actual color words.

Several rather different types of explanation have been offered to explain this interference effect, explanations that differ with respect to the locus of the effect in the information-processing system. A favorite one proposed that it was due to some type of interference that occurred at the time of the utterance of the response, but this seems unlikely since the effect is found even when no verbal response is required (see below for an example). To say simply that the perceiver could not suppress the color word because of some prepotency of words is not sufficient, although it appears as if something of this kind must be involved.

Morton (1969) explains the Stroop effect in terms of interference that occurs when naming one color while ignoring the name of another color, when both names are available after encoding. To test this notion, Morton and Chambers (1970) used a card sorting version of this task in which the perceiver had to sort cards into two piles depending upon whether ink used to print a color name at the top of the card was the same color as a patch at the bottom of the card. For example, the word "red" might be printed in green ink at the top of the card and a green patch might be at the bottom. The perceiver had to place this card in a pile in which ink and patch colors were the same, even when the color word at the top did not agree. Cards of this sort took longer to sort than ones which did not have a conflicting color name printed at the top. However, if the perceiver was instructed to look first at the bottom of the card and then at the top (instead of the typical top-to-bottom sequence), the interference disappeared. According to Morton, in this situation the perceiver processed only the color at the bottom, since that was the only information present, and then could easily have developed a strategy to match only the appropriate color at the top. Presumably, color information could be analyzed from the top without any interference. When the processing starts at the top, both the ink color and the spelled color get named and are available for comparison. This causes confusion or interference in the comparison step of the processing and, therefore, loss of speed.

Thus, according to Morton, the interference can be avoided by choosing an order of processing that delays the availability of the printed color name until the perceiver is ready to match colored inks. At that time, the color word probably gets processed, but it is too late by then—the match has already been made.

This chapter has followed from the previous one and leads into the next without any sharp divisions. Many of the same techniques will be used in Chapter 11 on recognition. The difference will be one of emphasis primarily. In the present chapter we have focused on selective mechanisms—what is encoded and in what way. In Chapter 11 we will look at the fate of the encoded information, especially as it might form the basis for a recognition or an identification response.

SUMMARY

Noting that not all components of the luminance discontinuities are perceived and responded to as objects in the visual world, this chapter has examined some of the mechanisms by which selective processes occur and function in visual perception. The principal technique for selection is via our direction of gaze—where we choose to look, what we look at, and for how long. But within each fixation or glance not all of the potential information is processed. We suggested that such selection occurs because of strategies employed for processing or encoding stimulations, which determine the order that information is extracted. Since the storage mechanisms in the early stages of information processing are of brief duration, information processed late is usually degraded or lost by then. This type of loss due to delayed processing can be shown to account for much of the selectivity in perception. Further, we showed that many tasks permit adequate responses in the absence of complete identification, so that selection can occur because of the level in the processing sequence required.

Five different kinds of selection processes were examined, each illustrating a different methodology and revealing a different facet of the processing sequence. The first of these focused on visual search tasks, in which a perceiver had to search a list of items to find a predesignated target character. Clear evidence is reported to show that perceivers can find targets without having to identify each item encountered, but rather that they can select some of the information to process without having to complete a full analysis.

The second task provides the perceiver with an instructional set, which tells him which dimensions or parts of the stimulus array are most important. Evidence was reviewed to show that such sets improved performance on the emphasized dimensions whenever they cause the perceiver to alter the order in which he encodes the dimension, because it appears as if accuracy is primarily a function of that order of encoding from iconic storage into short-term memory. Some suggestive evidence was also presented to indicate that a coding strategy which permits the perceiver to process different dimensions of each part of the visual display is more efficient or faster than one which requires that each instance of a dimension be extracted before going on to another dimension. Thus we find selective processes both with respect to order of encoding and in terms of the type of code used.

The third area of research has concerned tasks in which selective processes can be studied while the speed of information extraction is examined. These studies also support an ordered processing, usually one item at a time, at very high rates approaching 100 items per second.

The fourth area concerned character classifications. Although these tasks do not reveal the necessarily sequential nature of information processing, they do dramatically illustrate the separate processing stages involved. Thus, if the task permits a classification based only on the way characters look, without regard to their names or meanings, then perceivers can make such classifications. If names, meanings, or rules are needed, then the characters must be named, and no effect of their visual features can be detected in further processing.

The last area looked at the interference created by information that is irrelevant or that must be ignored in order for processing to proceed smoothly. Here again, whether interference occurs depends on whether the perceiver can use strategies which either let him avoid processing the irrelevant material or avoid completely that processing to the level at which interference is more likely.

Readings

We have already mentioned Moray's (1970) excellent text on attention and Broadbent's (1971) more general statement on information processing. The major part of a new book by Kahneman (1973) concerns selective attention, although most of the work concerns the auditory modality. He also includes an excellent summary of current work on vigilance. Neisser (1967) covers most of the work in this chapter. Treisman (1969) has perhaps the best theoretical review of this topic, even though it leans on concepts somewhat different from those used here. A recent collected volume by Mostofsky (1970) contains many very fine papers on selective process in perception.

INTRODUCTION

This chapter will apply our information-processing analysis to the recognition and identification of figures, objects, faces, symbols, letters, words, and sentences. These processes are most clearly described by the term "visual cognition" since recognition and identification necessarily involve more than the construction of an internal representation of the visual world around us—that internal representation must somehow make contact with memory. That is, contact must be made between the present input and the stored representation of previous inputs. The study of perceptual recognition and identification, therefore, concerns the nature of this contact with memory. This has broad implications for the study of cognition and learning. The nature of the contact with memory will depend not only on perceptual variables and the nature of perceptual processing, but even more on the nature of the representations in memory and the processes which manifest their effect on the input. In many ways, then, the study of visual recognition and identification may be thought of as the study of perception *and* memory.

The terms "recognition" and "identification" are often used interchangeably despite some important distinctions between them. Recognition describes a sense of familiarity—"I have seen that before"—whereas identification requires the production of a specific label or category name—"That is an apple." When reporting our perceptions of words, we identify the visual display, naming the words being read rather than simply noting that we recognize them as being familiar. Thus, it is possible to identify words we do not recognize—as when we read a new word—as well as to recognize objects we cannot identify. Much of the research reported in the previous chapter showed evidence of this distinction.

The early explanations of perceptual recognition and identification centered around the enhancement or inhibition of perception. For example, it was found that tachistoscopic thresholds were lower for familiar shapes and words (Henle, 1942; Solomon and Howes, 1951; Solomon and Postman, 1952); and it was generally assumed that this occurred because they were perceived better or faster. Proposals that perception can be inhibited (perceptual defense) or enhanced (perceptual vigilance) were also made for variables related to the motivational and affective state of the perceiver (for example, Bruner and Postman, 1949a, 1949b; Bruner, 1957). This evidence demonstrated that stimuli which were differentially related to internal states of the perceiver produced

247

differential tachistoscopic recognition thresholds. For example, a perceiver who was made anxious by words with sexual connotations might require longer exposure durations than normal to see these words.

While the early experimental findings clearly showed differences in responses as a function of these variables, the explanations were quickly attacked as too simple. One criticism was based on a distinction between "perceptual" and "response" effects. For example, the differences might not reflect perceptual events but events related to response availability or even to a willingness of the perceiver to make a response (Eriksen, 1957; Garner, Hake, and Eriksen, 1956). Indeed, Goldiamond and Hawkins (1958) were able to show that perceivers who expected to see words in a tachistoscope, but were shown smudges, nevertheless produced a word-frequency effect in their responses.

It is now clear that even the perception-response distinction is too simple. Neisser notes (especially 1967, pp. 118–124) that these terms are difficult to encompass in experiments because they are impossible to define. The solution proposed by Neisser is to attempt explanations in terms of "visual" and "verbal" processes. But even though this proposal by Neisser is an advance, it does not go far enough. The perceiver's responses in recognition experiments can only be understood by reference to a much more complex model of the sequence of processes, such as one like the model proposed in Chapter 7. Therefore, the research reviewed in this chapter will be interpreted in terms of the information-processing model proposed earlier. For example, the differences found in recognition experiments may be explained by processes of information extraction from the icon or visual image and the subsequent encoding into short-term memory, or by processes involved in the retention of this information prior to the response, as well as by processes involved in the construction of the visual image representation.

We will not discuss the entire range of phenomena relating to recognition and identification in this chapter. Instead, we will concentrate on variables which are loosely concerned with familiarity, but are more properly understood as variables relating the visual world to the perceiver's memory. Therefore, our discussion in the first part of this chapter will primarily involve experiments using letters and words as stimuli. The second part will concern variables which alter the motivational or affective state of the perceiver. These will be reviewed and interpreted within the same information-processing model. A final part on picture recognition will permit a comparison between processes involved in identifying linguistic material, in which verbal codes may be important, and those involved in picture recognition, in which such verbal codes may not be as relevant.

FAMILIARITY

Familiarity is the general term used to describe the fact that perceivers respond differently to novel stimuli than they do to stimuli with which they have had some experience. The degree of familiarity is not a property of the stimulus, but of the perceiver. Since different perceivers may have had different amounts of experience with the same stimulus, familiarity with respect to a particular stimulus may be different for different perceivers.

In applying these ideas to experiments on perceptual recognition and identification, familiarity is the general term which describes a set of variables used to study the processes involved in memory contact. For example, letters are more familiar than letter-like forms because we have seen letter-configurations many times in our lives and have rarely, if ever, seen the letter-like forms. Moreover, the letters have readily available verbal labels—their letter names. Thus, for simple patterns or configurations, variation in familiarity refers to differences in visual experience as well as in the availability of verbal labels. Familiarity may also be varied by combining letters in different ways. Letter strings may be formed by selecting letters at random or by following rules which reflect the distributional and sequential letter frequencies found in the natural language. Letters may be selected to produce strings which are more or less pronounceable or, finally, they may be selected to produce actual meaningful words, for which a single name can be used to represent a sequence of letters. Words may also be selected according to their frequency in print to represent differences in familiarity. Each of these stimulus patterns, then, represents a different way to vary familiarity and, therefore, each represents a different implicit assumption about the nature of the representation in the memory of the perceiver. For example, using word frequency to vary familiarity implies that the number of past contacts with each word is somehow represented in memory. In this sense, a frequent word is more familiar than a rare word not simply because it appears more often in print, but because this frequency is assumed to be represented in the perceiver's memory and, consequently, to affect memory contact during recognition.

We will begin our discussion of the role of familiarity in recognition with an analysis of the processes involved in matching single letters and letter-like forms. Next we will turn to processing letter strings that differ in the degree to which they approximate the structure of English words without being actual words. We will see that much of the data from experiments using letter strings can be explained by assuming a simple left-to-right letter-scanning mechanism. We will then consider this explanation for the processing of words.

Processing Single Letters

Posner and Mitchell (1967) compared performance in a letter-matching task with that for matching letter-like forms (Gibson, 1965) presented under the same instructions. Their purpose was to determine whether matching unfamiliar forms was similar to matching letters—forms which are highly familiar in both perceptual configuration and in name. They found that familiarity did not improve performance in the perceptual matching task—matching a pair of physically identical letters did not take less time than matching nonsense forms of similar complexity. Similar findings have been reported for matching mirror-image letters (Hochberg, 1968), for matching lines at different slants (Posner, 1969), and for matching pictures (Wingfield, 1968).

Hochberg (1968) found no difference in the number of looks needed to match upright letters and upside-down letters when the letters were presented next to each other. When the letters were separated by a distance large enough to require a movement of the eyes for both to be seen, matching upright letters took fewer glances. This change in response pattern suggests that the adjacent letters were matched using visual information while the separated ones were matched using the letter names. Hochberg concluded that memory did not play a role in perceptual matches when it was not necessary to encode the name of the stimulus to make the match. As soon as it became necessary for information about the letters to be stored in order to perform the match, the perceiver had to encode them and, therefore, to identify them. The easiest form of identification for matching is letter naming.

The analysis presented above assumes that visual matches are made on the visual representations of the stimuli. The finding that familiarity plays no role in these matches implies that familiarity plays no role in the construction of the visual image. Nevertheless, it is not necessary to abandon the idea that the visual image representation may be affected by the perceiver's familiarity with the stimuli being presented. The visual displays used in the experiments reviewed might not have provided an appropriate test for this proposition. The "unfamiliar" stimuli used were unfamiliar only in the sense of not having a readily available name or verbal category. But as far as being coherent forms or patterns whose organizational properties are well defined, they cannot be considered novel visual forms. It is true that they are not as familiar as the alphabetic shapes in the sense of having been seen as often, but they are certainly not unpredictable or unusual. Therefore, it is not surprising that the experiments did not yield differences in processing the visual representations of the "familiar" and "unfamiliar" materials used. A fairer test of familiarity with respect to the visual (organizational) properties of the stimuli would require forms completely unlike letters. Perhaps Chinese or Japanese characters or random-shaped polygons would provide a better evaluation of the role of familiarity in recognizing single forms.

Approximation to English

Another way to vary the familiarity of stimulus material is to construct sequences or arrays of letters that differ in the degree to which they approximate the distributional and sequential frequencies of English. Since we will consider a number of experiments which use such stimuli, we will describe the procedure for their construction in some detail.

Arrays of zero-order approximation to English are constructed by selecting letters for each position in the array independently from a distribution which contains each of the twenty-six letters. To pick a letter for the first position, we select one letter from the alphabet at random. To select a letter for the second position, we first return the letter selected for the first position to the distribution and then randomly select a second letter. This procedure continues until all of the positions in the array are filled. Using this procedure, each letter has one chance out of twenty-six of being selected for each position, and the selection of a letter for any one position is independent of the selection of a letter for any other position. Of course, a sequence of zero-order letters does not resemble English at all. It is zero-order because it does not reflect the different frequencies with which letters actually occur in English nor the typical sequences of letters found in actual words. The first column of Figure 11.1 illustrates some zero-order letter strings constructed in this way.

FIGURE 11.1 Pseudowords constructed at different orders of approximation to English (from Miller, Bruner, and Postman, 1954).

Zero-Order	First-Order	Second-Order	Fourth-Order
YRULPZOC	STANOGOP	WALLYLOF	RICANING
OZHGPMTJ	VTYEHULO	THERARES	VERNALIT
DLEGQMNW	EINOAASE	CHEVADNE	MOSSIANT
GFUJXZAQ	IYDEWAKN	NERMBLIM	POKERSON
WXPAUJVB	RPITCQET	ONESTEVA	ONETICUL
VQWBVIFX	OMNTOHCH	ACOSUNST	ATEDITOL
CVGJCDHM	DNEHHSNO	SERRRTHE	APHYSTER
MFRSIWZE	RSEMPOIN	ROCEDERT	TERVALLE
EJDYOEVZ	ISAAESPW	HEFLINYC	CULATTER
GFXRWMXR	ITYNENEE	EDINGEDL	PREVERAL
BHDTUNQK	OAENSTVT	LIKINERA	FAVORIAL
ANROAHOV	NHIDCFRA	RIPRYPLI	LYMISTIC
HHJHUFSW	YWDNMIIE	UMATSORE	OTATIONS
IJHBWSTT	IODTIRPS	SINEDSIN	INFOREMS
EAPMZCEN	NHGTTEDE	EDESENER	EXPRESPE

The first step in approximating some of the statistical properties of English prose is called first-order approximation to English. First-order letter arrays are constructed in the same way as zero-order except that the distribution from which the letters are selected is one in which the letters are represented in the same proportions they would appear in actual English prose. Thus the letters E and T would appear many more times than the letters X and Z and, therefore, the probability of selecting a T would be greater than the probability of selecting an X. First-order arrays approximate the distributional properties of English letters. Notice in column 2 of Figure 11.1 that relatively few infrequently used letters appear. But the letter sequences are still fairly unlike those found naturally in the language.

Second-order and higher approximations to English come closer and closer to approximating the sequential properties of English. They are all constructed in a similar fashion and we will illustrate it with second-order arrays. Recall that in the previous constructions, letters were selected to fill positions in arrays for each position separately. Now we want to introduce sequential relationships into our selection process; that is, we want the selection of a letter for a particular position to be influenced by the letters in its immediate neighborhood. In second-order arrays, we want the frequency of pairs of letters (digrams) in English prose to be represented in the selection process and therefore in the array.

In order to accomplish this, we sample digram frequency in actual written prose passages. For example, in order to select a letter for the first position in the array, we might open an English novel to some page selected at random, randomly select one position on that page as a starting point, and then search along the line for the first space. The letter immediately following the space would be our first letter. Presumably we are selecting randomly from a distribution in which pairs of letters are represented according to their frequency in English. To obtain the second letter, we follow the same procedure. We select a page and starting place at random, search along the line for an instance of the letter we had already picked for the first position, and then select the letter following it in the text as the next letter in the array. The next letter would be filled in by first finding an instance of the second letter and taking the one next to it. Third- and fourth-order arrays are constructed according to the same procedures, except that we sample trigrams or quadrigrams. To sample trigrams, for example, we search for the two letters previously selected and find the third letter from the text.

An early experiment, by Miller, Bruner, and Postman (1954), varied familiarity of stimulus arrays which differentially approximated the structure of English prose. They clearly showed that identification of letters was easier the higher the approximation. Figure 11.2 shows their results—the percentage

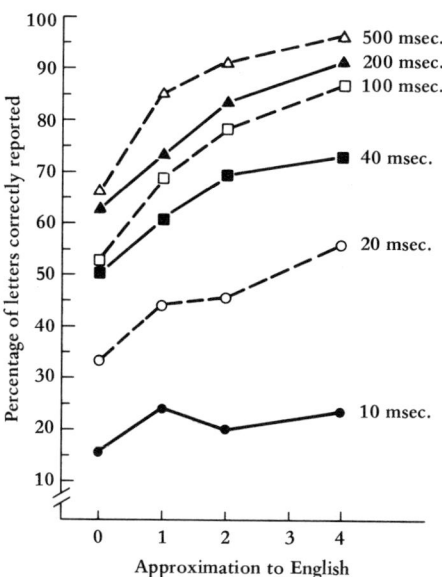

FIGURE 11.2 Percentage of letters correctly reported as a function of their approximation to English for six different exposure durations (from Miller, Bruner, and Postman, 1954).

of letters correctly reported increased as a function of approximation to English for each of the six exposure durations they used.

In another demonstration of this effect, Mewhort (1967) briefly presented pairs of letter arrays, of which each member could be either a zero-order or a fourth-order approximation to English. He used a partial report procedure in which one of two tones sounded after the presentation—a high tone indicated that the letters from the top row should be reported and a low tone that the letters from the bottom row should be reported. More letters were reported from fourth-order arrays than from zero-order arrays. Moreover, the familiarity of the row not reported also affected the accuracy of the report, suggesting to Mewhort that all of the stimuli were processed to some degree even if not reported.

In an attempt to determine how these differences are produced, Hershenson performed a series of experiments on recognition of seven-letter stimulus arrays differing in order of approximation to English. In the first experiment (Hershenson, 1969a), the previously reported differences in recognition accuracy as a function of approximation to English were reproduced (see the function for the naïve perceivers in Figure 11.3) and an interesting effect of letter position was also discovered. Not only was there a linear decrease in overall

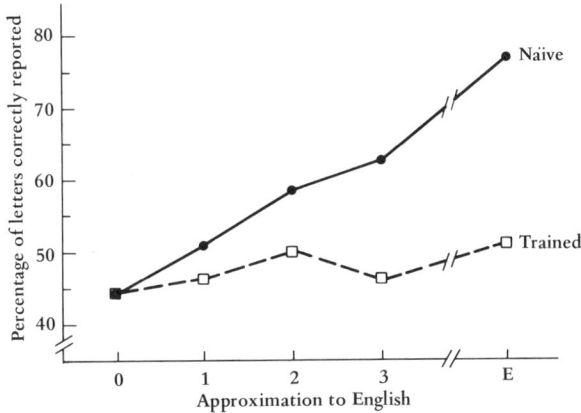

FIGURE 11.3 Percentage of letters correctly reported as a function of approximation to English for naïve and trained perceivers (from Hershenson, 1969a).

accuracy from position one to position seven—the order in which the letters were reported—but the accuracy decreased differentially as a function of approximation to English. There was only a slight decline for English words over the seven letter-positions, the decrease for zero-order was rather steep, and the other functions fell between these two (see Figure 11.4).

The position curves could be explained as a differential clarity of iconic or visual image representation as a function of approximation to English. They could also be explained as the product of differential encoding or retention

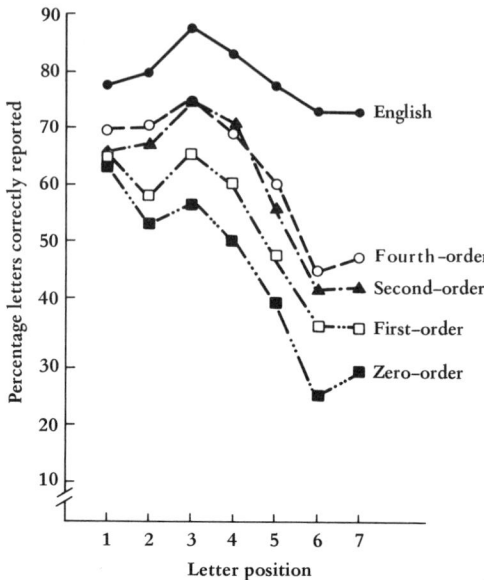

FIGURE 11.4   Percentage of letters correctly reported as a function of letter position in strings of letters of four different approximations to English and English words for naïve perceivers (from Hershenson, 1969a).

(forgetting) caused by serial encoding processes, or by the order in which they were reported. Hershenson attempted to distinguish these alternatives by manipulations designed to eliminate the latter effects. He argued that if the ease of encoding and remembering the letter arrays were equated, then the differences in identification of the letters should disappear. This was based on the assumption that differential clarity in the icon seemed quite unlikely. He demonstrated this with the use of another group of perceivers, tested in the same way. However, before the experiment proper, this group was required to memorize the stimuli to be used. Members of this group studied the lists until they could report correctly over 90 percent of the letters when presented with only one or two letters in each array. This group produced data which differed markedly from that of the first group. Figure 11.3 shows one effect of this training procedure—a sharp decrease in the effect of approximation to English for the trained group of perceivers. Thus, Hershenson's supposition was supported in the results, showing that the effect of different approximation to English was not on the initial representation in iconic storage or in the visual image representation but in subsequent processing.

This analysis was supported by two other differences between the two groups—the pattern of errors and the shape of the letter-position function. When the errors made by both groups of perceivers were analyzed, those made by the naïve perceivers were highly correlated with the frequency with which letters appeared in English. Perceivers who were trained did not show this pattern of errors. This difference suggests that the naïve perceivers were guessing and that their ability to predict the letters in the arrays accounts for their accuracy, rather than differential clarity of the iconic or visual image representation. With respect to letter position, accuracy of reporting each letter declined from left to right (shown for the naïve perceivers in Figure 11.4), an effect which could be due to the order of encoding or to differential forgetting. If so, then the trained perceivers, who would be able to encode more accurately and would forget less, should not show a decrease in accuracy over serial position. Figure 11.5 shows the verification of this prediction. Instead of a left-to-right effect, accuracy was an inverted U-shaped function of letter position—perceivers were most accurate for those items near fixation and least accurate for those farthest from fixation.

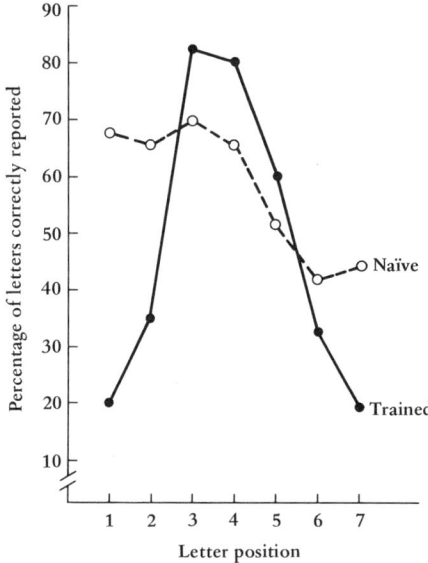

FIGURE 11.5   Percentage of letters correctly reported as a function of letter position for naïve and trained perceivers (from Hershenson, 1969a).

To show that the letter-position function for the trained group was due entirely to the relative perceptibility of the letters over retinal position, Hershenson (1969b) repeated the experiment but varied the fixation point. In this way the effects of position with respect to fixation point could be separated from left-right position in the sequence. With fixations presented over either the second, fourth, or sixth letter-positions, the inverted U-shaped functions followed the shifts in the positions of the eyes. For trained perceivers, then, the only differential accuracy that could be demonstrated depended on perceptibility and not on the predictability of the letter sequences. Thus there is strong reason to doubt that familiarity of letter strings has any effect on either the iconic representation or the visual image. The differences in responses as a function of approximation to English appear to be a manifestation of differential processing during information extraction from the icon or visual image or in subsequent processes.

Scanning

If we believe that familiar materials are not treated differently in their representation in iconic storage, then the advantage they subsequently enjoy might be due to a more rapid processing out of iconic storage into short-term memory. In essence, what is suggested is that with linguistic material the perceiver extracts information from the iconic storage by categorizing and attaching letter names to the shapes of patterns represented there. He does this sequentially, one name at a time, and in a spatially left-to-right order. Presumably the patterns are first segregated by preattentive processes into figural units which will ultimately correspond to letter units (see Chapter 8). The extraction process is a constructive one, as we have discussed it in this book. That is, the perceiver uses all of his knowledge of spelling patterns, word context, sequential redundancies, and the like to aid him in categorizing and naming each figural unit. Therefore, when the letters are in a familiar sequence (either because they are a high-order approximation to English, or form an English word in isolation, or, even more, a word in a context of other words), the perceiver is able to make predictions about what the next letter will be, and such hypotheses will reduce the time needed to name the next letter, and then verify that the name is correct. The higher the approximation of the word in iconic storage to the sequential redundancies of English words, the better the prediction and the less time will be needed to attach and verify the name of each of its letters.

The notion of processing is explicitly a sequential one, handling one letter at a time; and for each letter, processing takes more or less time depending on how much the perceiver can anticipate or predict. Although proposals of this type have been suggested in several forms, beginning with Heron (1957), Mewhort has provided some of the clearest evidence for such a possibility, using simple words which differ in their approximation to English as the stimulus material (for example, Mewhort, 1967; Mewhort, Merikle, and Bryden, 1969; Mewhort and Cornett, 1972). In his work he has called this model a scanning hypothesis, making explicit that the perceiver is shifting his attention rapidly from left to right, from one part of the icon to the next, attaching names to the forms as he goes.

We have already described Sperling's 1963 experiment on extraction of letter information from briefly presented arrays. When letter arrays are followed by a visual noise mask, the mask intrudes into the processing sequence so that only those letters already transferred from iconic storage to short-term memory are available for report. Those not yet processed are irretrievably lost. Sperling noted, moreover, that more letters were reported accurately as the duration of the display increased, presumably providing more time to process the information in the icon. The fact that the curves for two-, three-, four-, five-, and six-letter arrays all produce functions with the same slope suggested that the arrays were processed serially, that is, that the content of the iconic storage is scanned one letter at a time. Thus Sperling could calculate the rate of information extraction at about 10 milliseconds per letter.

Mewhort's first study (1967), mentioned earlier in this chapter, followed the assumptions proposed by Sperling's results. Since Mewhort found that perceivers could report more letters from a fourth-order row than a first-order row, this suggested a faster processing of the higher order array of letters.

In a more direct test of the scanning hypothesis, Mewhort, Merikle, and Bryden (1969) presented eight-letter arrays for 50, 125, or 200 milliseconds and a visual noise mask either 0, 75, or 125 milliseconds after the offset of the stimulus arrays. By combining the exposure duration with the delay of the masking field, the total time that information was available for processing could be calculated. It ranged from 50 to 325 milliseconds. Figure 11.6 shows the mean number of letters identified as a function of processing time. While accuracy of report increased monotonically as a function of processing time for both zero- and second-order approximations to English, the rate of increase was greater for second order. More letters were reported for second order than for zero order at all delays of the masking field. Mewhort, Merikle, and Bryden interpreted these results as indicating that familiar material is encoded more rapidly than unfamiliar arrays.

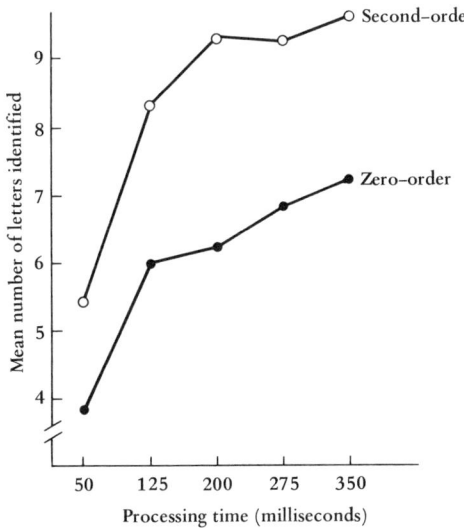

FIGURE 11.6 Mean number of letters correctly identified as a function of processing time for zero and second order of approximation to English (from Mewhort, Merikle, and Bryden, 1969).

In the second part of their experiment, Mewhort et al. attempted to demonstrate sequential left-to-right scanning more directly. They predicted that if information is processed from left to right, accuracy of report of information from the left half of the visual field should be better than from the right half when a visual noise mask is presented soon after the original display. They presented displays of zero- and fourth-order approximation to English, each containing eight letters. The mask was delayed for 0, 20, 40, 60, or 80 milliseconds and covered either the four letters to the left of fixation or the four letters to the right of fixation.

Figure 11.7 shows the mean number of letters identified as a function of delay of mask for the left and right sides of the arrays when left side or right side was masked. It is clear that, in all conditions, performance was better for letters on the left. For the letters reported from the left side of the sequence, the difference in accuracy as a function of left or right mask decreased as the delay of mask increased. This was not true of letters on the right. For letters reported from the left, masking on the left was more effective the shorter the delay. Thus the data strongly support the hypothesis of left-to-right processing. Moreover, the data suggest that the rate at which this sequential process operated was a function of the familiarity of the material.

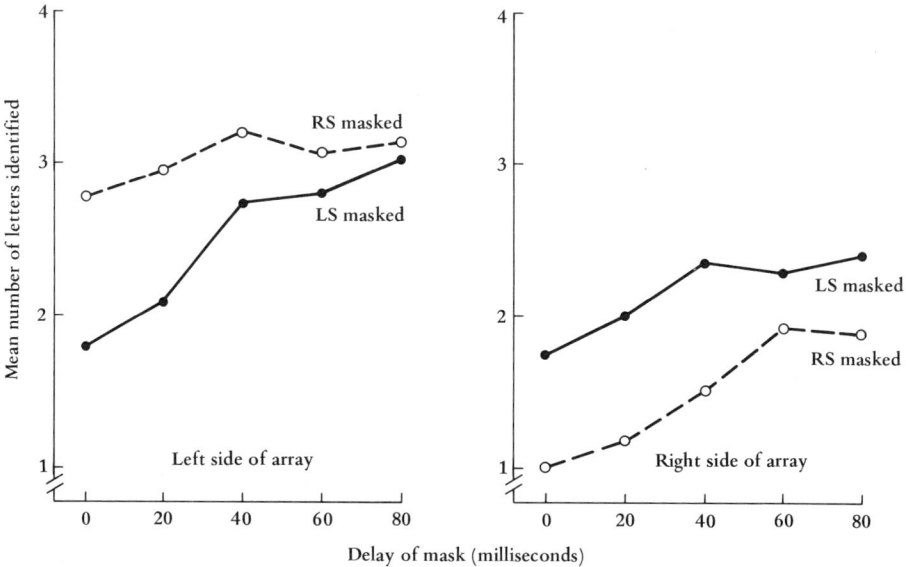

FIGURE 11.7   Mean number of letters correctly identified as a function of the delay of a visual noise mask for the left and right sides of the array of letters when the left and right sides were masked (from Mewhort, Merikle, and Bryden, 1969).

Krueger (1970) reported a comparable result in terms of the time needed to respond rather than the accuracy of response. He presented a six-letter word, with a target letter centered above the middle position (corresponding to the fixation point). The perceiver had to respond as quickly as possible as to whether or not the target letter was one of the six letters. On half of the trials the six letters spelled English words and on the other half they were randomly scrambled versions of the same words. Krueger found that the reaction times for the trials with words were up to 100 milliseconds faster than for the nonsense letter arrangements. That is, it took less time to find a target letter in a string of letters when the string spelled a meaningful word than when it made no sense. In an interesting comparison, Krueger showed that this effect did not hold when the letters were arranged in a vertical column. In the vertical arrangement, not only were all reaction times longer, but no differences were found between meaningful and nonsense arrays. Apparently the unusual arrangement (with respect to reading English) prevented the normal contribution due to meaningfulness. Mewhort (1966) showed the same loss when the spacing between the letters on a horizontal row was longer than normal.

These experiments are consistent with the suggestion that when processing meaningful arrays of letters of varying approximation to English words, perceivers scan the figural units in a left-to-right sequence, attaching a letter name to each configuration. These verbal labels are contained in short-term memory or transferred to a response organization process for verbal or written report, depending on the demands of the task.

The specific task demands are very important in these experiments. In virtually every instance, the letter arrays are nonmeaningful, they are presented without the context of other words, and the perceiver is required to use the names of letters in his report. Although it is easy to justify such restrictions in the laboratory as a way to gain experimental control, such tasks rarely if ever occur in nature, even for perceivers initially learning to read. Thus, we always have context, we are almost always reading meaningful words, and we invariably name, store, and repeat words, not letters. Therefore, the question still remains whether the scanning hypothesis can also be applied to the more typical tasks confronting a perceiver when he looks at meaningful contextual linguistic material.

Processing Words

There are two experimental findings which provide a beginning for understanding how words are processed. In a matching task, words are processed faster than nonsense strings of letters (Eichelman, 1970); and in a recognition task, perceivers are more accurate in identifying a letter from a word than from an array containing the same letters in scrambled order so as to be meaningless (Reicher, 1969). We will examine each of these findings in more detail.

Eichelman (1970) compared response latencies for matching words with those for matching letter strings of two, four, and six letters. He found that matching words was a faster process than matching letter strings and that the difference between the words and nonsense strings increased as the number of letters in the stimulus increased (see Figure 11.8). Eichelman also found that the reaction time was a decreasing linear function of the number of letters which were different in the stimuli to be matched. Since this function was not different for the nonsense and meaningful stimulus pairs, Eichelman doubted that the matches were being made on the basis of word names. He suggested that the availability of a name for the words could not account for the faster

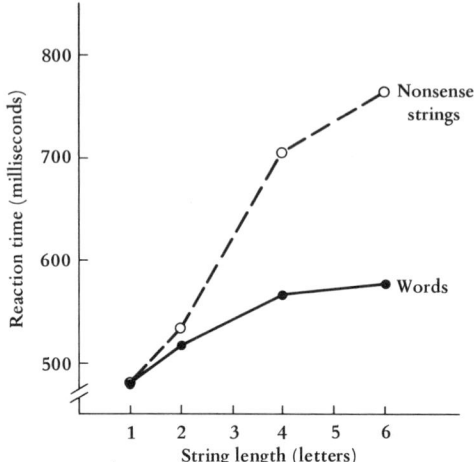

FIGURE 11.8 Reaction time to indicate that two strings of letters are physically identical or not, when they are either words or nonsense (from Eichelman, 1970).

overall response to the words. This conclusion was supported by the fact that physical identity matches for both types of stimuli were made faster than name matches for these stimuli. He concluded, therefore, that familiarity had its effect by making some physical characteristics of words more salient. Perhaps words are seen as "wholes" while letter arrays remain only strings of letters.

Reicher's (1969) experiment was also designed to clarify this problem. He presented a single word followed by a visual noise mask to limit the processing time. When the mask appeared, a pair of letters was presented above one of the letters in the word. The temporal sequence of this display is illustrated in the top row of Figure 11.9. The perceiver's task was to indicate which of the two letters were the same as the letter in the word. Reicher found that perceivers were more accurate in identifying a letter which had appeared in a word

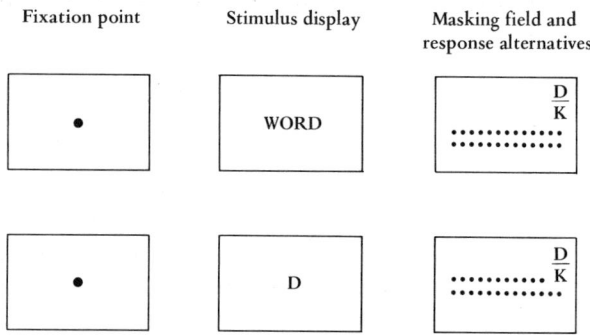

FIGURE 11.9 The display sequence for Reicher's (1969) experiment. The top row shows the sequence when a word was presented, followed by a mask and two alternatives above one of the letter positions. The bottom row is a comparable trial when only a single letter is presented.

than one which had been presented among the same letters scrambled to form a meaningless sequence. Unlike the experiments reported in the previous section (especially Krueger's) Reicher's results cannot be attributed to the information contained in the other letters since, as in the example in the figure, both *D* and *K* are equally predictable from *WOR–*. Since the perceivers did not know until after the presentation which position would be probed, theoretically all of the letters in the meaningful word would have produced a higher level of accuracy than those in its anagram.

This is a critical and important finding, but is almost lost sight of because of another one in his experiment, one which we feel is ungeneralizable to other contexts and hence irrelevant to the theoretical issues to which it is applied. Reicher had another condition, depicted in the bottom row of Figure 11.9. Here only a single letter is presented, again followed by the mask with the two alternatives. Since only a single letter has to be processed, rather than four, it would seem reasonable that this should be an easier task. However, he found it to be more difficult. Perceivers were more accurate in deciding which of two letters was in the display when the letter was part of a meaningful word than when it was presented alone. The letter alone and the nonsense anagrams were reported at about the same level of accuracy.

Wheeler (1970) replicated this strange finding (as well as the more important one previously described). At the same time, he showed that it could not be accounted for by response bias, difference in word frequencies of the different alternatives, letter frequencies, spatial position uncertainty, or interference between the letters and the alternatives. Thus, it appears that when a meaningful word is presented, *all* of its letters are processed faster (or at least better) than any single letter when presented alone. It would seem on the surface at least that a scanning model could not predict this finding since four letters cannot be scanned faster than one, no matter how much predictability is gained by the perceiver's knowledge of spelling patterns or sequential redundancies in the language. To suggest simply that with real words, all of the letters are processed together at the same time, rather than letter by letter, does not solve the problem, because both Reicher and Wheeler found that the accuracy was not merely equal, but *higher* for the words than for the single letters.

We feel this particular finding is an artifact of the experimental arrangements, and should not be generalized to larger theoretical issues. In fact, Wheeler's most plausible explanation (1970, pp. 83–84) is of this form, although he does not label it explicitly as an artifact. Even more important, however, the scanning hypothesis cannot be applied to single letter recognition tasks, since there is nothing to scan there. Thus, the perceiver probably adopts such a different strategy in extracting information from a display containing a single letter, that to compare the accuracy or the rate of processing of such arrays with those of larger arrays is quite inappropriate. Further work is obviously needed here, but we expect that a discontinuity in processing will also be found for single items or for multiple items that are not conducive to ordered scanning.

So let us return to the problems in processing words more directly. We have already hinted at the likelihood that one explanation for the differences in processing words and their anagrams is that processing may be faster or more accurate when letters form larger units for analysis. For example, one suggestion for the unit of analysis in letter strings which spell meaningful words is that of the clusters of letters which have an invariant pronunciation. To study the role of such units in visual recognition, Gibson, Pick, Osser, and Hammond (1962) varied the degree of pronounceability of stimuli which were exposed in a tachistoscope. Pronounceable arrays consisted of an initial consonant-spelling having a single regular pronunciation, a final consonant-spelling having a single regular pronunciation, and a vowel-spelling having a single regular pronunciation when between the consonant sounds. Arrays with low spelling-to-sound correlation were then constructed from these arrays by interchanging the initial and final consonant-spellings. For example, *DINK* became *NKDI*, and *GLURCK* became *CKURGL*. Figure 11.10 shows the percentage of words correctly identified as a function of exposure duration for both pronounceable and unpronounceable arrays. Pronounceable arrays were more easily identified regardless of the duration at which they were presented. Gibson et al. explained this effect in terms of differential sensitivity, suggesting that, in acquiring reading skills, people become sensitive to superforms which are organized according to the auditory-vocal temporal patterns inherent in the relationships between written and spoken English. This sensitivity implies that fewer units need to be processed when such spelling patterns are present, which thereby leads to improved accuracy of processing.

This experiment has recently been replicated with some clarification of

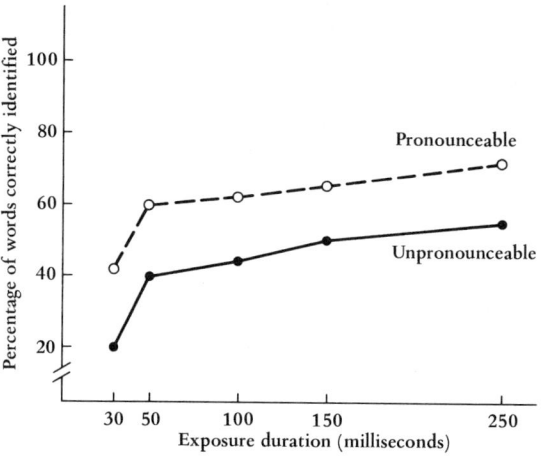

FIGURE 11.10 Percentage of words correctly identified as a function of exposure duration for pronounceable and unpronounceable arrays of letters (from Gibson, Pick, Osser, and Hammond, 1962).

the processes involved. Aderman and Smith (1971) showed that the spelling patterns were advantageous only if the perceiver was expecting words which contained such patterns. If they had been looking at words with low correspondence between letter sequences and pronounceability, then they performed no better on an unexpected word that had such correspondence. Hershenson (1972) found that a group of perceivers identified more letters from pronounceable arrays than from unpronounceable arrays when the arrays were unfamiliar. However, a second group which was very familiar with all of the stimuli (they had memorized the list of stimuli), did equally well regardless of the degree of pronounceability. Hershenson concluded that pronounceability plays a role in the retention and report of stimulus information and not in its representation in the icon or visual image.

We shall not pursue the spelling-pattern–pronounceability relationship further here, except to note that it has two rather separable components—the sequential redundancies among the letters in the language and the correspondence of these redundancies with invariant pronunciations. The evidence for the former's importance seems overwhelming, but, as Hershenson (1972) has noted, the role of pronounceability per se in perceptual recognition is still a very open question. This is especially true since Gibson, Shurcliff, and Yonas (1970) reported that the same spelling pattern results are found with deaf perceivers who have never heard an invariant pronunciation of these spelling patterns.

So, what conclusions are possible that can account for the differences in processing between words and nonword sequences of letters? Simply saying that the perceiver enlarges the unit of processing is not a sufficient explanation for describing how such changes take place. We have substantial evidence that letter extraction proceeds faster when the letters form a predictable or a meaningful unit such as a word, and further, that little or no extra time is needed for additional letters when the letters spell words.

The scanning hypothesis is compatible with these results, although it needs some qualifications. Its prediction of faster scanning of letters of words of higher order approximations to English finds good support in the experiments of Mewhort, of Krueger, and of Reicher and Wheeler. But the hypothesis says nothing explicitly about whether the unit of processing changes as well. Are the separate letters of real words scanned individually, no matter how rapidly? Or are several letters treated together as a unit (such as a spelling or pronounceability pattern)? Or are some letters not processed at all, being sufficiently redundant that the perceiver can predict them without even bothering to attend to them? All of these could be made consistent with some form of a scanning hypothesis, but the alternatives are quite different and need to be separated experimentally.

We have not carried this discussion very far into the realm of reading connected textural material. Most psychologists, educators, and linguists (for example, see Smith's book on reading, 1971) would resist the extrapolation implied here. Is reading connected discourse simply a letter-by-letter scan carried out at an even faster rate than for individual words, or nonsense, or single letters? It seems rather unlikely, and for at least three rather separate reasons. The redundancies in connected text are so high that the perceiver-reader can dispense with the processing of most of the letters, and even most of the words, and still achieve adequate understanding. A constructive model of reading predicts that this will happen. This is not inconsistent with a scanning notion, since it permits processing of a given item to be determined by the categorization of preceding items. One such determination might easily be not to process the next item at all—as it is perfectly predictable without any processing.

Second, as noted in Chapter 9, the pattern of eye movements in reading are rarely perfectly sequentially ordered from left to right, but rather show many regressive movements. Although the scanning hypothesis is explicitly concerned with information extraction from a single fixation, it would seem unlikely that we always proceeded sequentially from left to right item by item within a fixation, but use a far more variable sequence between fixations. This is a logical argument, without much evidence one way or another to decide whether two different processing modes are reasonable or not.

Finally, one can think of many examples of whole-word processing in reading—knowing a word by its configuration or some other characteristic which permits processing all of the letters simultaneously. Thus, it is not simply that the unit of analysis has gone from a single letter to multiletter groups, but that the unit may no longer have much to do with letters at all. Further, readers may make no effort to name, categorize, pronounce, or store letters, and may not need to know anything about the letters they are reading. Without going into more detail, this extrapolation from letter recognition to word recognition to reading must be considered tenuous at best. Smith (1971) summarizes a number of hypotheses about reading, none of which survives unscathed.

This concludes our discussion of the role of familiarity in perceptual recognition and identification. Some basic processes seem fairly clear but the more complex possibilities have not been worked out. Judging from the amount of current work on this problem, better answers should be forthcoming soon.

MOTIVATIONAL AND AFFECTIVE STATES

A second major source of information which has been shown to affect responses in perceptual recognition experiments is the motivational or affective state of the perceiver. The importance of this kind of information is derived from the fact that it reflects input from lasting characteristics of individual perceivers—usually described as the individual's personality—as well as the more immediate and transient states like hunger and thirst.

In the introduction to this chapter, we discussed the early views of perceptual defense and perceptual enhancement. We noted there the conceptual and methodological difficulties which were immediately apparent. But even if these difficulties were overcome, a logical problem remains for the notion of perceptual defense. How could a perceiver defend himself from perceiving a particular word until he became aware of it and identified it? But if he was aware of it, what could perceptual defense mean? One answer was that we have unconscious perception, that is, we can perceive something without having been aware of having done so. But this explanation simply changes the meaning of our notion of perception and moves the problem back into an earlier perceptual system. Other explanations have also been proposed but the seemingly logical inconsistency of the process of perceptual defense probably was one of the major reasons for the decline of research on this problem.

Erdelyi (1973) has proposed an alternative explanation of perceptual defense and vigilance by reinterpreting them in an information-processing framework. Erdelyi notes that a major premise of the information-processing approach is that the input is sequentially subject to different types of transformations and storages. It would only be natural, therefore, to assume that different selective processes might be operative at different stages of processing. Thus the information-processing approach has within it the implication that selectivity may occur at multiple loci. It is this conception which Erdelyi applies to explain the effects of inputs from motivational and affective systems. Thus it now becomes possible to explain perceptual defense, not merely in terms of a perception-response or visual-verbal distinction but as a fundamental expression of cognitive control processes exercising selective regulation throughout the information-processing sequence. Thus Erdelyi reframes the question of perceptual defense to ask about the locus and mechanisms of selectivity. In this way we can think of bias as part of the processing sequence rather than as artifact.

To illustrate the power of this analysis, Erdelyi catalogued a number of possible selective mechanisms that respond to motivational and affective variables. First, selectivity in looking strategies or in actual peripheral receptor mechanisms may control the information input to the system. These strategies include not only the direction and sequence of fixation, but also the shutting off of the input by closing the eyes. Pupil diameter and accommodation have also been shown to be responsive to internal states and may also be involved in input control. On the output side, selection may occur as a result of reporting strategies, including one of the simplest early explanations for perceptual defense, namely, that the perceiver suppresses his report of troublesome stimuli.

The major contribution of Erdelyi's explanation, however, is the inclusion of processes occurring between input and output. As we noted in our discussion of selectivity in Chapter 10, many of the effects produced by instructional sets can be explained by reference to encoding and transfer processes. Erdelyi extends this notion to include "chronic sets" or "personality dispositions" which become part of each individual through years of development. In addition to encoding strategies, the processing of certain material may be interrupted on the basis of partial analysis, or some other information may intrude into the processing sequence causing the original information to be lost. Similar events may take place in a later part of the sequence when information is being transferred to long-term memory. Dixon (1971) has proposed a similar analysis of subliminal perception—the situation in which a perceiver's behavior is modified as a consequence of stimuli which he has not yet fully analyzed or identified. Without going into detail, Dixon sees selective attention and subliminal perception as the end points on a continuum of information handling. This view supports the conception of many theorists that selective processes in attention occur prior to awareness.

The information-processing explanation of perceptual defense makes the paradox of defense a little less paradoxical. If a stimulus fails to be encoded or placed into permanent memory because of its emotional content, it becomes irretrievably lost to the perceiver after the iconic storage and visual image fade. Thus the perceiver can be said to have defended against the input since it is unavailable to him beyond a fleeting moment. Yet, at a different level, he did "perceive" it—after all, it was available, if only for a very short period of time. As Erdelyi notes, the viewer both perceived and defended against perceiving (further) the very same input. Thus, the combination of selective and recognitive processes makes many alternative outcomes possible.

RECOGNITION OF PICTURES AND SCENES

Thus far we have primarily been concerned with the perception of linguistic material—letters or words which have names and meaning. We have described one processing sequence to explain a large portion of the data: The visual information in the stimulus is represented internally and then encoded into short-term memory as letter or word names. While this description of recognition and identification processes is important for human perceivers, it only represents a portion of our perceptual experience. Therefore, this last section will discuss the perception and recognition of pictures and scenes. We shall see whether the information supplied by the environment of natural objects is processed in a fashion similar to that supplied by the symbolic environment.

We will turn first to two studies which show apparently contradictory results about the need to learn to recognize pictures. The experiment by Hochberg and Brooks (1962) suggests that picture recognition is an ability that requires little or no learning; the work of Deregowski (1972) suggests that learning may be very important. Hochberg and Brooks tested pictorial recognition in a 19-month-old infant who had seen very few pictures. The few he had seen had not been accompanied by the names of the depicted objects. Nevertheless, the infant was able to name or otherwise indicate recognition of nearly all of the objects depicted. This suggests that pictorial recognition is an unlearned ability.

Deregowski (1972), following work by Hudson (1967), observed that most African perceivers have great difficulty perceiving or interpreting depth in two-dimensional drawings in which familiar size, interposition, and linear perspective are available as cues (see Chapter 13 for a discussion of these cues). When questioned about the content of the drawings, African perceivers could recognize the objects without difficulty but were not always able to place them in their proper relationship with one another. Deregowski classified perceivers as two- or three-dimensional viewers, depending on the extent to which they correctly integrated the depth cues in the picture. He then showed that these two groups differed in predictable ways when asked to make a model of a two-dimensional drawing of a cube or in copying an impossible figure (the bottom example in Figure 8.6). When asked to adjust the apparent distance of a spot of light seen in one eye so that it was the same distance as different objects depicted in a two-dimensional picture seen by the other eye, the two-dimensional perceivers set the spot at the same distance for all of the objects in the picture, regardless of the depth cues available. The three-dimensional perceivers set the spot further from them when matching the distance of "more distant" objects in the picture. This suggests that the three-dimensional perceivers were not only able to interpret depth in the pictures, but that, in some sense, they perceived the depth directly.

It is possible that the differences in the two experiments are due to language learning, to specific naming experiences, or to the richness of exposure to pictures from an early age. It is also possible that recognizing and naming what an object is might be different from seeing depth in its two-dimensional representation.

Several studies have demonstrated the ability of perceivers to separate correctly a very large number of pictures into those which were previously seen and those which are being viewed for the first time. For example, Shepard (1967) presented 600 pictures one at a time to perceivers asking them to look at each for a few seconds so that they could remember them. He then presented a number of pairs of pictures, each composed of one member from the previously seen 600, and one new picture which had not been previously viewed. When tested immediately after seeing the last of the 600 pictures, accuracy for selecting the old picture from each pair was over 98 percent. Even after a week's delay in testing for recognition, accuracy remained above 90 percent. After four months, however, accuracy had dropped substantially. Standing, Conezio, and Haber (1970) showed perceivers more than 2500 pictures over a four day period. Even with that large a number, accuracy exceeded 90 percent correct and, if anything, the perceivers were more accurate on pictures they had seen on the first day (that is, four days before the testing) than on the last day. Moreover, it did not matter whether the old picture in each test pair was presented as originally shown or in its mirror image. The perceivers were still able to identify the mirror image of a picture they had seen before, and they could tell which of the old pictures had been reversed and which were in the same orientation.

The duration and accuracy of retention of information from pictorial presentations suggests that this information is processed differently from linguistic information. In one attempt to describe the difference, Shaffer and Shiffrin (1972) presented 120 pictures and varied independently the exposure duration of each picture from one to four seconds, and the time between one picture and the next. Accuracy increased with exposure duration but was unaffected by the time between presentations. This pattern is different from that found in experiments using linguistic stimuli, in which time between presentations greatly aids retention, presumably because it provides time for rehearsal. Because of this difference, Shaffer and Shiffrin argued that verbal rehearsal is not normally used in the retention of information from complex pictorial stimuli.

This is not to say that the representation of a picture cannot be visually rehearsed. Posner and Konick (1966) showed that the memory for the location of a dot on a line could be easily maintained unless the perceivers were prevented from rehearsal by having to perform an interpolated task. But there appears to be little verbal representation as part of picture memory. Otherwise providing more time to rehearse such a representation would have aided retention.

None of these studies on picture memory measured the similarity among the pictures or the ease with which verbal labels could be used to describe them. The only similarity among the pictures was that they were representational, that is, they were two-dimensional representations of objects or scenes which were familiar to the perceivers (although hopefully they had not seen any of the particular stimuli before). But it is likely that some similarity existed among some of the pictures, given the large number used.

On the basis of data such as these, Haber (1970b) suggested that recognition memory for pictures was virtually perfect, that it probably lasted indefinitely, and that it did not seem to be mediated by verbal coding or labeling of the content of the pictures. Except for the great accuracy of pictorial memory, the other conclusions have not gone unchallenged. The long-term character of the memory had, in fact, been previously mentioned by Shepard who found that even at four months accuracy fell off substantially. Until we know more about the role of intervening experiences on recognition memory (and can assess the likelihood that in the interim perceivers might have seen some of the "new" pictures, thereby making them "old" when retentive testing occurred), the longevity of picture memory should probably be treated more cautiously.

Daniel and Ellis (1972) examined the encoding processes in more detail. They presented randomly shaped polygons to two groups of perceivers. One group had to learn a different label for each shape while the other group was allowed simply to observe the shapes for the same amount of time. The exposure time was either one-half second or six seconds. A test for shape recognition was conducted either immediately, or fifteen minutes after the presentation, or one week later. In the test, the perceiver had to select the old shape from among four new ones and to recall the verbal labels they had previously learned. The shapes paired with labels were remembered better, as were those presented for the longer duration. Recognition for the shapes did not decline over the retention intervals tested, but the accuracy of recall of the labels did decline with time. Moreover, there was no correlation between retention of the shape and retention of its corresponding label.

Daniel and Ellis explained these results by suggesting that the labels helped the perceiver discriminate the relevant distinctive features of the shapes because he was forced to attach a different label to each. But once encoded, the presence of the label was of no further relevance, either for rehearsal or for retrieval. Thus, having a verbal label did not seem to be a necessary part of visual recognition memory, except in so far as it might alter the encoding strategy or the amount of information extracted at the time of initial encoding into a visual representation.

So far the studies reviewed minimize the role of verbal encoding in memory for pictures. Several experiments provide evidence suggesting a more positive role. Dallett and Wilcox (1968), Glanzer and Clark (1964), Tversky (1969), and Wyant, Banks, Berger, and Wright (1972) all have shown in one way or another that when old and new pictures are selected for recognition testing on the basis of both their visual similarity and the similarity of a verbal description of them, the latter is important. For example, Wyant et al. found that the higher the rated verbal discriminability of the differences between each pair of old and new pictures, the better the recognition accuracy. This implies that the perceivers were using a verbal code to remember the pictures. Only when viewing time was short (three seconds compared to ten seconds), was there any effect of rated visual similarity between the old and new members of each pair. Presumably when the perceiver has enough time to look at the pictures, he can notice enough of the visual features so as not to be confused by similar pictures. Wyant et al. presented no evidence that the two ratings made of the pictures were independent or that they were measuring what they were supposed to be measuring. Thus, it is possible that both ratings may be reflecting different aspects of visual similarity. Even without this objection, it is still possible that their effect may be comparable to that of Daniel and Ellis —the verbal descriptions, even though supplied by the perceivers themselves, may have been used primarily for initial encoding of visual features and not as a memory representation thereafter. Thus, the question of verbal mediation of pictorial representation in memory is still open.

Nevertheless, we do know some things about the visual representations themselves. In Chapter 9 we noted that pictures are searched in a nonrandom manner—the eyes fixate on high information and novel features. Moreover, fixation points are selected quickly, undoubtedly on the basis of information picked up in the periphery of the retina. It was also noted that multiple fixation suggests that the visual image is constructed.

One further set of experiments by Loftus (1972) can be mentioned in this context. He showed perceivers 180 pictures two at a time as pairs for them to study, and then showed them 360 pictures one at a time for them to classify as old or new. With several manipulations, he showed that the number of fixations was the critical independent variable affecting recognition accuracy. Even overall exposure duration did not increase accuracy unless it resulted in a greater number of fixations. Similarly, instructions that changed the value of different pictures had no effect on accuracy unless they also changed the number of fixations. These findings suggest that each new fixation is capable of adding new information or aiding the process of integration of information from successive fixations, and that this occurs much more from adding more fixations than by extending the length of each separate fixation.

One other comparison in the Loftus experiments is relevant to this discussion. In one condition, the perceivers were instructed to look at only one of the two members of the pair and never to look at the other one during their exposure. Further, they were led to believe that the other (not-to-be-looked-at) picture was a distractor and would not be tested later. In another condition, they could look at one or both in whatever proportion they wished. In this second condition, a number of pairs drew fixations to only one member. Hence, although the perceiver expected to be tested on both, he only looked at one. In this latter case, he had some memory for the nonfixated picture, but in the first condition, he had no memory at all. Since the number of fixations were zero in both cases, this difference shows a selectivity in which perceivers seem to be able to attend to peripheral information they do not look at when they believe it relevant.

In several earlier chapters, we pointed out the importance of an integration of the information processed from each fixation across many fixations, involving a construction of a picture from the segmentation of features or elements contained in each fixation. Hochberg has provided most of the reasoning and evidence for this argument, which is presented most clearly for picture perception in his 1972 paper.

A pair of very recent studies, one by Wiseman and Neisser (1972) and the other by Freedman and Haber (1973), investigated another important aspect of picture memory—the need for a coherent organization constructed by the perceiver. In both studies, the pictures to be remembered were faces (see Figure 11.11), but drawn so that only the highlights and shadows were represented. Some of these were rather easy to see as a face, others were more difficult; and for all, sometimes a face could be seen and sometimes it could not. The latter characteristic was the important variable in these studies. It was argued that if the perceiver saw an organized picture, such as a face, then he had a much greater chance of remembering it. If it was not organized, he would have to remember a large number of meaningless blobs, which would have no coherence or structure, in much the same way that a random array of letters lacks the organized structure that occurs when they are rearranged to spell a meaningful word.

In the two experiments, the perceivers were shown a number of the faces, one at a time, and simply asked whether they could see a face in it. When tested for recognition, they were shown the same set again, randomly mixed with an

FIGURE 11.11   Two examples of faces shown only in highlights constructed by Mooney (1954).

equal number of "new" pictures of the same nature. Now they were asked to indicate "new " or "old" for each and also whether they could see a face. Both studies found that recognition accuracy was significant only for pictures that perceivers reported they saw as a face both on the initial inspection and at the time of testing.

Thus, whether a picture will be remembered cannot be predicted solely from its stimulus properties. It also depends on the perceiver's ability to construct a meaningful visual image. For most pictures and scenes, such constructions are easy to make. When the construction is made problematical, as in these two experiments, then its importance can be seen more clearly.

In this same vein, we will mention one further study, by Biederman (1972). He took photographs of typical scenes and cut them up into six segments of three columns and two rows. He told the perceivers that they would be shown the pictures either with the pieces arranged in their proper organization or with the six pieces randomly placed together. They were told to attend to one of the six cells (specified by location) and to decide which of four alternative objects was in that part of the picture. The location and the list of alternatives might be given before the presentation or after, or one before and the other after, or vice versa. Under all conditions, perceivers were more accurate when the picture was coherently arranged than when the pieces were randomly arranged.

Although this might be an intuitively reasonable outcome, it is a stronger finding than we might have expected. For example, in a picture of some buildings, with a fountain in front, a path with a bicycle leaning against a wall, a person walking, and so forth, the perceiver is more accurate in recognizing that the bicycle was in the lower left hand corner when the other five pieces made a cohesive picture than when they did not. Further, this was true even when the location and the alternatives were known well before the presentation of the picture. Thus, even when the perceiver knew exactly where to look and what to look for, the coherence of the organization of the rest of the picture was still effective in determining his recognition accuracy.

SUMMARY

Recognition processes involve some reference to familiarity—a contact between the representation of current stimulation and that of prior stimulation or other aspects of memory. We considered only a small number of recognition tasks, specifically those that clearly involved the initial processing from the visual display.

First we looked at the role of familiarity in character classification tasks. A number of studies have shown that the verbal familiarity (the availability of a name or category for the form) does not affect the time needed to make a match based upon the visual shape alone. It clearly has a powerful effect when the classification has to be made in terms of the names or the categories of the items. We suggested that if visual familiarity was manipulated with visually novel forms, then the visual matching time might be shown to be a function of such familiarity.

Next we turned to the role of sequential redundancies among letter sequences and showed that when the perceiver has access to such redundancies, they aid him in his accuracy of reporting the letters. We described techniques for constructing strings of letters which differed in their approximation to sequential dependencies of words in the English language. Our analyses suggested that the effects were due not to a clearer iconic representation, nor entirely to a better retrieval, but to a more rapid processing of each letter. This was possible apparently because the perceiver can use his predictions of what the next letter might be to reduce the time it takes him to process and verify the name of the next letter. This process was described in terms of a scanning hypothesis, which also assumed that perceivers extracted information in a left-to-right sequence across a horizontal array of letters. Several experiments were described that provided support for the scanning hypothesis for nonmeaningful strings of letters.

The problems in understanding these processes are more complex when the letter strings spell meaningful words. Extraction of letters is even faster for word strings than for nonword strings, but the process appears discontinuous in several respects. We also looked at the role of pronounceability. Several studies have shown that pronounceable sequences of letters are reported better, but we questioned whether the data are yet sufficient to attribute this to pronounceability per se.

The next to last topic briefly explored the role of selectivity in perceptual defense and vigilance, the situations in which perceivers may show higher recognition thresholds for words which are threatening to them. We suggested ways in which these findings can be interpreted in information-processing terms of greater predictive and explanatory power.

Finally we considered several lines of work on recognition of pictorial rather than linguistic material. Evidence on the very accurate pictorial recognition memory was described and several factors that might account for this were mentioned. Specifically, we looked at studies that sought to discover whether pictures were processed and remembered in verbal or in visual representations alone. Although this issue is far from settled, substantial evidence is available for the independence of visual from linguistic representations. We also briefly examine the role of perceptual organization on perceptual recognition, showing that recognition depends on having a coherent organization of the form.

This chapter concludes the middle section of our study of visual perception, a section that focused primarily on the extraction of information from visual stimulation, using the concepts and language of information processing. Although we will not abandon this approach in the final section of the book, the focus will shift rather dramatically.

Readings

As in the previous several chapters, the best general source of work on perceptual recognition is Neisser (1967). Several of the papers considered in this chapter are also reprinted in Coltheart (1972). Posner's work on reaction time is best summarized in Posner (1969). For a more detailed discussion of approximations to English, see Attneave (1959) and Garner (1962). Erdelyi's (1973) review of perceptual defense is thorough and wide-ranging, and Dixon (1971) is virtually complete. Several more speculative and technical papers on picture-processing are collected in Lipkin and Rosenfeld (1970), and Loftus (1972) has an excellent review of the literature on eye movements and picture recognition.

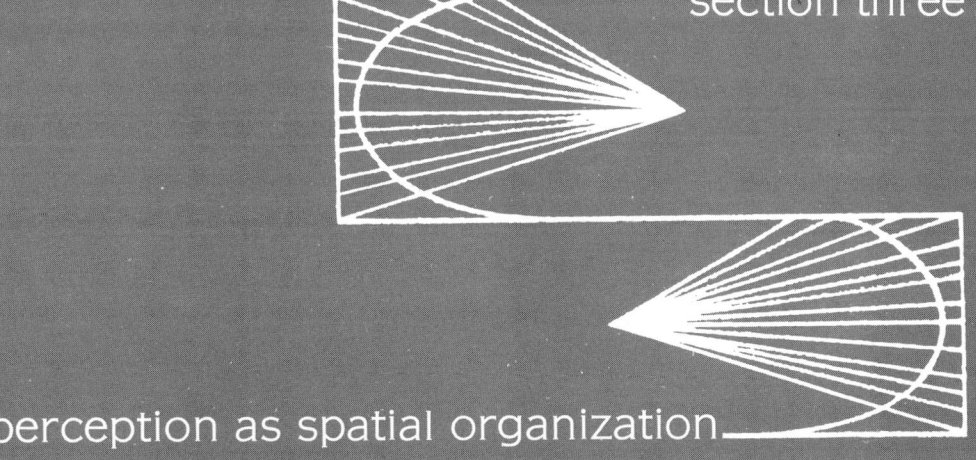

section three

perception as spatial organization

The last section, consisting of four chapters, will concentrate on the perception of the natural visual world around us. In several ways we have been building up to this point in the earlier sections, first by considering the basic coding processes for light in the visual system, and then by focusing on the ways in which more complex information is extracted from visual stimulation. But in many respects these chapters move beyond previous topics, in part because of the complexity of the problems, and in part because of the persisting strong theoretical differences. Although there has been controversy and disagreement on many of the topics in the earlier chapters, most of it has been focused on particular experiments rather than basic concepts and strategies of research.

Our approach in this last section will not be entirely eclectic—we have chosen sides to some extent. This will show up primarily in the way we will present ideas and research, and in the selection of things to talk about. In this sense, those readers who have already chosen the other side might find our presentation annoying. We hope, however, they will also find it convincing.

The two points of view which will be presented are illustrated in many ways. Basically, they differ in the importance they place on the retinal projection as a source of information about the visual world. One argues that, although luminance discontinues in the projection are rich in information, they are not sufficient to produce a unique perceptual experience of the visual world. Therefore, they usually have to be supplemented from other sources, especially past experience or expectations derived from past experience. Proponents of this view are often called empiricists, in order to denote their belief that perception is learned and is constantly anchored in reality by the outcome of previous commerce with the visual world.

The opposite view is that the content of the retinal projection is sufficient to determine virtually all perceptual experience, and except for objects with learned meanings, no references to past experience are necessary. This approach is often called a psychophysical view of space perception, because it looks for the physical dimensions in the retinal projection that determine perceptual experiences. The task is to find these psychophysical correlates. We tend to lean toward this second approach.

Chapter 12 outlines these two points of view in some detail, and provides several basic examples to illustrate their respective approaches. This sets the stage for Chapter 13, in which we provide a detailed analysis of the sources of information in the retinal projection, contrasting the two approaches as we go. Chapter 14 shifts our attention slightly so we can consider the perception of motion and movement, and so we can recognize that almost all perception takes place within a perceiver who is himself in motion. In this chapter we shall also note that the retinal projection may need some supplements, not from prior experience, but from nonvisual information, specifically the commands that produce self-initiated movements of the perceiver. Finally, in Chapter 15, we will consider how much of the perception of objects in space can take place in a human newborn. Recent evidence, less than a decade old, will strongly suggest that a newborn has a sophisticated functioning visual system, and that his perceptual experiences differ from that of adults only in a quantitative fashion.

12

two major points of view on the perception of space

INTRODUCTION

The task of students of visual space perception is to explain how we come to see a three-dimensional world containing objects which have stable sizes and shapes and are seen in particular locations in space. To study these aspects of perception, we have to distinguish between two conceptions of space. Physical space refers to the realm of the physical world studied by geometers, physicists, and engineers. Visual space is the space of perceptual experience, the space that we as psychologists, expecially those interested in perception will study in the remaining chapters.

Physical space is measured with straightedges, rules, and transits, following the laws of Euclidean geometry. These measurements are based on the assumption that an object may be displaced or rotated without deformation and without changing the relationships between its parts. Objects can be assigned positions in a Cartesian (rectangular) coordinate system. These simple assumptions provide the foundation for our conception of a rigid physical world.

The description of visual space is a problem for research—it cannot be assumed to be Euclidean. The exact geometrical representation of visual space must be empirically determined. Moreover, when the perceiving organism is taken into account, it is necessary to speak of positions of visual points in a space centered on the perceiver. Such a space is best described using a polar coordinate system, with the perceiver at the origin, and with measurement given in terms of angular and radial distance from the origin.

Since the patterning of the retinal projection in the two eyes can be predicted from the laws of geometrical optics, those retinal projections can be related directly to the spatial objects themselves and to their physical positions in space. In some sense, the projection contains the information that the perceiver requires in order to see objects in space. The study of how the perceiver acquires this information has generally been approached from one of two points of view. One view starts with an analysis of stimulation, sometimes describing characteristics of the actual physical object and sometimes of the retinal projection. Such a view then asks whether the informational component which has been isolated correlates with various aspects of the resulting perceptual experience. This procedure usually has led to the conclusion that the retinal projection does not provide the information necessary for the perception of objects in space. Therefore, other sources of information have been sought, usually in memory, which may determine the perceptual experience. This approach has been called empiricism and is usually traced back to the British philosopher Bishop Berkeley. Modern empiricists sometimes prefer to identify Helmholtz, the great nineteenth-century physicist and physiologist, as its contemporary founder. This view will be discussed primarily in terms of transactionalist theory (for example, Ittelson, 1960) since this group has developed empiricism most systematically.

The alternative view seeks stimulus correlates of visual space perception, starting with an analysis of perceptual experience. This is a psychophysical approach in its insistence on looking for correlates in the optical projection of light reaching the retina. This view requires an exhaustive study of stimulation before resorting to a concept of learning. The modern version of a psychophysical theory of space perception has its heritage in the nativism and relationism of Gestalt psychology and is best exemplified today by James Gibson (1950, 1966).

Since these two views differ in some fundamental ways, they will be presented separately. We shall first consider their major premises, beginning with the empiricist view and then turning to the psychophysical view as developed by Gibson. We shall not attempt a resolution or an integration of these viewpoints—the research base will not permit it. Instead, we will try to present a coherent picture of visual space perception, as well as can be done at the present time.

THE EMPIRICIST POINT OF VIEW

Empiricists typically begin their analysis with the physical Euclidean space consisting of lines and angles, with straight lines parallel to one another, and so forth. Presumably, this world extends outward from the eye in a straight line. In this view the size and shape of objects could be related to the pictures (configurations) on the retina, with the perception of distance as the main aspect of space perception that needed explanation.

To provide such an explanation, the classical empiricist view proposed that the organism responds to a specific set of ray-directions. Each light ray represented an individual point stimulus in space. This theory viewed distance as an attribute of the world perceived by means of cues present in the retinal picture. Each cue would be evaluated in isolation and then integrated to get the appropriate percept. Since the size of the retinal projection itself could not provide an adequate account of the distance, familiar size given by learning or past experience was necessary to determine size and distance. The sensed size could then be compared with remembered size, and the distance of the object could be obtained by an "unconscious inference" or computation, a view elaborated by Helmholtz (1850).

The more modern proponents of this view, the Transactionalists, begin with a study of the stimulus isolated in the laboratory and broken down into components as does classical empiricist theory. However they take the analysis one step further. After identifying the characteristics of the retinal projection of the stimulus, they ask what percepts could be like, given the particular projection. They attempt to show, by comparing the stimulation in the retinal projection with the perceptual outcome, that the information in the projection is not adequate to determine the outcome. If the stimulus projection is inadequate, then the percept must be determined by other factors, most likely memory, learning, or personality. Let us examine these concepts in more detail.

Equivalent Configurations and Stimulus Inadequacy

The relationship between an object in space and the luminance discontinuities it produces in the retinal projection is specifiable in terms of the physical characteristics of the stimulus and the light reflected from the objects which stimulates the retina. For example, Figure 12.1 shows a line of size S at distance

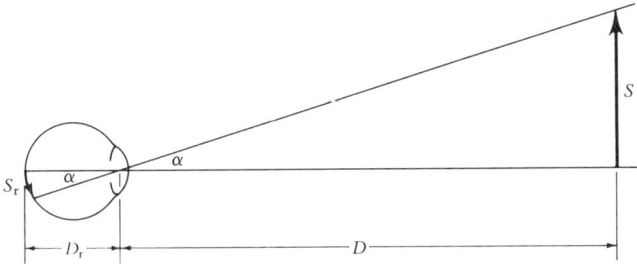

FIGURE 12.1   Geometrical relationships between a physical object of size S at distance D from an eye of diameter D_r to yield a retinal size S_r.

D from the perceiver. The size of the projection on the retinal surface will be a function of the visual angle formed by the light rays from the extremities of the object. This angle supplies important information about the stimulus object, but it is not unique to this object. Clearly this particular object at this particular distance is the only one which could give rise to the visual angle described. But is it the only object in space which could result in such a visual angle? Figure 12.2 shows that it is not. A number of objects of different sizes and different distances could give rise to an envelope of light rays entering the eye at that angle. When different slants are considered as well, the number of such objects is infinite. All stimuli in space which could give rise to the same pattern on the retina are said to be members of a family of equivalent configurations. Figure 12.3 shows some members of a family of equivalent configurations for a two-dimensional surface. The relationships described are simply statements of geometrical fact—no psychological statement has been made. Thus, in this analysis, any two members of the same family of equivalent configurations will supply the same stimulation at the retina.

Thus far the analysis has proceeded from the physical object to the retinal projection, a purely geometrical analysis. Now we may ask the psychological

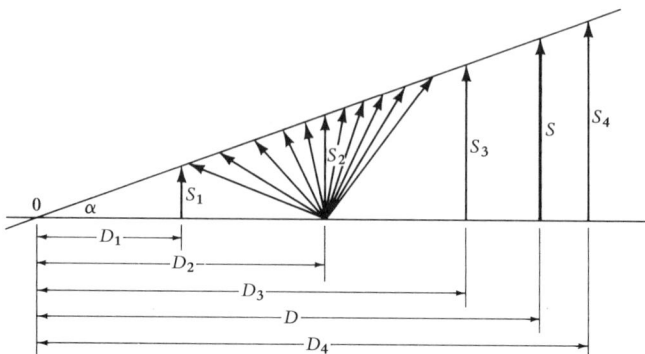

FIGURE 12.2 Objects of different sizes at different distances which could produce a given visual angle, α .

question: Given the stimulus on the retina, what is the nature of the percept—what is perceived to be out there? Other things being equal, two members of a family of equivalent configurations should be perceived as the same. As soon as the question is phrased in this way, it is clear that the concept of equivalent configurations implies that there is not enough information in the stimulus on the retina to determine a percept uniquely. Clearly any member of the family of equivalent configurations could have given rise to this retinal pattern, and therefore, it is not possible to tell which is the one out there, using retinal information alone. If two or more objects can give rise to the same stimulus on the retina, and if the stimulus determines the percept, then clearly the perceiver would be unable to discriminate between these objects. The only conclusion possible is that additional information must be supplied from other, presumably memorial, sources to supplement the retinal information.

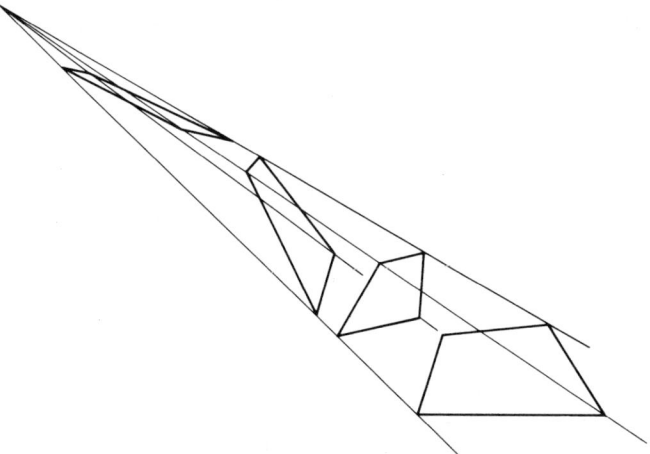

FIGURE 12.3 Some members of a family of equivalent configurations for two-dimensional (plane) surfaces.

Tests for the existence of equivalent configurations can be performed by identifying the retinal patterns produced by an object and then showing that the external stimulus can be altered while the pattern remains unchanged. In general, this test has been applied to stimulus cues in isolation (see Chapter 13 for a discussion of some of these cues). However, for empiricist theory to be generally applicable, it must be shown to hold for cues in combination. Adelbert Ames designed a number of demonstrations to support this position. We will consider one in some detail.

The Ames Chair Demonstration

Ames devised the chair demonstration to illustrate the relationships between a physical object in space, the retinal pattern of stimulation, and the resulting percept. It shows not only what these relationships might be, but also how they pose problems for the study of visual space perception. Figure 12.4 shows the stimulus arrangements for a string chair suspended in space. Thin black wires

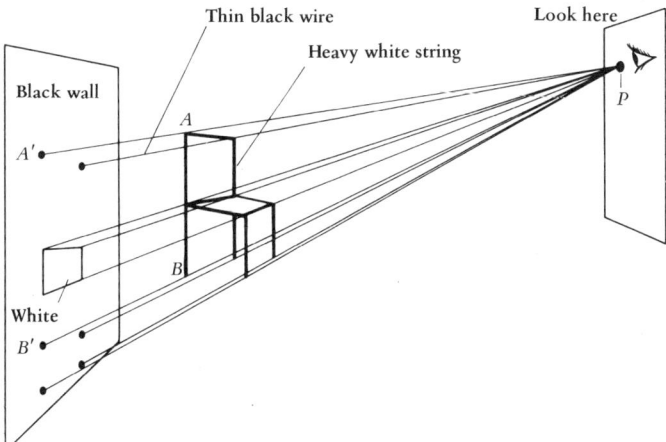

FIGURE 12.4   Real string chair suspended in space and the proper viewing point.

are stretched between point *P* and a black wall so that they represent the outermost rays reflected from various portions of the chair. The chair can then be suspended in space by connecting heavy white string to the appropriate thin black wires. For example, the rear left leg of the chair *(AB)* can be suspended by connecting a heavy white string between wires *PA'* and *PB'*. A seat of the chair is not suspended in space but is represented by a particular member of the family of equivalent configurations which would be produced by the real seat, namely, that configuration which is determined by the rear wall of the apparatus. This portion of the rear wall is painted white.

Figure 12.5 shows three different stimulus arrangements in the chair demonstration with a representation of the retinal pattern for each. The first panel shows the three-dimensional string chair suspended in space by wires,

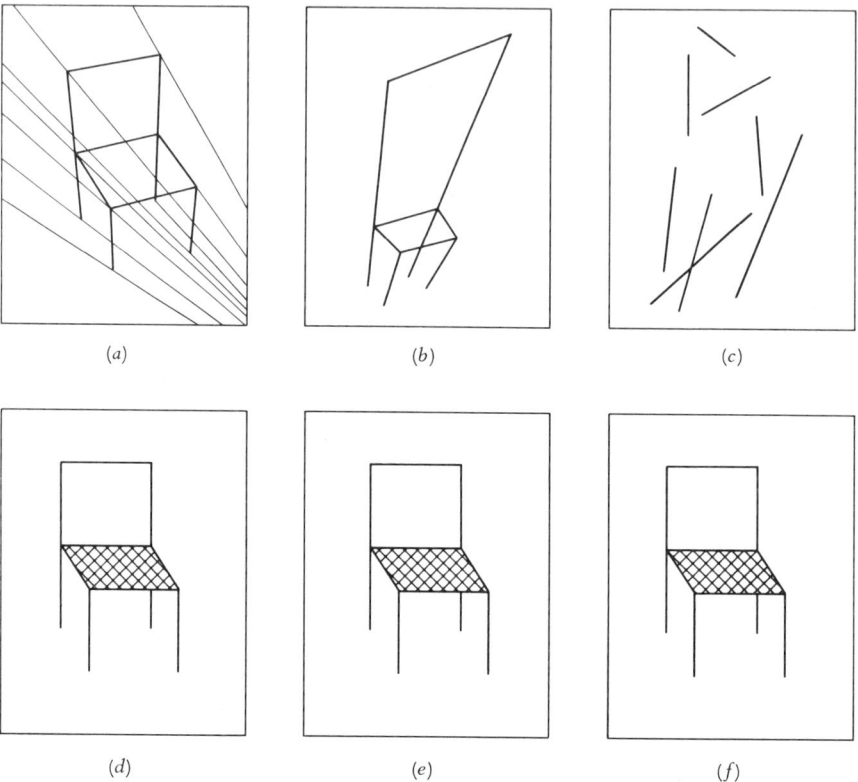

FIGURE 12.5 The three stimulus situations in the "chair" demonstration and their respective perceptual outcomes. *(a)* Real chair of strings suspended in space. *(b)* Same wires as in *(a)* but now cut with a plane. Strings are all connected between points intersected by the plane. *(c)* Same wires as in *(a)* but now each pair of wires is cut by a different plane at a different slant. Strings are connected between the two points of intersection of each plane with the pair of wires. *(d)* Representation of impinging stimulus on picture plane from real chair of strings. *(e)* Representation of impinging stimulation on picture plane from equivalent configuration in which all strings are in same plane. *(f)* Representation of impinging stimulus on a picture plane from wires cut by different planes at different slants.

as described in Figure 12.4. The second panel shows what the strings would look like if they were connected as follows: First, imagine a plane at some angle to the line of regard which passes through the wires. The plane in the illustration is tipped so that the top is further back than the chair was and the bottom is closer to the viewing point. Now connect string to pairs of wires corresponding to parts of the chair at the points at which they intersect the plane. This procedure will produce the physical arrangment of strings shown in the middle panel. The third panel shows what the strings would look like when they were connected as follows: First select a pair of wires corresponding to one part of the chair, say to the left front leg. Cut this pair with a plane at some angle to the line of regard and connect a string between the points of intersection. Now select another pair of wires corresponding to another part of the chair, say the left rear leg. Cut this pair with a plane at some other angle to the line of regard, which is different from the previous angle selected. Now connect these two points with a string. Continue in this fashion, selecting a different angle for the plane each time, until each pair of wires corresponding to each part of the chair is included. The pattern of strings would look something like that pictured in the right-hand panel.

Now we may ask, what are the different retinal patterns produced by these three different but related sets of strings? The answer is shown in the bottom row of panels—they each produce virtually identical patterns on the retina. These different sets of strings are all members of the same family of equivalent configurations, because they were constructed in that way. What do these three sets of strings look like when we place our eye at point *P*? All perceivers report that the three look the same, and that they all look like the original chair. The perceptual outcome is never *any* member of the family of equivalent configurations, but always a *particular* one, the three-dimensional chair. Since each of the three sets of strings produce the same pattern, why do we see only a single organization in space no matter what is producing the stimulus in reality? According to the empiricist view, the stimulus itself supplies insufficient information to determine the outcome in all three situations. Therefore, other sources of information must be present. We see chairs because our experience with this particular pattern always involved real chairs and we have learned to give this retinal pattern the organization implicit in the notion of a chair. Unless some outside source of organization is invoked, there would be no reason for seeing a chair rather than a random array of strings. This is true even in the one case where there presumably really was a random set of strings supplying the stimulation.

We will return below to a further consideration of some of the assumptions underlying the interpretation of this demonstration, when we compare the empiricist view with that of a psychophysical view of the perception of space.

THE PSYCHOPHYSICAL POINT OF VIEW

A logical alternative to the stimulus inadequacy view of the empiricists is to argue that the stimulus at the eye is entirely adequate to represent all of the information about the physical world. To pursue such a position, one performs psychophysical experiments, attempting to find psychophysical correlates which relate the pattern of information available in the retinal projection to aspects of our perception of the world around us. The psychophysics of space perception often seems different from psychophysical investigations such as those discussed in Chapter 5. In sensory psychophysics, there was little doubt about the stimulus variables to be correlated with, for example, perceived brightness—obviously, we are interested in the functions relating stimulus intensity, duration, area, and the like, to perceived brightness. In the psychophysics of space perception, however, the initial task is to discover the physical variables. What are the variables of importance? What aspects of the stimulus pattern are correlated with our visual experience of space? This task is very much more difficult.

The principal contemporary proponent of the psychophysical point of view is James Gibson (1950, 1957, 1966), and he remains its most forceful spokesman. Gibson views the visual system as responding to higher-order variables of stimulation directly. Thus the stimulus must contain sufficient information to determine our perceptual experience uniquely, without mediation by prior experience or memory. In attempting to account for the ordinary, familiar visual world of everyday life, Gibson's analysis stresses the role of transformations that take place when the observer moves while he is observing. Thus Gibson has attempted to describe this visual world carefully in order to direct the search for the proper correlates.

The Visual World and the Visual Field

In Gibson's view, the visual world we perceive is made up of solid objects which look solid and of slanted surfaces which are perceived at the appropriate slant. The visual world has no boundaries; it is continuous, and it has a panoramic character. This world has no center and no differences in clarity among its parts. The visual world is perceived by scanning—it does not move when we move our head and eyes, it is stable and shows constancy of size, shape, and form. Thus the visual world is dependent on eye movements rather than on a single fixation and, therefore, will require an explanation in terms of dynamic stimulus correlates, that is, correlates containing temporal patterning.

Gibson distinguishes between this perceived visual world and the contents of a single glance or fixation—the momentary visual stimulation which we usually do not experience. We may become aware of it by fixating the eyes on a point and paying attention to the whole area that can be seen, keeping the eyes fixed. If you now take the attitude of an artist, you will observe a two-dimensional picture, the visual field. Figure 12.6 shows a typical visual field for one eye. It is made up of colored patches and surfaces divided by contours. It has boundaries, it is oval in shape covering about 180 degrees horizontally and 150 degrees vertically. The visual field is sharp, clear, and fully detailed at the center but gets progressively vaguer and less detailed toward its boundary; that is, there is a center-to-periphery gradient of clarity. The visual field shifts as the eyes, head, and body move. Objects represented in the visual field show projective shape and, therefore, do not have constancy but change their size and shape when fixation changes.

This is a critical distinction, and failure to acknowledge it imposes an insurmountable barrier to any theory of visual space perception. The visual world has continuity but we sample it with the motions of our eyes—eyes which move in a head which in turn is also moving in space. In the normal state of affairs, with our eyes, head, and body moving through space, the visual

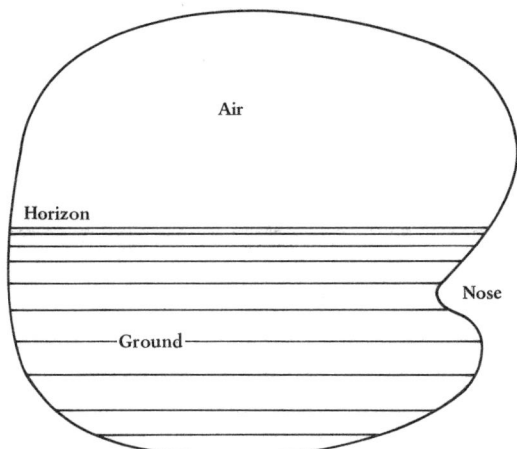

FIGURE 12.6   A typical visual field of an eye showing ground, air, horizon, and general shape of field.

field is in a state of flux. Clearly the analysis of visual space perception must involve successive retinal stimulation from successive fixations. The successive stimulations of the retina do not fuse with one another but are integrated over time in the same sense that the successive frames of a motion picture film are not blurred one into the other, but simply supply the stimulus over time for the perception of continuous motion. Thus it is necessary to understand the geometry of transformations on the retina in order to explain why successive changes can correspond to various aspects of visual experience. Because the successive retinal images are not entities but simply represent temporal samples of a stimulus constituting change-over-time, the visual world cannot be perceived all at once. The perception of visual space is based not on a succession of images, but on a continuous-but-changing set of images.

This relationship is illustrated in Figure 12.7, which shows the optical transformations that occur as a perceiver enters a room. The information contained in a particular retinal pattern at any moment in time cannot be understood in isolation. It must be analyzed in terms of the effects of the motions of the observer and of the transformations produced by these motions. We shall devote substantial space to an understanding of the regularities of these transformations in the latter half of Chapter 13.

The Ground Theory—Texture, Surface, Gradients, Transformations

Gibson's psychophysics rests on a conception of physical space as objects on surfaces, and it gives special recognition to a particular surface—the ground. Not only is the ground a surface that extends away from the observer in the third dimension, it also provides support for motor activity and is involved in the equilibrium of the body, upright posture, and locomotion in general. More-

FIGURE 12.7   The optical transitions when moving from one vista to another (from Gibson, 1966).

over, since man is a terrestrial animal, the lower portion of the visual field is almost invariably filled by a projection of the terrain (see Figure 12.6), while the upper portion is usually filled with a projection of the sky separated from the terrain by a skyline. The ground projects an image which is spread out on the retina rather than confined to a point.

Figure 12.8 illustrates the advantage of conceptualizing the visual information at the eye in terms of surfaces rather than in terms of points and lines as is commonly done by the empiricists. Analyzing the retinal projections in terms of points of stimulation causes a major difficulty in assigning depth values to points in space when they were aligned, as are points A, B, C, and D. The distance along the line of sight could not be translated into differential stimulation on the retina by any means. With an emphasis on the surface invariably below the eye, there is always a projection of an extended surface represented on the retina. Therefore, the points in the retinal pattern A', B',

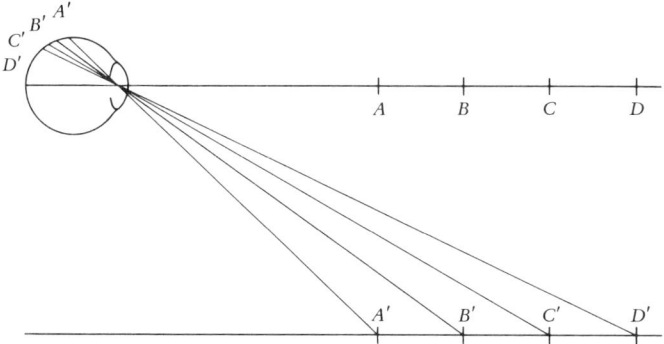

FIGURE 12.8 Two formulations of the problem of distance perception: one considering only points on the retina and the other emphasizing the image of a surface as a relationship among many points.

C', and D', which correspond to the points A, B, C, D in the surface, are always discriminable on the retina.

The Constant Scale of Space

The empiricists pose the question of the perceived constancy of size and shape in terms of their narrow analysis of the retinal projection. Thus the informational burden is placed upon that portion of the retinal projection which corresponds to the object itself. Since this aspect of the stimulus is easily shown to be inadequate, the empiricists are forced to look for other sources of information. Thus the problem of perceptual constancy is unsolvable without resort to learning and memory.

A psychophysics of visual space is not faced with this difficulty because the retinal projection is analyzed in terms of surfaces at slants which are in contact with the object in question. Constancy would be a direct consequence of our perception of textured objects on textured surfaces—the normal visual world. It would not be necessary to know what an object is, or to have come into contact with it in the past, in order to perceive it as having a constant size and shape when we move, or when it moves. Constancy would be given in the particular relationships in the changing retinal projection. It is the gradients and transformations in this projection which provide a constant scale for all of visual space. Within this metric, objects are perceived as attached to the underlying ground surface and thereby can be perceived in relation to its scale. Thus it is scale and not the size of specific objects which remains constant in perceiving objects in space.

Figure 12.9 illustrates the importance of scale provided by texture and perspective in determining the perceived size of the three objects. Each of the objects depicted subtends the same visual angle, which you can verify by measuring each of them with a ruler. They differ in their relative positions with

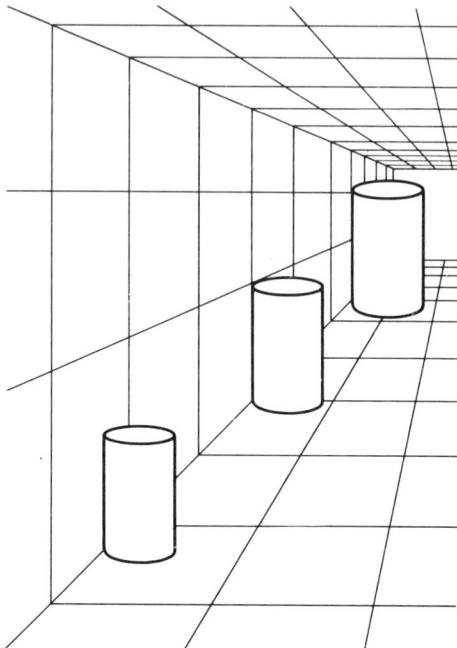

FIGURE 12.9   The size illusion showing the role of the scale provided by gradients of texture, size, and perspective in determining perceived size of three objects subtending the same visual angle.

respect to the gradients on the projection plane. Therefore they intersect the scale provided by these gradients at different points. Since the scale provides the metric of size-at-a-distance, the point of intersection of the object with the surface will determine its relative depth and its relative size. The retinal projection intersecting the projection of the ground surface low in the projection plane does so where the texture, size, and perspective all indicate "near." The same projection near the top of the plane will intercept the surface at a point indicating "far." Since the texture-size provides a constancy scaling as a decreasing size of the retinal projection, an unchanging size in the retinal projection will appear to be larger in the "far" position, and vice versa. Figure 12.10 shows what happens when the size of the retinal projection of the object decreases in the same proportion as does the gradient. Now the perception is clearly of three objects of the same size at different positions in depth.

There are other aspects to the perception of size and shape constancy, and many of them seem to be amenable to this type of analysis. The experimental literature is not very useful in clarifying these problems, however, since much of the research on constancy has studied outline shapes on textureless backgrounds. In this situation, the perceiver has a much more difficult task than in situations where texture is provided. These perceivers must turn to nonvisual sources of information because the retinal projection is made an inadequate source of information by the experimenter.

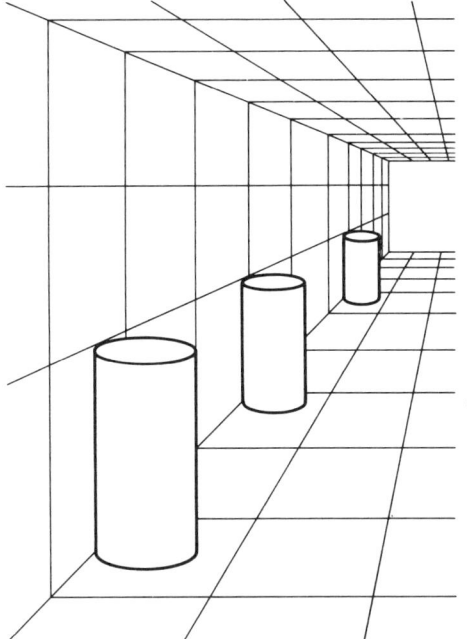

FIGURE 12.10 Perceptual constancy resulting from objects projecting different sizes onto retinal surfaces, but intersecting the ground plane at different levels and thereby scaled differently.

WHICH POINT OF VIEW IS CORRECT?

We have briefly considered the two points of view most concerned with the perception of the visual world. Both may be criticized as incomplete, but their deficiencies are somewhat different. The empiricists carry out an inadequate analysis of stimulation and then perform experiments using impoverished stimuli. The psychophysicists, on the other hand, suggest higher-order variables without demonstrating their effectiveness, and without specifying mechanisms by which these variables could operate. Let us examine these criticisms in a little more detail.

We may illustrate the criticisms of the empiricist position by reference to the chair demonstration. The effectiveness of that demonstration rested on a retinal projection of outline shapes on a fixed eye looking through a pinhole. But this does not represent the normal viewing situation. If the pinhole at P were enlarged to a centimeter or two and the head could move while looking through it, the three "chairs" would look very different. The view through the pinhole is only a portion of the view through the larger opening. If perception is accurate in the latter situation, in what sense can a portion of that stimulus be said to supply information? Moreover, if it does supply some information, should we be convinced that, if this information is inadequate, we must invoke a nonperceptual source? Since we are provided with stimulation to the entire retinal surface in the natural viewing situation, it would seem that the theorist has the responsibility of demonstrating that the entire normal retinal pattern is inadequate before invoking concepts such as learning and memory.

In the chair demonstration, all of the lines in Figure 12.5 may be equivalent in visual angle, but not in their thickness—the closer ones will be wider, and those at a slant will be tapered. The nearer ones will have a texture, and will overlap parts or all of ones farther away. If the eye or head should move, the retinal projection of the nearer ones will shift much more than the far ones. Thus the patterns in Figure 12.5 represent equivalent patterns on the retina only in a very contrived way. In the normal visual world, each will give rise to a different retinal pattern, and each will be perceived as different.

Nevertheless the empiricist position may be correct. Unfortunately, much of the experimental work rarely demonstrates all of the sources of information that are present in the retinal projection. One of the reasons for this is the empiricist's concept of perceptual cue. The visual experience of space must emerge in part from the information provided by features of the stimulus on the retina. Therefore, empiricists have sought such features within the two-dimensional pattern on the retina which may be used in conjunction with past experience to determine the perceptual outcome at any given moment. These features have been called "cues," or sometimes "clues," to incorporate in their name the notion that they do not uniquely determine perceptual experience in and of themselves. The problem arises with this conception because cues do not occur in isolation in the natural environment. Thus it is not clear whether the cues individually isolated in experiments ever operate in isolation in the natural environment. A number of cues will be discussed in more detail in the next chapter.

Perhaps the greatest deficiency in the empiricist position is their relegation of texture on surfaces to the status of cue, equal in importance to many of the other cues. It is more likely that surface texture plays a major role in providing a scale for visual space. Its importance comes from an appreciation of the fact that the visual world is experienced as extending away from a perceiver whose body rests on the same ground as other objects.

The psychophysicists are not vulnerable to these criticisms. However, the uncovering of plausible correlates of experience in the retinal projection cannot be accepted as sufficient proof that the stimulus is adequate. It must be accompanied by experimental support. A complete theory in this context must demonstrate two things. First, it must show that the variables discovered are in fact the ones responsible for our perceptual experience. In our present state of knowledge, the shapes of the psychophysical functions are not known and it is not clear whether every one of these variables suggested is actually used by the perceiver. Second, the theory must concern itself with the mechanisms by which these variables are used to construct an experienced visual world. The psychophysicist says these variables yield perceptual experiences directly. We know this cannot be true, even for very simple psychophysical relationships such as intensity and brightness. Those transformations within the visual system are extensive, even if none of them appears to involve learning or prior experience. The explanations for the perception of space must be even more complex. How are these variables processed? How is a construction made, especially one which draws upon the continuous changes across many fixations as the eyes, head, and body change their positions relative to the visual world?

Our analysis of visual space perception will lean more toward the psychophysical approach in the remaining chapters. Specifically, we will show in Chapter 13 the kind of information that is contained in stimulation, and in Chapter 14, we shall discuss the integration of the visual perceptual system with the motor system. In Chapter 15 we shall discuss the kind of information to which human infants can respond and the implications for perceptual development in general.

SUMMARY

We have reviewed the two major approaches to the study of visual space perception. We have noted the major similarity in the attempt to isolate the nature of the information at the retina, and the major difference in either establishing that the information is inadequate, or showing that it supplies sufficient information to yield the perception of a visual world without invoking learning or memory. The empiricist position was found to be lacking because it rests on incomplete analysis of the stimulus. It may be that the retinal pattern is inadequate, but that remains to be proved, especially when perceiving the normal visual world.

The psychophysical analysis of space perception assumes that the elementary impressions of the visual world have to do with surfaces and edges rather than points and lines. The search for stimulus correlates must take into account the fact that the visual world must be scanned in order to be perceived. Thus the retinal projection for a moving observer undergoes continuous transformations. The temporal patterning is an important part of the study. With scanning, the image becomes a continuous serial transformation which is unique, yielding the stable, panoramic, and unbounded visual world we normally perceive.

Readings

Hochberg's (1962) chapter provides a historical context for these theoretical disputes. Two principal books by Gibson (1950, 1966) are essential for a further understanding of his psychophysical position. Ittelson (1960) represents the transactionalist approach, and as such is the major empiricist viewpoint. There are many other books and articles which review, comment upon, or criticize these two positions, but most of these references are more appropriate for the next few chapters. Some earlier history of these controversies will be found in Boring (1942) and in Pastore (1971).

INTRODUCTION

Some of the information about objects in space may be found in the two-dimensional projection on the retinas. In this chapter, we will see how the retinal projection has been analyzed, first for a fixed pattern on a single eye, then for fixed patterns simultaneously present in two eyes, and finally for changing patterns in the two eyes. Perceivers' eyes, heads, and bodies are rarely, if ever motionless. Nevertheless, spatial information is contained in the retinal pattern of a single glance. The static sources of information to be reviewed in the first part include surface texture and the traditional monocular cues of outline perspective, retinal size, interposition, and aerial perspective. The traditional binocular cues include convergence and binocular disparity, the latter including double images and stereopsis. We will conclude with a discussion of the changing retinal patterns which provide the basis for the perception of the motion of objects and of movement of the observer.

INFORMATION IN A FIXED MONOCULAR
RETINAL PATTERN

Since we intend to describe the physical correlates of objects on surfaces as they are represented in the retinal projection, we must first focus on the properties of surfaces against which the objects are viewed. It should become clear that the characteristics of such surfaces provide most of the information about the perception of space.

We noted in Chapter 12 (especially Figure 12.8) that most surfaces project images that are spread out over the retina rather than confined to a point, a line, or an outline shape. It will be easier to visualize this stimulation, therefore, if the outline shapes of the surfaces in space are projected onto a fronto-parallel plane. Such an arrangement is illustrated in Figure 13.1. It shows a solid pyramid in space projected onto a two-dimensional surface which is perpendicular to the viewer's line of sight when he is looking straight ahead. This projection is similar to the one on the retina. It has the advantage of permitting us to perform our analyses on an enlarged and upright view of the pattern.

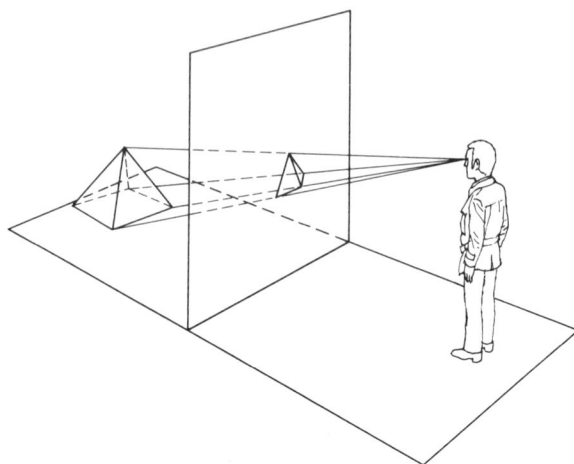

FIGURE 13.1 An object projected onto a fronto-parallel plane.

Surface Texture and Perspective

All surfaces in the physical world have texture. They possess a microstructure or a grain which can be thought of as units repeated over the entire surface. Thus the units are characteristic of the surface and must be represented in the information present in the retinal projection. If all elements of the surface are effectively equidistant from the perceiver, then the retinal projection of each of the units, as determined by principles of geometry, will be the same size. However, in the real world, we encounter surfaces which are almost invariably at a slant to our line of sight. Consequently, the units in surfaces are projected onto the retina according to the rules of perspective. There are two rules which govern the change in projective unit size, one having to do with the frontal dimension of the surface texture and the other with its longitudinal dimension.

When considering the projection of a textured surface, for example, one upon which the observer is standing and which stretches away from him, these rules tell us how the elements of the surface will change. In general, projected size will decrease with distance—the farther away an element is, the smaller its projection will be. As an example, assume that a ground surface is made up of square elements (as in a linoleum tile floor). Figure 13.2 shows these relationships for a viewer at point P looking down on a row of elements whose projective size is shown on a fronto-parallel plane. In order to make the two components of projective size change clearer, consider first the frontal dimensions of the squares. Figure 13.3 shows the rows of elements looking straight down on the surface and on the fronto-parallel plane. The frontal dimensions of the square elements decrease linearly as the distance from the projection plane increases. Looking back at Figure 13.2 it should be clear that this change corresponds to a decrease in unit size up the projection plane. This will be an important component in our understanding of the scale of space and the perception of constancy which is related to it. Moreover, this change in size in

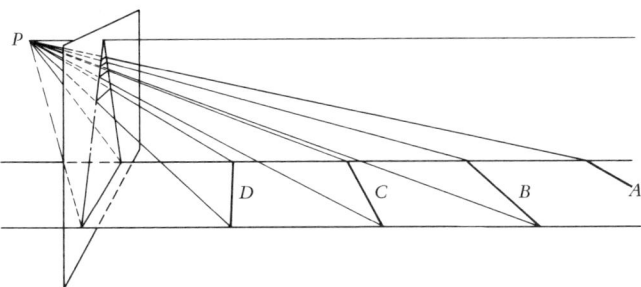

FIGURE 13.2 The principles of perspective for square units of the ground showing the combined force of changes in frontal and longitudinal dimensions.

the projection results in a change in outline shape—the squares project as trapezoids because the projections of their far edges are smaller than the projections of their near edges. The sides, which are physically parallel, are projected as converging with distance.

The longitudinal dimensions of the units are projected as the altitudes of the trapezoids on the projection plane. The altitudes are a negatively accelerated function of the distance and, therefore, this dimension is foreshortened in the projection—it is "compressed" in relation to the frontal dimension (see Figure 13.4).

Thus far we have described only the geometric transformations of elements in surfaces stretching away from the perceiver as they are represented in the retinal projection. As yet, no reference has been made to how or what a perceiver does with this perspective information. It should be reasonable, however, that a perceiver uses this gradient of texture in his retinal projection as a source of information about the structure of space.

Surface-at-a-Slant

We have seen that the units in a slanted surface supply a retinal projection at the eye which has continuous and systematic change in both the frontal and longitudinal dimension. This gradient is taken by the psychophysicist point of view to be the correlate for the perception of a surface-at-a-slant, that is, a surface in depth. These changes may be thought of as producing a gradient in

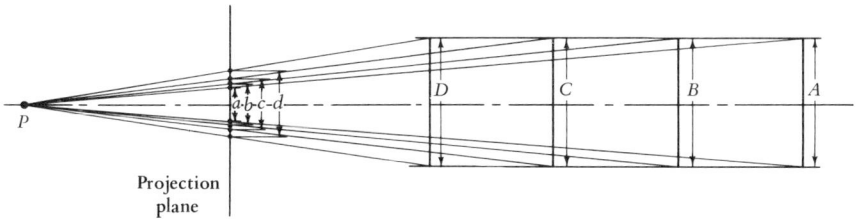

FIGURE 13.3 Top view of horizontal units of a surface showing changes in relative size of same sized frontal portions of units when projected onto fronto-parallel plane.

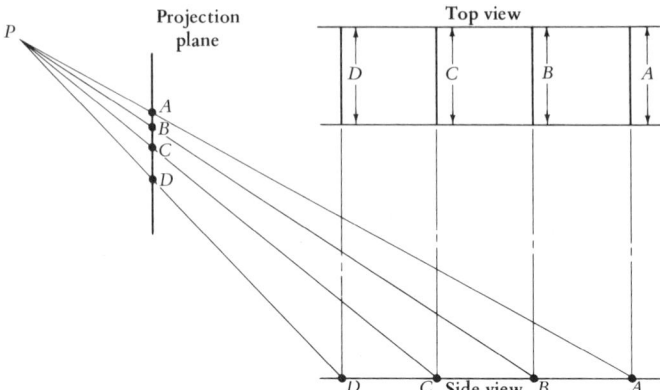

FIGURE 13.4   Side view of horizontal units of a surface showing changes in relative size of longitudinal dimensions of units when projected onto fronto-parallel plane. These units show "compression."

the density of texture on the retina. This gradient of density may be the adequate stimulus for the perception of continuous distance. If so, it would account for the distance of all parts of a surface simultaneously, rather than for only a single point, a single line, or a single shape-unit. Thus texture gradients provide a perceptual scale for the visual world, a scale that defines a dimensionality against which all other variations can be measured.

To illustrate the power of this analysis, contrast it with the empiricist analysis of the perspective relationships. These are usually broken down into separate analyses of size-distance, shape-slant, and linear perspective. In each case, the empiricists focus on one aspect of an object in an otherwise empty visual field. Figure 13.5 shows that, for example, the projection of outline shapes must be ambiguous when treated in isolation—the three different shapes at different slants all produce the same retinal projection. It should be clear why the empiricists' analysis concludes that the stimulus only provides

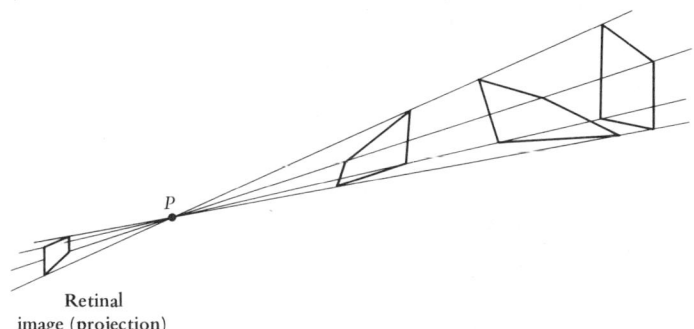

FIGURE 13.5   A family of configurations which are equivalent in the sense that they all could produce the same shaped projection on the retina. Given this retinal projection as a stimulus, any member of the family, that is, any of these shapes-at-a-slant, could be perceived.

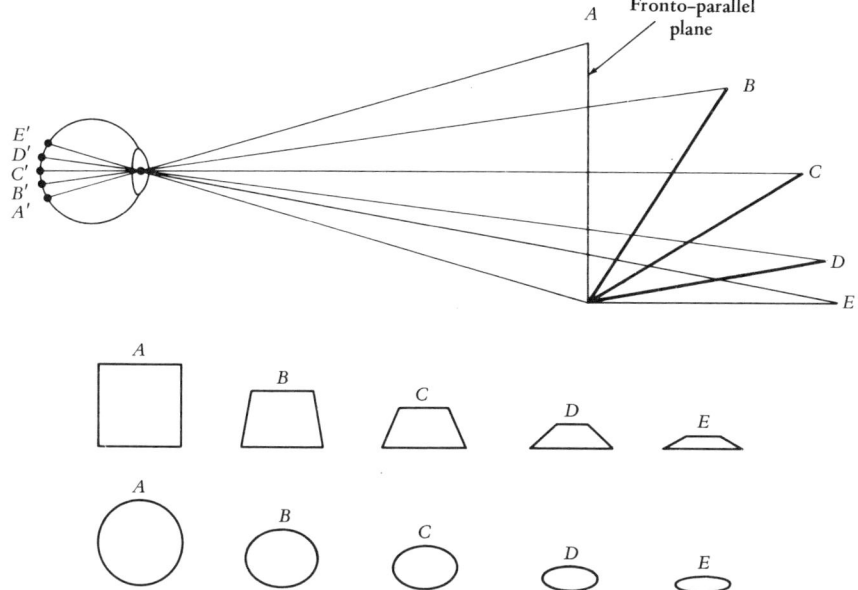

FIGURE 13.6 Illustration of the relationship between shapes-at-a-slant and the corresponding deformations of the retinal projection.

enough information to specify a family of equivalent configurations—trapezoids at different slants—and why it is inadequate to specify a particular surface-at-a-slant.

The systematic foreshortening, perspective, and compression of area which accompanies the relative slant of a rectangle (or circle) in space is illustrated in Figure 13.6. When presented as isolated outline shapes, they specify only different families of equivalent configurations. But notice what happens as soon as textural background is included and the outline shape is also given its texture. Figure 13.7 shows the same five trapezoidal projections taken from Figure 13.6, but now against a textured surface which provides a

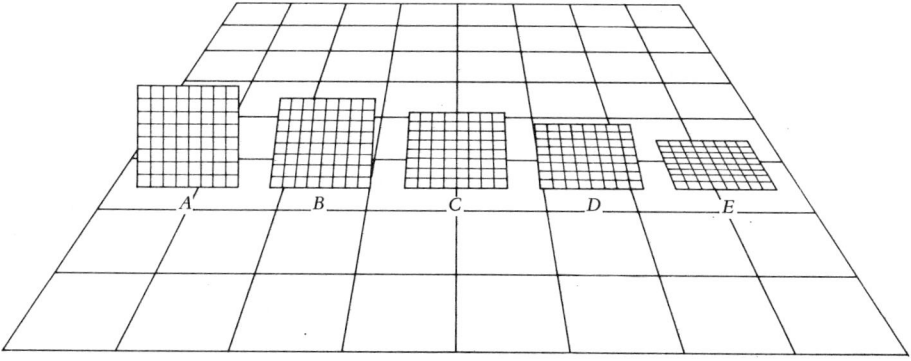

FIGURE 13.7 Textured shapes on a textured ground.

continuous scale of the visual world. Only shape *E* has a texture gradient which changes at the same rate as the surface—hence *E* is perceived on the surface, or parallel to it. Shape *A* has no texture gradient, and therefore it is perceived to be in a fronto-parallel plane, that is, standing upright on the surface rather than lying flat on it. Thus with texture gradients added, the shapes are perceived by their relationships to the scale of visual space. The stimulus—that is, the entire stimulus—now is sufficient to specify a particular surface-at-a-slant.

Size-at-a-Distance

In Figure 13.7, all five shapes appear to be equidistant from the perceiver. Before analyzing the information that allows us to perceive their distance, let us examine how such information is conveyed in the absence of textural backgrounds. In the typical analysis, the distance of an object is related to the retinal size of its projection. The trigonometric function relating object size *(S)*, object distance *(D)*, and the visual angle *(a)*—tan $a = S/D$— is illustrated in Figure 13.8. Since tan $a = s/17$, where *s* is the retinal size, $s = 17S/D$ in millimeters.

Given these relationships, it is clear that retinal size (or visual angle) alone does not supply enough information to determine a unique perceptual outcome. The perceiver only has enough information to determine a family of equivalent configurations such that the ratio of perceived size to perceived distance equals *s*/17. But since the perceiver usually reports seeing only one object at a single distance—and it usually is the actual physical distance of the physical object in space—empiricists have argued that other sources of information must be brought to bear. The simplest source has been called familiar size—the size of objects which is learned as a result of our associations with real, meaningful, and useful objects in space. Thus absolute retinal size could only serve as a cue to perceived distance if supplementary information is provided.

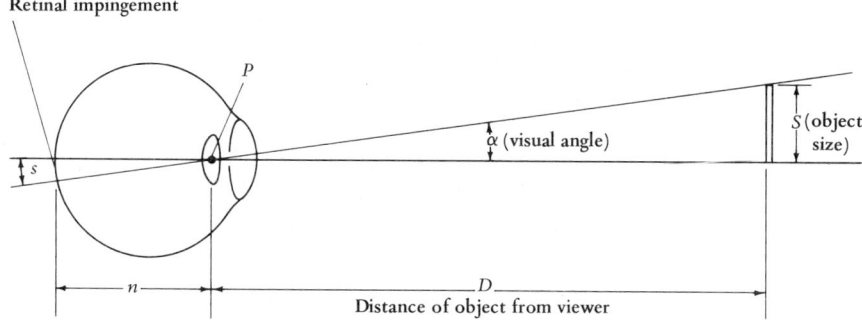

FIGURE 13.8 The relationships between the size *S* of a vertical object in space in a fronto-parallel plane at a distance *D* from an observer whose eye is at point *P*, showing the retinal projection size *s* and the angular subtense *a*, where tan $a = S/D$.

If there is not enough information in the geometry of size-distance relationships to yield depth directly for a single object in space, perhaps the
relative information in the stimulus provided by two objects would be sufficient. Figure 13.9 shows the visual projection of two objects S_1 and S_2 at two
distances D_1 and D_2, with their respective visual angles a_1 and a_2. If the perceiver can assume that the two objects have the same real size, through the use
of other depth information, past experience, or a guess, then $a_1/a_2 = D_2/D_1$.
In this case, the object producing the larger retinal size will be perceived at the
closer distance. Similarly, if the perceiver can assume that the two distances
are equal, then $a_1/a_2 = S_1/S_2$, and the two real sizes vary directly in the
same ratio as their retinal sizes.

The study of size-distance relationships has primarily been conducted
under viewing situations that provide only retinal size information to the
observer. For example, perceivers asked to judge the size (or distance) of a
luminous object seen monocularly in total darkness (for example, Holway and
Boring, 1941) must base their estimates entirely on retinal size. Thus observers
having no information about distance drop distance out of the equation
entirely. Such experiments are not very useful for understanding the perception
of space. What an observer will be forced to do in an impoverished viewing
situation need have no relation to the kinds of processes taking place in natural
environments. Denied all usual sources of information, a perceiver might be
forced to use retinal size in order to make judgments about depth. Nevertheless,
it is likely that the retinal size of objects represents only a small segment of the
information normally available.

Thus textureless objects in empty space provide a monocular retinal projection that does not supply enough information to determine perceived size

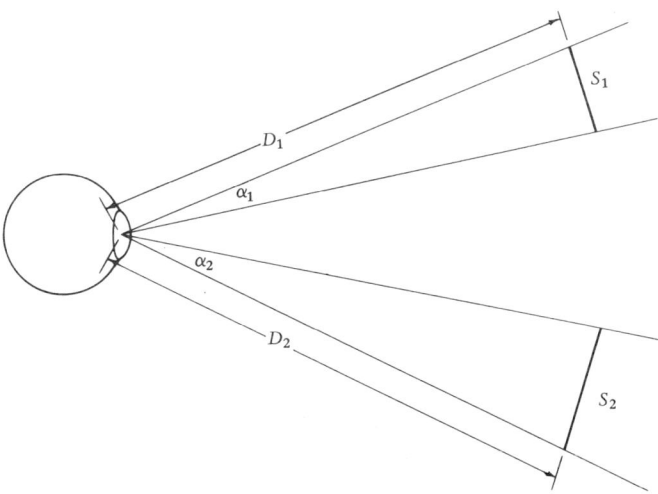

FIGURE 13.9   The information (a_1/a_2) supplied by two stimuli at different distances and in different directions.

and perceived distance uniquely. As soon as the object is given a texture and is placed on a textured surface, the inadequacy is greatly reduced. Look back at Figure 13.7. All of the objects are perceived to be at the same distance, not because of a retinal size comparison, but because all of them intersect the surface at a point where the textures of the object and of the surface are of the same density. The scale of space will place these objects at the same distance from the perceiver even if he has to turn around to see them all. Since every object can be located with respect to the scale, they can be located with respect to every other object.

Corner and Edge

Since the gradient of texture is a function of the slant of a physical surface away from an observer, the density of the texture on the retinal surface varies with the physical distance. Therefore, the intersection of two surfaces, or the abrupt change in slant of a surface, may be specified by changes in the gradient of texture. A corner is formed by the intersection of two planes with differing slants. This corresponds to an abrupt change in the gradient of the density of texture and gives the impression of a line across the field at the "corner." The stimulus for a corner is illustrated in Figures 13.10 and 13.11. An edge or a contour is specified by a change in the amount of density with the gradient remaining constant on either side of the change. This also gives the impression of a visual line (see Figures 13.12 and 13.13). Corners lend solidity to objects and contours make them stand out from the background. Together they provide part of the basis for the perception of solid objects in space. In this analysis, properties of visual space are specified by changes in the texture gradients alone, that is, without an edge or contour being present in the retinal projection. For example, there is no line defining the corner in Figure 13.11 or the contour in Figure 13.13, and yet we perceive these as if a line were present.

Epstein and Park (1964), in a review of the evidence pertaining to some of the psychophysical hypotheses, noted that the perception of surface and hardness was related to intensity gradients when looking at a Ganzfeld (see Chapter 8) or when looking at a coarse-textured plasterboard under full illumination (Gibson and Dibble, 1952). In both situations, perceivers reported seeing a fog —that is, no surface or form—with low illumination of the plasterboard or when intensity gradients were absent from the Ganzfeld. Epstein and Park concluded, therefore, that texture was a sufficient stimulus for the perception of surface.

But Epstein and Park noted some limitations in the power of texture as a source of information. A number of experiments were found in which perceived slant increased as the texture gradient increased, but it could produce perception of a single surface at a particular slant only when supplemented by additional stimulus information. Moreover, a texture gradient alone was not as effective as outline perspective as a stimulus for perceived slant. Epstein and

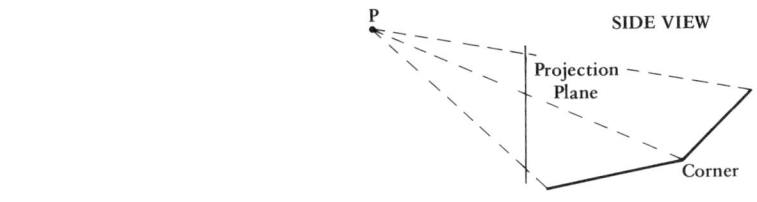

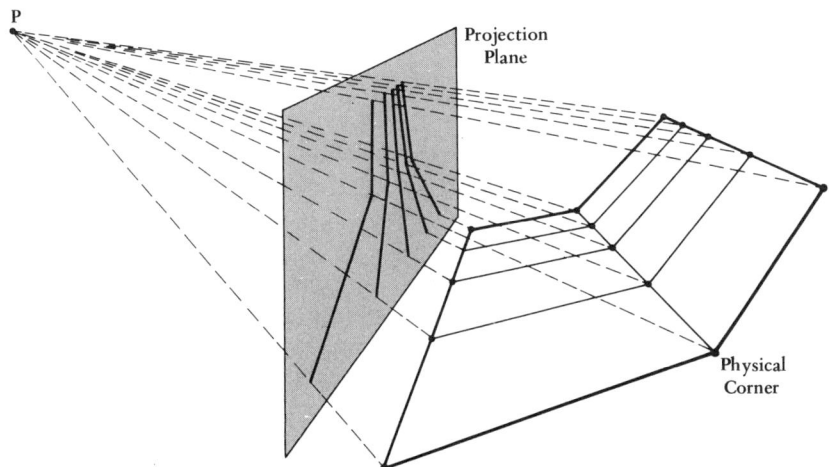

FIGURE 13.10 Perspective drawing showing the projection of optical texture from two planes with the same texture intersecting in a "corner" and the consequent optical pattern: an abrupt change in the gradient.

Park concluded that a gradient of texture density was not sufficient for veridical perception of slant.

But the research reviewed by Epstein and Park may not be appropriate to test psychophysical hypotheses in terms of the concepts developed in this chapter. As the previous chapter tried to show, it seems unlikely that our perception of objects in space is based on the processing of only one or a few cues, but rather depends on the generation of a scale of space from which all references are made. Since in the natural environment all of the information about space is consistent, we probably make use of it all in an integrated fashion, rather than separately, cue by cue. What seems most unlikely is that cues are processed individually and then added together in some manner.

One of the limitations that stem from these narrower investigations into individual sources of information is that narrow questions are asked. For example, much of the research done on perception of space has measured perceived distance as the dependent variable. The logic for this is reasonable. Since the retinal projection is only two-dimensional, the process to account for in perception is how well the third dimension of depth or distance is construct-

FIGURE 13.11 Fronto-parallel plane view of optical texture gradients provided by a surface changing its direction. This produces the perception of a corner.

ed, estimated, inferred, or perceived. But this is rarely a very interesting variable, and it certainly is not a central component of an organized perception of objects on surfaces extending away from the perceiver.

This illustrates a more general problem in the study of space perception.

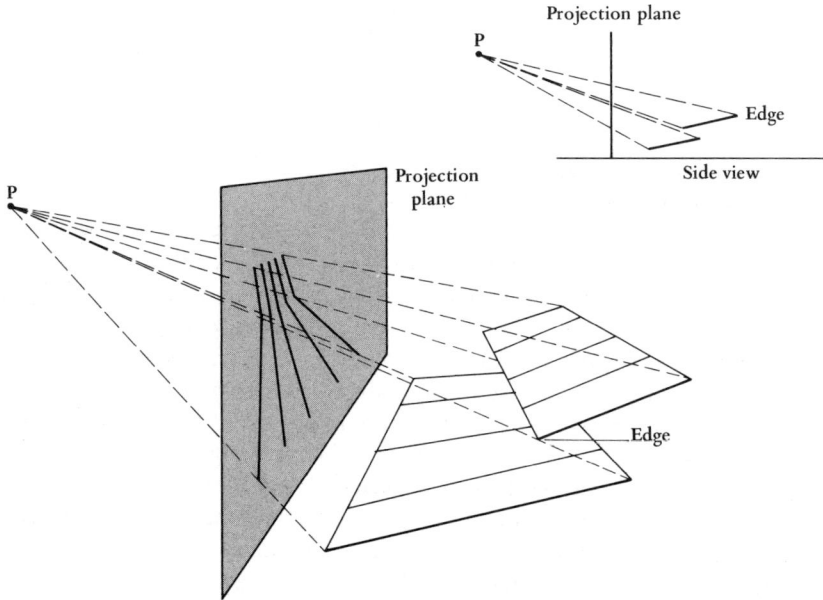

FIGURE 13.12 Perspective drawing showing the projection of optical texture from two planes, one in front of the other, and the consequent optical pattern: an abrupt change in the amount of density.

FIGURE 13.13   Fronto-parallel plane view of optical texture gradients provided by two surfaces, one in front of the other. This produces the perception of an edge.

Researchers have assumed that they could simulate natural visual environments with simple outline drawings of single objects on otherwise featureless surrounds. Further, they assumed that they could add, subtract, and bring into conflict sources of information about this environment by making subtle changes in these outline drawings or in the arrangements among simple objects seen against even simpler backgrounds. Finally, they assumed that by identifying a stimulus variable that produced a change in a perceptual response they had uncovered a cue to the perception of space. This is an adequate argument for the simple environment being manipulated, but generalization to the natural visual environment is dangerous at best.

These criticisms apply equally to the research generated by proponents of both the empiricist and the psychophysical point of view. They apply specifically to the experiments reviewed by Epstein and Park. Thus, it seems unreasonable to conclude that texture is or is not a sufficient cue for slant, where the experiments are ones which add and subtract texture and other cues in isolation. The psychophysical argument is that slant will be perceived from information about the scale of space, a scale given in part by the texture gradients, in part by perspective changes in outline shapes, in part by the relative textures of object and background surface at their intersections, and so forth. None of these alone need be powerful enough, or consistent enough to uniquely define a perceptual organization such as the slant of a surface.

Occlusion, Overlay, and Interposition

Objects on a textured surface will always occlude a portion of the surface—they will block part of the texture so that it will not be represented in the reti-

nal projection. Figure 13.7 illustrates such occlusion where portions of the surface which are directly behind the forms cannot be seen. Occlusion supplies
information about relative depth—what is in front and what is behind. We will
see later that occlusion will be an important component of the transformations
taking place in the retinal projection when the observer or the world is in
motion.

The occlusion resulting from the juxtaposition of objects in space has been
called overlay or interposition. This cue has been shown to be extremely
powerful in determining the perceived relative distance of textureless objects
in a textureless space. Figure 13.14 shows the relative positions of the borders
for three arrangements of circles and rectangles. The figure with the continuous border is perceived to be an object in front of another object whose border
is partially occluded. The occlusion occurs in such a way that the occluded
portion of the more distant object corresponds exactly to the portion cut off
by the front object. This is shown in the top of the figure.

The second row shows two figures in the same relative positions as those
in the top row except that they now share a common border. In this case, the
perception is of two objects at the same distance from the perceiver. This
situation is sometimes called "coincidence of edge." The third row shows the
force of the continuity of the border in determining which figure is perceived
as the object in the front and which is seen behind. Even though the figures on
the right side have a discontinuity in their borders, they are continuous at the
point of intersection with the borders of the other figures. This continuity
appears to be associated with the nearer object.

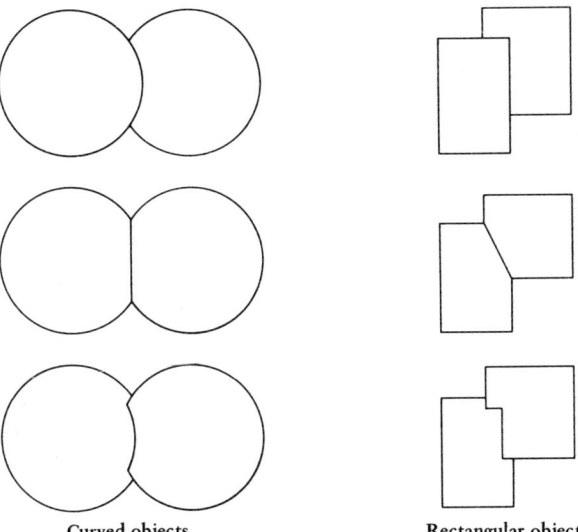

Curved objects   Rectangular objects

FIGURE 13.14 The relative positions of the borders of figures in the retinal projection is a strong
cue for relative depth. The figure with the continuous border is perceived to be in front of the other
object.

Other things being equal, two outline shapes in the retinal projection will be perceived closer together in depth the closer they are laterally in the retinal projection (Gogel, 1965). The limiting case is when the objects share a common edge in their projection on the retina. In this case, the objects are perceived as having an edge in common at the same depth. Gogel called this relationship the "equidistance tendency" and has provided strong evidence for the functioning of this cue, at least with textureless objects.

Gradients of Illumination

Brightness, shading, color, shadow, and aerial perspective all are capable of supplying some information about the relative depth of objects. All things being equal, bright objects appear to be closer than dim ones. Shading appears to be a strong cue for solidity—the shadow depending on the direction of the light source and the distribution of light. Aerial perspective refers to the fact that the retinal projections of distant objects are less sharp and less saturated in color than near objects. In general, the more the color of an object approximates the background, the more it tends to recede into it and to appear far away.

A gradient of illumination results from the relationship of the light source to the surface reflecting the light. The gradient does not vary with the distance of the surface from the source but with the degree of curvature of the surface. It provides, in the retinal projection, information that objects are not flat. Shading produces the perception of protuberances and indentations in surfaces as a function of gradients of illumination. Figure 13.15 shows how adding shading transforms ambiguous shape into clear three-dimensionality. A relief map correlates shading with the perception of protuberances (hills) and indentations (valleys) in a surface. The shading in one part of the map is related to shading in other parts by the direction of illumination. All protuberances must be shaded on the same side and all indentations on the other or they will not result in proper perceptions.

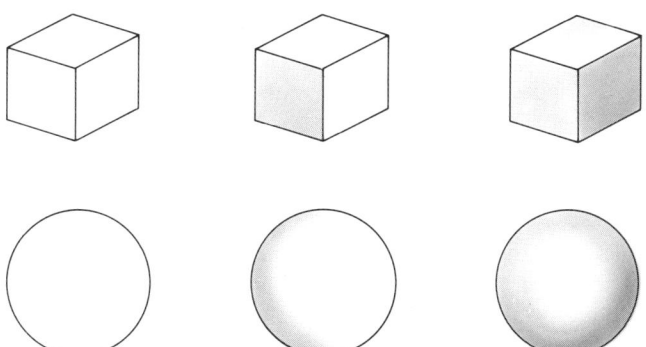

FIGURE 13.15 Rectilinear and spherical objects showing the impression of solidity resulting from gradients of illumination (shading).

We have now considered each of the important sources of information about the perception of space that are available in the retinal projection of a stationary eye. We have also focused on several aspects of how that information is used. Now we will enlarge our discussion by adding a second eye to the analysis.

INFORMATION IN FIXED BINOCULAR RETINAL PROJECTIONS

Two major components to depth perception—the direction in which an object is seen and its distance from the observer—can be directly related to the projection spread out over the retinas of the eyes. In this section, we will first review the information which underlies the perception of direction and then the information supplied to the two eyes which yields the perception of depth.

Visual Directions

We noted in Chapter 12 that perceptual space will be described using a polar coordinate system with the perceiver at the center or origin. In this system, direction can be measured as angular displacement from the straight ahead and distance can be measured radially, that is, out from the center. This system is particularly useful in describing the perception of visual directions because, as we will see, perceived direction is almost invariably related to the perceived straight ahead.

First let us examine the visual directions associated with each eye separately. We can think of visual lines which connect all points in space with various points on the retina. There will be a line for each direction and there will be an infinite number of points on each line, each at a different distance. We can single out one line for special consideration—the one which passes through the center of the lens and fovea. This line is called the principal visual line or visual axis of the eye. The subjective direction associated with the visual axis is called the principal visual direction. All other directions are experienced in relation to this direction. To say that we are fixating on an object means that the eye is oriented in such a way that the object is on the visual axis of the eye and that the projection of the object falls on the fovea.

This becomes a more difficult problem when we realize that we have two eyes, set about two and one-half inches apart. Consequently, what is straight ahead for one eye will be off to the side for the other, especially if the object in question is quite close. Both eyes can converge on the same fixation point, but then neither eye has its principal visual axis "straight ahead," at least in relation to any part of the rest of the body.

But localization of visual direction does not occur for each eye separately. The directions from the two eyes are jointly referred to some kind of body image, so that directions arrange themselves in relation to the perceiver's "mind." Thus every object is seen in a single subjective visual direction. The directions of all points appear to be arranged about a definite center so that the bundle of visual directions appear to converge to a point between the two eyes. This point is called the Cyclopean eye. Thus the two eyes localize jointly as if from a point located between them through which all visual directions pass. There is only one direction for each point in space with respect to the Cyclopean eye. These directions are called primary subjective visual directions to differentiate them from the directions associated with each eye separately.

These relationships are shown schematically in Figure 13.16. The two eyes are fixating point F in space and the respective foveas are stimulated. The subjective visual direction is illustrated as a direction pointing straight at F from between the two eyes (D_f). Similar relationships are indicated for points A and B which are not being fixated. Their subjective directions are also shown $(D_a$ and $D_b)$, and they suggest the cone of directions emanating from the Cyclopean eye.

But this does not entirely solve the problem of defining visual directions. If both eyes are fixating a nearby object, there will be substantial disagreement between the two subjective visual directions given by each of the two eyes and the primary subjective visual direction emanating from the Cyclopean eye in the middle. In such cases, the perceived direction corresponds to that of the Cyclopean eye. The law of identical visual directions, attributed to the nineteenth-century physiologist Hering, states that all objects lying on the two

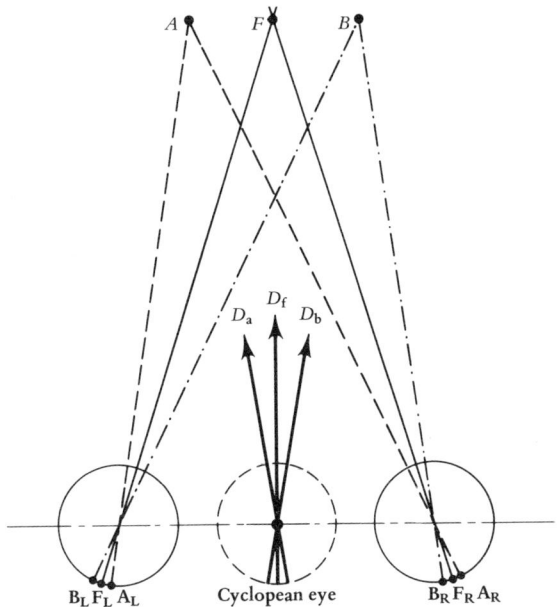

FIGURE 13.16   Visual directions are perceived as if there were a single "Cyclopean" eye situated between the two eyes.

principal visual directions will be perceived in the same primary subjective visual direction, irrespective of their angular position relative to the observer. This law refers to other parts of the retina also—the subjective visual directions of other points will be determined relative to those which occupy the central portion of the retina. This relationship suggests that every retinal point in the binocular field of one eye has a partner in the retina of the other eye with identical directional value.

The law of identical visual directions can be observed by performing a simple experiment which Hering first described. Figure 13.17 shows two cases where the law operates, one for near fixation and one for far. For far fixation, the viewer looks through a pane of glass at some distant point. He then makes two marks on the glass to correspond with the principal visual direction of each eye. Now clearly these two marks are separated laterally with respect to the viewer, but since they both fall on corresponding retinal areas of the two

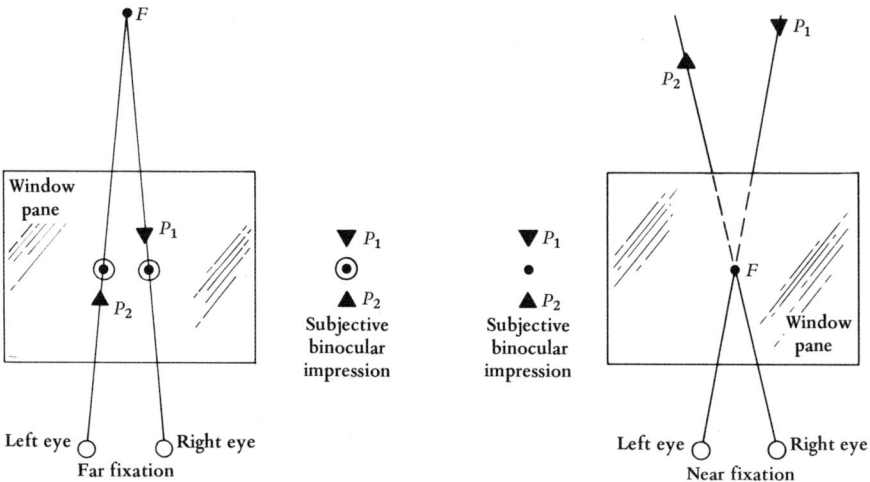

FIGURE 13.17 Hering's experiment showing the operations of the law of identical visual directions.

eyes, they will be seen in the identical visual direction. The same is true when, with near fixation, two far objects are separated spatially but fall on corresponding retinal points. Figure 13.18 gives detailed instructions for reproducing Hering's experiment.

Convergence

Since the two eyes are separated, and since they have to converge in their orientation for near objects, it seems reasonable that the angle of convergence will be a binocular cue to depth. Gregory (1969) suggests that convergence acts like a range-finder mechanism, telling the perceiver how far away an object is by the angle that he sets between two eyes so that each is directly fixating on

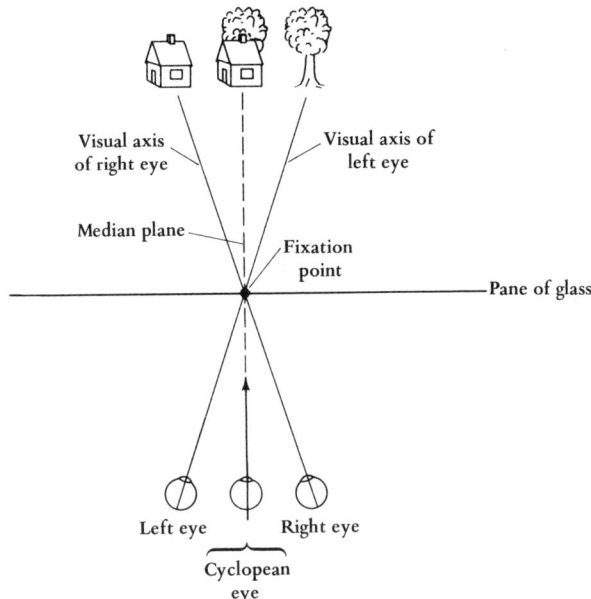

FIGURE 13.18 Instructions for the Hering experiment. (1) Stand in front of a window. Holding the head steady, close one eye (say, the right) and look at an object (say, a tree) in the distance to the right. While fixating the tree, place a small mark on the window pane so that it is in the direct line with the tree. (2) Now close the other eye and fixate the spot on the window pane. Then pay attention to some object in the distance (say, a house and chimney) which is in line with the dot on the pane. (3) With both eyes open, and directed at the spot on the window pane, the house, chimney, and tree will all be seen in the same visual direction, and that will be the direction of the spot from the center of the two eyes.

the object. If prisms are placed in front of each eye, so that the light path from object to eye is bent, thereby changing the angle of convergence, then the perceiver misjudges the distance of the object by the amount predicted from the optical displacement.

    This evidence notwithstanding, Ogle (1962) concludes that convergence appears to provide by itself relatively little information about depth. We should not expect it to be a powerful source of information since the muscle control systems are relatively slow and imprecise, compared to the accuracy of the perception of space. Therefore, convergence occurs as a way to bring the projection of the important parts of the visual world onto the fovea. We do not directly monitor that control system—we only attend to its results.

Corresponding Points on the Two Retinas

    The overlap of the two monocular fields is called the binocular field of vision. The two monocular fields, superimposed and projected onto a fronto-parallel plane, are shown in Figure 13.19. All areas within the overlapping fields stimulate both eyes. The maximum width of the monocular field is between 90

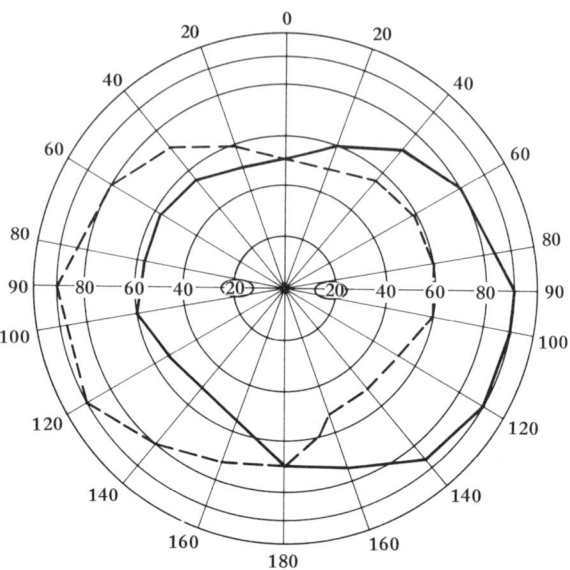

FIGURE 13.19   Binocular field of vision projected onto a fronto-parallel plane.

degrees and 115 degrees of visual angle, depending on the size of projection of the nose. The binocular field is flanked on both sides by a monocular field of about 30 to 35 degrees.

When the eyes fixate a point in space there is a retinal element in one eye which is associated with a retinal element in the other eye so that, when stimulated, they both give rise to the same subjective visual direction. These elements are said to be corresponding points. Thus, when the two retinas are stimulated on corresponding points (by any means whatever), the object is seen localized in space at the intersection of the lines of direction from the two eyes. These relationships are illustrated in Figure 13.20. When an object in space stimulates corresponding points, it is perceived as a single object localized at a single place in space. Thus the notion of corresponding points incorporates within it the notion that stimulation of the two eyes in a particular way results in singleness of perception.

There is a strong neuroanatomical basis for the singleness produced by stimulation of corresponding points of the two retinas. The receptive fields of most ganglion cells in one eye are represented in the same column of area 17 cortical cells as the receptive field from the corresponding retinal area of the other eye. In addition, most of the cells recorded from area 18 are binocularly driven, that is, respond to stimulation from either eye. In such cases, they are responsive only to stimulation falling on corresponding points of the two eyes. As we will soon see, this forms part of the basis for stereoscopic depth as well.

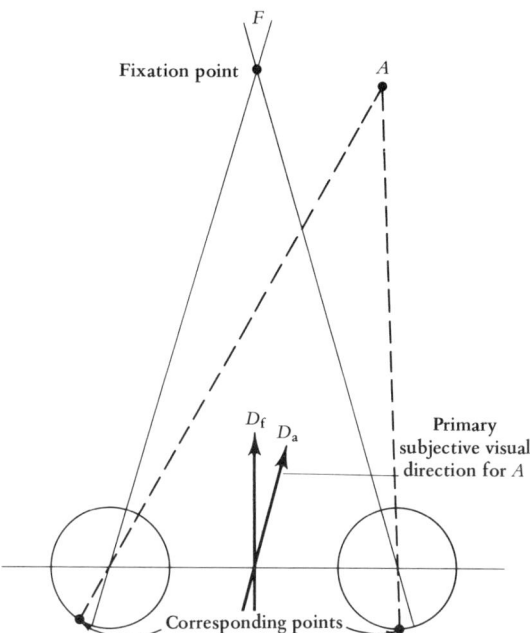

FIGURE 13.20   Relationships between points in the field, the fixation point, corresponding points, and subjective visual directions.

Stereopsis

If stimulation of corresponding points in the two retinas leads to a perception of singleness, what happens when a particular object in space does not stimulate corresponding points in the two eyes? To answer this, we must first consider the circumstances in which noncorresponding points are stimulated by a given object.

If both eyes fixate on object F, as in Figure 13.20 above, the object A will fall on corresponding points of each retina—its projections will be as much to the right of the projection of F in the left as in the right eye. Empirically, all objects that lie along a line passing through the point of fixation roughly in the frontal parallel plane will project onto corresponding points of each retina. This locus is called the horopter. All objects on the horopter will be seen as equidistant from the perceiver, as they should be, since they are roughly equally distant.

But notice what happens to objects which are nearer or farther than the horopter for a given fixation point, as in Figure 13.21. Now when fixating A, the projection of B is much closer to A in the left eye than in the right eye. Geometrically this must occur because the points are not equidistant from the two eyes. The projection of C is reversed between the two eyes, being to the left of A in the left eye and to the right of A in the right eye. In terms of

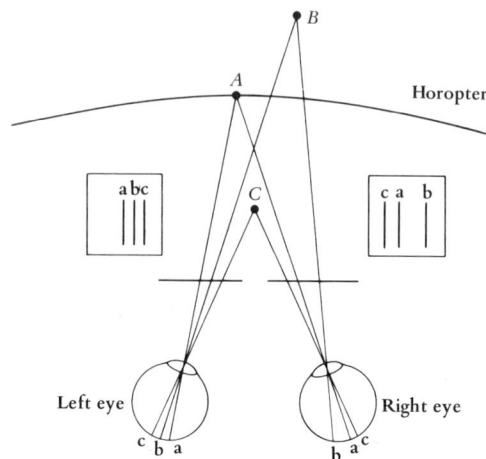

FIGURE 13.21 The geometrical relationships which give rise to disparity between retinal projections in the two eyes.

geometry, this will occur whenever *C* is closer than the fixation point. Any failure for an object to project on corresponding points of the two retinas is called binocular disparity. Disparity is the source of information for stereopsis.

Stereopsis provides depth information whenever both eyes are used and are fixated on the same object. Then all other objects not on the horopter for that fixation point will produce disparate projections and be seen in depth. Stereoscopic perception can be demonstrated in several ways. Focus a camera on an object and take a picture of a nearby scene. Then displace the camera about two and one-half inches laterally and take a second picture. Then show the two pictures, one to each eye, by means of a device such as a stereoscope. The objects in the pictures will pop into three-dimensional depth. If the two pictures were taken from more than two and one-half inches apart, this depth will be accentuated.

Stereopsis occurs over the entire binocular visual field—it is not confined to the region about the point of fixation. It has been demonstrated in dim illumination and therefore works with rods as well as with cones. Because of the geometrical and anatomical relationships involved, stereopsis provides information for relative depth only for objects up to about 135 meters from the viewer. Stereoscopic acuity is greatest near the fovea and generally follows the decrease in visual acuity with peripheral angles.

Julesz (1970) has demonstrated that retinal disparity of dot patterns is a sufficient stimulus for stereoscopic depth perception. He used random-dot stimulus patterns which were constructed via a computer program which filled each cell of a 100 × 100 cell matrix with either a black or a white dot. Obviously with these random properties, no meaningful pattern could be represented. If two identical copies of one of these random-dot patterns are presented, one to each eye, they will not be seen in depth. But if an entire section of one of them is displaced laterally, then viewing them stereoscopically will produce a disparity in their retinal projections and, therefore, a clear perception of depth. The section that has been moved on one of the copies will be seen in front of or behind the rest of the pattern, depending on whether it was moved toward the nose or the ears. Those dots that fall on corresponding locations—the unshifted section—will all be seen on a flat surface, as they should be. The dots that fall on noncorresponding locations are those that pop out or recede.

The depth does not change as the perceiver moves his eyes over the display. But we already know that it should not, because virtually any location on the entire retina can be assigned a corresponding location in the other retina. Hence, the depth can be seen even if the entire pattern is viewed by the peripheral areas of both retinas.

The important part of Julesz's demonstrations is what they tell us about the factors that affect stereopsis. For example, it is impossible to see any depth at all by looking at either half of the pairs alone, or even by looking at them together with both eyes. Only when they are separately seen by the two eyes does depth appear. Thus none of the other sources of information about depth reviewed in this chapter appear to be relevant to stereopsis. Since the patterns are not meaningful, stereoscopic depth does not depend upon any type of familiarity. Nor does it need convergence, since depth can be seen with only a 1-millisecond flash of a stereo pair. In sum, the only source of information necessary for stereoscopic depth is binocular disparity, even if it is only disparity among elements of texture.

In this sense, stereoscopic depth appears to be an independent aspect of depth available to us, available because we have two eyes with partially overlapping projections. It adds some resolution to our perception of depth, but it clearly is not the most important part. We have quite adequate perception of space with only one eye. This can be verified by covering one eye to see how easy it is to locomote and to perceive correctly the spatial arrangements in the visual world. Stereopsis does increase the vividness of depth—near objects are seen more vividly in front of far ones when seen with two eyes than with one. But even with one, the visual world rarely deceives us. Stereopsis also permits very precise close judgments of depth for stationary perceivers. This may be important to a creature that works with its hands. Thus, in terms of the evolution of the human brain, disparity may have played an important role.

INFORMATION IN A CHANGING RETINAL PATTERN

If the observer moves in space or if objects move with respect to the observer, there is a flow of stimulation as the retinal projection shifts across the retinal surface. We usually move about in the world and move our heads and our eyes, so that the stimulation on the retinas is constantly changing. Therefore, in order to understand how we perceive the three-dimensional world in these situations, we must learn something about the nature of the flow of stimulation on the retina as a function of the changes in eye, head, and body position. We will discuss changes that occur when the relative motion is either radial (toward or away from the observer) or tangential (directed laterally with respect to the observer), or some combination of these. We will see that movement introduces parallax—an apparent change in the position of an object resulting from the change in direction from which it is viewed. It also produces transformations of perspective that occur as a result of continuous movement of the field or of the observer. In this chapter, we will not make a distinction between movement in the physical world and movement of the observer. That will be a central problem of Chapter 14. Instead, this section will focus on the nature of the transformations in the retinal projection when there is any kind of motion present.

Radial Movement

When an object moves directly toward or away from an observer's eye, or when an observer moves directly toward or away from a stationary object, we have the simplest case of radial movement. This situation is illustrated in Figure 13.22 for an object of size S at various momentary distances from an eye. The change in real distance of an object of fixed size (S) results in a change in retinal size s_1 to s_5. If we think of this as a continuous change, when the object moves away from the viewer, the retinal extent of the consequent stimulation decreases symmetrically. When the object moves toward the observer, the retinal extent increases symmetrically.

A pattern increasing in size symmetrically is perceived as an object of unchanging size moving directly toward the observer on a "collision" course. Such an object appears as if it were "looming." The converse is called "zooming." If the increase in the retinal pattern is asymmetrical, the resulting percep-

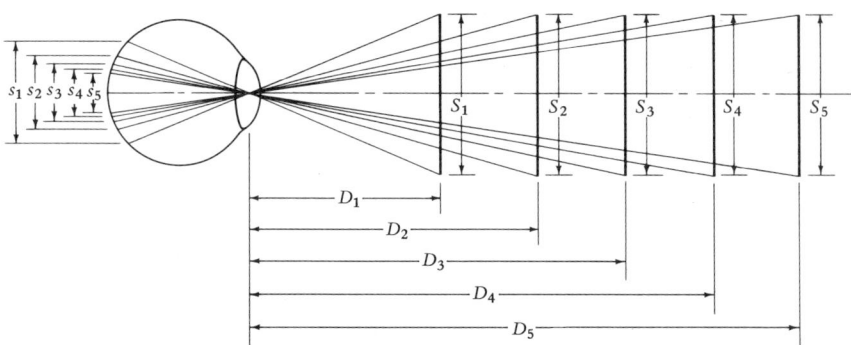

FIGURE 13.22 Schematic representation of the relationships between the momentary positions of lines of fixed size (S) moving away from (or toward) an observer and the corresponding retinal impingement. The physical change in distance is translated into an expansion and/or compression of the projected size.

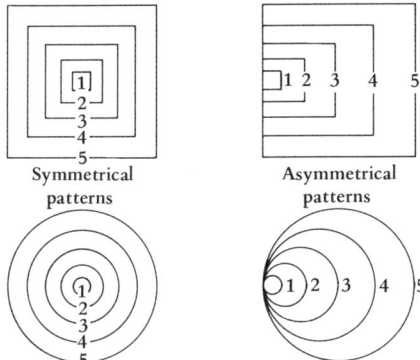

FIGURE 13.23 Successive momentary stimulus patterns for the perception of objects on collision paths (symmetrical patterns) and for objects on miss paths (asymmetrical patterns).

tion is of an object of fixed size which is approaching the general direction of the observer, but on a "miss" path. The degree of symmetry will determine how much the path will deviate from collision.

These relationships are illustrated in Figure 13.23. It should be clear from the illustration that the information at the retinal surface is simply a continuous change in the retinal extent of the stimulation, that is, an optical expansion or contraction pattern. There is no depth in the stimulus, nor is any specific size specified by the momentary stimulation. Yet the perceptual system organizes such a stimulus in a way that results in the perception of an object of constant size which is changing its relative position in depth.

Motion Parallax

The information provided by the relative movements of the projections of objects on the retina as an observer moves laterally is called motion parallax. The extent and direction of these movements will depend upon their relation to the point of fixation. This can be illustrated by analyzing the stimulus pattern on the retina for two objects in space, first when fixation is at an intermediate distance, and then when it is on a very distant object.

Figure 13.24 shows the former case. The observer moves his head from side to side, changing its location from point P_1 to P_2, while he maintains his fixation on some point in space somewhere between a near and a far object. In this case the retinal pattern at P_1 will have all three points overlapping since P_1, the fixation point, and both objects are in line. When the head moves the eye to a new position P_2, the objects and fixation point are no longer in line but have moved laterally in the visual field and in the retinal projection in a particular way. The motion of the displacements will be a direct function of the position of the objects with respect to the fixation point and of the direction of movement of the eye. The far object will be displaced in the same direction as

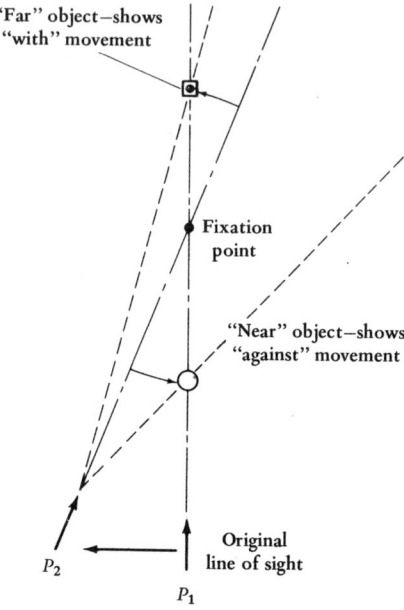

FIGURE 13.24   The transformation on the retina when viewing objects from two points of view, P_1 and P_2 and the corresponding visual fields, when fixating on a point of intermediate distance.

the eye was displaced ("with" movement) and the near object will move in the opposite direction ("against" movement).

With fixation on the far object, a different pattern of motion across the retina will occur. In this case, the projection of the far object will not be displaced on the retina, while the projection of the near one will move against the observer's movement. If the eye is fixated beyond the far object, then all objects will be displaced in the direction opposite to the observer's movement, and the nearer the object, the greater the displacement.

This continuously changing situation is schematically represented in Figure 13.25 where a viewer moves across a scene containing a man, a house, and a tree while maintaining his fixation on the house. Five momentary retinal fields are depicted at the bottom of the figure. These show that, with fixation on the house, the near object moves from left to right across the retinal projection, the far object moves from right to left across the field, and the house remains in the same relative position. This stimulus is perceived as an apparent movement of the world about the fixation point, the house, and is also perceived as movement of the eye. If fixation were changed to a distant object, say a tree on the horizon, all objects in the field would appear to move in the same direction—opposite to the direction of movement of the observer, with the nearest object moving the fastest. It should also be apparent from the dia-

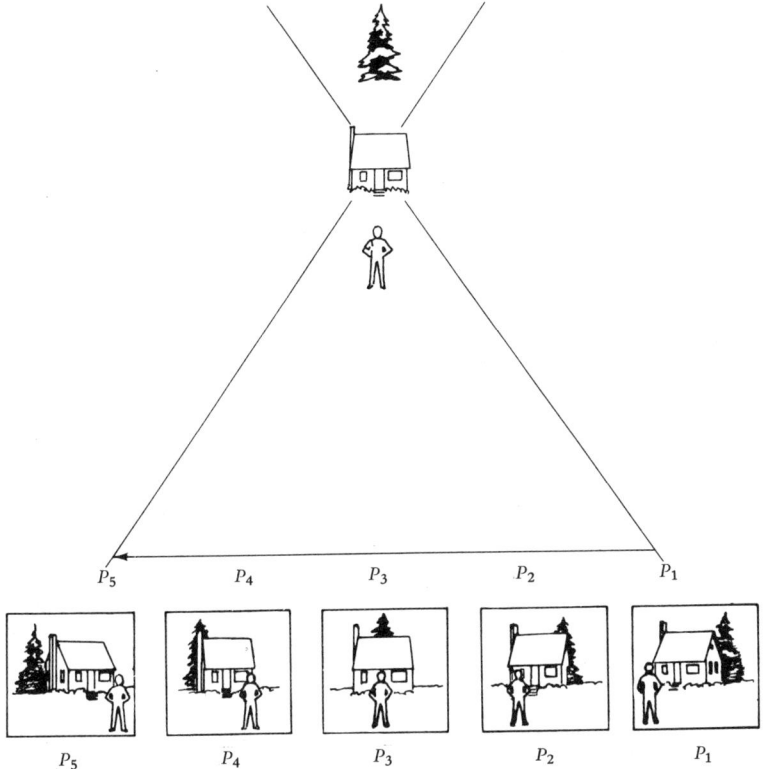

FIGURE 13.25 The transformations on the retina when moving through a sequence of positions while fixating a point of intermediate distance.

gram that occlusion is an essential aspect of parallax. The movement causes a shift in relative position in the projection and also causes occlusion and · changes in occlusion.

Motion Perspective

The stimulation of the retinas of an active observer is continually changing. These changes follow certain patterns which are a direct result of the structure of the physical world and the nature of the movements of the observer. We usually walk forward, with out heads erect and our eyes looking ahead. When we turn our head (and eyes) to the side, the consequent flow of stimulation is altered.

When an observer shifts from one position to another, the pattern on the retinas changes from one momentary stationary array to another. But more frequently we move continuously through space, and the corresponding retinal images are better described as flowing according to certain systematic rules.

Gibson (1950, 1966) has described the flow pattern obtained when a perceiver is walking along the ground. The directions of flow of the optic array are illustrated in Figure 13.26 for an observer moving forward. For this observer, the transformations of the visual field appear as projected on a spherical surface surrounding the head. The horizon, stars, and field of view upward do not move. However, the ground below him and the world flow past him in a continuous stream. This flow is a continuous transformation of the surface of the earth, and no matter which way the observer looks, the flow decreases upward in the visual field and vanishes at the horizon. In this sense there is a perspective in the flow. The rate at which an element flows, holding the loco-motion constant, is inversely proportional to its physical distance from the observer so that the flow decreases the farther away are the stimulus objects. The geometry of this decrease is the same as that for stationary objects. In this sense the flow produces a gradient or change in parallax.

The gradients of continuous transformation of angular separations of points in the field, which is a consequence of the movement of the perceiver, is called motion perspective. It is a transformation of pattern rather than a simple comparison of velocities as is motion parallax. Parallax arises when the perceiver moves his head from side to side in order to obtain depth informa-tion. The relative velocities of the displacement of two objects associated with such movements is conceived of as a cue. Motion perspective arises when a perceiver is locomoting in space and the retinal gradients of velocities are associated with the movement across the ground surface. Thus motion per-spective is the more general source of information.

The direction and speed of motion within this perspective flow vary independently. The direction of the flow as a visual impression depends on

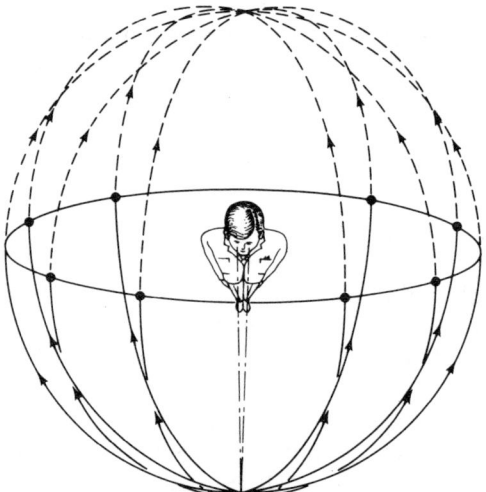

FIGURE 13.26 The directions of deformations in the visual field during forward locomotion as projected on a spherical surface around the head (Gibson, 1950).

the physical direction of movement of the spot in question and the direction of regard. When looking ahead, the flow is downward, when looking to the right the flow is to the right, when looking to the left the flow is to the left, and when looking behind the flow is upward. Thus the visual field ahead appears to expand outward from a focus, the focus being that point toward which the observer is moving. If he changes direction, the focus also shifts. In this sense the visual perceptual system always provides a "point of aim" for a perceiver who is moving in space. Thus the direction of movement is always present in the stimulation reaching the eye, even if it is sensed directly as change in body position rather than change in perceptual qualities.

Figures 13.27, 13.28, and 13.29 show the motion perspective for a perceiver moving straight ahead when he looks forward, to the side, and in the middle distance, respectively. The gradients of velocity and direction depicted here are invariably concomitants of locomotion on the surface of the earth.

Figure 13.29 shows the relationship between the fixation point and the amount of flow and its direction. At the fixation point, the velocity of projected flow is zero, since the movement of the eye compensates for the movement of the physical world with respect to the body of the perceiver. All points above fixation in the projection plane flow in the direction of movement of the observer. All points below flow in the direction opposite to the per-

FIGURE 13.27 Motion perspective for a perceiver moving straight ahead down a country road and fixating at the horizon.

FIGURE 13.28 Motion perspective for a perceiver moving from right to left and looking to his right, fixating at the horizon.

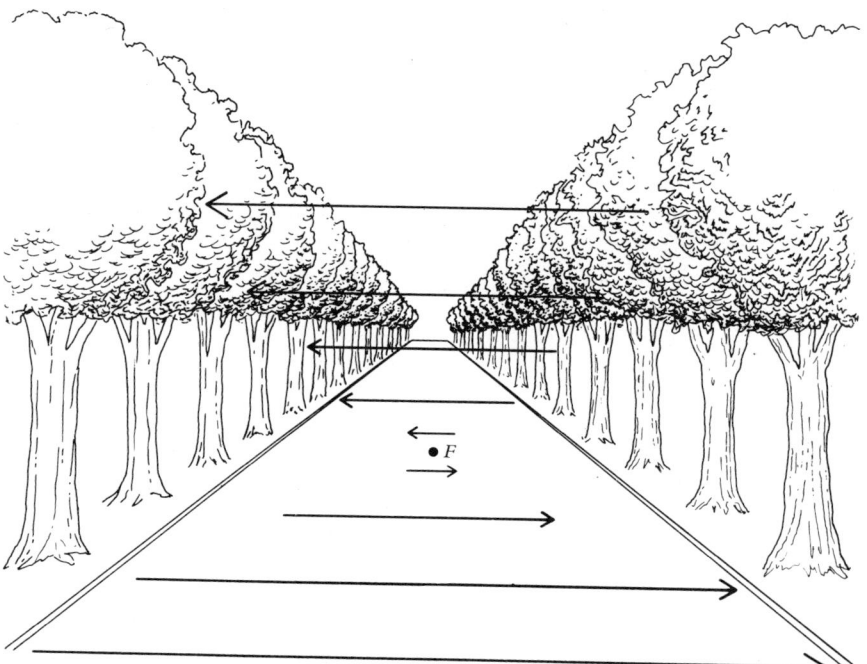

FIGURE 13.29 Motion perspective for a perceiver moving from right to left, looking to his right and fixating at an intermediate distance.

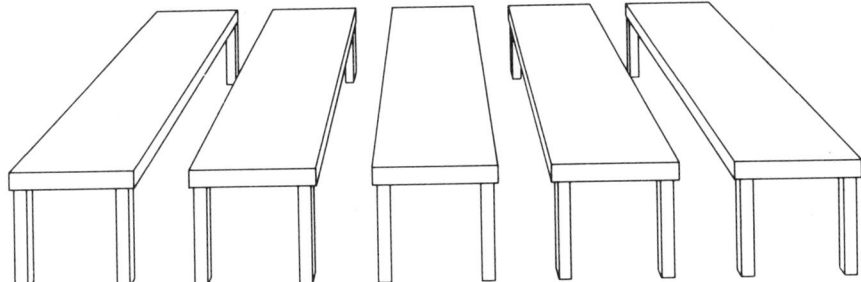

FIGURE 13.30 Five momentary views of a table showing the perspective transformations which would occur in the retinal projection when an observer walks by.

ceiver. Once again the relationship to motion parallax is apparent. Thus, in perspective there is a gradual change in the rate of displacement of texture elements or of contours in the visual field. The change is from motion in the direction of the observer, through a line of no motion, to motion in the opposite direction.

Continuous Perspective Transformation

When an observer or an object is in motion, there will be a continuous transformation of the perspective in the shape of the projection of the object on the retina. Figure 13.30 illustrates five time samples of the transformations which would occur in the retinal projection of an observer who was walking by a table. There is a continuous change in the size and shape of the projection of the rectangular table top. A similar pattern would be produced if the observer were stationary and the object were moving—as with a swinging door—or if both were moving.

The Psychophysics of Retinal Change

The previous pages and figures have described some of the changes that occur in the retinal patterns of stimulation as an observer's eye moves through space, either as a result of shift in his head position or during locomotion. We have not distinguished binocular effects but it should be obvious that taking into account the disparities between the patterns on the two retinas will yield even more visual information about the locations and arrangements of objects in space.

Gibson has placed great emphasis on the potential information available when the perceiver moves through visual space. It is clear that, regardless of what other information the perceiver may have, he has access to changes in the visual input which are directly correlated with the characteristics of the visual world in which he is moving. The nature of this correlation is quite impressive. For example, the geometry of perspective is such that the relative parallax of any pair of objects in space is exactly proportional to their relative distances from the perceiver, for any given fixation point. Thus, those that shift more on the retina are that much closer, by exactly the ratio of their displacement. Furthermore, linear perspective (for example, parallel lines converging at the horizon) changes at exactly the same rate as do the relative displacements produced by parallax. Thus, the trees in the distance of Figure 13.28 are nearer to each other in the same ratio as their rate of change on the retina when the perceiver moves forward. The examples could go on and on.

What is the implication of all this? For Gibson, this tremendously informative (although complex) stimulation produces a scale for the visual world. The changes in this scale over the pattern and across time over changing patterns could only arise if the scale of the visual world were constant—the space between objects in the distance is specified in the same units as that between near objects. It is the recognition of this scaling as a consequence of the spatial and temporal patterning of the information at the retina that has led Gibson to argue that perception of space is given directly. The "superstimulus" contains all the information necessary for direct perception of space and our movement within it.

If a psychophysical theory of visual space perception is to be taken seriously, the correlates in stimulation which yield perception directly must yield consistent, relatively unvarying percepts and, in addition, the percepts must be in good correspondence with the objective properties of the sources of stimulation. There are experiments which lend support for the psychophysical position in general, but there are also many questions remaining (Epstein and Park, 1964).

Optical expansion and contraction patterns in the retinal projection are sufficient stimuli for the perception of radial motion (Ball and Tronick, 1971; Bower, Broughton, and Moore, 1970; Schiff, Caviness, and Gibson, 1962). Motion perspective in isolation may not be adequate to specify the unique perception of depth, slant, or the relative order of surfaces in space. However, a continuous sequence of perspective transformations in the retinal projection does produce the perception of a rigid surface changing its slant. For example, in the kinetic depth effect (Wallach and O'Connell, 1953), a sequence of transforming shadows projected on a translucent screen invariably produced the perception of a rigid object having internal depth and turning in space. This experiment and others (see Epstein and Park, 1964) provide evidence that a continuous sequence of transformations in the retinal projection is sufficient to determine the perception of a rigid turning form and, moreover, that stimulation undergoing continuous change is the useful information for perceiving a stable visual world having size and shape constancy. Thus it seems clear that motion and sequence are also crucial aspects of the construction of a scale of space which provides the foundation for the perceptual world. The relation of this type of stimulation to our perception of motion and of our own movements will be the major topics in the next chapter.

SUMMARY

We have reviewed in this chapter the information available to a perceiver in the luminance discontinuities in the retinal projection in each eye. Three main stimulus classes were analyzed—the fixed monocular retinal projection, the fixed binocular retinal projection, and the changing retinal projection. The fixed monocular retinal pattern was analyzed in terms of its texture, and the gradients of texture and illumination. These were related to the perception of surface-at-a-slant, size-at-a-distance, and the intersections and occlusions of various portions of the visual field. The fixed binocular pattern was analyzed to show the relationship between stimulation of the two eyes and the perception of visual directions. We saw that direction is perceived in relation to a single point between the two eyes—the Cyclopean eye. We also noted that stereoscopic depth is produced by the stimulation of noncorresponding points on the two retinas—a situation which produces disparity in the two retinal projections.

The information in changing retinal patterns is more complex. Change in the retinal projection such as optical expansion and contraction patterns and continuous perspective transformations produce the perception of a visual world having a scale which yields size and shape constancy. One additional factor—the perception of movement within this space—remains for the next chapter.

Readings

In addition to the books suggested at the end of Chapter 12, several other books will provide an excellent extension of the content of this chapter. Epstein (1967) covers many of these topics, emphasizing the empiricist approach. The two chapters by Hochberg in Kling and Riggs (1971) are useful for a more eclectic approach. Howard and Templeton (1966) also cover much of this material and provide a slightly different perspective from that taken here. Matin (1972) discusses at an advanced level the relation of eye movements to perceived visual direction.

chapter
14
the perception of motion and movement

INTRODUCTION

This chapter concerns the problems associated with movement—both the motions of objects in the physical world and the movements of our eyes, head, and body in space. In the previous chapter, we discussed the stimulation at the eye when the retinal projection was stationary and when it was changing. In centering the discussion on the retinal pattern, however, we avoided the difficult problems relating to the perception of external motion and of our own movements. How is it that we are able to perceive a stable world in which objects move and in which we, as perceivers, can move? Is visual information sufficient for veridical perception of motion and movement, or must it be supplemented by information about our motor activity?

This chapter will describe some answers to these questions. Three points of view concerning the perception of motion and perception while moving will be discussed. Some representative experiments supporting each view will be presented. This discussion sets the stage for a description of experimental studies in which the visual input is systematically altered. Such work has led to substantial changes in our understanding not only of motion perception, but of the organization of perceptual processes in general.

THREE VIEWS OF MOTION PERCEPTION

What are the phenomena to be accounted for? Considering the visual world first, we need to account for how we notice that an object moves, such as seeing a bird fly across an otherwise motionless forest or across a scene in which all of the leaves and branches are also in motion. We might want to know about the threshold for detection of motion—how fast must an object move for a perceiver to be able to notice that it moved, and for him to see it as moving? Further, how do we detect changes in rate of motion?

These phenomena appear to become more complex when we take the perceiver into account. Since the perceiver is rarely if ever completely motionless himself, the retinal projection of stimulation from the visual environment will be constantly shifting, changing, stretching, and transforming. Hence, in perceiving movement in the visual world, we have to be able to distinguish it unequivocally from our own eye, head, and body movements. As we are rarely if ever fooled, this distinction must be an easy one to make under normal circumstances.

As with many topics in this book, our understanding of motion perception is influenced by the way we phrase our questions about it. There have been three major viewpoints expressed. The first two are related to the theories of space perception we have already discussed. One view sees the source of information used in the perception of motion as the successive stimulation of adjacent retinal points. Thus, in some way the visual nervous system codes successive changes across the retina as movement. As we will see, explicit neurophysiological mechanisms have been found that accomplish this neural coding.

The second viewpoint argues that the cue to motion is a relative transformation in the retinal projection, so that one part is shifted relative to another part. Thus, object motion is perceived when there is a relative displacement *in* the retinal projection, not a displacement *on* the retina. This view is consistent with the analysis of space perception developed by Gibson.

The third viewpoint argues that neither source of information is sufficient to achieve a unique and stable perception of our motion or of object motion, or to enable the perceiver to distinguish between the two. Rather, such a view argues that, in order to perceive motion or movement, we must also have a special type of information related to our own movements—either reafferent visual information or efferent nonvisual information. Reafferent information is obtained by observing the consequences of our own movements. The term "reafference" is used to emphasize the correlation between the changes in the input and the changes in eye, head, and body position. The efferent nonvisual information is obtained from the efferent commands issued by the central nervous system to induce the movements of our eyes and body. By knowing the ways in which we intend to move, we can distinguish between motion in the retinal projection that was caused by our own movements and that was caused by the movement of objects in the world.

Psychologists frequently must distinguish between real and apparent motion. Real motion would be specified by a physicist as the continuous displacement of an object from one location to another at a particular velocity or acceleration. If the perceiver's eye is stationary when observing real motion, a luminance discontinuity in the retinal projection will be displaced at the same angular velocity as the object in motion. But if the perceiver's eye is not stationary, the angular velocity of the projection of the object might be very different. It could even be zero if the eye is pursuing the moving object. In that case, however, the retinal projections of all of the stationary objects in the visual environment would be displaced in the opposite direction to the path of pursuit. Thus, in this case, displacement in the retinal projection occurs in the absence of physical motion in the visual world. Normally perceivers attribute such displacements to their own movements and not to object motion.

Apparent motion refers to circumstances in which motion is perceived when there is no physical movement in the visual world, at least not of the objects being seen in motion. We will consider several instances of apparent motion as a means of learning about the nature of the information in the retinal projection that leads to the perception of motion.

MOTION-DETECTION SYSTEMS

The motion-detection system is the simplest explanation of the perception of an object in motion by a stationary observer. Light falling on a set of receptors at one instant, and on a nearby set in the next instant, and so forth, successively stimulates adjacent retinal points (loci). This sequence of events could be the necessary and sufficient source of information for a motion-detection system which signals that something was moving out there. All that would be needed is a coding device that could detect this change.

The discovery of cortical cells which respond to displacements in the retinal projection of the stimulus has lent strong support to the view that motion perception is a result of the detection of successive stimulation on adjacent retinal loci. For example, in studying the visual system of cats, Hubel and Wiesel (1962) found cortical cells with relatively large receptive fields that were primarily responsive to movement. The cell did not respond when its receptive field was stimulated by a stationary bar of light. But if the bar was moved over that field, the cell did respond. Hubel and Wiesel found cells whose responsivity was specific to stimuli of a given width, length, orientation, direction of motion, and velocity of motion, although most cells were not specific to all of these variables simultaneously.

The evidence that motion-detection systems of this sort exist in humans is based in part on the study of motion aftereffects. A motion aftereffect is an apparent motion in the visual field which is induced by the prolonged viewing of motion. One example is the waterfall illusion. If you watch the water descending over a fall for a minute or two, and then look at a motionless visual field, the objects in the field will appear to be moving up — that is, in the direction opposite to the original motion. In the laboratory this is usually studied by viewing a rotating spiral disk, or the lateral movement of vertical bars rotating around a drum. For example, Spigel (1962) reported that after viewing a spiral pattern rotating slowly at ten revolutions per minute, all perceivers saw the spiral rotating in the opposite direction when the actual physical rotation was stopped. This aftereffect lasted nearly ten seconds on the average.

Sekuler and Ganz (1963) had perceivers view stripes that moved in one direction for five seconds. They did this under stabilized retinal presentation (see Chapter 8) so that the only motion over the retina would be from objective stimulus movement, and not from eye movements. They then tested the luminance threshold for the movement of stripes when the stripes moved in the same direction or in the reverse direction. They argued that if motion was perceived because of a cortical motion detector, then viewing motion in one direction should decrease the sensitivity of that detector, and elevate the threshold for

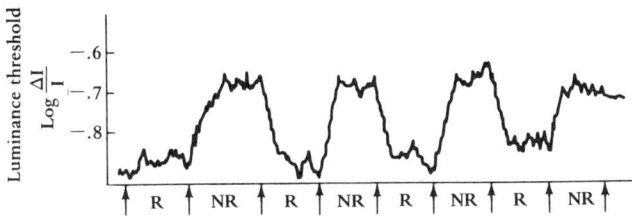

FIGURE 14.1 A continuous record of luminance threshold values during one session for both same (NR) and reverse (R) directions (from Sekuler and Ganz, 1963).

that pattern of motion. Figure 14.1 shows a dramatic change in this threshold. In every case they found that the threshold for motion in the same direction as that of the previously viewed pattern was elevated. This finding strongly supports the argument that there are unitary motion-detecting systems in humans —systems whose sensitivities are momentarily changed as a function of stimulation.

Sekuler and Ganz went to some effort to remove the effects of eye movements on motion sensitivity, so that their results would be due only to motion detectors sensing a displacement across the retina caused only by objective movement. Presumably under normal viewing conditions, we do not lose too much sensitivity to motion after prolonged viewing of motion, because our eyes are continuously in motion relative to the stimulus. This would shift the stimulus from one motion-detecting receptive field to another, assuming the eye movements were large enough. But to the degree to which motion aftereffects are found, and they are very common, some sensitivity loss is always occurring.

The discovery of motion-detector systems has lent strong support to the view that motion perception is the result of detecting successive stimulation of adjacent retinal loci. But even before this evidence was available, this view had led to substantial research which explored the thresholds for motion. If the retinal projection of a luminance discontinuity moves across the retina too slowly, it will not be seen to move (although the perceiver might notice later that it is in a new position). If it moves too fast, the object moving will not be seen as anything except a blur.

These lower and upper thresholds for motion have been found to be a function of a number of variables—so many in fact, that it would be misleading to imply that there is a single value for each. Under optimal conditions a minumum displacement threshold approaches the resolution acuity for the object itself. This means that if the thickness of the line elements in the object are thirty seconds of arc wide, and if the object is displaced by as little as thirty seconds, the perceiver will say it has been moved. But he will not necessarily say he sees it moving—only that it is in a new position. Whether it will be perceived as moving or not will depend upon its size, the illumination on it, its contrast, and the number of nearby objects. For example, any variable that increases the sharpness of the object will increase the chances of the perceiver noticing it moving—hence increases in illumination and contrast will lower motion threshold. Object size, however, has the reverse effect—smaller objects are easier to see in motion than larger ones.

More important even than acuity is the heterogeneity of the visual field. It is very difficult to perceive motion of the object moving over a homogeneous or textureless field. If the object is seen through a window, it is much easier to notice it moving when it is near the edge of the frame than when it is in the center of the window, away from all other objects or contours. This clearly suggests some relational properties to motion perception, comparing the change of position of one object to that of another.

The importance of the field in stabilizing stimulation is shown by the phenomenon known as autokinetic movement. If a small light is presented in an otherwise dark room, the light will appear to move about, usually in an unpredictable and erratic manner. The most common explanation has been in terms of eye movements. In the dark, the viewer has difficulty in maintaining his orientation and he cannot distinguish between movements of his own eyes and movements of the light. Since the eyes do move, and the observer has no visual frame of reference, he attributes some of the movement to the stimulus. Furthermore, it is nearly impossible to perceive real motion when such a light really does move in the dark. In the absence of a visual frame of reference, real movement is almost impossible to detect.

On the other hand, if two nearby stationary lights are alternately flashed, the viewer will report seeing a single light rapidly moving back and forth. In this case, there is no motion in the stimulus but, for certain recycling rates, we invariably perceive motion. In addition, we perceive the light during its flight across the space between the two sources, even though there is no objective stimulus in any of those positions. This phenomenon has been called phi motion and it is the basis for the motion seen in the flashing lights on theater marquees or on "moving" signs. The motion we perceive when a series of separate scenes are flashed in rapid succession—as in motion pictures—is related to this phenomenon. The motion-picture projector presents a rapid succession of slightly displaced scenes. The visual system fills in the temporal gaps to produce the perception of continuous motion.

Frisby (1972) has argued that phi motion might be interpretable in terms of motion detectors in the cortex. Thus, just as real motion might be detected by a light moving over a receptive field at a particular rate, a cortical cell might be induced to fire if the light first fell on one region and then on another, without transversing the space between. As long as the same cortical cell responded to both cases, real and apparent (phi) motion would be determined in the same way.

The major problem for the perception of motion from this first viewpoint is to show how a perceiver differentiates successive stimulation of adjacent retinal loci caused by object motion as distinct from the motion of his eyes or body. Both will produce displacements of the retinal projection, yet we rarely attribute our motion to that of the visual world, or vice versa. The other two viewpoints provide somewhat different answers to this question. The second one, as a psychophysical model, represents a relatively complete theory of motion perception, and as such covers much more than the differentiation of object motion. It will be considered next.

THE PSYCHOPHYSICS OF MOTION AND MOVEMENT

The psychophysical view developed by Gibson (1966) includes not only the direct perception of a three-dimensional visual world containing solid objects but one in which the motion of objects and the movements of the viewer are perceived and differentiated. In the previous chapter we discussed the correlates for the direct perception of space which are found in the retinal projection. The correlates for the perception of motion and movement are also part of this effective stimulation.

If the observer moves in space or if space or objects move with respect to the observer, there is a flow of stimulation across the retinal surface. We usually move about in the world, especially our eyes and head, so that the stimulation on the retina is constantly changing. Therefore, in order to understand how we perceive the three-dimensional world in these situations, we must learn something about the nature of the *flow* of stimulation on the retina as a function of changes in eye, head, and body position.

Before looking more formally at Gibson's theory, consider some very simple circumstances in which displacement occurs in the retinal projection. If we look at a stationary scene that has no movement in it, and we hold our eyes, head, and body momentarily motionless, this will yield a particular momentary pattern of stimulation in the projection on the retina. We will consider this the baseline and discuss the transformations it might normally undergo.

Consider first the change in which the entire pattern is shifted to the right. The extreme right-hand edge will disappear and a new part of the visual world will come into view on the left. Only one circumstance can produce this change —a movement of our eyes to the left without change in the position of our head or body, and without motion in the scene. This is the only possible natural circumstance that can produce this transformation of the pattern in the projection on the retina. In a psychophysical sense then, this should be a completely adequate source of visual information to distinguish this type of movement from any other. Visual information alone should be adequate to tell us it was our eye and not the world that moved.

In another type of change, the baseline pattern remains stationary except for one part of it which is displaced to the right. Only one circumstance can produce this change—an object in motion in an otherwise stationary visual world. Any time there is a relative displacement of part of the pattern in the absence of any other changes, there must be something out there moving.

Again, this is conveyed by visual information alone as a displacement in part of the retinal pattern of stimulation.

As another and more complex example, suppose that the pattern is shifted to the right, but different components in the pattern shift relative to each other at different rates. Thus some components are occluded sooner than others. There is only one set of circumstances that can produce this change—viewing a stationary scene with a moving eye. This is not an uncommon stimulus, for example, looking at a stationary scene out of the window of a train moving laterally to the left, without any movement of your eyes, head, or body. Another might be when you are walking or running ahead while looking at a 90-degree angle to the path of motion. The specific circumstance depicted here is one in which fixation is on near space, a speck of dust on the glass window of the train, for example. The trees near the track will flash across our stationary retina at a high rate while distant hills will be displaced slowly.

The previous conditions can be complicated by permitting some eye movement or head movement as well as bodily displacement laterally. The details become more complex but the principle is the same. Each particular type of motion, whether of specific objects, or the entire visual world, or of the eyes, head, or body, or any combination of these, produces a unique pattern of change in the stimulation in the retinal pattern. Thus, there is visual information which always is correlated with the perceived change in the visual world.

The major point here is that perceivers should never have any trouble distinguishing their own motions from motions in the visual world, and should be able to do this from information available in the changes that occur in the transformations within the retinal projection in addition to the displacement of that projection across the retina.

Therefore, according to Gibson, the motion of an object with respect to other objects is perceived when the retinal projection contains a perspective transformation associated with kinetic optic occlusion. As an object moves, it progressively covers and uncovers the texture of the surface behind it. The consequence of this motion in the retinal projection is described by Gibson as a "wiping out" of texture at the leading border, an "unwiping" at the trailing border, and a "shearing" of texture at the lateral borders. Thus the perspective transformation is invariably associated with a break in the continuity of the texture of the background. This kinetic retinal projection is the normal stimulus situation. The kinetic occlusion specifies the existence of an edge, of depth at the edge, and the existence of one surface behind another. The continued existence of the hidden surface may be a component of object constancy —the belief in the permanence of objects which momentarily disappear from view.

Thus an object in motion produces transformation in its own perspective projection on the retinal surface and also relative changes with respect to its texture and that of the background. If the observer is stationary, the remainder of the optic array will be relatively stable. When the observer moves, however, the optic array becomes alive with motion. There is a flow of velocities of retinal points—a global motion parallax; there is a perspective transformation of each form projected on the retinal surface; there is a displacement among the elements of texture; and there are breaks in the flow of texture as surfaces cut across one another. All of these changes in the retinal projection are related to each other and to the actual movements of the observer.

These systematic transformations in the retinal projection specify the perception of movement of the observer himself. For example, look back at Figure 13.27. It showed the directions of deformations in the visual field during forward locomotion. The flow in the retinal projection from the forward pole to the rear pole specifies the locomotion of the viewer with respect to the world and, simultaneously, the layout of that world. The focus of optical expansion specifies the point toward which the movement is directed.

When moving from one place to another, the viewer changes his vista and new kinds of transformations are introduced which specify more complex kinds of environmental changes. For example, the successive transformations in the retinal projection of a person approaching a doorway were illustrated earlier in Figure 12.7. The sequence of pictures illustrates the relationship between the movement of the observer and the changes in the array. As the observer moves forward, a number of objects will appear to emerge from behind the aperture. The doorframe will expand to uncover the array in the new room—another aspect of kinetic occlusion. All apertures in the visual world—doors, windows, spaces between objects—open on optically denser patterns. This ability to perceive openings and spaces as a direct correlate of properties of the retinal projection permits locomotion without collision.

Thus, for Gibson, it is not necessary for the retinal projection to be interpreted in order to perceive motion and movement. The consequences of self-produced movement for change in the retinal projection are different from those of an object in motion, and therefore, each can be perceived directly.

Gibson's explanations for the perception of object and observer motion represent substantial improvement over the narrow motion-detector model considered first. Of course, since Gibson does not discuss the mechanisms by which the transformations in the retinal projection are detected, he has not had to face the problem of how the visual nervous system does this. One possibility is that we possess higher-order motion detectors. The inputs to such a higher-order detector would be a number of outputs of the lower-level type of detector systems described by Hubel and Wiesel. Thus, if all lower-level detectors signaled the same velocity over all parts of the retina, the higher-order detector might not respond, since the circumstances creating this invariant pattern of inputs comes from an eye movement and not object motion. On the other hand, if one of the inputs signaled the presence of motion over its receptive field while the others did not, then the higher-order detector would respond, since there is objective motion. One could continue this theoretical description of combinations of motion detectors so that each of the phenomena described by Gibson would be covered. There does not appear to be anything more complex in this proposal than has already been discussed for other aspects of coding of spatial dimensions of the retinal projection, such as shown by the cascading of simple, complex, and hypercomplex cortical cells (see Chapter 3).

What should be clear from these arguments is that a model of motion perception such as the first one is doomed if it only deals with a narrow portion of the retina, or ignores the remainder of the retinal projection against which one part is changing. Since these two viewpoints of motion correspond rather closely to the two we have been considering in the two previous chapters on space perception, most of the evaluative comments there apply here as well. Here too, the psychophysical approach of Gibson seems to be a more complete explanation since it is capable of covering a far wider range of circumstances.

Both of the views of motion perception considered so far assume that we can perceive all aspects of object and observer motion based on visual information alone. There have been a number of proposals that argue that visual information by itself is inadequate and we must have something more, usually in the form of information about movements that we will make or have made. The last viewpoint of motion perception represents this argument in its general form.

INTEGRATION OF VISUAL
AND MOTOR INFORMATION

Helmholtz (1867), who sponsored the first viewpoint, attempted to solve the problem of differentiating observer from object motion by postulating some type of unconscious computation or feedback from eye position or body position, so that these changes can be subtracted from the retinal displacement. Thus, if there was a displacement of the projection on the retina of 10 degrees to the right, but there was also feedback from the eye muscles providing information that the eye had moved 10 degrees to the left, these two would be subtracted. The net result of zero would then be interpreted to mean that no object motion occurred. Other combinations would be interpreted in a similar manner.

Without denying that we potentially may have feedback information about the current position of our eyes, head, or other parts of our body, there are enough reasons to doubt the usefulness of this form of a perceptual-motor integration. Spigel (1965) has reviewed some of this evidence, primarily noting that the position sense of the eye is not precise enough to provide the input needed for the type of computation proposed by Helmholtz. In addition, since the latency to initiate a saccadic eye movement is about 200 milliseconds, feedback from an actual change in eye position would be very slow, far slower than permissible given the precision of our movement perception. In a more direct test of this theory, Brindley and Merton (1960) covered the eye, and anesthetized its surface, so that only the muscles attached to the eye could provide feedback about the movements of the eye. Under such circumstances, perceivers could not tell that the eyes, singly or together, were being moved mechanically.

There is another sense in which Helmholtz might be correct. If instead of using the feedback from the eye position, one used the efferent or outgoing signals from the brain which control the eye, head, and body movements, then those objections would not be so serious. In addition, another troublesome problem of motion perception would be solved—how to account for the perceptual consequences of eye movements which were not self-initiated. If you move your eye intentionally over a stationary scene, you perceive it as a stationary scene—it does not shift or jump in any way. However, if you put your finger against the side of your eye and press it so as to rotate the eye back and forth, the visual world jumps around in correspondence with the externally initiated movements. This would not be expected if feedback from the eye position were being monitored, but it would be predicted if the efferent signals to the eye muscles were involved. When you press on your eye, there are no efferent signals (except to your fingers, which are probably too indirect), and hence the displacement is sensed as belonging to the world and not to the eye.

Von Holst (1954) reported some experiments which support this observation and interpretation. First he replicated an experiment by Helmholtz (1867). The eye muscles of a perceiver were paralyzed so that the eye could not move in a given direction, and then the perceiver was instructed to move his eye in that direction, say to the right. This instruction, which presumably produces an efferent command but no resulting displacement on the retina (the eye could not execute the command), resulted in the perception of the visual world moving to the right. In a second experiment, von Holst moved the paralyzed eye mechanically to the right instead of instructing the perceiver to move it. In this case, there should be no efferent command, but now there is retinal displacement. Here also, the perceiver reported seeing movement of the visual world, but now he saw it moving to the left, as would be expected. In a third study, von Holst instructed the perceiver to move his paralyzed eye, and at the same time von Holst moved the eye mechanically in the same direction. In this case there will be both an efferent command and a retinal displacement. Thus, the effects found in the first and in the second studies just canceled, and the perceiver reported that the visual world was stationary.

These three studies provide very clear evidence that the perception of motion, at least under some circumstances, must include a comparison or correlation between the efferent commands to muscles with the resulting visual afferent consequences—a perceptual-motor integration. Note that Gibson argues that the visual afferent information is entirely adequate to account for all instances of perception of object and observer motion. In light of the above studies, Gibson's claim appears to be insufficient but the degree to which efferent commands are routinely used in perception remains to be seen.

Nevertheless, there is strong evidence that an efferent-afferent correlation is involved in movement perception (Gyr, 1972). If the copy of the efferent signal and the resulting visual changes are involved in movement perception, the perceiver must have processes which compare these two signals so that the perceptual and motor information can be integrated. One way in which this process could work is for the brain to store a copy of the commands for movements at the time it sends them out. When the input from the receptors reaches the brain, it could then be automatically compared with the stored copy. If it matches, the input is taken as feedback (reafference), so that the effect of retinal displacement is attributed to eye movements. If it does not match, it is taken as the consequence of independent external events, with the consequent perception of motion in the visual world.

The important point about efferent commands is that they imply self-initiated movement. We will turn now to the even broader importance of self-initiated movements with a consideration of the ways in which perceivers adjust to stimulation which has been transformed or distorted.

ADAPTATION TO SYSTEMATIC VISUAL DISTORTION

One major technique used to study the nature of perceptual-motor functioning is to distort the visual input in a systematic way and to follow the adaptations which occur. This may be accomplished in a number of ways, using mirrors, prisms, and lenses. First, we will cover the studies performed at Innsbruck since they describe almost all phases of the adaptation phenomenon. In subsequent discussion, we will deal more directly with the questions of the locus of adaptation and the role of the perceiver's own movements.

Innsbruck Studies

These studies describe the experiences of Erismann and of Kohler (1951), who wore distorting prisms and mirrors for extended periods of time. Their descriptions of the concomitant changes have supplied the foundation for the more precise studies of each of the effects discovered by these investigators. These include the systematic variation in perception which occurs immediately upon introduction of the distortion, and the gradual changes in perception which occur after wearing the distorting instrument for a while. These gradual changes are referred to as adaptation because the distortion in perception disappears. Aftereffects of the distortions also are found—distortions reappear in perception as a result of the removal of the distorting instrument.

In order to understand the effect of distorting the input to the visual system, the locus of distortion must be clearly pinpointed. In the experiments to be discussed here, the input to the visual system is systematically altered by placing a prism or a mirror in a pair of goggles and attaching the goggles to the head. Thus the change in input is introduced between the eye and the environment. This produces a fixed change between the light entering the eye and the position of the head; that is, since the goggles are attached to the head, this distortion is fixed. Both the eyes and the body may move with respect to the head and, therefore, with respect to the distortion. Thus, the light still carries information about the environment, but that information is biased in some way. Kohler and Erismann studied the long-term consequences of this bias.

In one set of studies, Kohler wore mirrors attached to his forehead in such a manner that he could only see the world in front of him by looking up into the mirrors. Consequently, the stimulation coming to his eyes was inverted in the up-down direction. To imagine the kind of reversal this is, you may think of moving your eyes upward but having the stimulation reaching your eye being that from moving your eye downward over the same scene. The pattern and flow is upside-down.

The results of this distortion of visual inputs were dramatic. The immediate experience was directly predictable from the distortion introduced—everything appeared to be upside-down. Errors were made in attempting to touch objects. The viewer felt unsure of himself and needed an escort in order to walk about. Even then his step was halting. Over the first three days his behavior gradually became normal (or at least looked normal to another person). By this time, he was able to ride a bicycle without help and on the sixth day he was able to ski.

The perceptual effects as reported by Kohler are even more interesting. During the first few days, perceptions appeared to be right-side-up only sporadically. But this was not random. There were special cases when the perceptual world would right itself. Objects would appear in their proper orientation when they were simultaneously viewed and touched, or when a plumb line was present in the visual field, or when the object was in the perceiver's immediate vicinity so that he could see his feet.

When the mirrors were removed, objects immediately reverted to their previous upside-down position and for a few minutes, people and furniture appeared "suspended from the ceiling, head downward." After about half an hour, the aftereffects started to go away.

There were some interesting disturbances in eye-head coordination which resulted from wearing the spectacles. When they were on, the perceiver had to raise his head and eyes somewhat to see at all. As time went on and the perceptual adaptation took place, the kinesthetic sensations (of the head and eyes raised) were no longer felt to be unusual. After removal of the goggles, when it was again necessary to look in the actual straight-ahead direction to look at the world ahead, the viewer felt that he was looking down, or that the floor was giving way under his feet. This aftereffect caused Kohler to maintain his head in a curiously crooked position, lowering his head by about 30 degrees to place his eyes in the previously "normal" position. Thus the orientation of the eyes and head involves the distortion not only of the accompanying perception but also of the felt position of the eyes with respect to the head and with respect to the objective straight ahead.

In general, the adjustment of overt behavior—the motor reactions—preceded the adaptation of perception. There were three main types of information which were essential in mediating the perceptual adaptation—touch, alignment with gravity, and familiarity. Whenever Kohler reached for and touched an object in his immediate vicinity, the object which was first seen as inverted suddenly appeared to be upright. This also occurred when the object was touched with a stick—essentially an extension of the arm. In general, the hands were the first objects to be seen as upright.

The second feature of information which corrected the inverted perceptual experience was information about gravity. A plumb line was seen in its correct direction as soon as Kohler held the string himself. Once this took place, he could use the plumb line to correct the perception of other objects. Whenever information about gravity was available, such as when he was driving uphill in a car, the world appeared upright. Specific objects would right themselves when appropriate gravity information was available. For example, a candle would appear upside-down but would change to its proper orientation when a flame was added. This would also occur with a cigarette which could be perceived in any orientation until the smoke would supply information about gravity. Then the cigarette would be perceived in its proper orientation.

These comments and observations represent only a small segment of Kohler's findings, both upon himself and on other perceivers. The essential point is that complete perceptual adaptation can occur in a relatively short time when one is wearing inverting mirrors, so that the visual world comes to look perfectly normal, as long as the perceiver is permitted free self-initiated movement. We will see the importance of this below.

The up-down inversion just described is a gross change in the visual input. Suppose a small change is introduced in the direction of stimulation reaching the eye. How similar would the concomitant visual effects be to those for inversion of up and down? These questions were answered by Erismann and Kohler in a series of experiments in which a perceiver (usually Kohler) wore prisms over his eyes for long periods of time.

The distortion of the visual input caused by prisms is different from that caused by inverting mirrors. Figure 14.2 shows a prism with base *ABCD* and apex *EF*. When a viewer looks through the prism at a point in space, that point will be perceived as if it were in a direction closer to the apex of the prism than is the actual point. The visual direction of that point will be displaced by an angle equal to one-half the apex angle of the prism. Therefore, the more distant the point is from the perceiver, the greater the displacement. This alteration in stimulation represents the simplest aspect of the distortion that takes place in a prism experiment.

It is clear from an analysis of the patterns of light that the distortion introduced into the retinal projection by wearing wedge prisms of this sort is much more complex. For example, contours appear to be surrounded by color bands as a result of the differential diffraction of light as a function of wavelength as it crosses from one medium to another. More important, however, is

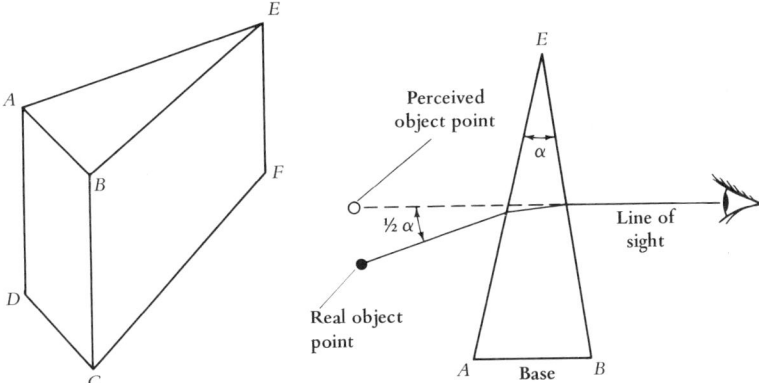

FIGURE 14.2   Displacement caused by prism with base *ABCD*, apex *EF*, and apex angle *α*. The image of a real object point is displaced by ½ *α*.

the complex distortion of contour. Figure 14.3 shows the type of distortion introduced when looking at the left-hand figure through wedge prisms with the base on the left-hand side. Notice the curvature introduced in the image—straight lines are no longer straight and right angles are no longer 90 degrees. Moreover, there is a contraction on the left and an expansion on the right half of the field (for base-left prisms). In this figure, all of the vertical lines would have colored fringes.

Figure 14.4 shows this distortion in more detail. It contains photographs taken through prisms and shows the distortion introduced when the prisms are placed in a position so as to simulate looking in different directions. The first plate *(a)* is a photograph of the stimulus configuration without prisms. This can be compared with *(b)* looking straight ahead through the prism, *(c)* and *(d)* looking to the left and to the right, and *(e)* and *(f)* looking up and down. Figure 14.5 shows the same type of distortion of the retinal projection when looking at the real world and rectangular objects in it. The expansion, compression, and distortion of rectangularity are obvious. Less obvious but equally

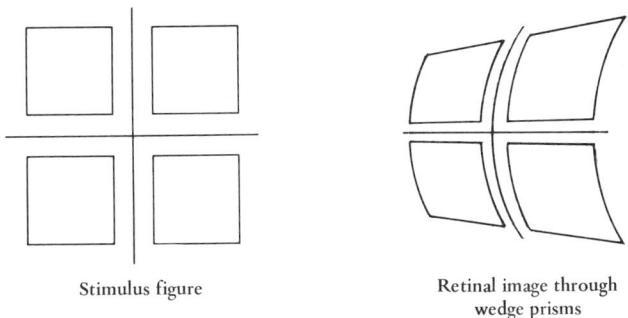

Stimulus figure

Retinal image through
wedge prisms

FIGURE 14.3   Schematic representation of distortion introduced into retinal projection when wearing wedge prisms.

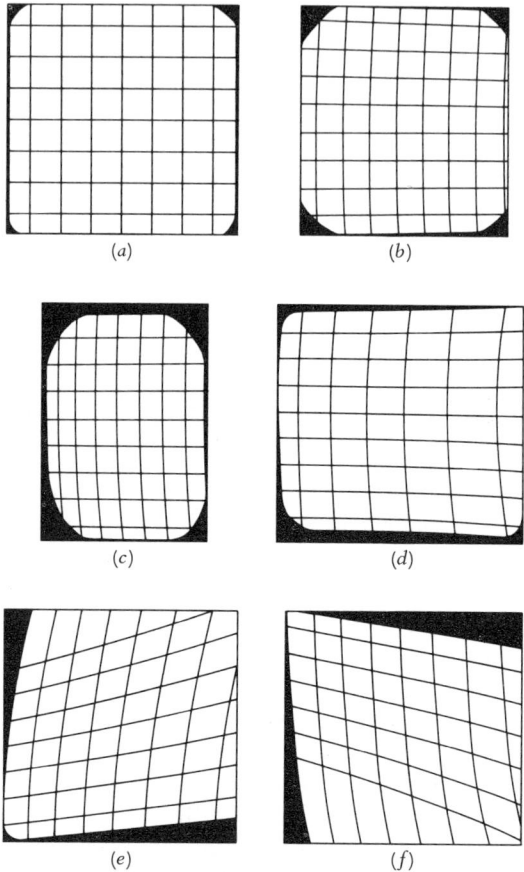

FIGURE 14.4 Systematic distortion introduced by looking through wedge prisms: *(a)* without prisms, *(b)* visual projection looking straight ahead, *(c)* contraction when looking left, *(d)* expansion when looking right, *(e)* looking up, *(f)* looking down (from Kohler, 1951).

important are the curvatures of gradients, the warping of slopes, and the distortions of angles.

When an experiment is begun and the perceiver first puts on the wedge prisms, there is a close correspondence between the newly formed retinal projections and the perceptions accompanying them. The properties of objects change as the properties of the projections received from them change on the retina. Illusions of depth and distortions occur. The perceiver experiences the world as "rubbery" and feels "drunk" when walking on the street. Thus, the photographs in Figures 14.4 and 14.5 may be taken as fairly good representations of the momentary perceptual experience of a person who has just put on the spectacles containing the wedge prisms for the first time.

In the experiments by Kohler, a number of different kinds of prisms were used varying in displacement from 10 degrees to 20 degrees in visual direction. In some experiments Kohler wore the spectacles for as long as 124 days. Once again we can divide the results into observations of the perceptual-motor behavior of the person wearing the spectacles, and the subjective reports of that person about what his perceptual experience is like. With respect to perceptual-motor behavior, all difficulties such as the errors made in reaching for objects disappeared within one day. Within six days, Kohler was skiing.

FIGURE 14.5 Systematic distortion in a real picture introduced by looking through wedge prisms (from Kohler, 1951).

The adaptation effects took longer to begin. Within two days Kohler reported the disappearance of the apparent visual motion which he perceived when the spectacles were first put on. At this time, curved surfaces began to appear flat and figures looked less distorted than at first. After ten days, all surfaces appeared to flatten out and objects no longer appeared distorted.

When the spectacles were removed, aftereffects occurred immediately. Kohler reported the return of curvature and distortion in viewing surfaces and figures as well as the return of the apparent movement of the world. The experience was very similar to when the goggles were first put on. These aftereffects continued in general for four days and curvature aftereffects were noted for as long as twenty-three days.

The most striking discovery was what Kohler called the situational after-effect. This was an aftereffect whose characteristic depended on a particular condition, such as on the direction of the line of sight. As an example of this type of aftereffect, recall that the deflection of light by a prism is minimal when the viewer is looking directly through the center of the prism and that the distortion increases as one looks away from this position, both vertically and horizontally. The important point is that the quality of the perceptual change depends on the direction of vision, that is, whether the observer is looking to his left or to his right to see the object. The same object would appear thin when viewed in one direction and thick when viewed in the other. Moreover, whether looking at the object to the left or to the right, the eyes turn in the head in such a way that the stimulation is falling, in general, on the same central portion of the retina. Thus the adaptation which takes place in some way corrects for the difference in distortion introduced into the projection when looking one way or the other. The situational aftereffects are a special kind of negative aftereffect because they occur only when the situation is the same as the one in which the prism-induced alterations originally took place. Consequently, after the prisms are removed, perceptual anomalies will occur whenever the head and eyes are moved. These anomalies will be opposite to the ones which occurred in the same head-eye posture when the prisms were worn. The effect is as if the perceiver were now wearing spectacles with prisms exactly opposite to the ones used in the original experiment.

Suppose now that the goggles were altered so that only the upper half had prisms while the lower half contained plain glass. Thus when the viewer looked straight ahead, his visual field would be bisected by a line demarking the difference between the prism and the glass. Now distortion would be introduced into the retinal projection when the viewer is looking up; while when one is looking down, the image would be exactly the same as if no goggles were worn. This distortion is illustrated in Figure 14.6 for a grid and for a number of scenes.

In the case of the half-prisms, the presence or absence of distortion will depend on the direction in which the viewer is looking. Objects will contract in the upper left and expand in the upper right. When he is looking down, the retinal surface is stimulated by normal, undisturbed rays of light, and the consequent vision should be undisturbed. Notice that when the viewer is looking up or down, the entire retina becomes stimulated either by normal or by distorted impinging light. When he is looking straight ahead (see Figure 14.6) there is a break in the continuity of stimulation. The upper parts of objects are suspended above and to the right of the lower parts.

Initially, the world looked as represented in the pictures. When some adaptation took place to the distortion introduced by the prisms, it would be lost when the eyes were lowered to look down through the lower portion of the spectacles. This was probably due to the aftereffect of looking through the prisms, since shifting from looking up to looking down had the same effect in terms of stimulation as removing the prisms. Thus there appeared to be little adaptation over the first few days. Gradually, there was an increase in adaptation to the prismatic distortion without disturbing the normal vision when looking down. That is, the initial aftereffect which occurred when looking down disappeared. This was noticeable after about ten days. It indicates differential adaptation as a function of direction of regard.

Even after two months, however, there was still no adaptation at the

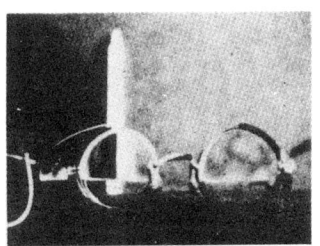
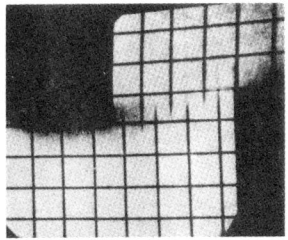

FIGURE 14.6 Distortion caused by wearing spectacles with prisms in upper part only (from Kohler, 1951).

transition zone. If the viewer deliberately looked across the transition zone, the perceptual experience immediately broke into two parts displaced by about 5 degrees from one another—exactly the same experience as that on the first day. There was adaptation to the apparent movement. For example, on the first day, when a point moved across the dividing line it would jump visually from one place to another. This no longer happened even when the point crossed the transition line. When the spectacles were removed for a short period of time after two months, points jumped once again when the head was moved up and down. Even more interesting, the viewer noticed that when he scanned a vertical edge, his eyes always moved unexpectedly to the left and right. He felt as though his eye movements were not vertical but along a diagonal. Therefore, the direction of eye movement was an integral part of the adaptation.

After wearing the half-prisms for fifty days, adaptation was almost complete. Looking up and down did not introduce any noticeable distortion into the perceptual experience of the viewer, nor were there errors in prehension of note. Even though the retinal projections were displaced systematically when looking up and down, there must have been some adjustment which occurred as a function of the experience of the observer which corrected this difference automatically. When the spectacles were removed after fifty days, aftereffects occurred when looking up and down or right and left. The apparent movement was most striking—looking up produced the perception of objects moving peculiarly, swaying in strange fashion. Looking down produced no apparent motion. Once again, we see a specific situational aftereffect, with the perceptual experience tied directly to the direction of regard.

Figure 14.7 shows the quantitative measurements which were taken during the course of the half-prism experiment. Four graphs are presented showing the magnitude of the "prismatic sensation" and of the aftereffect as a function of the number of days the spectacles were worn and then removed. The viewer was required to adjust an apparatus until a desired visual effect was obtained. For example, he was to adjust the positions of two vertical lines, one above the other, until they looked straight. The graphs for "prismatic sensation" show the amount of discrepancy in measurements of this type. The four graphs shown measured the perception of curvature, of distortions, errors in aiming at targets, and the apparent lateral movements of targets.

The abscissa on each graph is in days. The spectacles were worn for the first fifty days and measurements were taken for an additional forty days. The positive ordinate is a measure of the magnitude of prismatic sensation. The negative ordinate is a measure of the aftereffect. The thick solid line represents the measurements taken when the perceiver looked up through the prisms and, therefore, it represents the course of adaptation to the prisms in the upper half of the visual field. This line shows a clear and steady decrease over the course of the experiment although the rate is different for the different types of perceptual tests. The thin solid line is a measure of the perceiver's performance in the same tasks when looking up without the spectacles, that is, it measures the aftereffects. There appears to be a more or less constant distance between the prismatic effect and the aftereffect, indicating that the aftereffect was almost always equal and opposite in effect to the adaptation. Therefore, as perception improved while the viewer was wearing the prisms, it got worse when they were removed.

The dotted lines show the results of measurements taken when the viewer was looking down through the glass part of the spectacles. This kind of measurement is instructive because it is not the same as measuring the aftereffect. This measurement takes into account the fact that the viewer never received distorted input when looking down. It measures whether the distortion introduced into the system when looking up affects the system when looking down. From the graphs it is clear that the distortion does affect the perceptions when looking down in the initial stages of the experiment. Clearly for the first few days, the position of the eyes made no difference—the effects were the same as if they were aftereffects (that is, measured while looking up). When this curve separates from that for aftereffects, it indicates the action of the direction of regard. When the viewer was looking down, less and less distortion was found

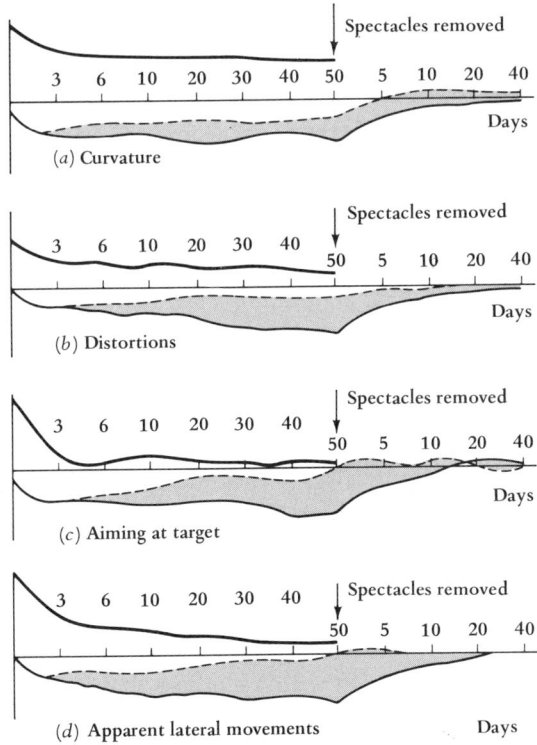

FIGURE 14.7 Measurements of curvature, distortions, aiming at targets, and apparent lateral movements for looking up through prisms (solid dark lines), looking up without spectacles (solid light lines), and looking down through plain glass (dotted line). Shaded area shows situational aftereffect (from Kohler, 1951).

in the perception while more and more (the aftereffect) was found when looking up. Thus spatial vision becomes more and more differentiated as a function of the direction of regard and the "situational" aftereffects gain in strength.

When the spectacles were removed, the same objects could give rise to different perceptions depending on the direction of regard. The aftereffects of form, movement, and orientation all depended on the direction of gaze. Objects occupying the whole visual field appeared bisected at first, and the viewer adapted to this situation by looking diagonally instead of up and down. This type of movement resulted in the perception of a continuous, vertical object. The discontinuity returned when the eye movements stopped.

Clearly the situational aftereffects raise a serious question for perceptual theorists. How can the same retinal projection arouse different perceptions when the ocular system is directed toward a different point in space? The answer cannot be in terms of isolated retinal projections or isolated retinal areas. The total stimulus situation must be considered and this must include the direction of regard, a motor component to be combined with the information from the visual system. Thus somehow, the activity of the organism itself in directing the gaze must be taken into account in the ultimate perception. The following sections will illustrate some modern attempts to provide this type of explanation.

VISUAL VERSUS PROPRIOCEPTIVE CHANGE

The first step in attempting to understand the mechanisms involved in the perceptual-motor adaptation which occurs when the visual input is systematically altered is to pinpoint the changes taking place. Two major possibilities have been suggested. The adaptation may represent a change in the visual experience of the perceiver so that he sees the object differently, or it may represent a proprioceptive change so that the perceiver senses the position of the parts of his body differently, and thereby sees the world from a different perspective.

The problem can be more easily understood when measuring adaptation in a simple pointing task. Figure 14.8 shows the apparatus used by Harris (1965) to measure visual and proprioceptive adaptation differentially. A perceiver viewed five upright pegs at the far edge of a horizontal plate of glass which was just below the level of his eyes. There were three tasks—pointing at visual targets, pointing at sounds, and pointing straight ahead. His normal performance in these tasks was measured before putting on the prisms. In this pretest, the glass was covered with a cloth so that the perceiver could not see his hand under the glass.

After the pretests, the perceiver wore wedge prisms for about three minutes. He was required to point repeatedly at the center target with one hand which was visible through the glass. Over the course of the three minutes, the direction of pointing, inaccurate at first, became accurate. The retest provided a measure of the effects of adaptation which could be compared to the pretest data. All retests were made without prisms. The results showed a large shift in pointing with the adapted hand, but little or no shift with the other hand for each of the three tests. Harris concluded, therefore, that the change involved in adaptation was in the felt position of the specific hand and arm which had been involved in the adaptation. He argued that the change could not be perceptual because, if it were visual, there should be no difference in direction of pointing between the two hands in the visual task and there should be no shifts in pointing to the sound—the nonvisual stimulus.

To determine whether the adaptation was a change in sensed position of hand and arm or a learning to correct motor responses, Harris (1965) performed some additional tests. In one test, he had the perceiver estimate the distance between his hands while he was blindfolded. These judgments were made before and after one arm had been adapted as before. However, the perceiver was blindfolded during the pretests and posttests and the experimenter moved the hand to the appropriate position. Then the perceiver was required to place his unadapted hand at a specific distance from his adapted hand. Thus he could only use information from the position sense to determine where his hand was. The results indicated that the perceiver felt his hands farther apart after the adaptation than before. Therefore, Harris argued, the perceiver's position sense had been altered. Notice that Kohler had also commented in several of his experiments that, as adaptation occurred, he changed the position or orientation of some part of his body. With the inverting mirrors, the orientation of the head was a principal component of the adaptation.

FIGURE 14.8   An apparatus used by Harris to test visual and motor adaptation.

Harris (1965) reviews a number of instances of the proprioceptive component of adaptation, and shows how it will explain the reported visual experiences.

Hay and Pick (1966) studied the change in reaching behavior which accompanied wearing wedge prisms that produced a lateral displacement in stimulation. At first, each perceiver made many errors in reaching for objects, but within a few hours of active walking, they were able to reach for objects fairly accurately. In devising the experimental tasks, Hay and Pick reasoned that a change in reaching behavior or in proprioception of the hand should be manifest in reaching for nonvisual targets as well as visual targets. Therefore, if a perceiver who has adapted to wearing the prisms is asked to indicate the direction of a sound rather than a visual stimulus, they could tell whether the visual impression had changed or whether the felt position of the hand had changed. Furthermore, if the change was visual in nature, this could be determined by having the perceiver make a verbal indication of where he saw an object, for example, naming the position on a scale behind which a sound appeared to be. Thus, while these investigators were studying the adaptation which took place in eye-hand coordination, they separated it into ear-eye coordination and ear-hand coordination in order to discover the major factor which had changed.

The results are illustrated in Figure 14.9, in which performance on the three tasks is plotted as a function of the duration of prism exposure. Changes in both ear-eye and ear-hand coordination occurred and these added up to the total change in eye-hand coordination. Thus there is evidence for both visual and proprioceptive adaptation. The two types of adaptation do not progress in the same way over time, however. The rate of proprioceptive adaptation grows rapidly during the first twelve hours and then slowly decreases until it levels off at about seventy-two hours. The visual shift grows rapidly over the first twenty-four hours, then less rapidly until it too levels off at about seventy-two hours. Thus the immediate adaptation includes both visual and proprioceptive changes, whereas later changes are largely visual.

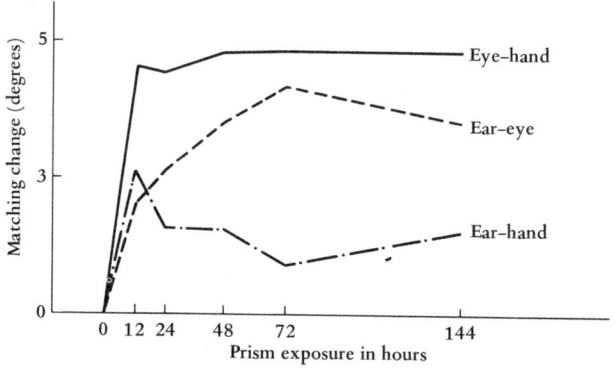

FIGURE 14.9 Magnitude of adaptive change for three intermodal comparisons as a function of length of prism exposure (from Hay and Pick, 1966).

Thus far the studies have been concerned with the alteration of visual information about visual direction—the stimulus was displaced laterally by use of wedge prisms. Rock (1966) introduced a different kind of distortion—distortion of size and of shape—to test whether these kinds of changes might produce visual perceptual changes. The change in size was produced by a lens and the change in shape was produced by a cylindrical optical device which made the stimulus narrower. In the experiment on perceived size, naïve perceivers saw a one-inch white plastic square through the lens and touched it from below through a cloth (see Figure 14.10). They could not see their hands. Three tests were used: *(a)* they were to draw the size of the square as accurately as they could; *(b)* they were to match the size from a series of visually presented squares, and *(c)* they were to match the size from a series that they could touch but could not see. The average size of the matched object or of the drawing was smaller when vision and touch were in conflict than when touch alone was involved. The matched size was about the same when visual information was available and when touch was providing information in one case and not in another. Thus touch had almost no effect on the visually perceived size of the object. In the experiment on shape in which similar conditions were involved, the information provided the perceiver with a rectangular visual object and a square tactual object. Once again the results showed that vision completely dominated the responses—not only did most of the perceivers say they saw a rectangle, but they claimed that the object felt like one also.

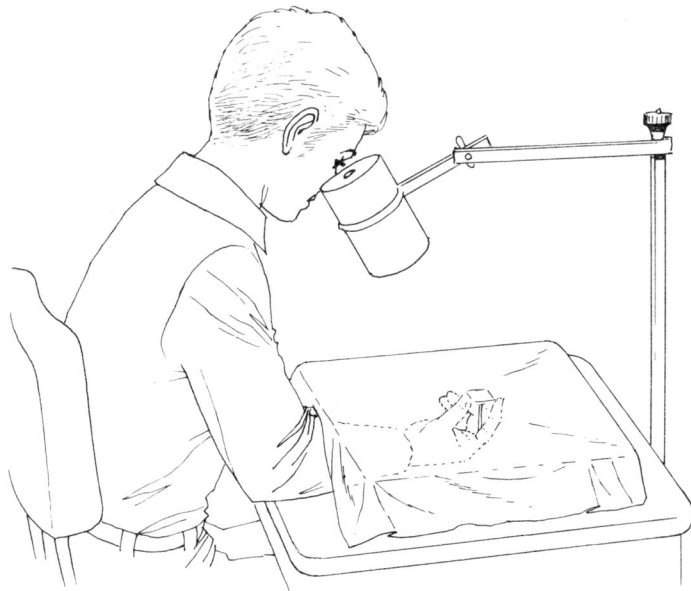

FIGURE 14.10 An appratus used by Rock to provide conflicting visual and touch information about the size and shape of an object.

PASSIVE VERSUS ACTIVE MOVEMENT

The alteration which takes place during adaptation to the distorted input appears to be a realignment of the motor-kinesthetic portion of perceptual-motor acts. In order to reach, point, walk, run, or ski, the person wearing distorting goggles must have information about the relationships of the systems involved and must readjust the internal correlation. This information can be provided visually by reafference—the visual consequences of movements of the observer initiated by the observer.

In the Innsbruck studies, the perceiver wearing the goggles was permitted free movement, almost entirely self-initiated. Such movement would be an important source of efferent and reafferent information. Is this movement necessary, or will adaptation take place with only visual input? Held and Hein (1958) compared performances of a perceiver wearing prisms for three minutes while he looked at his hand when it was stationary, when it was moved by a mechanical device that simulated real movements, and when it was moved by the perceiver himself. In pretests and posttests, the perceiver marked the position of the intersections of lines as illustrated in Figure 14.11. Clearly the active movement produced substantial adaptation—most perceivers showed complete adaptation within half an hour. No adaptation was shown by those receiving passive movement. Thus even though the visual information was the same in both conditions, there was no relationship between the efferent motor signals and the afferent sensory signals in the passive condition. This suggested to Held and Hein that contingent reafferent stimulation was the critical factor in adaptation to displacement. Similar results were found when movement of the entire body was involved (Held and Bossom, 1961; Held and Freedman, 1963).

A slightly different viewpoint concerning active movement asserts that the information obtained from a record of certain outgoing motor nerve impulses is available for use in adaptation. Specifically this would mean that the perceiver would know the direction in which the eye was looking because it had a record of where the eye had been directed to go. For example, Festinger and Canon (1965) found that the accuracy of pointing at the location of a target was better when the target appeared suddenly than when the target moved slowly toward its destination. They took this as evidence that the efferent information was available and useful in judging target direction.

In this view, then, perception need not involve the actual motor activity as much as the central concomitant of a readiness to activate a programmed efferent signal. The consequence of this view is that the visual information present in the psychophysicist's superstimulus must still be supplemented by nonoptic information of some sort for precise perceptual-motor behavior to take place. As Gyr (1972) points out, for adaptation to take place, the organism must actively confront the production and/or the reception of input from the environment. Thus, while the information need not be motor activity, or

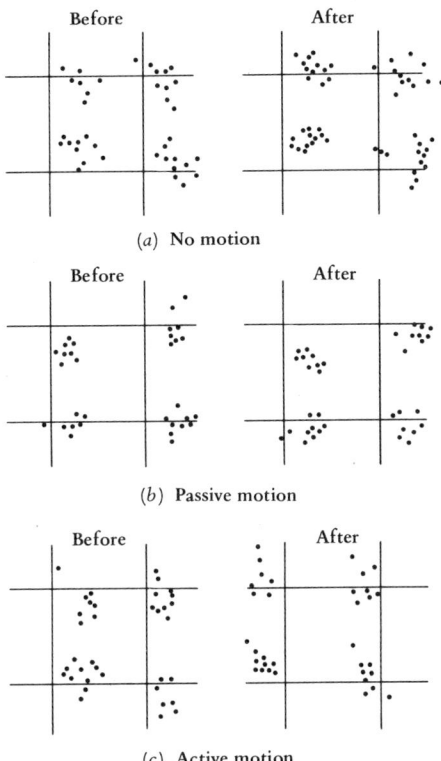

Before   After

(a) No motion

Before   After

(b) Passive motion

Before   After

(c) Active motion

FIGURE 14.11 Before and after tests for marking the intersection of lines when wearing prisms and after looking at their hand when it was (a) stationary, (b) moved by a mechanical device, and (c) actively moved by the subject (from Held and Hein, 1958).

even its consequence in stimulation—reafference—an additional component must be present for adaptation—and, indeed, for perception—to take place.

SUMMARY

We have reviewed the three major views of motion and movement perception. Several tentative conclusions are possible. First, there is evidence that human beings possess cortical motion-detecting systems that respond to a displacement of a luminance gradient over a retinal receptive field. Second, evidence has been reviewed to suggest that relational qualities are critical for the perception of any kind of motion, real or apparent. Motion of an object on a textureless dark background is virtually undetectable, while such a stationary object will appear to move unpredictably. Gibson's theory of motion and movement perception rests entirely on the relative displacements in the retinal projection. His explanation is internally consistent and possesses great power. However, we have also seen that the literature on adaptation to distorted input suggests the third conclusion, namely that nonoptic information, is also necessary for visual perception to take place.

Readings

General coverage of the problem of perceived movement may be found in Spigel's (1965) book. Gyr's (1972) article contains a sophisticated discussion of the theories of movement and motion perception as well as reviews of the experimental evidence. A detailed discussion of the problems of adaptation to distortion may be found in Rock (1966). A new book by Kolers (1972) covers much of this material, but interprets it as part of a constructive theory of perception.

the development of visual space perception

INTRODUCTION

It is perhaps natural to ask of any psychological process how it came to be the way it is—did it appear full blown in its adult form at birth or did it develop in successively more sophisticated forms as the newborn matured? If it developed, did it change with experience or practice, or was the growth quite independent of these factors? Unfortunately, we will not be able to discuss this type of problem in this book, as it requires substantially more space than we have available. Rather, we will confine our attention to a very specific problem—what are the perceptual abilities of humans at birth and shortly thereafter? Can we learn anything about the way in which the visual world appears to a newborn? Is it the "booming, buzzing confusion" postulated by James (1890) or similar to the world seen by adults?

PREREQUISITES FOR PERCEPTION
IN THE NEWBORN

We have observed in earlier chapters the close relationship between the structure of the visual system and the resulting perceptual experience. In studying perceptual development, therefore, it becomes necessary to ask, first, whether the organism possesses the basic anatomical and neurophysiological mechanisms necessary to produce the different types of perceptual experience, and second, whether the organism is able to produce responses which can demonstrate the existence of these processes. The latter question is frequently answered in terms of the ingenuity of the experimenter in using whatever responses or actions the young organism is able to make at different ages. The answer to the first question requires systematic analysis of each stage of the visual system of the very young organism. This work has recently been surveyed by Hershenson (1967), and we will look briefly at its salient conclusions.

Anatomical and functional studies show that the retina of the newborn infant (one to five days of age) contains rods and cones, and that both the photopic and scotopic systems are functional at birth. The level of development of the central components of the newborn's visual system have been evaluated using both the electroencephalogram (EEG) of the newborn and the visual cortical evoked response. The newborn's EEG shows distinct sleep-wake stages and, apparently, mechanisms for coordination between the cerebral hemispheres have also matured. Measurements of cortical evoked responses indicate that at least some intact pathways exist between the eye and the cortex. This measurement has been made in many newborn infants and some investigators have reported that they can always produce an evoked response if they use stimuli intense enough. Since the differences between the evoked responses of infants and of adults are primarily quantitative, the visual system of the infant is probably well organized and functional at birth.

The evidence about convergence, accomodation, and conjugate movement of the eyes is not as clear. Newborn infants have been observed to follow a moving target with both eyes but, when looking at stationary targets, their eyes frequently appear to wander independently. Thus, while newborns can direct their eyes at a single point in space, it probably takes a compelling target to keep them there for any length of time. The attempts to assess accommodative ability differ in their results depending on the measurement technique used. It is clear, however, that by two months of age or so, the infant is able to accommodate fairly well. This is supported by data measuring the visual acuity of newborns which indicate that the image is at least sharp enough for a fair amount of resolving power for the newborn eye (loosely about 20/200).

Hershenson (1967) concluded that the human newborn infant probably possesses the necessary muscular control and detector apparatus to bring the projection of an object onto the fovea and to hold it there. This could be done reasonably well even when the object was moving. Convergence and accommodation were not as clearly demonstrable. Nevertheless, it seemed clear that the potential for perception in the human being is present at birth, and that the differences which exist between newborns and adults are only quantitative.

PERCEPTUAL ABILITIES
OF THE HUMAN INFANT

It seems reasonable to assume that soon after birth the infant is able to extract and utilize complex visual information from the environment. This is not to say that perceptual abilities do not improve with experience, nor to deny that the developing organism is learning to use different kinds of information to supplement or replace its repertoire of innate mechanisms. It is quite likely that the visual discrimination of the adult and child could be different from those of the infant. In this sense, perhaps Fantz (1965) was correct in his belief that perception is "innate in the neonate and learned in the adult." In this section, we will look at a number of different abilities, from simple to complex.

Intensity

Brightness sensitivity has been measured in infants up to 113 days of age. The results show rapid development in the first two months of life (Doris, Casper, and Poresky, 1967; Doris and Cooper, 1966). Visual preferences, as assessed by the number of fixations to three intensities of light differing by one log unit, have been found in human newborns in the first week of life (Hershenson, 1964a).

Simple Stimulus Features

The possible existence of feature analyzers in the human must be investigated by indirect methods since electrophysiological procedures cannot be used. One fruitful method, illustrated in Figure 15.1, uses photographs or television recordings of the eyes of infants in order to determine their direction of gaze. When markers are placed in the field, the fixations can be located fairly precisely.

In a study using photographic recordings, Kessen, Salapatek, and Haith (1972) presented newborns with a single contour in either vertical or horizontal orientation located off the center of the visual field. Fixations on the blank

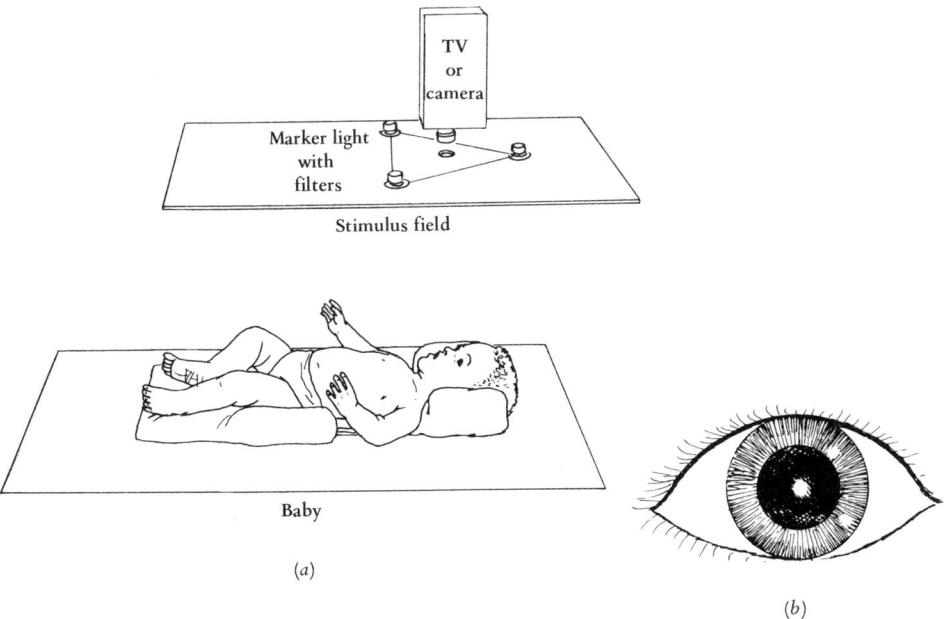

FIGURE 15.1 Schematic representation of method for obtaining pictures of the eyes of infants looking at forms on a screen and of the type of pictures obtained. *(a)* Typical apparatus for observing the corneal reflex of infants. *(b)* Typical photo frame showing eye directed at one angle of a triangular stimulus, indicated by light reflected from marker lamps.

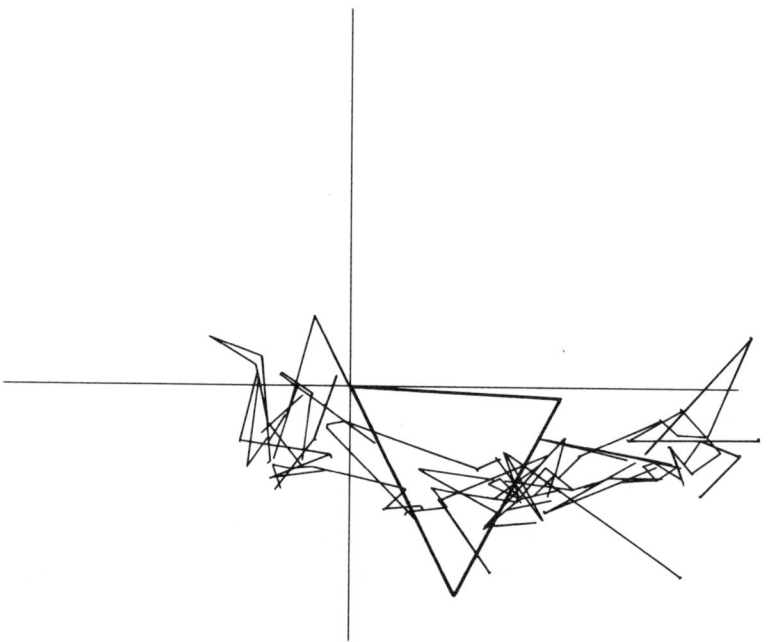

FIGURE 15.2   Visual scanning pattern of human newborn of a homogeneous field. Each dot represents one time sample of eye orientation (from Salapatek and Kessen, 1966).

control field were distributed fairly normally around the center of the field. The distributions of eye fixations for the horizontal contour were virtually identical to those for the blank screen. However, the vertical contours were clearly attractive to the babies—for the left-of-center contour, the distribution of eye fixations showed a sharp peak in the region of the contour. For the right-of-center contour, the distribution of fixations shifted to the right, and the peaking occurred to the right of the contour region. Thus, infants appeared to be attracted to those contours which could be easily crossed. These results suggest that some kind of excitation occurs when an edge is crossed, and that this stimulation is implicated in the mechanism which maintains fixation around the contour. Like adults, it appears to be easier for an infant to move his eyes horizontally across a vertical edge than vertically across a horizontal edge.

When figures are introduced into the visual field of newborns, a slightly different kind of visual behavior occurs. Salapatek and Kessen (1966) presented newborn infants with a large black triangle and photographed their eye fixations. Fixation points were plotted with respect to the real stimulus triangle presented to an experimental group and with respect to an imaginary triangle for the control group. Figure 15.2 shows responses to a blank homogeneous field. Each dark point represents a fixation and these are connected in sequence. The eye moved almost every second, and much more in the horizontal than in the vertical direction. Figure 15.3 shows the response of a typical infant. Eye movements were much shorter and the fixations tended to cluster around one of the three vertices. Thus, the infants appear to have responded to the angle rather than to the total form. In a subsequent experiment (Nelson and Kessen, 1969), three stimuli were shown to newborn infants—a complete outline triangle, only the sides of the triangle, and only the angles of the triangle. In this situation, the infants typically looked toward a single angle component—the angular elements attracted the infants' gaze whether the sides of the triangle were present or not. Taken together, these experiments suggest that the infants sought out those areas of greatest change or discontinuity—the angles in this case. Perhaps we could even argue that they were guided by the presence of angle detectors.

In an attempt to separate the important aspects of stimulation which were attracting the newborns' gaze, Salapatek (1968) varied size, angularity, figure-ground contrast, and figure type (solid or outline). The ocular response was subjected to detailed analysis by measuring the location of gaze, dispersion of gaze, number of shifts in gaze, direction of shifts, length of shifts, and time spent looking at the total figure, part of the figure, contour versus center of circles, and sides versus angles of triangles. The results did not indicate that either specific figures as wholes, or specific parts of figures were more attractive than others. Nonetheless, the experiment did supply firm evidence in support of the earlier studies.

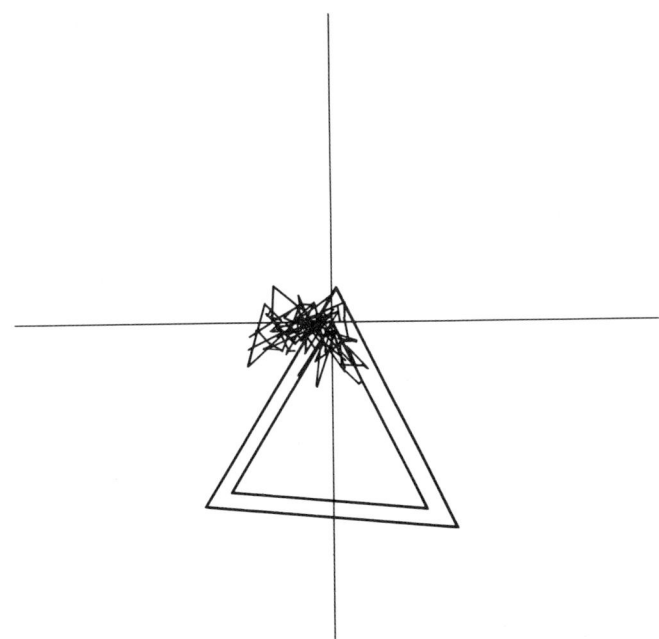

FIGURE 15.3 Visual scanning of human newborn of large black equilateral triangle. Each dot represents one time sample of eye orientation (from Salapatek and Kessen, 1966).

Salapatek (1968, 1969) characterized the visually naïve newborn's response to patterned two-dimensional surfaces in terms of several salient aspects. Visual scanning was more dispersed in the horizontal than in the vertical dimension of the visual field under all stimulus conditions, whether a stimulus was present or not. In the absence of a stimulus, the broad automatic scan occurred reliably, in all infants and for extended periods of time. Introduction of a geometric figure into the newborn's visual field resulted in a decrease in the horizontal dispersion of visual scanning and a decreased difference between the horizontal and vertical dispersion of scanning. More specifically, newborns modified the pattern of visual scanning to fit the physical features of the stimulus.

Within a very short time after a figure or pattern was introduced into the visual field, the majority of newborns ceased their scanning and fixated the figure's contour, typically coming to rest on some limited segment or feature of the contour. Localization of fixation occurred for the majority of the infants within three or four seconds and often involved an eye movement across some portion of the figure. This pattern of behavior suggests that the newborn is able to discriminate pattern in its peripheral visual field, and that this determines the direction of eye movements. In this respect, angles appear to be particularly salient.

In two recent experiments, Salapatek (1969) followed the development of visual scanning through the first ten weeks of life. In the first experiment, two groups of infants were studied—one group ranging from four to six weeks of age and the other between eight and ten weeks. The stimuli used were a homogeneous field, a circle, a square, a triangle, a regular 12-turn shape, and a random 11-turn shape. With the homogeneous field, all infants either fixated the extreme portions of the visual field, became fussy, or fell asleep. When a geometric figure was introduced, infants rapidly fixated and scanned the figure for an extended period of time. In general, the scan was directed toward an angle, if one was present in the figure.

Of the two groups Salapatek studied, the younger infants concentrated most of their visual scanning on a small portion of the stimulus with a more focused scan as compared to the older infants who directed their scan more loosely. Although all infants fixated the contour rather than the center of the geometric patterns, the younger infants limited their gaze to a very small segment of the contour, whereas the older infants showed a tendency to direct some fixations toward the centers of the figures.

In the second study, Salapatek presented thirty-three infants between four and ten weeks of age with several different geometric patterns. Some of these stimuli had internal and external contours—they might even be thought to have internal features similar to those of a face. Salapatek found that older infants fixated more on the internal features than did younger ones, and for longer periods of time.

In summary, then, it seems clear that the human infant responds to elements or stimulus features from birth and that this response is specific to some types of elements selected for fixation or scansion. As the infant grows older, more and more extensive portions of figures are scanned actively. Thus, immediately upon being exposed to the world, the infant actively seeks stimulation rather than passively receiving it. As the infant matures, more and more information about the environment is sought and dealt with (Bond, 1972).

Natural Patterns of Looking

The research just reviewed used eye movements as a dependent variable when specific stationary geometric patterns were placed in the visual field. These results are difficult to interpret because the experimental situations were imposed upon the infants by the experimenters. We are just beginning to learn about the natural visual field of infants and their patterns of looking at it.

The natural patterns of integrated head and eye movements of infants between three and fifteen weeks of age were studied by Tronick and Clanton (1971) using electrooculographic recordings of eye movements, and recording head position by measuring displacements of a light, free-moving gimballed harness. By combining these signals, accurate records of eye position, head position, and line of sight were obtained. Figure 15.4 shows a schematic representation of the apparatus they used. The three objects in the field were

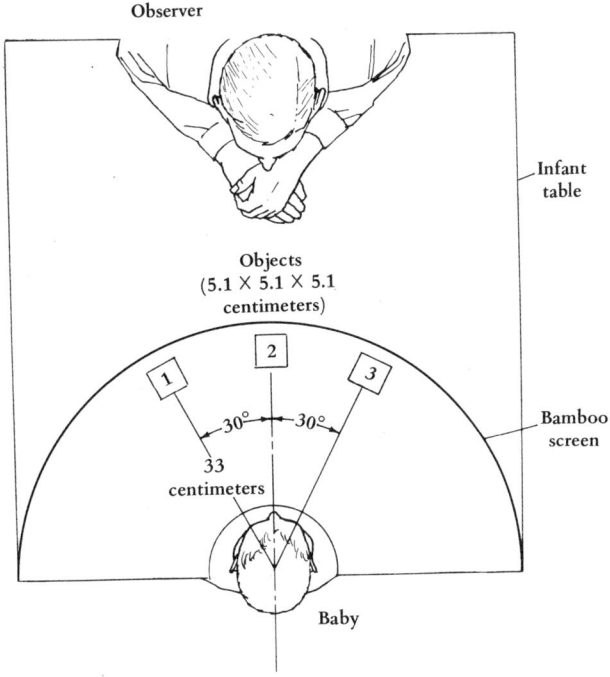

FIGURE 15.4 Apparatus used by Tronick and Clanton (1971) to study infant looking patterns.

brightly colored cubes, about five centimeters on a side, mounted on small motors to that they could be made to move somewhat.

Four looking patterns were observed in the records of these infants: First, the "shift" pattern in which a saccadic movement of the eyes was integrated with a smooth and fairly rapid movement of the head. The lead of either the head or the eye did not appear to be related to the motion of the target. Second, the "search" pattern in which a slow displacement of the head was coordinated with a series of eye fixations and saccades. These movements produced a step-like looking pattern which covered a large sector of the visual field. Third, a "focal" pattern in which the head remained stable while a series of small saccades and fixations covered a limited portion of the visual field. In this pattern, sometimes the eyes remained fixated for only brief periods whereas there were many cases in which eyes and head remained stable for long periods of time. Fourth, the "compensation" pattern in which the eyes and head moved slowly and continuously in opposite directions and then returned to their original positions. The resultant of the two movements was no change in the line of sight.

In general, integration of head and eye movements were well executed by all infants. The movements were smooth and the looking patterns appeared better organized than either component alone. The major differences between the infants of different ages appeared to be quantitative in that the fixations of younger infants were typically of smaller amplitude and there were longer periods in which no change of gaze occurred. Thus the looking patterns indicated that infants even at twenty days of age possess a visual system that is adapted for the exploration and extraction of information from the environment. The system appears to deploy attention to new loci, or to maintain attention at a particular locus, by shifting or stabilizing a visual line of regard with coordinated head and eye movements. The youngest infants explored less of the environment than the older infants. Their looks were of shorter duration and they looked to fewer places. The older infants were more skillful in the exploration of the visual environment but this increased capability did not require a qualitative change in the patterns of looking.

The Visual Field of Infants

The effective visual field is a measure of how far a stimulus can be in the periphery and still register information for the control of exploratory fixations. If this effective visual field changed with age, it would have important consequences for our understanding of perceptual development. To study these changes, Tronick (1972) presented two- to three-week old infants with fixation stimuli in the midline, and then with a stimulus at some position in the periphery. They were allowed fifteen seconds in which to change fixation. The infants were tested weekly for nine weeks.

Figure 15.5 shows how far off midline a stimulus object could be to elicit a fixation, as a function of age of the infant, for four stimulus presentation

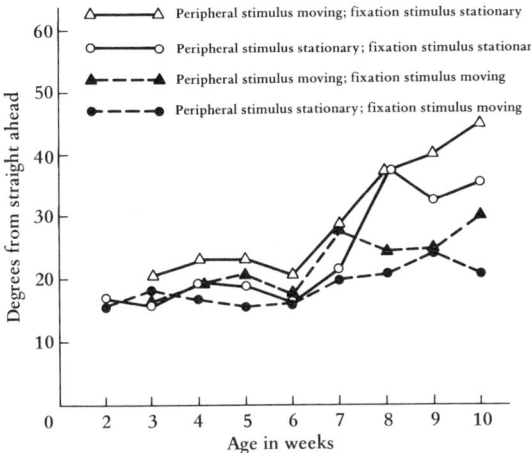

FIGURE 15.5 Looking patterns as a function of age for moving and stationary stimuli (from Tronick, 1972).

conditions. Initially the infant's effective visual field was not much greater than 15 to 20 degrees to either side of his line of regard. When the fixation object was in motion and the peripheral object was stationary, the size of the field changed only slightly over the first ten weeks. In contrast, when the peripheral object was in motion and the fixation object was stationary, the visual field at ten weeks was 20 degrees larger than it was initially, and more than 20 degrees larger than it was in the reversed movement condition. At every age, the effective visual field was larger when the object in the periphery was moving. The other two conditions—both objects in motion and both objects stationary—fell between the two extremes. In general, the area of the effective visual field remained approximately constant until about six weeks of age, at which time it began to expand. This relationship was found in all conditions. Motion was a more effective stimulus for attention; it was more easily registered in the periphery, and was more compelling in the focal field.

The increase in the size of the visual field appears to reflect both an increase in stimulus control and a growing functional capacity of the infant. This developmental trend may also explain the change from an obligatory to a voluntary looking pattern in infants noted by some investigators (Hershenson, 1967). Now, rather than a transition, it may be seen as a result of a quantitative growth in the effective visual field.

Space

We have seen that the infant possesses a visual system which enables him to look around the visual world. Does this infant perceive a three-dimensional world of surfaces, edges, and solid objects? Some recent experiments have shown how capable the young infant is in doing this. Empiricist theory argues that the discrimination of depth is dependent upon activity in space. Consequently, in order to see space, and objects in space, an organism would first have to move around.

To test one aspect of this, Bower (1964) trained infants (seventy-five to eighty-five days old) to turn their heads to one side to see an experimenter's head pop up above the table and say "peek-a-boo." Figure 15.6 shows a schematic representation of the apparatus and experimental arrangement used. The "peek-a-boo" functioned as a reinforcement for the infant's response of turning his head toward the stimulus—a 30-centimeter cube placed nearly one meter from the infant's eyes. This cube provided a standard against which the generalization tests could be compared.

The training and four generalization test situations are represented schematically in Figure 15.7. Two different sized cubes—one 30 centimeters and one 90 centimeters—were each placed at one meter or three meters from the infants to provide the four test conditions in which projective size could be pitted against real size. After the infant had been trained to turn his head whenever the 30-centimeter cube was presented at one meter, generalization was tested by measuring the number of responses made to each of the four test stimuli. The first test stimulus was a 30-centimeter cube at one meter— the same stimulus as in training. In this case, therefore, both the real size and the projective size of the test stimulus was the same as the real size and the projective size of the training stimulus. The second test stimulus was the 30-centimeter cube placed at three meters from the infant. For this stimulus the real size was unchanged, but the size of the cube projected onto the retina was very much smaller than when it was at one meter. In the third stimulus situation, a 90-centimeter cube was placed one meter from the infant. This test cube was much larger than the training stimulus in both real size and in projective size. The fourth stimulus was the 90-centimeter cube placed at three meters from the infant. While this cube was much larger than the training stimulus in reality, its projective size was now equal to that of the 30-centimeter training stimulus at one meter.

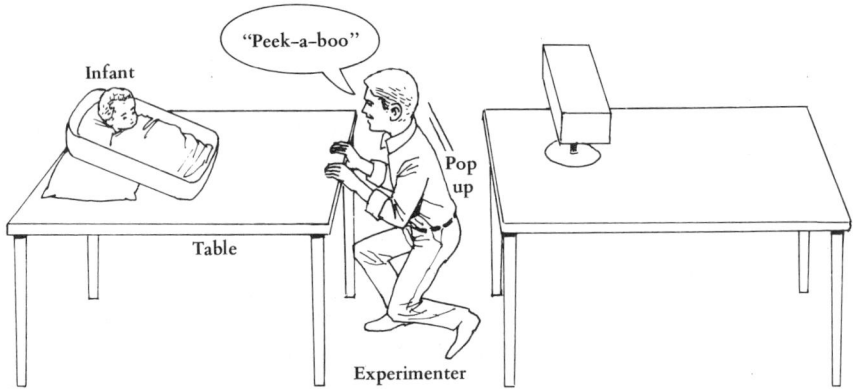

FIGURE 15.6 Arrangements in Bower's (1964) experiment with different sized objects in which experimenter pops up to say "peek-a-boo."

The number of conditioned responses in the four test conditions were 103, 66, 54, and 23 respectively, showing that, while the infants clearly responded less when any change was made, they responded more when real size was the same than when projective size was the same but real size was not. Thus, at least some of the information specifying distance and size-at-a-distance was received and used by the infants. Since they were not old enough to locomote and, therefore, had no opportunity for action in space, their discriminations of depth must have been made on the basis of information other than the learning associated with the projective size of objects displaced in depth. Since the infants responded to objects that were changed in their spatial positions in a manner which was independent of the spatial change, we may conclude that they showed a form of perceptual constancy.

In a subsequent study, Bower (1965) showed that motion parallax was the necessary stimulus for perceptual discrimination in infants between one and two months of age. These infants were also trained to turn their heads to one side to see the experimenter saying "peek-a-boo." There were three groups: a monocular group, a binocular group, and a group which saw only a projection

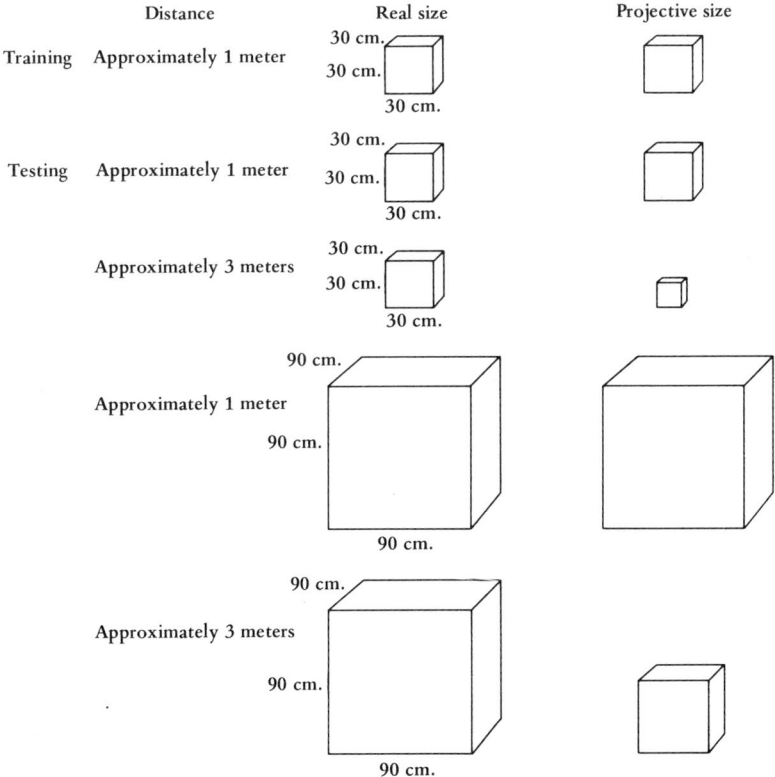

FIGURE 15.7 Schematic representation of the stimuli used in Bower's (1964b) experiment on constancy.

of the real scene. All groups were able to make a discrimination based on changes in the size of the retinal projection. Only the first two groups, however, could discriminate among presentations where the retinal size was not changed. This response can be interpreted to mean that the infants could not only detect spatial position but could also detect size-at-a-distance, that is, they manifested size constancy. The ability to perceive size as invariant, with distance transformed, appears to have been based on information due to motion parallax. For both the binocular and monocular groups, head movements could produce relative displacements of objects and spaces in the visual field sufficient for the judgment.

In a similar experiment, Bower (1965) trained two-month-old infants to turn their heads whenever they were presented with a particular wooden block in a particular orientation. The infants were then tested for generalization with four different stimulus situations. In the first, the original block was presented in its original 45-degree orientation. This was simply a generalization test using the original stimulus with no change in orientation. The second test used the original block but now aligned with the fronto-parallel plane. This situation provided a stimulus with the same objective shape, but with a different projective shape and in a different orientation from the original. The third stimulus was provided by an object shaped like a trapezoid in the fronto-parallel plane whose retinal projection was equal to that of the original block at 45 degrees. This object had a different objective shape from the original block but it provided a stimulus having the same projective shape as the original, although the orientation was different. The fourth stimulus was the trapezoid placed at 45 degrees. In this orientation, it provided a stimulus which had a different objective shape and a different projective shape from the original, but the orientation was the same.

The infants responded approximately twice as much to the original stimulus in the generalization test as they did to the stimuli which projected a retinal shape identical to it. They responded almost as much to the same objective shape in the different orientation as they did to the original stimulus. Thus, Bower argued, the infants had not learned to respond to a projective or retinal shape but to an objective shape which could be recognized in a new orientation. To this extent, they showed shape constancy.

The fact that three-month-old infants display some degree of perceptual constancy suggests that distance information was not simply registered but was used appropriately in structuring space such that the perception of size and shape were reasonably unaffected by distance. Aronson and Tronick (1970) argue that perceptual structuring of this sort cannot be explained by assuming that distance perception develops within the first two months of life because, first, the reaching behavior that has long been the presumed learning mechanism for this accomplishment is not typically displayed at three months, and second, the infants would have had to learn to correlate distance information with the changes in the retinal projection that are created by the same object at different distances, in addition to learning to perceive distance.

To see whether infants respond appropriately to objects with respect to change in spatial position, Bower, Broughton, and Moore (1970) observed the adaptive responses of infants six to twenty days of age when an object approached them. This response consisted of the eyes opening wide, the head going backwards, and both hands coming up between the object and the face. The eyes generally remained straight ahead during the entire response.

In one experiment, they exposed infants to two foam-rubber cubes of different sizes moving directly toward the infants. The near-approach condition upset the infants sufficiently that the experiment had to be abandoned. Nevertheless it suggested that the infants were able to discriminate enough about the approaching cube to make an adaptive response. The next experiment used a visual expansion pattern projected onto a screen in front of the infants (aged ten to twenty days). A red and black bulls-eye pattern initially attracted their gaze to the screen. On each trial an object moving away from the screen toward a point source of light produced an expansion pattern. Since the infants viewed the screen binocularly, they received the same pattern in both eyes—a situation somewhat different from the natural world where there would be binocular parallax associated with the stimulation to the two eyes. Figure 15.8 shows a typical shadow-casting device for producing an optical expansion pattern. Eight of the nine infants showed some avoidance responses to the expansion pattern. The responses were not as fully developed as when actual objects approached, although the same components were found. An additional experiment was performed to see whether the lower intensity of

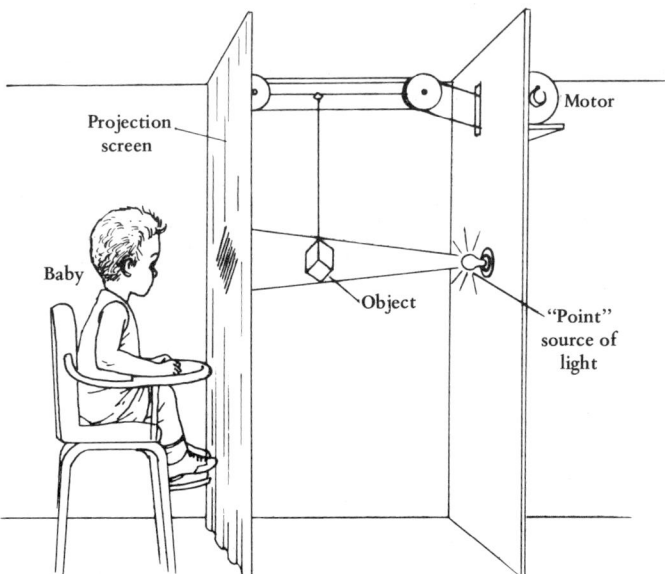

FIGURE 15.8 Typical shadow casting apparatus for producing optical expansion patterns used by Bower, Broughton, and Moore (1970) and by Ball and Tronick (1971).

response was due to the lack of an air-pressure change. Four infants were exposed to air-pressure changes which approximated those produced by approaching objects. The air movement alone produced a response which was quite opposite to that produced by approaching real objects.

The adaptive response of infants to approaching objects was clearly demonstrated by Ball and Tronick (1971). They found that infants two to eleven weeks of age responded with an integrated avoidance response and with "upset" when viewing symmetrically expanding shadows—the optical stimulus which specifies an approaching object. This response did not occur when the infants were presented with asymmetrically expanding shadows—the optical patterns which specify an object approaching but on a miss path. The response also did not occur for contracting shadows—the optical pattern specifying a receding object. These responses were observed in infants at all ages. In a second experiment, infants reacted defensively to the approach of a real object on a collision path, but not to one on a miss path. Apparently these infants were able to detect the direction and relative depth of approach, and could differentiate a collision path from a miss path, for both real objects and their optical equivalents.

This series of experiments shows that the newborn infant displays a functionally appropriate avoidance response to approaching objects, and that visual stimuli control the response. While there are many experiments which show that infants can discriminate spatial variables, they do not show whether infants are perceiving objects-at-a-distance, or whether they are merely responding to proximal variables per se. For example, the demonstration that infants prefer to fixate solid objects rather than their two-dimensional representation does not differentiate between discrimination mediated proximally by information at the retina or distally by the perceived spatial qualities of the object. That is, it cannot tell us whether the infants are fixating solids, as mediated by motion parallax and binocular parallax, or motion parallax and binocular parallax per se. This series of experiments on response to optical expansion found distally appropriate responses coordinated with distal variables—it was a response to the approach of an object, mediated by such variables as the optical expansion pattern. It was not merely a response to the proximal variables.

Configurational Meaning

Two different kinds of relationships occur between stimulus configurations and the meaning associated with them. The meaning could be an integral part of the configuration, not separable from it and, therefore, not arbitrary, or the meaning could be arbitrarily assigned to a configuration which may or may not have some natural significance. Faces are illustrations of the first kind of relationship, and letters and words are examples of the second kind. In this section, we shall discuss only the first kind of relationship.

The literature on human infants' response to human faces is of great interest but as yet does not portray a consistent set of facts. A number of different dependent variables have been used to measure the infants' responsiveness to real faces, pictures of faces, schematic representations of faces, and even scrambled collections of facial features. For example, Hershenson (1964b) and Hershenson, Kessen, and Munsinger (1967) measured preferential looking time in newborn infants one to five days old to a picture of a woman's face, a distorted face which maintained the overall outline (hair and chin) configuration but changed the arrangement of the features (the eyes, mouth, and lips), and a scrambled face which mixed all features, including pieces of hair and chin (Figure 15.9). While there were some consistent individual preferences, there were no consistent preferences among the three types of facial stimuli.

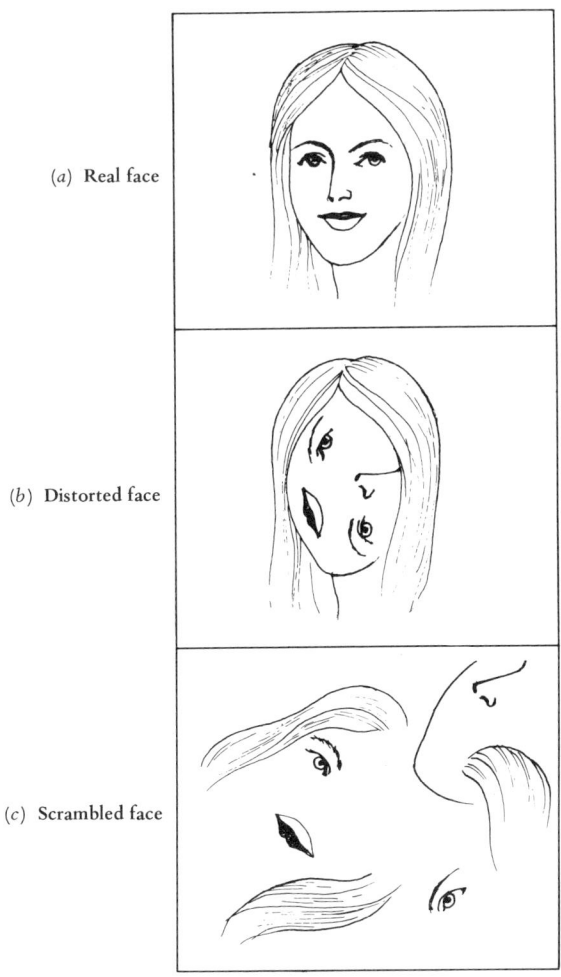

(a) Real face

(b) Distorted face

(c) Scrambled face

FIGURE 15.9   Three stimuli used by Hershenson (1964b) to test newborn response to the organization of facial components.

In light of Salapatek's results with internal versus external features of forms, Bergman, Haith, and Mann (1971) examined the eye fixations of infants who could view real faces. The infants could observe either their real mother, or a stranger, who either remained still, moved slightly, or talked. They found that the youngest infants directed their gaze toward contours around the perimeter of the configurations, such as the hairline. At about seven to nine weeks of age, fixations were equally likely on internal contours, especially if their contrast was high. The internal fixations were directed to the eyes rather than the contours and, while brief excursions were made to the mouth, they returned to the eyes when the mother spoke (see Figure 15.10). There were no differences in looking patterns as a function of movement or the presence of speech.

In general, then, it is probable that infants less than two months of age do not respond to faces as stimuli in terms of the meaning we normally attach to faces as objects. Perhaps by about two months of age the infant is able to perceive the entire face as a configuration, and selectively fixates this Gestalt in order to receive the greatest amount of information from it. For the most part, the eyes serve as this source.

While the developmental pattern shown by human infants in response to faces suggests that the configurational meaning is not manifest at birth, we should not generalize this result to include all possible meaningful configurational patterns. A remarkable experiment by Sackett (1966) with monkeys

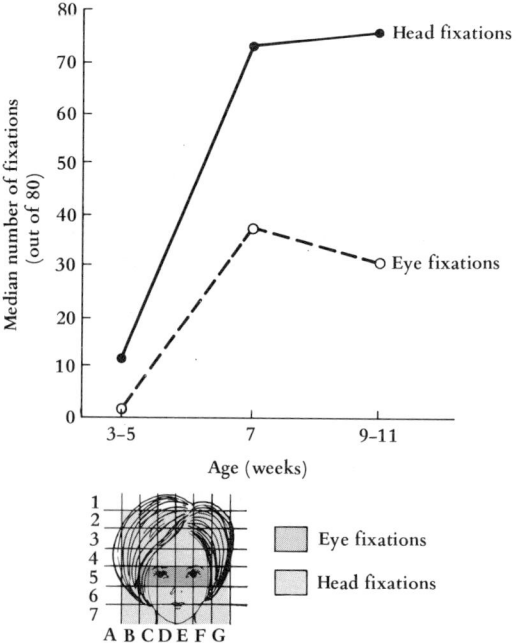

FIGURE 15.10 Median number of fixations by infant on eye and head of mother as a function of age in weeks (from Bergman, Haith, and Mann, 1971).

illustrates the fact that complex innate mechanisms may be involved in visually mediated behavior. Sackett raised monkeys in isolated cages from birth to nine months of age. On the fourteenth day of their lives, the monkeys were shown pictures of other monkeys in various activities and expressing various emotions. The pictures included monkeys in a threatening posture, in a fearful posture, playing with other monkeys, exploring, and having sexual relations. There were also pictures of other infant monkeys, a mother and an infant together, and monkeys just doing nothing. The responses to these pictures were compared with responses to control pictures of a living room, a sunset, an outdoor scene with trees, an adult female human, and various geometric patterns. Responses categorized as exploration, play, vocalization, and disturbance occurred most frequently to pictures of monkeys threatening and to pictures of other infants. From two and one-half to four months of age, the threat pictures produced a high frequency of disturbance level. If the monkey was given control of his viewing of the stimulus so that he could turn it on when he wanted, this picture was rarely looked at during this period.

Thus, pictures of infant monkeys and of threat appear to have nonlearned prepotent general activating properties for socially naïve infant monkeys. Pictures of threat appear to be able to release a maturationally determined innate fear response. These results suggested to Sackett that there exist innate recognition mechanisms which are species specific.

Thus the recent evidence about the perceptual abilities of infant monkeys and human beings indicates that they possess a more developed perceptual system than the early empiricists had been willing to grant. Nevertheless, there is still a great deal of perceptual change which must take place. Therefore, theories of perceptual learning and differentiation, and theories dealing with building perceptual and cognitive structures or schemata (for example, Piaget, 1952; Kagan and Lewis, 1965) may still play important roles in determining the kind of perceptual system we observe in adults.

THE SCALE AND THE METRIC OF VISUAL SPACE

The data from experiments with human infants strongly support the psychophysical view. However, it is clear that perceptual development does take place—infants change their looking habits as they grow older and we suspect that they see things differently as a consequence.

One of the major developments which may be taking place during this period is the acquisition of a metric for the scale of space which they already possess. This would explain the infant's ability to respond to the constancy of objects and would still leave room for the integration of information available to the infant only as a consequence of his own movements. The relational information provided by the retinal projection alone could be sufficient to produce perceptual constancy but it may not be sufficient to produce the exceptionally fine acts of perceptual-motor coordination of adults. Certainly the pinpoint accuracy in motor skills achieved by athletes in many sports—shooting in basketball and hockey, pitching in baseball, passing in football—requires more than the maturation of fine muscle control. The visual space we perceive must have a very precise metric and that metric must be related to the size of our body and its parts.

A system which responded to relational information as a consequence of its structure, and to metric information as a consequence of development (learning, adaptation, or differentiation), would be precisely suitable to an organism gradually maturing and growing over a number of years. The basic spatial information—the ground with objects having constancy of size, shape, and position spaced out on it—would be available immediately and would provide a foundation for later development since it is based on those qualities of space which are permanent. The metric of this space would be changeable and could be continually modified as the organism's body size changes with age. Thus at every age, the organism would supply his own metric to the relational qualities of the scale of space depending on his size within that space. In this sense then, the perception of space is both innate and acquired.

SUMMARY

It appears that the human infant has a fairly well-constructed visual system but that his responses are mostly to aspects of stimuli (to features) rather than to entire forms. At an early age, the attention is directed to simple features of the environment. Moreover, the young infant appears to be able to respond to spatial information in a spatially appropriate way. Gradually the infant comes to respond to more global aspects of stimuli, to have his selective attention tempered by his past experience with objects, presumably because these objects acquire meaning. Perhaps his movements in space permit the infant to supplement the early experience of space with a metric which can be calibrated to the relative sizes of his own body. Regardless of whether these guesses about the precise course of perceptual development are correct, it is clear that the human infant is a pretty good perceiver in every sense of the term—the infant is active, selective, and a seeker after knowledge. His rapid acquisition of knowledge probably also rapidly alters his perceptual experience.

Readings

Details about the perceptual abilities of infants can be found in review articles by Hershenson (1967) and Bond (1972) and in a chapter by Hershenson (1971). Epstein (1967) covers many different topics in perceptual development in his book. Gibson's (1969) book is probably the most complete source for both theory and experimental findings.

references

Aderman, D., and Smith, E. E. Expectancy as a determinant of functional units in perceptual recognition. *Cognitive Psychology*, 1971, *2*, 117–129.

Aguilar, M., and Stiles, W. S. Saturation of the rod mechanism at high levels of stimulation. *Optica Acta*, 1954, *1*, 59–65.

Allport, D. A. The rate of assimilation of visual information. *Psychonomic Science*, 1968, *12*, 231–232.

Allport, D. A. Parallel encoding within and between elementary stimulus dimensions. *Perception and Psychophysics*, 1971, *10*, 104–108.

Alpern, M. Metacontrast. *Journal of the Optical Society of America*, 1953, *43*, 648–657.

Alpern, M. Muscular mechanisms. In H. Davson (Ed.), *The eye*. Vol. 3. New York: Academic Press, 1962.

Alpern, M. Effector mechanisms in vision. In J. A. Kling and L. A. Riggs (Eds.), *Woodworth and Schlosberg's experimental psychology*. (3rd ed.) New York: Holt, Rinehart and Winston, 1971. Pp. 369–394.

Alpern, M. Eye movements. In D. Jameson and L. M. Hurvich (Eds.), *Handbook of sensory physiology*. Vol. VII/4. *Sensory psychophysics*. Berlin: Springer-Verlag, 1972.

Aronson, E., and Tronick, E. Perceptual capacities in early infancy. In J. Eliot (Ed.), *Human development and cognitive processes*. New York: Holt, Rinehart and Winston, 1970.

Atkinson, R. C., and Shiffrin, R. M. Human memory: A proposed system and its control processes. In G. H. Bower and J. T. Spence (Eds.), *The psychology of learning and motivation*. Vol. 2. New York: Academic Press, 1968.

Attneave, F. Some informational aspects of visual perception. *Psychological Review*, 1954, *61*, 183–193.

Attneave, F. *Application of information theory to psychology*. New York: Holt, Rinehart and Winston, 1959.

Averbach, E., and Sperling, G. Short-term storage of information in vision. In C. Cherry (Ed.), *Symposium on information theory*. London: Butterworth, Ltd., 1961. Pp. 196–211.

Ball, W., and Tronick, E. Infant responses to impending collision: Optical and real. *Science*, 1971, *171*, 818–820.

Barlow, H. B. Some possible principles underlying the transformations of sensory messages. In W. A. Rosenblith (Ed.), *Sensory communication*. New York: John Wiley, 1961. Pp. 217–234.

Barlow, H. B. Light and dark adaptation: Psychophysics. In D. Jameson and L. M. Hurvich (Eds.), *The handbook of sensory physiology*. Vol. VII/4. *Sensory psychophysics*. Berlin: Springer-Verlag, 1972.

Beck, J. Perceptual grouping produced by line figures. *Perception and Psychophysics*, 1967, *2*, 491–495.

Beck, J. Similarity grouping and peripheral discriminability under uncertainty. *American Journal of Psychology*, 1972, *85*, 1–20.

Bekesy, G. von. *Sensory inhibition*. Princeton: Princeton University Press, 1967.

Bergman, T., Haith, M. M., and Mann, L. Development of eye contact and facial scanning in infants. Paper presented at the meeting of the Society for Research in Child Development, Minneapolis, April 1971.

Berlyne, D. E. Attention. In E. Carterette and M. Friedman (Eds.), *Handbook of perception*. Vol. 1. *Historical and philosophical roots of perception*. New York: Academic Press, 1973.

Biederman, I. Perceiving real-world scenes. *Science*, *177*, 77–79.

Blackwell, H. R. Psychophysical thresholds: Experimental studies of methods and measurements. *Bulletin of the Engineering Research Institute*, University of Michigan, 1953, No. 36.

Bond, E. K. Perception of form by the human infant. *Psychological Bulletin*, 1972, *77*, 225–245.

Boring, E. G. Apparatus notes: A new ambiguous figure. *American Journal of Psychology*, 1930, *42*, 444.

Boring, E. G. *Sensation and perception in the history of experimental psychology*. New York: Appleton-Century-Crofts, 1942.

Bower, T. G. R. Discrimination of depth in premotor infants. *Psychonomic Science*, 1964, *1*, 368.

Bower, T. G. R. Stimulus variables determining space perception in infants. *Science*, 1965, *149*, 88–89.

Bower, T. G. R., Broughton, J. M., and Moore, M. K. Infant responses to approaching objects: An indicator of response to distal variables. *Perception and Psychophysics*, 1970, *9*, 193–196.

Boynton, R. M. Some temporal factors in vision. In W. A. Rosenblith (Ed.), *Sensory communication*. New York: John Wiley, 1961. Pp. 739–756.

Boynton, R. M. Color vision. In J. A. Kling and L. A. Riggs (Eds.), *Woodworth and Schlosberg's experimental psychology*. (3rd ed.) New York: Holt, Rinehart and Winston, 1971. Pp. 315–368.

Boynton, R. M. Discrimination of homogeneous double pulses of light. In D. Jameson and L. M. Hurvich (Eds.), *Handbook of sensory physiology*. Vol. VII/4. *Sensory psychophysics*. Berlin: Springer-Verlag, 1972.

Boynton, R. M., and Boss, D. E. The effect of background luminance and contrast upon visual search performance. *Illuminating Engineering*, 1971, *66*, 173–186.

Boynton, R. M., and Bush, W. R. Laboratory studies pertaining to visual air reconnaissance. Wright Air Development Center, Technical Report 55-304, Part 2, 1957. Pp. 1–46.

Boynton, R. M., Elworth, C., and Palmer, R. M. Laboratory studies pretaining to visual air reconnaissance. Wright Air Development Center, Technical Report 55–304, Part 3, 1958. Pp. 1–61.

Boynton, R. M., and Seigfried, J. Psychophysical estimates of on-responses to brief light flashes. *Journal of the Optical Society of America*, 1962, *52*, 720–721.

Boynton, R. M., Sturr, J. F., and Ikeda, M. Study of flicker by increment threshold technique. *Journal of the Optical Society of America*, 1961, *51*, 196–201.

Briggs, G. E., and Blaha, J. Memory retrieval and central comparison times in information processing. *Journal of Experimental Psychology*, 1969, *79*, 395–402.

Brindley, G. S. *The physiology of the retina and the visual pathway*. (1st ed.) London: Arnold Press, 1960.

Brindley, G. S. Afterimages. *Scientific American*, 1963, *209* (Oct.), 84–93.

Brindley, G. S. *The physiology of the retina and the visual pathway.* (2nd ed.) London: Arnold Press, 1972.

Brindley, G. S., and Merton, P. A. The absence of position sense in the human eye. *Journal of Physiology*, 1960, *153*, 127–130.

Broadbent, D. E. *Perception and communication.* London: Pergamon Press, 1958.

Broadbent, D. E. Stimulus set and response set: Two kinds of selective attention. In D. I. Mostofsky (Ed.), *Attention: Contemporary theory and analysis.* New York: Appleton-Century-Crofts, 1970. Pp. 51–60.

Broadbent, D. E. *Decision and stress.* New York: Academic Press, 1971.

Bruner, J. S. On perceptual readiness. *Psychological Review*, 1957, *64*, 123–152.

Bruner, J. S., and Postman, L. Perception, cognition and behavior. *Journal of Personality*, 1949, *18*, 14–31. (a)

Bruner, J. S., and Postman, L. On the perception of incongruity: A paradigm. *Journal of Personality*, 1949, *18*, 206–223. (b)

Buswell, G. T. Fundamental reading habits: A study of their development. *Education Monograph Supplement*, 1922, *21*.

Buswell, G. T. *How people look at pictures.* Chicago: University of Chicago Press, 1935.

Campbell, F. W., and Green, D. G. Optical and retinal factors affecting visual resolution. *Journal of Physiology*, 1965, *181*, 576–593.

Carterette, E., and Friedman, M. (Eds.), *Handbook of perception.* Vol. 1. *Historical and philosophical roots of perception.* New York: Academic Press, 1973.

Carterette, E., and Friedman, M. (Eds.), *Handbook of perception.* Vol. 3. *The biology of perceptual systems.* New York: Academic Press, 1974, in press.

Cheatham, P. G. Visual perceptual latency as a function of stimulus brightness and contour shape. *Journal of Experimental Psychology*, 1952, *43*, 369–380.

Cheatham, P. G., and White, C. T. Temporal numerosity: I. Perceived number as a function of flash number and rate. *Journal of Experimental Psychology*, 1952, *44*, 447–451.

Chomsky, N., and Halle, M. *Sound patterns of English.* New York: Harper & Row, 1969.

Cohen, W. Spatial and textural characteristics of the Ganzfeld. *American Journal of Psychology*, 1957, *70*, 403–410.

Coltheart, M. (Ed.) *Readings in cognitive psychology.* Toronto: Holt, Rinehart and Winston, 1972.

Corcoran, D. W. J. *Pattern recognition.* Baltimore: Penguin Books, 1971.

Cornsweet, T. N. Stabilized images techniques. In M. A. Whitcomb (Ed.), *Recent developments in vision research.* Washington: National Academy of Science—National Research Council Publication No. 1272, 1966.

Cornsweet, T. N. Information processing in the human visual system. *Stanford Research Institute Journal*, 1969 (Jan.), Feature Issue No. 5.

Cornsweet, T. N. *Visual perception.* New York: Academic Press, 1970.

Corso, J. *The experimental psychology of sensory behavior.* New York: Holt, Rinehart and Winston, 1967.

Crawford, B. H. Visual adaptation in relation to brief conditioning stimuli. *Proceedings of the Royal Society* (London), Series B, 1947, *134B*, 283–300.

Crozier, W. J., and Holway, A. H. Theory and measurement of visual mechanisms: I. A visual discriminometer. II. Threshold stimulus intensity and retinal position. *Journal of General Physiology*, 1939, *22*, 341–364.

Dallett, K., and Wilcox, S. Remembering pictures versus remembering descriptions. *Psychonomic Science*, 1968, *11*, 139–140.

Daniel, T. C., and Ellis, H. C. Stimulus codability and long term recognition memory for visual form. *Journal of Experimental Psychology*, 1972, *93*, 83–89.

Davey, E. The intensity-time relation for multiple flashes of light in the peripheral retina. *Journal of the Optical Society of America*, 1952, *42*, 937–941.

Davidson, M. L. Perturbation approach to spatial brightness interaction in human vision. *Journal of the Optical Society of America*, 1968, *58*, 1300–1309.

Davson, H. (Ed.) *The eye*. New York: Academic Press, 1962. In 4 volumes.

de Groot, A. D. *Thought and choice in chess*. The Hague: Mouton, 1965.

Deregowski, J. B. Pictorial perception and culture. *Scientific American*, 1972, *227* (Nov.), 82–88.

DeValois, R. L., Abromov, I., and Jacobs, G. H. Analysis of response patterns of LGN cells. *Journal of the Optical Society of America*, 1966, *56*, 966–977.

Ditchburn, R. W. Eye movements in relation to retinal action. *Optica Acta*, 1955, *1*, 171–176.

Ditchburn, R. W., and Ginsburg, B. L. Vision with a stabilized retinal image. *Nature*, 1952, *170*, 36–37.

Dixon, N. F. *Subliminal perception: The nature of a controversy*. London: McGraw-Hill, 1971.

Dodwell, P. C. *Perceptual processing: Stimulus equivalence and pattern recognition*. New York: Appleton-Century-Crofts, 1971.

Donchin, E. Retroactive visual masking—the effect of test flash duration. *Vision Research*, 1967, *7*, 79–89.

Doris, J., Casper, M., and Poresky, R. Differential brightness thresholds in infancy. *Journal of Experimental Child Psychology*, 1967, *5*, 522–535.

Doris, J., and Cooper, L. Brightness discrimination in infancy. *Journal of Experimental Child Psychology*, 1966, *3*, 31–39.

Dowling, J. E. The site of visual adaptation. *Science*, 1967, *155*, 273–279.

Dowling, J. E., and Boycott, B. B. Organization of the primate retina: Electron microscopy. *Proceedings of the Royal Society* (London), Series B, 1966, *166*, 80–111.

Efron, R. The duration of the present. *Annals of the New York Academy of Science*, 1967, *138*, 713–729.

Egeth, H. Selective attention. *Psychological Bulletin*, 1967, *67*, 41–57.

Eichelman, W. H. Familiarity effects in the simultaneous matching task. *Journal of Experimental Psychology*, 1970, *86*, 275–282.

Epstein, W. *Varieties of perceptual learning*. New York: McGraw-Hill, 1967.

Epstein, W., and Park, J. Examination of Gibson's psychophysical hypothesis. *Psychological Bulletin*, 1964, *62*, 180–196.

Erdelyi, M. H. A new look at the new look. *Psychological Review*, 1973, in press.

Eriksen, C. W. Unconscious processes. In M. R. Jones (Ed.), *Nebraska symposium on motivation*. Lincoln, Neb.: University of Nebraska Press, 1957.

Eriksen, C. W. Discrimination and learning without awareness: A methodological survey and evaluation. *Psychological Review*, 1960, *67*, 279–300.

Eriksen, C. W. Temporal luminance summation effects in backward and forward masking. *Perception and Psychophysics*, 1966, *1*, 87–92.

Fantz, R. L. Ontogeny of perception. In A. M. Schrier and H. F. Harlow (Eds.), *Behavior of nonhuman primates*. Vol. 2. New York: Academic Press, 1965. Pp. 365–403.

Fechner, G. *Elements of psychophysics*, 1860. English ed. of Vol. 1, edited by H. E. Adler, D. H. Howes, and E. G. Boring. New York: Holt, Rinehart and Winston, 1966.

Fehrer, E., and Biederman, I. A comparison of reaction time and verbal report in the detection of masked stimuli. *Journal of Experimental Psychology,* 1962 *64,* 126–130.

Fehrer, E., and Raab, D. Reaction time to stimuli masked by metacontrast. *Journal of Experimental Psychology,* 1962, *63,* 143–147.

Festinger, L., and Canon, L. K. Information about spatial location based on knowledge about efference. *Psychological Review,* 1965, *72,* 373–384.

Fiorentini, A. Mach band phenomena. In D. Jameson and L. M. Hurvich (Eds.), *The handbook of sensory physiology.* Vol. VII/4. *Sensory psychophysics.* Berlin: Springer-Verlag, 1972.

Forsyth, D. M., and Chapanis, A. Counting repeated light flashes as a function of their number, their rate of presentation, and retinal location stimulated. *Journal of Experimental Psychology,* 1958, *56,* 385–391.

Fraisse, P. *The psychology of time.* New York: Harper & Row, 1963.

Freedman, J., and Haber, R. N. Why we never forget a face: The role of organization in perceptual memory. Unpublished paper, University of Rochester, 1972.

Frisby, J. P. Real and apparent movement—same or different mechanisms? *Vision Research,* 1972, *12,* 1051–1056.

Galanter, E. H. Contemporary psychophysics. In *New directions in psychology.* New York: Holt, Rinehart and Winston, 1962.

Garner, W. R. *Uncertainty and structure as psychological concepts.* New York: John Wiley, 1962.

Garner, W. R., Hake, H. W., and Eriksen, C. W. Operationism and the concept of perception. *Psychological Review,* 1956, *63,* 317–329.

Geer, J. P., and Moraal, J. Peripheral pattern identification (an experiment on dynamic vision). *I.Z.F. Report,* 1962, Number 18.

Geyer, J. J. Perceptual systems in reading: The prediction of a temporal eye-voice span. In H. K. Smith (Ed.), *Perception and reading.* Newark, Del.: International Reading Association, 1968.

Gibson, E. J. Learning to read. *Science,* 1965, *148,* 1066–1072.

Gibson, E. J. *Principles of perceptual learning and development.* New York: Appleton-Century-Crofts, 1969.

Gibson, E. J., Pick, A. D., Osser, H., and Hammond, M. The role of grapheme-phoneme correspondence in the perception of words. *American Journal of Psychology,* 1962, *75,* 554–570.

Gibson, E. J., Shurcliff, A., and Yonas, A. Utilization of spelling patterns by deaf and hearing subjects. In H. Levin and J. P. Williams (Eds.), *Basic studies in reading.* New York: Basic Books, 1970. Pp. 57–73.

Gibson, J. J. *The perception of the visual world.* Boston: Houghton Mifflin, 1950.

Gibson, J. J. Optical motions and transformations as stimuli for visual perception. *Psychology Review,* 1957, *64,* 288–295.

Gibson, J. J. *The senses considered as perceptual systems.* Boston: Houghton Mifflin, 1966.

Gibson, J. J., and Dibble, F. N. Exploratory experiments on the stimulus conditions for the perception of visual surface. *Journal of Experimental Psychology,* 1952, *43,* 414–419.

Gilinsky, A. S., and Cohen, H. H. Reaction time to change in visual orientation. *Perception and Psychophysics,* 1972, *11,* 129–135.

Glanzer, M., and Clark, H. The verbal loop hypothesis: Conventional figures. *American Journal of Psychology,* 1964, *77,* 621–626.

Gogel, W. C. Equidistance tendency and its consequences. *Psychological Bulletin*, 1965, *64*, 153–163.

Goldiamond, I., and Hawkins, W. I. Vexierversuch: The log relationship between word-frequency and recognition obtained in the absence of stimulus words. *Journal of Experimental Psychology*, 1958, *56*, 457–463.

Goldwater, B. C. Psychological significance of pupillary movements. *Psychological Bulletin*, 1972, *77*, 340–355.

Graham, C. H. (Ed.), *Vision and visual perception*. New York: John Wiley, 1965.

Graham, C. H., and Bartlett, N. R. The relation of size of stimulus and intensity in the human eye: II. Intensity thresholds for red and violet light. *Journal of Experimental Psychology*, 1939, *24*, 574–587.

Green, D. M., and Swets, J. *Signal detection theory and psychophysics*. New York: John Wiley, 1966.

Gregory, R. L. *Eye and brain*. New York: McGraw-Hill, 1969.

Gyr, J. W. Is a theory of direct visual perception adequate? *Psychological Bulletin*, 1972, *77*, 246–261.

Haber, R. N. A replication of selective attention and coding in visual perception. *Journal of Experimental Psychology*, 1964, *67*, 402–404. (a)

Haber, R. N. The effects of coding strategy on perceptual memory. *Journal of Experimental Psychology*, 1964, *68*, 257–262. (b)

Haber, R. N. The nature of the effect of set on perception. *Psychological Review*, 1966, *73*, 335–350.

Haber, R. N. (Ed.), *Information processing approaches to visual perception*. New York: Holt, Rinehart and Winston, 1969.

Haber, R. N. A note on how to choose a mask. *Psychological Bulletin*, 1970, *74*, 373–376. (a)

Haber, R. N. How we remember what we see. *Scientific American*, 1970, *222* (May), 104–115. (b)

Haber, R. N. Perceptual memory for pictures—do we use words, images or both? Paper presented at the XXth International Congress of Psychology, Tokyo, August 1972.

Haber, R. N. Information processing. In E. Carterette and M. Friedman (Eds.), *Handbook of perception*. Vol. 1, New York: Academic Press, 1973.

Haber, R. N., and Hershenson, M. The effects of repeated brief exposures on the growth of a percept. *Journal of Experimental Psychology*, 1965, *69*, 40–46.

Haber, R. N., and Nathanson, L. S. Post-retinal storage?—Parks' camel as seen through the eye of a needle. *Perception and Psychophysics*, 1968, *3*, 349–355.

Haber, R. N., and Standing, L. G. Clarity and recognition of masked and degraded stimuli. *Psychonomic Science*, 1968, *13*, 83–84.

Haber, R. N., and Standing, L. G. Direct measures of short-term visual storage. *Quarterly Journal of Experimental Psychology*, 1969, *21*, 43–54.

Haber, R. N., and Standing, L. G. Direct estimates of apparent duration of a flash followed by visual noise. *Canadian Journal of Psychology*, 1970, *24*, 216–229.

Harris, C. S. Perceptual adaptation to inverted, reversed, and displaced vision. *Psychological Review*, 1965, *72*, 419–444.

Harris, C. S., and Gibson, A. R. Is orientation-specific color adaptation in human vision due to edge detectors, afterimages, or "dipoles"? *Science*, 1968, *162*, 1506–1507.

Harris, C. S., and Haber, R. N. Selective attention and coding in visual perception. *Journal of Experimental Psychology*, 1963, *65*, 328–333.

Harter, M. R., and White, C. T. Perceived number and evoked cortical potentials. *Science*, 1967, *156*, 406–408.

Hartline, H. K., and Ratliff, F. Inhibitory interaction of receptor units in the eye of Limulus. *Journal of General Physiology*, 1957, *40*, 357–376.

Hay, J., and Pick, H., Jr. Visual and proprioceptive adaptation to optical displacement of the visual stimulus. *Journal of Experimental Psychology*, 1966, *71*, 150–158.

Hebb, D. O. *The organization of behavior.* New York: John Wiley, 1949.

Hecht, S. Vision: II. The nature of the photoreceptor process. In C. Murchinson (Ed.), *A handbook of general experimental psychology.* Worcester: Clark University Press, 1934. Pp. 704–828.

Hecht, S., and Mintz, E. U. The visibility of single lines at various illuminations and the retinal basis of visual resolution. *Journal of General Physiology*, 1939, *22*, 593–612.

Hecht, S., Peskin, J. C., and Patt, M. Intensity discriminations in the human eye: II. Relationship between Δ I/I and intensity for different parts of the spectrum. *Journal of General Physiology*, 1938, *22*, 7–19.

Hecht, S., Shlaer, S., and Pirenne, M. H. Energy, quanta, and vision. *Journal of General Physiology*, 1942, *25*, 819–840.

Heckenmuller, E. G. Stabilization of the retinal image: A review of method, effects and theory. *Psychological Bulletin*, 1965, *63*, 157–169.

Heinemann, E. G. Simultaneous brightness induction as a function of inducing- and test-field luminances. *Journal of Experimental Psychology*, 1955, *50*, 89–96.

Heinemann, E. G. Simultaneous brightness induction. In D. Jameson and L. M. Hurvich (Eds.), *The handbook of sensory physiology.* Vol. VII/4. *Sensory psychophysics.* Berlin: Springer-Verlag, 1972.

Held, R., and Bossom, J. Neonatal deprivation and adult rearrangement: Complementary techniques for analyzing plastic sensory-motor coordinations. *Journal of Comparative and Physiological Psychology*, 1961, *54*, 33–37.

Held, R., and Freedman, S. J. Plasticity in human sensorimotor control. *Science*, 1963, *142*, 455–462.

Held, R., and Hein, A. V. Adaptation of disarranged hand-eye coordination contingent upon re-afferent stimulation. *Perceptual and Motor Skills*, 1958, *8*, 87–90.

Helmholtz, H. von. *Physiological optics*, 1850. (J. P. C. Southall, Ed.) Optical Society of America, 1925.

Helmholtz, H. von. *Treatise on physiological optics.* Vol. III. (Translated from the 3rd German ed., 1867, J. P. C. Southall, Ed.) New York: Dover, 1962.

Henle, M. An experimental investigation of past experience as a determinant of form perception. *Journal of Experimental Psychology*, 1942, *30*, 1–22.

Hering, E. *Outlines of a theory of the light sense*, 1877. Cambridge, Mass.: Harvard University Press, 1964.

Heron, W. Perception as a function of retinal locus and attention. *American Journal of Psychology*, 1957, *70*, 38–48.

Hershenson, M. Visual discrimination in the human newborn. *Journal of Comparative and Physiological Psychology*, 1964, *58*, 270–276. (a)

Hershenson, M. Visual discrimination in the human newborn. Unpublished doctoral dissertation, Yale University, 1964. (b)

Hershenson, M. Development of the perception of form. *Psychological Bulletin*, 1967, *67*, 326–336.

Hershenson, M. Stimulus structure, cognitive structure, and the perception of letter arrays. *Journal of Experimental Psychology*, 1969, *79*, 327–335. (a)

Hershenson, M. Perception of letter arrays as a function of absolute retinal locus. *Journal of Experimental Psychology*, 1969, *80*, 201–202. (b)

Hershenson, M. The development of visual perceptual systems. In H. Moltz (Ed.), *The ontogenesis of vertebrate behavior.* New York: Academic Press, 1971. Pp. 29–56.

Hershenson, M. Verbal report and visual matching latency as a function of the pronounceability of letter arrays. *Journal of Experimental Psychology,* 1972, *96,* 104–109.

Hershenson, M., Kessen, W., and Munsinger, H. Ocular orientation in the human newborn infant: A close look at some positive and negative results. In W. Wathen-Dunn (Ed.), *Models for the perception of speech and visual form.* Cambridge, Mass.: M.I.T. Press, 1967.

Hirsh, I. J., and Sherrick, C. E. Perceived order in different sense modalities. *Journal of Experimental Psychology,* 1961, *62,* 423–432.

Hochberg, J. Nativism and empiricism in perception. In L. Postman (Ed.), *Psychology in the making.* New York: Alfred A. Knopf, 1962.

Hochberg, J. In the mind's eye. In R. N. Haber (Ed.), *Contemporary theory and research in visual perception.* New York: Holt, Rinehart and Winston, 1968. Pp. 303–331.

Hochberg, J. Attention, organization and consciousness. In D. I. Mostofsky (Ed.), *Attention: Contemporary theory and analysis.* New York: Appleton-Century-Crofts, 1970. Pp. 99–124.

Hochberg, J. Perception: I. Color and shape. In J. A. Kling and L. A. Riggs (Eds.), *Woodworth and Schlosberg's Experimental Psychology.* (3rd ed.) New York: Holt, Rinehart and Winston, 1971. Pp. 395–474. (a)

Hochberg, J. Perception: II. Space and movement. In J. A. Kling and L. A. Riggs (Eds.), *Woodworth and Schlosberg's Experimental Psychology.* (3rd ed.) New York: Holt, Rinehart and Winston, 1971. Pp. 475–550. (b)

Hochberg, J. The representation of things and people. In E. H. Gombrich, J. Hochberg, and M. Black (Eds.), *Art, perception and reality.* Baltimore: John Hopkins University Press, 1972. Pp. 47–94.

Hochberg, J. Organization and the Gestalt tradition. In E. Carterette and M. Friedman (Eds.), *Handbook of perception.* Vol. 1. New York: Academic Press, 1973. Chapter 10.

Hochberg, J., and Brooks, V. The psychophysics of form: Reversible-perspective drawings of spatial objects. *American Journal of Psychology,* 1960, *73,* 337–354.

Hochberg, J., and Brooks, V. Pictorial recognition as an unlearned ability: A study of one child's performance. *American Journal of Psychology,* 1962, *75,* 624–628.

Hochberg, J., and McAlister, E. A quantitative approach to figural "goodness." *Journal of Experimental Psychology,* 1953, *46,* 361–364.

Hochberg, J., Triebel, W., and Seaman, G. Color adaptation under conditions of homogeneous stimulation (Ganzfeld). *Journal of Experimental Psychology,* 1951, *41,* 153–159.

Holst, E. von. Relations between the central nervous system and the peripheral organs. *British Journal of Animal Behavior,* 1954, *2,* 89–94.

Holway, A. H., and Boring, E. G. Determinants of apparent visual size with distance variant. *American Journal of Psychology,* 1941, *54,* 21–37.

Howard, I. P., and Templeton, W. B. *Human spatial orientation.* New York: John Wiley, 1966.

Hubel, D. H., and Wiesel, T. N. Receptive fields, binocular interaction, and functional architecture in the cat's visual cortex. *Journal of Physiology,* 1962, *160,* 106–154.

Hubel, D. H., and Wiesel, T. N. Receptive fields and functional architecture in two non-striate visual areas (18 and 19) of the cat. *Journal of Neurophysiology*, 1965, *28*, 229–289.

Hubel, D. H., and Wiesel, T. N. Receptive fields and functional architecture of monkey striate cortex. *Journal of Physiology*, 1968, *195*, 215–243.

Hudson, W. The study of the problem of pictorial perception among unacculturated groups. *International Journal of Psychology*, 1967, *2*, 89–107.

Hurvich, L. M., and Jameson, D. An opponent-process theory of color vision. *Psychological Review*, 1957, *64*, 384–404.

Hurvich, L. M., and Jameson, D. *The perception of brightness and darkness.* Boston: Allyn and Bacon, 1966.

Ittelson, W. H. *Visual space perception.* New York: Springer-Verlag, 1960.

James, W. *The principles of psychology.* New York: Holt, Rinehart and Winston, 1890.

Jameson, D., and Hurvich, L. M. (Eds.), *The handbook of sensory physiology.* Vol. VII/4. *Sensory psychophysics.* Berlin: Springer-Verlag, 1972.

Judd, D. B., and Wyszecki, G. W. *Color in business, science, and industry.* (2nd ed.) New York: John Wiley, 1963.

Julesz, B. *The Cyclopean eye.* New York: Academic Press, 1970.

Kagan, J., and Lewis, M. Studies of attention in the human infant. *Merrill-Palmer Quarterly*, 1965, *11*, 95–127.

Kahneman, D. Time intensity reciprocity under various conditions of adaptation and backward masking. *Journal of Experimental Psychology*, 1966, *71*, 543–549.

Kahneman, D. Method, findings and theory in studies of visual masking. *Psychological Bulletin*, 1968, *70*, 404–425.

Kahneman, D. *Attention and effort.* New York: Prentice-Hall, 1973.

Kandel, G. L. A psychophysical study of some monocular and binocular factors in early adaptation. Unpublished doctoral dissertation, University of Rochester, 1958.

Keesey, U. T. Effects of involuntary eye movements on visual acuity. *Journal of the Optical Society of America*, 1960, *50*, 769–774.

Kelly, D. H. Visual responses to time-dependent stimuli. *Journal of the Optical Society of America*, 1961, *51*, 422–429.

Kelly, D. H. Flicker. In D. Jameson and L. M. Hurvich (Eds.), *The handbook of sensory physiology.* Vol. VII/4. *Sensory psychophysics.* Berlin: Springer-Verlag, 1972.

Kessen, W., Salapatek, P., and Haith, M. M. The visual response of the human newborn to linear contour. *Journal of Experimental Child Psychology*, 1972, *13*, 9–20.

King, S. J. A system for separating objects from the background in automatic picture processing. Unpublished doctoral dissertation, Cornell University, 1971.

Kinsbourne, M., and Warrington, E. K. Further studies on the masking of brief visual stimuli by a random pattern. *Quarterly Journal of Experimental Psychology*, 1962, *14*, 235–245.

Klein, G. S. Semantic power of words measured through the interference with color naming. *American Journal of Psychology*, 1964, *77*, 576–588.

Kling, J. A., and Riggs, L. A. (Eds.) *Woodworth and Schlosberg's experimental psychology.* (3rd ed.) New York: Holt, Rinehart and Winston, 1971.

Koffka, K. *Principles of Gestalt psychology.* New York: Harcourt Brace Jovanovich, 1935.

Kohler, I. *The formation and transformation of the perceptual world.* (Tr. by H. Fiss.) International Universities Press, 1964. Originally *Über Aufbau und Wandlungen der Wahrnehmungswelt.* Vienna: R. M. Rohrer, 1951.

Kolers, P. A. Three stages of reading. In H. Levin and J. P. Williams (Eds.), *Basic studies in reading*. New York: Basic Books, 1970. Pp. 90–118.

Kolers, P. A. Reading pictures: Some cognitive aspects of visual perception. In T. S. Huang and O. J. Tretiak (Eds.), *Picture bandwidth compression*. New York: Gordon Beach, 1972.

Kolers, P. A. *Aspects of motion perception*. New York: Pergamon, 1972.

Kolers, P. A., and Eden, M. *Recognizing patterns: Studies in living and automatic systems*. Cambridge, Mass.: The M.I.T. Press, 1968.

Kopfermann, H. Psychologische Untersuchungen über die Wirkung zweidimensionaler Darstellungen korperlicher Gebilde. *Psychologische Forschung*, 1930, *13*, 293–364.

Kristofferson, A. B. Attention and psychophysical time. *Acta Psychologica*, 1967, *27*, 93–100.

Krueger, L. E. Search time in a redundant visual display. *Journal of Experimental Psychology*, 1970, *83*, 391–399.

Lappin, J. S. Attention in the identification of stimuli in complex visual displays. *Journal of Experimental Psychology*, 1967, *75*, 321–328.

Latour, P. L. Visual threshold during eye movements. *Vision Research*, 1962, 2, 261–262.

Lefton, L. A. Metacontrast: a review. *Perception and Psychophysics*, 1973, *13*, 161–171.

Lefton, L. A. Probing information extracted from briefly presented displays. Unpublished doctoral dissertation, University of Rochester, 1972.

Le Grand, Y. *Light, colour and vision*. London: Chapman and Hall, 1957.

Leibovic, K. N. *Information processing in the nervous system*. New York: Springer-Verlag, 1969.

Lettvin, J. Y., Maturana, H. R., Pitts, W. H., and McCulloch, W. S. Two remarks on the visual system of the frog. In W. A. Rosenblith (Ed.), *Sensory communication*. New York: John Wiley, 1961. Pp. 757–776.

Liberman, I. Y., Shankweiler, D., Orlando, C., Harris, K. S., and Bell Berti, F. Letter confusions and reversals of sequence in the beginning reader; implications for Orton's theory of developmental dyslexia. *Cortex*, 1971, *7*, 127–142.

Lindsay, P., and Norman, D. *Human information processing*. New York: Academic Press, 1972.

Lipkin, B. S., and Rosenfeld, A. (Eds.), *Picture processing and psychopictorics*. New York: Academic Press, 1970.

Liss, P. Does backward masking by visual noise stop stimulus processing? *Perception and Psychophysics*, 1968, *4*, 328–330.

Loftus, G. R. Eye fixations and recognition memory for pictures. *Cognitive Psychology*, 1972, *3*, 525–551.

Long, G. E. The effect of duration of onset and cessation of light flash on the intensity-time relation in the peripheral retina. *Journal of the Optical Society of America*, 1951, *41*, 743–747.

Luria, A. R. *The mind of a mnemonist*. New York: Basic Books, 1968.

Lythgoe, R. J., and Tansley, K. The relation of the critical frequency of flicker to the adaptation of the eye. *Proceedings of the Royal Society* (London), 1929, *105B*, 60–92.

Mackworth, N. H. Visual noise causes tunnel vision. *Psychonomic Science*, 1965, *3*, 67–68.

Mackworth, N. H., and Kaplan, I. T. Visual acuity when eyes are pursuing moving targets. *Science*, 1962, *136*, 387–388.

Mackworth, N. H., and Morandi, A. J. The gaze selects informative details within pictures. *Perception and Psychophysics*, 1967, *2*, 547–552.

Matin, L. Eye movements and perceived visual direction. In D. Jameson and L. M. Hurvich (Eds.), *The handbook of sensory physiology*. Vol. VII/4. *Sensory psychophysics*. Berlin: Springer-Verlag, 1972.

Maxwell, J. C. On the theory of compound colors, and the relation of the colors of the spectrum. *Philosophical Transactions of the Royal Society of London*, 1860, *150*, 57–84.

McCollough, C. Color adaptation of edge detectors in the human visual system. *Science*, 1965, *149*, 1115–1116.

McFarland, J. *Perception of line forms.* Chicago: University of Chicago Press, 1973.

McKinney, J. P. Disappearance of luminous designs. *Science*, 1963, *140*, 403–404.

Metzger, W. Optische Untersuchungen am Ganzfeld: II. Zur Phänomenologie des homogenen Ganzfelds. *Psychologische Forschung*, 1930, *13*, 6–29.

Mewhort, D. J. K. Sequential redundancy and letter spacing as determinants of tachistoscopic recognition. *Canadian Journal of Psychology*, 1966, *20*, 435–444.

Mewhort, D. J. K. Familiarity of letter sequences, response uncertainty, and the tachistoscopic recognition experiment. *Canadian Journal of Psychology*, 1967, *21*, 309–321.

Mewhort, D. J. K., and Cornett, S. Scanning and the familiarity effect in tachistoscopic recognition. *Canadian Journal of Psychology*, 1972, *26*, 181–189.

Mewhort, D. J. K., Merikle, P. M., and Bryden, M. P. On the transfer from iconic to short-term memory. *Journal of Experimental Psychology*, 1969, *81*, 89–94.

Miller, G. A. The magical number seven, plus or minus two. *Psychological Review*, 1956, *63*, 81–97.

Miller, G. A., Bruner, J. S., and Postman, L. Familiarity of letter sequences and tachistoscopic identification. *Journal of General Psychology*, 1954, *50*, 129–139.

Milner, P. *Physiological psychology.* New York: Holt, Rinehart and Winston, 1970.

Monk, G. S. *Light.* (2nd ed.) New York: Boulder, 1963.

Mooney, C. M. Age in the development of closure ability in children. *Canadian Journal of Psychology*, 1957, *11*, 219–226.

Moray, N. *Attention: Selective processes in vision and hearing.* New York: Academic Press, 1970.

Morton, J. The effects of content upon speed of reading, eye movements and eye-voice span. *Quarterly Journal of Experimental Psychology*, 1964, *16*, 340–355.

Morton, J. Categories of interference: Verbal mediation and conflict in card sorting. *British Journal of Psychology*, 1969, *60*, 329–346.

Morton, J., and Chambers, S. Personal communication with authors, 1970.

Mostofsky, D. I. *Attention: Contemporary theory and analysis.* New York: Appleton-Century-Crofts, 1970.

Mueller, C. G. Frequency of seeing functions for intensity discriminations at various levels of adapting intensity. *Journal of General Physiology*, 1951, *34*, 463–474.

Nachmias, J. Signal detection theory and its application to problems in vision. In D. Jameson and L. M. Hurvich (Eds.), *The handbook of sensory physiology.* Vol. VII/4. *Sensory psychophysics.* Berlin: Springer-Verlag, 1972.

Neisser, U. Decision-time without reaction-time: Experiments in visual scanning. *American Journal of Psychology*, 1963, *76*, 376–385.

Neisser, U. *Cognitive psychology.* New York: Appleton-Century-Crofts, 1967.

Neisser, U., and Beller, H. K. Searching through word lists. *British Journal of Psychology*, 1965, *56*, 349–358.

Neisser, U., and Lazar, R. Searching for novel targets. *Perceptual and Motor Skills*, 1964, *19*, 427–432.

Neisser, U., Novick, R., and Lazar, R. Searching for ten targets simultaneously. *Perceptual and Motor Skillls*, 1963, *17*, 955–961.

Neisser, U., and Stoper, A. Redirecting the search process. *British Journal of Psychology*, 1965, *56*, 359–368.

Nelson, K., and Kessen, W. Visual scanning by human newborns: Responses to complete triangle, to sides only, and to corners only. Paper presented at the meeting of the American Psychological Association, Washington, D.C., September 1969.

Norman, D. A. *Models of human memory*. New York: Academic Press, 1970.

Noton, D., and Stark, L. Scanpaths in saccadic eye movements while viewing and recognizing patterns. *Vision Research*, 1971, *11*, 929–942.

Ogle, K. N. The optical space sense. In H. Davson (Ed.), *The eye*. New York: Academic Press, 1962. Pp. 211–417.

Pastore, N. *Selective history of theories of visual perception: 1650–1950*. New York: Oxford University Press, 1971.

Piaget, J. *The origins of intelligence in children*. New York: International Universities Press, 1952.

Pirenne, M. H. *Vision and the eye*. London: Chapman and Hall, 1948. (Second edition, 1967.)

Polyak, S. L. *The retina*. Chicago: University of Chicago Press, 1941.

Polyak, S. L. *The vertebrate visual system*. Chicago: University of Chicago Press, 1957.

Posner, M. I. Abstraction and the process of recognition. In G. H. Bower and J. T. Spence (Eds.), *The psychology of learning and motivation*. New York: Academic Press, 1969. Pp. 44–100.

Posner, M. I., Boies, S. J., Eichelman, W. H., and Taylor, R. L. Retention of visual and name codes of single letters. *Journal of Experimental Psychology*, 1969, *79*, (Monograph Supplement 1), 1–16.

Posner, M. I., and Keele, S. W. Decay of visual information from a single letter. *Science*, 1967, *158*, 137–139.

Posner, M. I., and Keele, S. W. Retention of abstract ideas. *Journal of Experimental Psychology*, 1970, *83*, 304–308.

Posner, M. I., and Konick, A. F. Short-term retention of visual and kinesthetic information. *Organization Behavior and Human Performance*, 1966, *1*, 71–86.

Posner, M. I., and Mitchell, R. F. Chronometric analysis of classification. *Psychological Review*, 1967, *74*, 392–409.

Posner, M. I., and Taylor, R. L. Subtractive method applied to separation of visual and name components of multiletter arrays. *Acta Psychologica*, 1969, *30*, 104–114.

Pritchard, R. M. Stabilized images on the retina. *Scientific American*, 1961, *204*, (June), 72–78.

Pritchard, R. M. Physiological nystagmus and vision. In M. B. Bender (Ed.), *The oculomotor system*. New York: Harper & Row, 1964. Pp. 321–331.

Purkinje, J. *Beobachtungen and Versuche zur Physiologie der Sinne*. Zweiter Bachchen. Berlin: G. Reimer, 1825.

Rabbitt, P. M. A. Learning to ignore irrelevant information. *American Journal of Psychology*, 1967, *80*, 1–13.

Ratliff, F. *Mach bands*. San Francisco: Holden-Day, 1965.

Reicher, G. M. Perceptual recognition as a function of meaningfulness of stimulus material. *Journal of Experimental Psychology*, 1969, *81*, 275–280.

Riggs, L. A. Visual acuity. In C. H. Graham (Ed.), *Vision and visual perception*. New York: John Wiley 1965. Pp. 321–349.

Riggs, L. A., Armington, J. C., and Ratliff, F. Motions of the retinal image during fixation. *Journal of the Optical Society of America*, 1954, *44*, 315–321.

Riggs, L. A., Ratliff, F., Cornsweet, J. C.. and Cornsweet, T. N. The disappearance of steadily fixated visual test objects. *Journal of the Optical Society of America*, 1953, *43*, 495–501.

Robinson, D. A. The mechanics of human smooth pursuit eye movements. *Journal of Physiology*, 1965, *180*, 569–591.

Robinson, D. A. Eye movement control in primates. *Science*, 1968, *161*, 1219–1224.

Robson, J. G. Personal communication to the authors, 1972.

Rock, I. *The nature of perceptual adaptation*. New York: Basic Books, 1966.

Rosenblith, W. A. *Sensory communication*. New York: John Wiley, 1961.

Rubin, E. *Visuell wahrgenommene Figuren*. Copenhagen: Glydendalske, 1921.

Rushton, W. A. H. Visual pigments in the colour blind. *Nature*, 1958, *182*, 690–692.

Rushton, W. A. H. Peripheral coding in the nervous system. In W. A. Rosenblith (Ed.), *Sensory communication*. New York: John Wiley, 1961. Pp. 169–182.

Sackett, G. P. Monkeys reared in isolation with pictures as visual input: Evidence for an innate releasing mechanism. *Science*, 1966, *154*, 1468–1473.

Salapatek, P. Visual scanning of geometric figures by the human newborn. *Journal of Comparative and Physiological Psychology*, 1968, *66*, 247–258.

Salapatek, P. The visual investigation of geometric patterns by the one- and two-month-old infant. Paper presented at the meeting of the American Association for the Advancement of Science, Boston, December 1969.

Salapatek, P., and Kessen, W. Visual scanning of triangles by the human newborn. *Journal of Experimental Child Psychology*, 1966, *3*, 155–167.

Sanders, A. *The selective process in the functional visual field*. Institute for Perception, RVO-TNO, Soesterberg, The Netherlands, 1963.

Scharf, B., and Lefton, L. A. Backward and forward masking as a function of stimulus and task parameters. *Journal of Experimental Psychology*, 1970, *84*, 331–338.

Schiff, W., Caviness, J. A., and Gibson, J. J. Persistent fear responses in rhesus monkeys to the optical stimulus of "looming." *Science*, 1962, *136*, 982–983.

Schiller, P. H. Single unit analysis of backward visual masking and metacontrast in the cat lateral geniculate nucleus. *Vision Research*, 1968, *8*, 855–866.

Schmidt, M. W., and Kristofferson, A. B. Discrimination of successiveness: A test of a model of attention. *Science*, 1963, *139*, 112–113.

Sekuler, R. W., and Ganz, L. Aftereffect of seen motion with a stabilized retinal image. *Science*, 1963, *139*, 419–420.

Sekuler, R. W., and Pantle, A. A model for aftereffects of seen movement. *Vision Research*, 1967, *7*, 427–439.

Shaffer, W. O., and Shiffrin, R. M. Rehearsal and storage of visual information. *Journal of Experimental Psychology*, 1972, *92*, 292–296.

Shannon, C. E. A mathematical theory of communication. *Bell System Technical Journal*, 1948, *27*, 379–423; 623–656.

Shepard, R. N. Recognition memory for words, sentences and pictures. *Journal of Verbal Learning and Verbal Behavior*, 1967, *6*, 156–163.

Smith, F. *The understanding of reading*. New York: Holt, Rinehart and Winston, 1971.

Solomon, R. L., and Howes, D. H. Word frequency, personal values, and visual duration threshold. *Psychological Review*, 1951, *58*, 256–270.

Solomon, R. L., and Postman, L. Frequency of usage as a determinant of recognition thresholds for words. *Journal of Experimental Psychology*, 1952, *43*, 195–201.

Sperling, G. The information available in brief visual presentations. *Psychological Monographs*, 1960, *74* (11, Whole No. 498).

Sperling, G. A model for visual memory tasks. *Human Factors*, 1963, *5*, 19–31.

Sperling, G. Successive approximation to a model for short-term memory. *Acta Psychologica*, 1967, *27*, 285–292.

Spigel, I. Relation of movement aftereffect duration to interpolated darkness intervals. *Life Science*, 1962, *6*, 239–242.

Spigel, I. (Ed.), *Visually perceived movement*. New York: Harper & Row, 1965.

Standing, L., Conezio, J., and Haber, R. N. Perception and memory for pictures: Single trial learning of 2500 visual stimuli. *Psychonomic Science*, 1970, *19*, 73–74.

Sternberg, S. High-speed scanning in human memory. *Science*, 1966, *153*, 652–654.

Stevens, C. F. *Neurophysiology: A primer.* New York: John Wiley, 1966.

Stevens, S. S. (Ed.), *Handbook of experimental psychology.* New York: John Wiley, 1951.

Stroop, J. R. Studies of interference in serial verbal reactions. *Journal of Experimental Psychology*, 1935, *18*, 643–662.

Stroud, J. The fine structure of psychological time. In H. Quastler (Ed.), *Information theory in psychology.* Glencoe, Ill.: Free Press, 1956. Pp. 174–207.

Sutherland, N. S. Visual discrimination of shape by octopus: Squares and crosses. *Journal of Comparative and Physiological Psychology*, 1962, *55*, 939–943.

Sutherland, N. S. Object recognition. In E. Carterette and M. Friedman (Eds.), *Handbook of perception.* Vol. 3. *Biology of perceptual systems.* New York: Academic Press, 1974, in press.

Taylor, S. E. Eye movements in reading: Facts and fallacies. *American Educational Research Journal*, 1965, *2*, 187–202.

ten Doesschate, J., and Alpern, M. The effect of photo-excitation of the two retinas on pupil size. *Journal of Neurophysiology*, 1967, *30*, 562–576.

Torgerson, W. S. *Theory and method of scaling.* (2nd ed.) New York: John Wiley, 1963.

Treisman, A. M. Strategies and models of selective attention. *Psychological Review*, 1969, *76*, 282–299.

Tronick, E. Stimulus control and the growth of the infant's effective visual field. *Perception and Psychophysics*, 1972, *11*, 373–376.

Tronick, E., and Clanton, C. Infant looking patterns. *Vision Research*, 1971, *11*, 1479–1486.

Tversky, B. Pictorial and verbal encoding in a short-term memory task. *Perception and Psychophysics*, 1969, *6*, 225–233.

Uttal, W. R. The psychobiological silly season—or—what happens when neurophysiological data become psychological theories. *Journal of General Psychology*, 1971, *84*, 151–166.

Uttal, W. R. *Sensory coding: Selected readings.* Boston: Little, Brown and Co., 1972.

Volkman, F. C. Vision during voluntary saccadic eye movements. *Journal of the Optical Society of America*, 1962, *52*, 571–578.

Volkman, F. C., Schick, A. M. L., and Riggs, L. A. Time course of visual inhibition during voluntary saccades. *Journal of the Optical Society of America*, 1968, *58*, 362–369.

Wald, G. The receptors of human color vision. *Science*, 1964, *145*, 1007–1017.

Wald, G., and Brown, P. K. Human color vision and color blindness. *Cold Spring Harbor Symposia on Quantitative Biology*, 1965, *30*, 345–361.

Wallach, H., and O'Connell, D. N. The kinetic depth effect. *Journal of Experimental Psychology*, 1953, *45*, 205–217.

Wattenbarger, B. L. The representation of the stimulus and character classification. Human Performance Center Technical Report #22, University of Michigan, Ann Arbor, August 1970.

Weisstein, N. Backward masking and models of perceptual processing. *Journal of Experimental Psychology*, 1966, *72*, 232–240.

Weisstein, N. What the frog's eye tells the human brain: Single cell analyses in the human visual system. *Psychological Review*, 1969, *72*, 157–176.

Weisstein, N. Metacontrast. In D. Jameson and L. M. Hurvich (Eds.), *The handbook of sensory physiology*. Vol. VII/4. *Sensory psychophysics*. Berlin: Springer-Verlag, 1972.

Werner, H. Studies on contour. *American Journal of Psychology*, 1935, *47*, 40–64.

Werner, H., and Wapner, S. Toward a general theory of perception. *Psychological Review*, 1952, *59*, 324–338.

Westheimer, G. H. Eye movement responses to a horizontally moving visual stimulus. *Archives of Ophthalmology*, 1954, *52*, 932–943.

Westheimer, G. Visual acuity and spatial modulation thresholds. In D. Jameson and L. M. Hurvich (Eds.), *The handbook of sensory physiology*. Vol. VII/4. *Sensory psychophysics*. Berlin: Springer-Verlag, 1972.

Wheeler, D. D. Processes in word recognition. *Cognitive Psychology*, 1970, *1*, 59–85.

White, C. T., Cheatham, P. G., and Armington, J. C. Temporal numerosity: II. Evidence for central factors influencing perceived number. *Journal of Experimental Psychology*, 1953, *46*, 283–287.

Whiteside, J. A. Eye movements of children, adults and elderly persons during inspection of simple dot patterns. Unpublished doctoral dissertation, University of Rochester, 1972.

Williams, L. G. The effect of target specification on objects fixated during visual search. *Perception and Psychophysics*, 1966, *1*, 315–318.

Williams, L. G. The effects of target specification on objects fixated during visual search. In A. F. Sanders (Ed.), *Attention and performance*. Amsterdam: North Holland Publishing Co., 1967. Pp. 355–360.

Wingfield, A. Effects of frequency on identification and naming of objects. *American Journal of Psychology*, 1968, *81*, 226–234.

Wiseman, S., and Neisser, U. Perceptual organization as a determinant of visual recognition memory. Paper presented at the meeting of the Eastern Psychological Association, Boston, April 1972.

Woodrow, H. The effect of pattern upon simultaneous letter span. *American Journal of Psychology*, 1938, *51*, 83–96.

Woodworth, R. S. *Experimental psychology*. New York: Holt, Rinehart and Winston, 1938.

Woodworth, R. S., and Schlosberg, H. *Experimental psychology*. (2nd ed.) New York: Holt, Rinehart and Winston, 1954.

Wulff, V. J., Adams, R. G., Linschitz, H., and Abrahamson, E. W. Effect of flash illumination on rhodopsin. *Annals of the New York Academy of Science*, 1958, *74*, 281–290.

Wyant, S., Banks, W. P., Berger, D., and Wright, P. W. Verbal and pictorial similarity in recognition of pictures. *Perception and Psychophysics*, 1972, *12*, 151–153.

Wyszecki, G. W., and Stiles, W. S. *Color science, concepts and methods, quantitative data and formulas*. New York: John Wiley, 1967.

Yarbus, A. L. *Eye movements and vision*. New York: Plenum Press, 1967.

Young, F. A., and Lindsley, D. B. *Early experience and visual information processing in perceptual and reading disorders*. Washington: National Academy of Science, 1970.

Young, T. On the theory of light and colours. In *Lectures in natural philosophy*. Vol. 2. Printed for Joseph Johnson, St. Paul's Church Yard, by William Savage, 1807.

Zusne, L. *Visual perception of form*. New York: Academic Press, 1970.

name index

subject index